NH

SCOTTISH INDUSTRIAL POLICY

SERIES: 2

Editors: Neil Hood and Stephen Young

INDUSTRY, POLICY
AND THE
SCOTTISH ECONOMY

edited by Neil Hood and Stephen Young
for the University Press

EDINBURGH

© Neil Hood and
Stephen Young 1984
Edinburgh University Press
22 George Square, Edinburgh

Printed in Great Britain by
Clark Constable, Edinburgh, London, Melbourne

British Library Cataloguing
in Publication Data
Hood, Neil
Industry, policy and the Scottish economy
—(Scottish industrial policy series; no.2)
1. Industry and state—Scotland
I. Title   II. Young, Stephen, *19* –
III. Series
338.9411   HD3616.G74S3

ISBN 0 85224 465 7

m.r.

CONTENTS

v

Contents

Contents

LIST OF TABLES

LIST OF FIGURES

PREFACE

There seems little doubt that the 1970s will be seen as a turning-point in the history of the modern world economy. Events which took place during this period – successive oil price shocks, the breakdown of the old international monetary order, the rise of the 'new protectionism', the enlargement of the EC, the growing competitiveness of the newly in-dustrialised countries, and the diffusion of the ubiquitous electronics technology – conspired to send shock waves around the globe. These events truly exposed the fundamental lack of competitiveness of British (and Scottish) industry, which had been obscured for much of the post-World War II period by a buoyant world economy. For Scotland, the 1970s thus saw a substantial (some would say catastrophic) erosion of the country's traditional industrial base. More optimistically, the period also saw the emergence of the so-called 'Silicon Glen', indicating at least a partial restructuring of the economy in line with changes in international comparative advantage, costs and competitiveness.[1] For industry in Scotland, the 1970s were noteworthy too for the emergence of new institutions with responsibilities in the areas of industrial policy and regional development. Adam Smith may have argued two centuries earlier that 'little else is requisite to carry a State to the highest degree of opulence from the lowest barbarism, but peace, easy taxes, and a tolerable administration of justice; all the rest being brought about by the natural course of things';[2] but reliance on the 'invisible hand' to begin the climb back to economic respectability has to be seen alongside the success of many countries, industrialised and newly industrialising alike, in pursuing a guided, interventionist approach to economic and industrial development.

Against this background, the objectives of this book are twofold. First, it seeks to evaluate industrial performance and industrial policy in Scotland over the recent past and especially from the early 1970s. Secondly, it attempts to point the way ahead by the formulation of possible new initiatives which might enhance future performance. In so doing, it is hoped that it will focus attention on the opportunities which exist for creative co-operation between industry and Government agencies in Scotland, thereby improving the quality of the debate on the ways in which industry can prosper in the very changed economic circumstances of the 1980s and beyond.

The book represents the second in the Scottish Industrial Policy series produced by Edinburgh University Press, the first being *Multi-*

nationals in Retreat, published in 1982. While the latter looked at one sector of industry only, the present volume takes a much wider view: the principal focus of attention is manufacturing industry, although chapters are also included on oil and related industries and on the finance sector, both of which are of vital importance to Scotland. Even within manufacturing industry, complete coverage has not been attempted, so no consideration is given to the Scottish operations of UK public sector enterprises. The nationalised industries such as steel, shipbuilding and aerospace are largely, therefore, excluded, except insofar as their performance impinges upon sectors such as engineering. To give some impression of the scope of coverage, the book discusses sectors accounting for some eighty per cent of manufacturing employment in 1982 and in total covers activities employing about forty per cent of employees in employment in Scotland in that year.

There are two distinct types of chapters in the book, one covering sectors defined by Standard Industrial Classifications (SICs) or Minimum List Headings (MLHs) and the other dealing with types of firms (small firms and foreign-owned enterprises) on a cross-sectoral basis. This approach has been taken deliberately to highlight the differing frameworks within which policy measures are constructed. Aside from these chapters, Chapters 1 and 2 set the scene for the industry studies by considering past trends in Scottish industry and future projections through to 1988, and by describing the industrial policy framework within the UK and Scotland.

The book is written within the context of the existing policy environment in the UK, assuming that the institutional set-up will remain broadly unchanged and that the Scottish economy will continue to receive a fairly similar proportion of overall UK economic resources for industrial development in the next decade. No hypothesised additions (or subtractions) arising from Scottish control over taxation are, therefore, envisaged. Within this context, the final chapter of the book – Chapter 12 – attempts to draw together the contributions of the various authors and derive some recommendations for policy action. A series of alternative scenarios for industrial policy are also briefly presented. The book concludes with some comments on the employment question, despite the fact that there is only an indirect and certainly longer-term linkage between industrial efficiency and employment levels.

The various chapters of *Industry, Policy and the Scottish Economy* have been written by authors with specialist knowledge of the Scottish economy or of particular sectors of the economy. Inevitably, within the guidelines provided to them by the present editors, their approach has varied, reflecting their own backgrounds, present employment and basic philosophy. It is hoped, nevertheless, that this enhances rather than detracts from the overall package. The various draft chapters were discussed at a series of meetings held from September 1982 through to the Summer of 1983, and our thanks are due to the authors, many of whom were under severe work pressures in their own organisations during this time. For their financial support for this project, we would like to thank the Scottish Development Agency; The Committee of Scottish Clearing Bankers, representing the Bank of Scotland, The Royal Bank of Scotland plc and the Clydesdale Bank PLC; and the *Glasgow Herald*. In an undertaking of this magnitude the editors and authors represent simply the equivalent of the tip of a large iceberg. We could not list all those, from company executives to library assistants, who were of assistance to us. However special mention should be made of the staff of Edinburgh University Press for their encouragement and tolerance; to officials of the then Scottish Economic Planning Department including Messrs Bill McNie, Stephen Hampson and Peter Scrimgeour; and to our secretary Betty McFarlane, now word-processor-equipped to meet future challenges.

Neil Hood, Stephen Young

NOTES AND REFERENCES
1. Yet it is disturbing that in the U K as a whole only four production industries – computers; water supply; petroleum and natural gas; and radio, radar and electronic goods – increased employment by more than 10 000 in the decade to 1983. Moreover, between them the four created only 84 000 new jobs. Source: *Sunday Times Business News*, 11 December 1983, quoting a Government report to the National Economic Development Office.
2. *An Inquiry into the Nature and Causes of the Wealth of Nations*, 1776.

TRENDS IN SCOTTISH INDUSTRY

DAVID BELL

Introduction

Like most Western economies, the Scottish economy has undergone radical structural change during the last thirty years. It has also suffered severe dislocation as a result of various external shocks, most notably the rise in the price of oil in 1973. Such shocks have tended to strengthen the momentum of structural adjustment. Indeed, the process of change may accelerate in the future as the developing nations, particularly the newly industrialised countries (NICs), force a fundamental shift in the international division of labour. It can no longer be assumed that a select group of Western countries will continue to dominate the production of manufactured goods. Scotland has been a member of this group, though its role has tended to decline. Once pre-eminent in steelmaking and shipbuilding, manufacturing production in Scotland now accounts for only 0·7 per cent of total OECD production. Scotland is thus a peripheral member of a group of industrialised countries whose comparative advantage in the production of manufactures has been considerably eroded. The restoration of this comparative advantage through the discovery of new directions for Scottish enterprise is the fundamental problem to which industrial policy in Scotland should be addressed.

This chapter is not concerned with the formulation of such policy, however. Subsequent chapters will deal with policy in some considerable detail. Rather, it is here intended to describe and analyse some of the major changes in Scotland's industrial performance which have taken place in the recent past and to project these tentatively into the future. This chapter should thus be seen as providing a backdrop to the more detailed discussion of industrial policy which will follow.

There are two main sections in the chapter, one concerned with assessing past trends, the other with making projections. In the initial part of the first section a brief summary of the symptoms of Scotland's industrial decline is set out. This discussion begins with a consideration of general indicators of welfare and economic performance. This is followed by a description of trends in international trade which have contributed to the current state of the Scottish economy. Another major influence on Scotland's recent economic history is the shift in emphasis away from the production of goods towards the provision of services. This development is analysed in the next subsection. The first section is concluded with a discussion of more fundamental explanations for the continuing decline in the relative performance of the Scottish economy. The second section begins with a description of the model and the assumptions used in the projections. Results for the period 1982–88 are then described and the concluding comments include a consideration of their implications for the labour market.

Recent Trends in Scottish Industry

The Symptoms of Decline. After 1945, the Scottish economy had to acclimatise to existing in an essentially peaceful world. Since then some industries have died, other have flourished; and the composition and industrial distribution of the labour force have altered dramatically. Yet, it is arguable that the changes which have taken place have either not been radical enough or have been completely misdirected. For, in the period since World War II, the U K and Scottish economies have gradually slipped down the international league table in terms of all the important economic indicators.

Immediately following World War II, output and productivity levels in Britain easily surpassed those in Continental Europe. While it was accepted that the U K would continue to lag behind the U S A and Canada, it was wrongly believed that Britain could maintain its position in the first rank of industrial powers. The Scottish economy, while not so robust as that in other parts of the U K, was forecast to benefit from the 'spillover' effects of this continuing prosperity. In what follows, it will be apparent that such 'spillover' linkages are extremely strong. Thus, on almost all standard indicators, Scotland's economic performance more closely resembles that of other parts of the U K, than of any of its international competitors.

Countries such as France, Japan and West Germany, which had lost much of their industry during the war, were expected to narrow the large gaps in income and output levels which existed in the early fifties. What was not expected, however, was the rapidity with which the U K would be overtaken and then left trailing by these nations. During the fifties, sixties and early seventies, the performance of the U K and Scottish economies lagged well behind the average for the industrial world. Some comparative statistics are shown in Table 1.1.

Scotland and the U K have moved closely together on most main economic indicators, with Scotland having perhaps a somewhat better growth performance over the whole period (once the effects of North Sea oil are excluded) and a slightly poorer record on unemployment. Yet, by comparison with the other major industrial countries, the record of the U K and Scotland is dismal. The rate of growth of real incomes in

2

Scotland lags way behind that in the USA, France, West Germany and Japan. And this is true whether one considers the period prior to the first major rise in oil prices or the period of slower growth which followed the OPEC intervention. These countries have also, by and large, provided a continuous growth in employment to absorb any increase in labour supply. (The case of West Germany is somewhat special because of the 'guest worker' phenomenon.) In Scotland, employment opportunities have tended to decline even though labour supply has increased, leaving little option but emigration or unemployment.

Table 1.1. Some indicators of economic performance.

	Real GDP growth (%)		Employment growth (%)		Average unemployment rate (%)	
	1963–72	1973–81	1963–72	1973–81	1963–72	1973–81
Scotland	2·9	0·4	−0·5	0·0	4·0	7·6
UK (incl. oil)	2·6	0·7	−0·1	−0·3	2·4	5·2
UK (excl. oil)	2·6	0·2	n.a.	n.a.	n.a.	n.a.
USA	4·0	2·7	2·1	2·3	4·7	6·7
France	5·5	2·8	0·8	0·4	1·9	4·8
West Germany	4·5	2·3	0·0	−0·3	0·9	3·4
Japan	10·5	4·4	1·2	1·0	1·2	1·9

Sources: IMF, *World Economic Outlook 1983*; C.Lythe and M.Majmudar, *The Renaissance of the Scottish Economy*, Allen and Unwin (London), 1982; London Business School, *Economic Outlook*, vol.7, no.1, 1982; *Scottish Abstract of Statistics*, 1983.

The effects of slow growth are not academic. The real income which individuals enjoy is dependent not only on the level of income but also on its distribution. However, the attainment of high rates of growth and consequently high average levels of income at least give a society the ability to choose how to distribute a somewhat larger cake. With faster growth, greater public spending on health, education, etc., need not necessarily be traded off to the same extent against greater private income. Faster growth also raises the level of demand in the labour market. The unemployment consequences of zero or even negative growth have become apparent with the Scottish jobless total rising by 500 per cent between 1962 and 1982.

A consistently poor growth performance has resulted in Scotland slipping gradually into the economic backwaters of Europe. It now lags behind the major EC countries to such an extent that it is considered one of the poorest regions of Europe and as such is eligible for many forms of

EC regional assistance. This decline, as mentioned earlier, is more the result of the consistently poor performance of the whole of the U K relative to other industrial countries rather than being the result of an inadequate showing by Scotland compared with other parts of the U K.

Table 1.2. Gross domestic product (£m) for Scotland and U K, 1971–81.

	1971	1972	1975	1976	1979	1981
Scotland	4281	4856	8468	9937	14677	18146
U K (less cont. shelf)	49079	55302	94346	110970	162257	198816
Scotland as % of U K	8·7	8·8	9·0	9·0	9·0	9·1

Sources: C.Moncur, 'Regional Accounts: Scottish Trends 1971–1980', *Scottish Economic Bulletin*, No.25, Summer 1982; *Scottish Abstract of Statistics*, 1983.

In fact, the Scottish economy has tended to outperform the rest of the U K since the mid sixties on a number of counts. Scotland's share of U K national output moved fairly steadily upward during the 1970s. This occurred even though Scotland's population fell by 1·9 per cent over the decade to 1981, while at the same time U K population actually rose by one per cent. Thus the increase in G D P per capita in Scotland was even faster relative to the rest of the U K than the figures in Table 1.2 suggest. A number of reasons have been forwarded for this relative improvement. First, there has been a tendency throughout the U K towards convergence of wage levels. Wages in the depressed regions moved closer to those in the more affluent areas. Perhaps this is partially the result of successful trade union activity to ensure parity of payment between workers in different parts of the U K. Alternatively, it may be the result of faster-than-average productivity improvements in the depressed regions. In turn, this may be the result of the success of regional policy in lowering the relative price of capital in the less affluent areas. Table 1.3 demonstrates that capital expenditure by Scottish manufacturing industry at least kept pace with that in the rest of the U K during the 1970s.

Capital spending in food, drink and tobacco has been consistently high in Scotland relative to the rest of the U K, even when the slightly higher proportion of employees in this sector is taken into account. The share of spending in the chemicals industry has tended to grow through time as a result of the growing importance of the North Sea in providing basic chemical feedstocks. In engineering, however, capital spending has been declining heavily in real terms. Between 1975 and 1979 the price of investment goods rose by about sixty per cent. Capital spending by the Scottish engineering industry only rose by nineteen per cent in nominal terms over the same period. In the textile and clothing industries, capital spending in Scottish firms has tended to increase as a share of that in the

U K as a whole. The greater preponderance of high-quality clothing and textile products in Scotland, more able to resist foreign competition, has undoubtedly played some part in this development. Thus, though there have been marked year-to-year fluctuations in Scotland's share of capital expenditure in U K manufacturing industry, the overall tendency has been upward.

Table 1.3. Net capital expenditure by industry group, 1963–79.

	Food, drink, tobacco	Coal, petroleum, chemical products	Engineering and allied	Textiles, leather and clothing	Other manu-facturing	Total manu-facturing
Expenditure (£m current prices)						
1963	16·4	24·6	30·3	6·6	14·9	92·8
1973	56·1	18·9	94·0	19·4	41·4	229·8
1975	86·1	75·5	183·7	19·3	60·8	425·6
1977	94·6	66·7	244·7	22·7	64·6	493·3
1979	123·0	109·4	218·3	33·8	112·0	596·6
Scotland as % of UK						
1963	11·8	8·6	9·1	7·8	8·2	9·0
1973	15·7	9·1	9·4	8·4	8·8	10·1
1975	19·1	12·7	9·1	8·4	8·7	12·0
1977	13·4	12·0	8·7	9·6	8·0	10·3
1979	13·5	10·9	7·7	10·3	8·3	8·6

Sources: Summary Reports of the Census of Production, *Business Monitor*, PA1002, various issues.

Having built up a newer and more adequate supply of capital, one might expect the level of productivity in Scottish manufacturing to rise relative to that in the U K. Figure 1.1 shows that this has indeed been the case. The graph demonstrates how rapidly output per worker in manu-facturing industry has been growing in Scotland relative to the rest of the U K in the period 1960–82. While sufficient statistics are not yet available to demonstrate whether, in absolute terms, output per worker is now higher in Scotland than in the rest of the U K, a great deal of the leeway which did exist has now been made up. Partly, this improvement in productivity is the result of a more severe 'shake-out' of labour from the Scottish manufacturing sector. However, the overall reduction in em-ployment has not been so marked in Scotland as has been the case in the U K, as is clear from Table 1.4.

The Scottish share of total U K employment has fluctuated around nine per cent, and if anything has tended to rise even though the popu-lation has fallen relative to that of the rest of the U K. One explanation

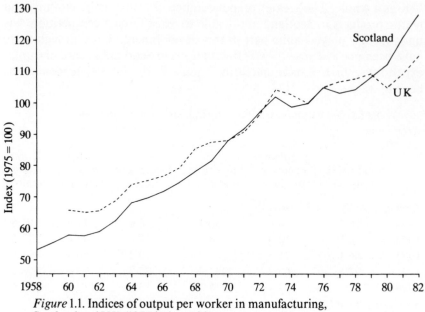

Figure 1.1. Indices of output per worker in manufacturing, Scotland and U K (1975 index=100).

of this change is that participation rates have grown more rapidly in Scotland – the evidence certainly suggests that women have a higher propensity to enter (or re-enter) the labour market in Scotland than in the rest of the U K. Another possible explanation of the expanding Scottish share of U K employment is that unemployment has grown less rapidly in Scotland. This can be judged from Table 1.5.

Table 1.4. Employment in Scotland and the U K (mid-year estimates in thousands).

	1971	1973	1975	1978	1981
Scotland	2003	2050	2076	2067	1931
U K	22122	22664	22710	22757	21192
Scotland as % of U K	9·05	9·05	9·14	9·08	9·11

Sources: *Regional Trends*, various issues; *Department of Employment Gazette*, February 1983.

Between 1971 and 1981, unemployment grew far less rapidly in Scotland than in the rest of the U K, with its share of total unemployment falling from 16·0 per cent in 1971 to 11·4 per cent in 1981. Though this comparison seems to point to a substantial improvement in Scotland's fortunes, the absolute rise in unemployment throughout the U K has been dramatic. The improvement is more attributable to a more serious deterioration in labour market conditions in the rest of the U K rather than any real improvement in Scotland.

Taken together, all the indicators discussed above suggest that Scotland's economic performance relative to the rest of the U K has shown a distinct improvement during the last decade. Nevertheless, these changes of relative performance between Scotland and other parts of the U K are minuscule by comparison with the differences in economic performance between the U K and other industrial countries.

Table 1.5. Unemployment in Scotland and the U K, 1971–82
(June each year, in thousands).

	1971	1973	1975	1978	1981
Scotland	116	91	100	187	306
U K	724	575	866	1446	2681
Scotland as % of U K	16·02	15·83	11·55	12·93	11·41

Source: *Department of Employment Gazette*, various issues.

Trade. The failure to emulate the economic progress made by many countries since the last war has been accompanied by a signal inability to maintain our position as a major trading nation. Though there is not a great deal of reliable information on Scottish trade patterns, since many goods are shipped into or out of Scotland via the rest of the U K, there is no reason to believe that Scottish trading performance over the last thirty years has been substantially different from that of the U K as a whole. Had Scotland performed markedly better or worse, those comparative indicators of Scotland and the rest of the U K, described above, would show much more significant disparities.

The term 'de-industrialisation' has been interpreted in a number of ways, the most common of which is the inability of a country to maintain a favourable trade balance in manufactured goods. A brief glance at the statistics confirms that the de-industrialisation process in the U K is well advanced. In 1983, for the first time since the beginning of the industrial revolution, the U K imported more manufactured goods than it exported. The U K trade balance in manufactured goods is shown in Figure 1.2. Of course, export failure and import penetration have not been uniform across all sectors of the economy. The recent U K record in the production of motor vehicles has been catastrophic, while in foodstuffs and drink, there has been little significant change in recent years. If anything, the increased import penetration has been less devastating in its effects on Scotland than in other parts of the U K. Without a vehicle industry of any size, for example, Scotland had less to lose when foreign imports began to decimate the British motor industry.

7

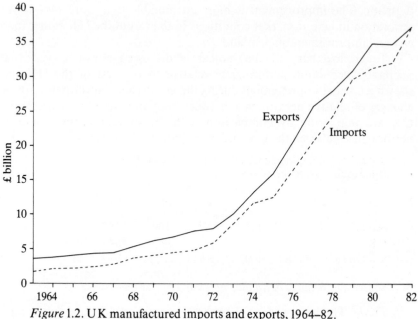

Figure 1.2. U K manufactured imports and exports, 1964–82.

Many explanations of the failure of the U K to establish a secure basis in international trade have been forwarded. Some of these are connected to its overall failure to reap the potential benefits of industrialisation. These will be touched on in the next section. Others are more directly related to trading behaviour and are worth discussing here since they have an important bearing on how Scotland has encountered difficulty in international markets. Factors determining export and import flows have been studied in some considerable detail at the U K level. The conventional wisdom holds that prices matter in international trade and hence the level of domestic prices relative to those worldwide when converted at the going exchange rate will be a critical factor in determining export success. Econometric modelling tends to confirm this view, though some modellers (notably those at the London Business School) hold that any benefits gained from devaluation will be temporary since the domestic price level will eventually rise to offset the advantage gained from an initial devaluation. Under this view, manipulation of the exchange rate by the authorities confers only temporary benefits to the domestic economy, which are eroded as wage bargainers strive to return to the pre-devaluation value of their real wage. Although there is clearly some erosion of benefits from devaluation, the empirical evidence does not presently suggest that these benefits are completely nullified. Thus, exchange-rate-induced boosts to competitiveness are still widely regarded as resulting in a more favourable balance between exports and imports.

8

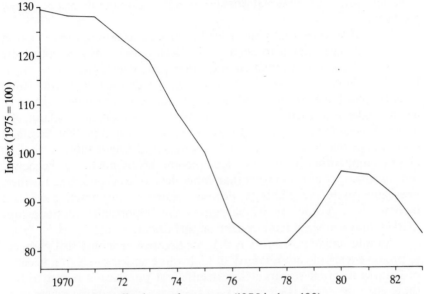

Figure 1.3. U K effective exchange rate (1975 index=100).

This approach somewhat oversimplifies the situation that exporters must deal with in the real world. Not all international markets are truly competitive. If this is the case, the major effect of devaluation will be to increase the profitability of foreign trade *vis-à-vis* domestic trade. While this may have long-run effects on firms' investment strategies, there may be no immediate quantity repercussions affecting output and employment.

Devaluation effects are concentrated on affecting the level of demand for a particular product. They may bring forward increased supply in the future. Such a development, however, is critically dependent on entrepreneurs' expectations of the future course of the exchange rate since that is what will be relevant when any increased supply comes on the market. Obviously, a high volatility in exchange rates will tend to make firms cautious and unwilling to invest in additional capacity because of the uncertainty which surrounds their future returns. Devaluation will obviously not bring forward any quantity effects immediately from firms which are supply-constrained.

Further, a long run of devaluations may only serve to fossilise the existing industrial structure. Weak industries producing low value added goods will be protected by devaluation and there will be no great incentive to innovate toward higher value products. Figure 1.3 shows that the general trend of sterling over the last decade has been downward. And one of the implications which would seem to follow from the above

9

argument is that the external pressure to restructure the British economy has been relatively weak.

If devaluation actually succeeded in producing a long-run reduction in the real wage offered to Scottish workers, perhaps as a result of the successful long-term implementation of an incomes policy, one might find that the economy would tend toward the production of low value added goods. For example, a sufficient devaluation of sterling might, once again, make low-quality textiles a viable proposition in Scotland. To accept this outcome or even to welcome it is to accept that Scotland should continue to move down the international league table so that its closest competitors in terms of real income levels might be the newly industrialising countries rather than other developed economies. Further, low-value products are likely to become relatively less attractive as world income rises. A country which spurns the opportunity to trade 'up-market' may sooner or later lose the opportunity to trade.

An alternative possibility is that the Scottish economy still manages to produce a significant quantity of high value added goods, but because of failures in other sectors it has insufficient purchasing power to buy these same products. High-quality knitwear is a case in point where most Scots can only afford to buy down-market, with the result that the bulk of high-quality Scottish woollens are sold to countries whose average income is considerably higher than that of Scotland. Of course, a small country such as Scotland must expect a high proportion of its products to be exported. What is disturbing is that the performance of the Scottish economy has been so poor as to have led to a situation where fewer Scots can afford to purchase the traditionally high-quality goods which are produced in Scotland.

Another problem with the conventional analysis of devaluation is that it is largely static. It does not take into account dynamic effects on trade conditions. There is a body of thought which argues that product innovation is more important than the traditional comparative advantage explanation of trading patterns. Countries which can successfully introduce new products to world markets are not vulnerable to competition until other countries are able to replicate the technology. This process confers a temporary advantage on the innovating country. This advantage can be maintained for a considerable length of time, however, when the product goes through a 'cycle' of development and the innovator maintains a lead in moving through its various stages. Eventually, when the technology of production becomes commonplace and easy to instal, the forces of comparative advantage will play a fuller role in determining trading patterns. By this point, the original innovating country will have hoped to move on to some new product in the initial stages of its 'product cycle'. This is a process which Japan has exploited in the post-war era, particularly in shipbuilding, cameras and consumer electronics.

To maintain a strong position in international trade, Scottish industry must look beyond the hope that devaluation will give it respite from increasingly oppressive competition. Most econometric equations describing UK exports have time trends built into them which generally exert a negative influence on export volume. These trends are assumed to proxy the complex of non-price factors which are difficult to quantify, but which clearly have not been working in the UK's favour in the post-war era. Successful action to raise the level of non-price competitiveness of Scottish goods requires more detailed analysis than that provided by a simple time trend.

Several studies, most notably that of NEDO,[1] have shown that British exports rate very poorly in terms of their non-price competitiveness. Poor performance on quality, delivery dates and marketing have all contributed to the catastrophic decline in Britain's share of world trade. Hard evidence on the relative importance of these factors is difficult to come by. Studies, such as that by Kravis and Lipsey,[2] do show how much importance businessmen place on non-price factors. Interviewing US exporters, they found that only 27 per cent attributed their success to price advantages, whereas 37 per cent suggested the critical factor was product superiority, 12 per cent cited after-sales service and 10 per cent product uniqueness. While these statistics clearly demonstrate the importance of non-price factors, it is worth bearing in mind that price and non-price elements are unlikely to be entirely distinct. Firms which are able to maintain a large surplus of price over direct costs have the opportunity to 'reinvest' some of this surplus in improving their non-price competitiveness. This may mean improving quality, upgrading after-sales service, additional marketing effort etc. If improved market share is the result of increased attention to non-price factors, the firm may be able to realise economies of scale in production and maintain a high surplus of unit price over direct costs. UK exporters seem to have consistently had difficulty in finding the correct balance between price and non-price factors with the result that many have dropped out of the export trade, claiming it to be insufficiently profitable.

To conclude this section on the decline in Scotland's position as a trading country, there is no doubt that the level of sterling does play an important role in the short-run determination of export demand. However, in the longer run, continual attempts to bolster a trading position through manipulation of the exchange rate are likely to be self-defeating. Continual devaluation may retard the pace of structural change by protecting industries whose long-term prospects are questionable. Few export markets are of the perfectly competitive form assumed in standard texts. Significant economies of scale, barriers to entry and non-homogeneity of products are as common in international markets as in domestic markets. Hence considerable attention must be paid to non-price factors such as delivery dates and after-sales service if market shares are to be maintained or expanded.

The Growth of the Service Sector. Another significant change which has paralleled Scotland's economic decline during the last thirty years has been the explosion of growth in the service sector. Some would argue that failure in the manufacturing sector is partly the result of the success-ful expansion of services. This is a matter of some contention and is best discussed following a quantification of the scale of service growth in recent Scottish economic history.

In 1962, the service sector accounted for 45 per cent of employment in Scotland. By 1982, that proportion had grown to 53 per cent. Through-out the sixties and for most of the seventies, the decline in manufacturing employment was matched by a rise in services, and consequently total employment remained almost static.

Table 1.6. Percentage distribution of household expenditure in Scotland, 1967–77.

Category	1967	1971	1974	1977
Housing	11·5	12·8	13·8	14·4
Fuel & light	6·3	6·0	5·2	6·1
Food	27·3	25·9	24·5	24·7
Alcoholic drink	4·2	4·7	4·8	4·9
Tobacco	5·4	4·2	3·6	3·6
Clothing	8·8	9·0	9·1	8·0
Durables	6·4	6·5	7·8	6·9
Other goods	7·2	7·5	7·7	7·4
Transport	12·5	13·7	13·4	13·5
Services	10·0	9·4	9·6	9·7
Miscellaneous	0·4	0·3	0·5	0·8

Source: *Family Expenditure Survey*, various issues.

A number of explanations for the rapid growth in services have been put forward. First, it has been argued that services are income-elastic and hence will inevitably outstrip other industries during a prolonged period of growth. As an argument, this is not wholly convincing since the evi-dence in Scotland does not suggest any substantial increase in household consumption of services as income has increased. Table 1.6 lists budget shares for different categories of consumer spending for a representative sample of recent years. The evidence does not show any dramatic surge in household spending on services even though real incomes increased considerably over this period. Yet this refutation of the 'high income elasticity' hypothesis of service-sector growth is predicated on the assumption that private households are the major consumers of services.

In fact, there are four major groups of consumers of Scottish services. These are:

(1) private households – who buy services for personal consumption.
(2) public agencies – who buy services on behalf of the public or provide services directly to the public.
(3) producers – who use services in the course of production or in the provision of other services.
(4) external consumers – those who buy Scottish services from outwith Scotland.

Service establishments are generally specialised in providing for these groups. For example, firms specialising in refrigerated transport will most probably be linked to the food-producing sector of manufacturing whereas many removal firms will deal only with the public. Scientific services for farmers are provided by the Government to the farming community, while many of the Scottish life-insurance companies find the bulk of their business outside Scotland. These distinctions between the different categories of consumers of services are crucial to the appreciation of recent developments in the Scottish service sector and to its likely future course. Further, the wide differences in the functions which the service sector provides means that there are wide disparities in the potential for productivity gains.

The presumed lack of potential for productivity growth in services has been put forward as another explanation of the phenomenal growth in service-sector employment in recent years. Yet again there are considerable differences between different types of services. Some service sectors are quite capital-intensive, notably transport and communications. Although these industries are subject to considerable Government regulation, there is potential for productivity gain as more efficient equipment becomes available. Some industries have experienced a substantial productivity gain without the benefit of increased capital intensity. Employment in distribution has fallen from 283 000 in 1965 to 193 000 in 1981 even though the volume of retail sales increased by approximately 33 per cent during this period. The trend toward larger and more efficient retail outlets is the major cause of this trend. Some service industries such as educational and legal services are heavily labour-intensive and are likely to remain so.

The general argument that the expansion of service employment is the result of the poor productivity record of the service sector as a whole relative to manufacturing seems contradictory. So, unless the demand for services is independent of their price, one would expect that poor productivity would lead to higher prices and hence reduced demand relative to manufactures. However, not only has the level of employment in services been rising relative to that in manufacturing, so also has the level of output. In 1971 service output accounted for 43 per cent of Scottish GDP. By 1981, this proportion had risen to 50 per cent. Thus the demand for services seems to have been strong, irrespective of any productivity effects. Nevertheless, there is an argument that certain categories of service, say those provided by the authorities for public consumption, are not susceptible to competitive pricing influences. However, those services exported from Scotland and those supplied to consumers and producers generally have to be priced competitively. Even those subject to considerable regulation regarding their pricing behaviour frequently attempt to use non-price competition to differentiate their product from that of their rivals.

Whatever the cause, the Scottish economy, like that of most Western nations, has experienced a considerable shift in resources away from manufacturing and into services in recent years. While this may be a natural response to a changing pattern of public and private demand, it is certain to cause difficulties if growth is to be restored as the top economic priority.

The difficulty is that a service-based economy generally finds it difficult to take advantage of external demand in generating growth. International markets for services are notoriously uncompetitive. Although the UK is extremely successful in the export of services, notably transport and financial services, much of this success is based on the convenience and reputation of London as a centre for international business. There are undoubtedly some opportunities for export of services in areas where Scotland has a comparative advantage, such as medicine, insurance and education. However, it is perhaps unrealistic to expect a sudden freeing of world trade in markets which previously have been highly regulated. This is particularly true at a time when the world seems gradually to be slipping toward a greater degree of protectionism. It is, therefore, wishful thinking to expect that a sudden expansion in the export of services can provide some sort of panacea to Scotland's present economic ailments.

The Causes of Decline. In seeking to explain the long-term decline of Scottish manufacturing industry, commentators normally extend beyond the narrow quantitative explanations which are commonly used to describe the current short-term problems of the British economy. The immediate causes of these short-term problems are then viewed more properly as symptoms of the UK's longer-term economic failure. The search for the underlying causes must inevitably probe somewhat deeper into the structure of our society and also will remain essentially speculative since this is an area where definitive answers are rare.

The first point to make is that the long-term problems of Scottish industry should not be viewed simply as a failure to maintain a constant level of employment in the manufacturing sector. There is no reason to expect constancy in the level of employment during a period where rapid technical change enables considerable expansion of productivity. Productivity gains are to be welcomed as increasing the scope for profitable business expansion. Thus employment levels should not be taken to be the main symptom of economic decline. Rather, one should think of decline in terms of Scotland and the U K's increasing inability to maintain a favourable balance on trade in manufactured goods. Britain was the first nation whose wealth was derived from its ability to successfully exchange manufactured goods for raw materials and food. Now, due to the eccentricities of the Common Agricultural Policy and the chance discovery of oil in the North Sea, the balance is swinging toward the export of foods and raw materials and the importation of manufactures.

· Secondly, it is clear that Scotland's economic ailments cannot be very different in character from those of the U K as a whole. Were it the case that the explanation of Scotland's relatively poor performance during the last thirty years was of a markedly different nature from that of the rest of the U K, one would have expected some significant differences in economic performance between Scotland and the rest of the U K during this period. Yet, as mentioned at the beginning of the chapter, while there have been some divergences between economic indicators, these have been minor compared to the gaps in growth and income which have opened up between the U K and most other developed nations.

It is also apparent that one should not be particularly surprised by this coincidence of economic malaise. Scotland and the rest of the U K share a common monetary system, a common administrative structure and a common institutional environment, each of which is bound to heavily influence the course of economic development. Scotland does further suffer from its peripheral position in the European market, though this peripherality is itself simply a reflection of past failures. Until recently, California could hardly have been accused of being at the centre of a great trading area. Yet, its own success partly explains the growing importance of trade round the Pacific basin. Peripherality is a relative, not an absolute concept.

The immediate explanation of Scotland's failure to produce sufficient goods to bring it into serious competition with the income levels of the major European countries is a lack of sufficient industrial capacity. There is insufficient capital in the Scottish economy to provide the necessary levels of output. Scotland certainly does not suffer from any shortage of labour. An excess supply of labour, manifested in high levels of emigration, has been a recurrent feature of Scotland's economic history. Since 1931, migration from Scotland has totalled 972 000 – more than the combined population of Highland, Grampian and Tayside regions. In 1963, net emigration amounted to 42 000 – more than 0·8 per cent of the population in a single year.

A failure to install sufficiently productive capital is thus the major obvious cause of Scotland's low output. Given that, relative to most of Europe, Scotland survived the Second World War with most of its capital intact, some have argued that it was the chronic slowness with which this capital was replaced that caused the lag in performance. Failure to adapt to new industries, to change the structure of Scottish industry, initiated the decline into mediocrity. It is obvious that Scottish industry is burdened by an excess of resources being poured into industries which cannot realistically expect to produce the types of goods likely to be in high demand in world markets twenty years from now. Even so, failure to adapt the structure of Scottish industry is not a full explanation of present problems. A complete explanation requires us to consider why such resistance to change has become a characteristic of the Scottish economy.

Perhaps the explanation of this inertia lies in the failure of Government policy to concern itself sufficiently with economic growth and with industrial investment. It is certainly true that post-war U K Governments have tended to be preoccupied with demand-management policies rather than industrial policy. In particular, demand-management has been used to handle the balance of payments problems which have plagued the British economy since the 'convertibility crisis' of 1947. The instinctive reaction of nearly all Governments when confronted by a drain on foreign reserves has been to devalue sterling and/or introduce deflationary measures in the domestic economy. Both of these cause negative repercussions on industry. As mentioned earlier, devaluation is a prescription for the preservation of the industrial status quo and an encouragement to trade 'down-market'. Successive rounds of 'stop-go' policies leave industries uncertain as to future prospects. Uncertainty breeds caution as far as investment and innovation are concerned.

Further, post-war Governments have always sought to maintain consumption during periods of restraint and have placed much less emphasis on maintaining investment. In turn, this reflects an attitude amongst the British people that investment and industry are not worthy of particular concern. The interests of industry are expendable. This attitude is deeply rooted in the national consciousness of Scotland. This may seem surprising given that Scotland was one of the first areas in the world to experience the Industrial Revolution and led the way in the introduction of many new products and processes.

Yet Weiner[3] has argued persuasively that, in England, support for industrialisation and an economy based on manufacturing was already declining in the latter half of the nineteenth century. His view is that the Industrial Revolution was thwarted by the lack of any coincident revolution in social attitudes and relationships. A romantic, rural view of England persisted amongst the ruling classes which was at odds with the ethos of industrialisation. Based on this view, education made no concessions to the needs of an industrial society, but rather stressed the disciplines which would only be useful for an academic or professional career. Further, industrialists failed to find an effective political voice. The Conservative Party was dominated by the landed gentry, whose aspirations certainly did not coincide with those of industry, while the emergent socialist and trade union movements were founded on opposition to the excesses of industrialisation.

Scottish culture has been increasingly dominated by that of England since the union of 1707 and thus it is not surprising that many of the views ascribed to English society by Weiner are also applicable in Scotland. In literature, politics and education the 'British' view has tended to swamp that of Scotland. Also, in Scotland as in England, the industrial revolution was confined to industry. It did not cause a reordering of the power structure of Scottish society. Thus industrialists never became a dominant force in Scottish politics. Therefore, unlike other industrial nations which have been forced to change their institutions and aspirations, Scotland has tended to a position where those who use their advocacy to support the cause of greater industrial efficiency and production have been heavily outweighed by the apathy and hostility of other sections of society.

If it is the attitudes and aspirations of society which are the cause, then the explanation that growth has been retarded by the 'stop-go' policies of successive post-war Governments must be discarded or at least heavily discounted. Further, the growth of the service economy which some have argued has caused a 'crowding out' of resources from manufacturing may simply be a reflection of the attitudes which play down the contribution of industry to society. One can explain such 'crowding out' in terms of the pressure placed on the financial markets by Government spending to fund activities which tend to be concentrated in the service sector. However, such spending is itself a reflection of the political priorities of Government. While some Governments, under the influence of Keynes, have argued that state spending can benefit the industrial sector, such benefits are generally regarded as secondary spin-offs rather than being the primary purpose of expenditure programmes. Industries which have been successful in the UK have been left, by and large, to fend for themselves. Aid has been channelled to some declining sectors largely as a result of the political pressure which organised labour can exert. The rarely-stated argument used implicitly in defence of declining industry is that change is undesirable because instability and uncertainty will inevitably accompany such change. The hard facts of changing international comparative advantage, which make change and uncertainty inevitable whether the status quo is maintained or some other option is chosen, are generally subliminated. From workers whose only apparent option is the dole queue, such a view is understandable. Yet this resistance to change is no different in essence from the inertia which has characterised British institutions during the last hundred years.

If the problems of Scottish industry are as deep-seated as the above argument suggests, then the success of Scottish industry is contingent on a great many fundamental changes in attitude to the process of production. Important changes can be made at the industry level as are discussed in other chapters. But wider changes are necessary, particularly at the educational level, in reassessing the role and contribution of industry in Scottish society, elevating it from its current low status.

This concludes the examination of past trends in Scottish industry. In the next section, attention is turned to the future and some future trends in Scottish industry are discussed.

Projections of the Scottish Economy

Methodology and Assumptions. Making accurate projections for the Scottish economy is extremely difficult because of the paucity of information on its structure and behaviour. There are wide areas of ignorance of Scottish economic experience rendering forecasting a more than usually hazardous procedure. In particular, since there is no comprehensive information on wages and prices, it is difficult to build a model which can adequately represent anything other than fairly simple quantity adjustments. It is thus difficult to take account of improved competitiveness resulting from increased productivity except in a fairly *ad hoc* fashion.

The model used in the present projection exercise has been constructed at the Fraser of Allander Institute and is essentially Keynesian insofar as it emphasises quantity, rather than price, adjustments. There are no supply constraints, a feature which in general terms is fairly reasonable, though undoubtedly there have been certain instances when it has been invalid. The model is multi-sectoral, recognising forty-two different industrial sectors, of which twenty-eight are within manufacturing. It is demand-driven, with twenty separate categories of final demand expenditure which can be individually assigned or set to grow at predetermined rates. The full list of final demand categories is contained in an appendix to this chapter. Inter-industry relationships are represented by the input/output tables which have been constructed for the Scottish economy in conjunction with the Scottish Council (Development and Industry).

The programmes which operate the model allow for the incorporation of different input/output matrices each year as the structure of the economy changes. Different allocations of final demand categories between commodities are also allowable each year, as are different rates of growth or levels of final demand.

Thus, although lack of knowledge of the Scottish economy is a serious obstacle to 'precise' and mechanistic forecasting, the model described here is sufficiently flexible to incorporate a wide range of alternative patterns of development for the Scottish economy.

Constructing a Forecast. This section of the chapter is concerned with the normal procedures which are used in making parameter changes in the model. Most of the changes are concerned with the allocation of final demands and the logical way in which to proceed with the discussion is to consider the major categories of final demand in turn.

The treatment of consumers' expenditure is crucial to the overall performance of the model since consumption accounts for approximately sixty per cent of total final demand. There are twelve separate categories of consumption and variation in total expenditure on these categories accounts for most of the variation in the pattern of industrial demand emanating from consumers' demand as a whole. Thus, a switch in spending away from food towards housing will result in increased demand for construction and reduced demand for food processing. In the model, this change is accommodated simply by increasing the total expenditure on housing relative to that on food. In turn, this means that those industries which are geared to supplying the housing industry will be faced with an increase in demand relative to those supplying food products. There is no need to change the pattern of industrial demands within a single expenditure category since food and housing have distinct profiles of industrial demand which are fully reflected within the model.

The position does become more difficult when a single consumers' expenditure category includes types of spending which one believes are likely to behave quite differently in the future. For example, the drink and tobacco category of expenditure encompasses types of consumer goods for which the demand is likely to grow at different rates. While the budget share of drink is likely to remain stable or even increase, the change in tastes away from cigarettes is likely to result in a sharp fall in the budget share of tobacco.

Since this development must be accommodated within a single expenditure category, it is necessary to change the allocation of demands to industries within this category. This simply means that, within consumer spending on drink and tobacco, a relatively greater weight must be allocated to demands on the drinks industry and relatively less to demands on tobacco production.

It would be desirable to have a sufficiently fine disaggregation of consumers' expenditure such that the only changes required were those to the relative weights given to different components of consumers' demand. Without this, the necessity to change some of the industrial allocations within a single spending category seems unavoidable, given the level of aggregation inherent in currently available statistics. Thus for the present one must accept the different treatment accorded to categories of expenditure which are classified to distinct expenditure aggregates within the model, as compared with that given to categories which are classified within wider aggregates.

Other categories of expenditure are not broken down in the same detail as consumption. However, Government spending comprises expenditure by Central Government, by Local Government and other Government spending. Thus, one can easily accommodate changes in the relative weight given to Central Government spending as opposed to that on Local Government using the same method as that outlined above for a change in the balance of consumer spending between food and housing.

Many of the adjustments require the use of data which is frequently unavailable for Scotland separately. For example, there are no regularly published data on inventories held by different Scottish industries. The procedure normally followed when such changes are necessary is that base year Scottish figures are changed in line with the changes which are taking place in the corresponding UK aggregates. So, for instance, changes in imports from the rest of the world into Scotland are assumed to follow the changes which are taking place in the UK market, where import penetration of manufactured goods has increased rapidly, particularly since 1979. Rates of increase in UK import penetration ratios by industry are thus applied to baseline Scottish figures to give an idea of the market penetration of imports. To give an example, suppose that imports from the rest of the world accounted for 50 per cent of the supply of new cars in Scotland in the base year. Since that time, import penetration in the UK as a whole has increased by 25 per cent. Then the assumed current import penetration ratio for Scotland is 62·5 per cent.

Information on Scottish exports is similarly limited by data deficiencies. While one can adopt reasonable assumptions for the aggregate growth in exports to the rest of the UK and to the rest of the world, there is little doubt that the industrial composition of these has changed drastically since the base year figures were compiled. As with imports, one is forced back on *ad hoc* approaches such as using growth rates which apply to the UK as a whole or concentrating on particular sectors (such as electronics in Scotland) where export growth is known to have been abnormal.

Even greater difficulties confront the treatment of sectors which are known to be highly volatile, both in terms of level and composition. The prime example of such a category of final demand is inventory change. Here the base year figures are undoubtedly of little value because of the extreme fluctuations in stocks which have occurred during the intervening business cycles. The practice here has been to rely completely on UK sources to estimate changes in the levels of Scottish stocks. Firstly, aggregate inventory change in Scotland is expressed as a fraction of UK change for some base year. This fraction is assumed constant throughout the forecast. Next, the allocation of stock change to industries is made on the basis of recent U K stock changes by industry. These figures tend to be aggregated over industrial sectors and figures have to be apportioned according to base year output weights in order to arrive at figures for individual industries. Though this is admittedly an arbitrary procedure, it is reasonable to argue that, for long-run forecasts, so long as the underlying stock/output ratio is not changing radically, the effects of the stock cycle will be neutral. Therefore it is appropriate to gradually reduce any stock change effects as the forecasts move further into the future.

Finally, the treatment of fixed investment is also problematic. Again, one can adjust Scottish aggregates in line with U K trends but there is little information on shifts in the industrial composition of fixed investment demands. Substitution away from purchases of building into plant and equipment has taken place in recent years and can be incorporated into the model parameters but information is only available at this very high level of aggregation.

Projections of the Scottish Economy 1984–88. The forecasts described in this section take, as their starting point, a view as to how economic development in the U K and the world as a whole will proceed over the period 1982–86. Such a view, of course, will be heavily conditioned by recent experience. The views expressed here draw heavily on those of the London Business School who have a long history of forecasting world and U K economic developments.

A cornerstone of these views is the belief that the rate of growth of the world economy will only be moderate by historical standards over the next four years. While the developed countries are keen to see a return to faster growth rates in order to alleviate the problem of unemployment, their overriding concern has been to overcome inflation, mostly through the use of tight fiscal and monetary policies. These policies have radically constrained short-term growth potential. Further, because of the generally high rates of interest necessary to enforce monetary discipline, debtor countries have been forced to take drastic measures to maintain solvency. With credit mostly flowing from the developed to the under-developed world, it has been mostly the poor countries of the Third World who have suffered debt repayment problems. Naturally, their reaction has been to try to expand exports in order to raise the foreign currency necessary for debt servicing. Some have been successful in this endeavour, particularly the NICs. Yet the overall debt is so great and the demand for foreign currency so voracious that many of the established industrialised countries have become extremely concerned that these exports, generally produced at very low cost, will pose a substantial threat to their domestic industrial base. Having not given sufficient attention to the necessity of forcing rapid structural change, the industrialised nations are adopting

21

the more simple expedient – protectionism. Free trading arrangements are giving way to a multiplicity of bilateral deals, which GATT seems incapable of adequately policing. This slide toward protectionism could partly be arrested if the dollar were less overvalued. Yet the balance of argument suggests that a dramatic decline in the value of the dollar is unlikely. Hence the outlook for world trade remains gloomy over the short to medium term.

The slackness of world demand will restrict the scope for export-induced growth. A reduction in the value of sterling might go some way to compensate for this weakness and the London Business School expects a reduction of around ten per cent in its effective exchange rate between 1982 and 1986 as a result of relatively rapid monetary growth in the U K. As a result, their forecast implies that exports will grow at an average of 3·4 per cent each year during this period.

By contrast, the forecast for Government spending is that the average annual rate of increase will only be 0·9 per cent. This is essentially a political judgement, though it seems clear, following the result of the 1983 election, that any dramatic increases in Government spending are unlikely. Public investment should increase, particularly as the offsetting effects of council house sales are reduced, at an annual rate of about 2·5 per cent. Consumer spending is unlikely to grow rapidly because the weakness of the labour market will continue to exert downward pressure on real wages. Further, because inflation is already at a historically low level, the savings ratio will not fall so rapidly as it has in recent years. Thus an annual growth rate of 1·6 per cent in consumers' expenditure for the period 1982–86 is expected. The final element of demand worthy of consideration is private investment. This should exhibit fairly steady growth because of improved profitability in the manufacturing sector.

The scenario of development described above is specified numerically in Table 1.7 which outlines the final demand assumptions for the Scottish economy during the period 1983–88. The sectoral results of a projection based on this scenario are shown in Table 1.8, which gives projected growth rates for Scottish industries based on the patterns of final demand listed in Table 1.7. The first six columns show real growth rates between pairs of years from 1982 to 1988, while the final column gives projected total growth in real terms over the period 1982 to 1988.

The results are by no means uniform across industries, suggesting that the process of structural change described at the beginning of the chapter is likely to continue over the projection period. High-technology industries, such as computers, electronics and aerospace, are likely to thrive, while iron and steel, shipbuilding and construction equipment will encounter further difficulties. The food industry is expected to grow slightly faster than the economy as a whole, which, in turn should benefit Scottish agriculture. Within the textile industries, a widely disparate performance is forecast. Synthetic fibres, textiles and clothing are expected to experience severe difficulties while woollens grow quite rapidly. The performance of the service sector is quite sluggish, probably because the model structure partly embodies the earlier argument that it is difficult to generate independent growth within the service sector. Similarly, the rates of growth likely to be experienced by the utilities are close to the average across industries, since they largely respond to developments elsewhere in the economy. However, their growth is likely to be partly retarded because the new, rapidly developing industries are less energy-intensive than those whose future seems to be in serious jeopardy. Note that although these results are presented at a 43-sector level of disaggregation, there is still considerable scope for variation within each sector, by groups of firms or individual companies. Some companies will thrive in industries where prospects appear poor and some new high-technology firms will go to the wall. While it is useful to produce goods for which demand appears to be rising, there is no substitute for effective and innovative management skills in ensuring continuing profitability in individual enterprises.

Table 1.7. Forecast assumptions for growth rates in Scottish final demand aggregates.[1]

Item	Percentage change					
	1982–83	1983–84	1984–85	1985–86	1986–87	1987–88
Consumption	2·5	0·9	1·3	1·7	1·7	1·7
Government	1·6	0·9	0·7	0·7	0·7	0·7
Investment	3·0	5·3	2·9	0·0	0·0	0·0
Exports to rest of UK	2·0	1·2	1·6	1·7	1·7	1·7
Exports to rest of world	2·9	3·5	3·1	2·6	2·4	2·2
Tourism	0·0	1·0	1·2	1·5	1·5	1·0
Stock change (£m)	−29·0	174·2	57·5	14·4	−11·5	8·1

[1] All values based on constant 1975 prices.
Source: Fraser of Allander Institute.

Finally, note that the overall rates of growth for the Scottish economy implied by this forecast are well in excess of the rates experienced during the late seventies and early eighties. In this sense the forecast is optimistic. However, an increase in the production of goods and services does not necessarily imply that the demand for labour will increase. If productivity continues to rise as it has since 1979, there will be little scope in the near future for reducing the level of unemployment. Recent Department of

Table 1.8. Projected industry growth rates in Scotland, 1982–88.

Sector	Percentage rate of growth						
	1982–83	1983–84	1984–85	1985–86	1986–87	1987–88	1982–88
Agriculture	1·52	2·62	2·00	1·63	1·68	1·73	11·83
Forestry and fishing	1·97	2·35	1·88	1·28	1·30	1·32	10·62
Coal mining	1·23	0·90	0·75	0·65	0·63	0·60	4·86
Other mining	-0·32	-0·20	-0·41	-0·77	-0·86	-0·96	-3·46
Oil and gas exploration	-0·14	1·52	0·94	0·45	0·46	0·48	3·78
Sugar and food products	2·26	2·00	1·87	1·62	1·62	1·63	11·63
Drinks	0·78	1·40	1·09	0·65	0·66	0·68	5·41
Tobacco	2·13	2·15	2·60	1·98	1·98	1·99	13·69
Oil products and general chemicals	0·87	1·06	0·66	0·15	0·11	0·06	2·95
Pharmaceuticals	0·56	0·07	-0·02	-0·44	-0·61	-0·80	-1·25
Paint, other chemicals and fertilisers	1·36	1·41	1·20	0·80	0·78	0·76	6·51
Iron, steel and aluminium	-1·53	-1·72	-2·06	-2·63	-2·91	-3·23	-13·13
Other non-ferrous metals	2·03	2·22	2·07	1·74	1·75	1·75	12·26
Vehicles & other mechanical engineering	0·03	-0·23	-0·42	-0·80	-1·00	-1·23	-3·58
Construction equipment	-1·94	-3·11	-3·34	-3·60	-4·14	-4·80	-18·89
Office equipment	1·00	0·32	0·48	0·33	0·27	0·19	2·63
Industrial plant and steelwork	2·30	2·30	2·25	1·99	1·99	2·00	13·69
Instrument engineering	1·46	1·39	1·36	1·15	1·15	1·15	7·97
Computer and electronics	10·56	10·74	10·61	10·33	10·34	10·36	87·66
Elec. mach., com. equ. & other elec. good	0·69	0·03	-0·01	-0·41	-0·79	-1·25	-1·73

Domestic electrical appliances	0·01	-0·94	-0·84	-0·97	-1·20	-1·46	-5·25
Shipbuilding	-2·85	-0·67	-1·23	-1·68	-1·45	-1·20	-8·69
Aerospace	4·16	4·48	4·27	3·92	3·94	3·96	28·06
Wire products and other metals	1·80	1·84	1·77	1·48	1·51	1·54	10·46
Man-made fibres and textiles	-0·87	-1·64	-1·58	-1·72	-1·90	-2·10	-9·33
Woollen and worsted	3·15	3·72	3·47	3·13	3·26	3·40	22·30
Leather and footwear	0·88	-0·01	-0·08	-0·38	-0·51	-0·66	-0·76
Clothing	-1·34	-2·25	-2·28	-2·60	-3·05	-3·57	-14·01
Building materials	0·95	0·95	0·84	0·40	0·37	0·33	3·92
Timber and furniture	1·41	1·92	1·45	1·23	1·26	1·30	8·95
Paper and board	-0·36	-0·95	-0·88	-0·96	-1·04	-1·11	-5·16
Printing and publishing	1·61	1·35	1·28	0·94	0·93	0·94	7·31
Rubber and other manufacturing	1·04	0·73	0·69	0·41	0·35	0·29	3·59
Construction	1·03	0·73	1·20	0·95	0·96	0·98	6·03
Gas	1·66	1·80	1·37	1·45	1·46	1·46	9·64
Electricity	1·40	1·34	1·00	1·06	1·06	1·07	7·17
Water	2·22	1·21	1·43	1·26	1·26	1·26	9·04
Transport	1·75	1·31	1·32	1·14	1·14	1·14	8·10
Communications	1·85	1·43	1·37	1·09	1·09	1·10	8·25
Distribution	2·06	0·91	1·19	1·54	1·54	1·55	9·20
Finance services	1·96	1·72	1·58	1·21	1·22	1·23	9·34
Other services	1·86	0·99	1·06	1·10	1·11	1·12	7·49
Household	2·72	0·97	1·43	1·60	1·60	1·60	10·43

25

Employment projections suggest that, under current policies, the Scottish labour force will rise by 60 000 between 1981 and 1986. With no increase in demand, there will thus be little scope for reducing unemployment unless new policies can be rapidly introduced to curtail labour supply. Thus, while the Scottish economy may grow somewhat more rapidly for the rest of the decade than was the case in the early eighties, it is difficult to avoid the conclusion that unemployment is a problem which will continue to trouble policy makers in the forseeable future. The policies which are described in succeeding chapters are intended at least to ameliorate the problem by making Scottish industry more resilient to the pressures of national and international competition.

These projections can only give a general impression of how the Scottish economy may develop over the next few years. Sudden major shocks to the world economy, such as a substantial rise in the oil price, may pull the economy away from its projected path. More hopefully, since the forecasts are inevitably based on historic trends and behaviour patterns, beneficial changes in policy and attitudes to the process of production may make them seem to have been unduly pessimistic.

Appendix: Final Demand Categories Used in Projections

Household Expenditure on (1) Food

                      (2) Clothing

                      (3) Housing

                      (4) Fuel and Light

                      (5) Drink and Tobacco

                      (6) Transport and Communications

                      (7) Durables

                      (8) Other Goods

                      (9) Other Services

(10) Indirect Taxes less Subsidies

(11) Tourism

(12) Fixed Investment

(13) Stock Changes

(14) Defence

(15) Local Government

(16) Other Central Government

(17) Offshore Oil (optional)

(18) Exports to Rest of World

(19) Exports to Rest of U K

(20) Imports from Rest of World

NOTES AND REFERENCES

1. NEDO, *International Price Competitiveness, Non-price Factors and Export Performance*, National Economic Development Office (London), April 1977.
2. I. B. Kravis and R. E. Lipsey, *Price Competitiveness in World Trade*, National Bureau of Economic Research (New York), 1981.
3. M. J. Weiner, *English Culture and the Decline of the Industrial Spirit 1850–1980*, Cambridge University Press, 1981.

2

INDUSTRIAL POLICY AND THE
SCOTTISH ECONOMY

STEPHEN YOUNG AND NEIL HOOD

Aside from reviewing and analysing the position of Scottish industry in the very changed circumstances of the 1980s, the major objective of this book is to take a new look at industrial policy in Scotland – to undertake a constructive evaluation of policy as presently implemented and provide some specific pointers to new initiatives. In the same way that Chapter 1 provided the background for the discussions on sectoral and company performance which are to follow, so this chapter is designed to provide an overall view of industrial policy in Scotland, within its United Kingdom context, to set the scene for later, more specific evaluations and suggestions. The chapter begins with some brief comments on the meaning of industrial policy and then looks at the history of industrial strategy in the UK and Scotland, focusing on instruments, expenditures and institutions.

The Meaning of Industrial Policy; Scottish Industrial Policy

There has been a tendency in the UK to use the term 'industrial policy' rather loosely, so that it could encompass almost all aspects of economic strategy. In part perhaps reflecting criticism along these lines, early in 1983 a paper was produced by the Department of Industry (DoI) summarising the Department's strategic aims and policies for industry (see Figure 2.1). This was intended to show the central aim of the DoI ('a profitable, competitive and adaptive productive sector in the UK') and the policies being pursued to achieve this aim, as well as providing a framework within which more detailed programmes could be developed with other departments of Government and other interested parties. Figure 2.1 shows very clearly the way in which macro- and micro-policies impact upon industry; and the former is important to bear in mind since historically fluctuations in the macroeconomic environment have been the most significant forces in uncertainty and change in the economy and in affecting the level and pattern of industrial activity. Yet industrial policy is much narrower than this and is here used in its more conventional sense to refer to industrial support, regulatory measures and programmes initiated by Government or its agencies to influence industrial

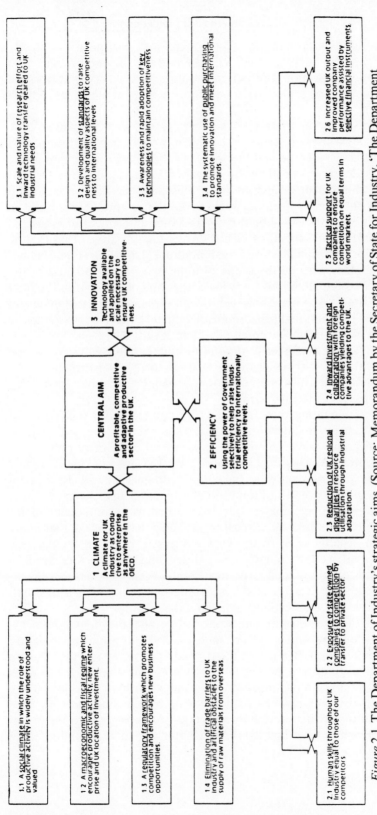

Figure 2.1. The Department of Industry's strategic aims. (Source: Memorandum by the Secretary of State for Industry, 'The Department of Industry's Strategic Aims', NEDC (83)13, NEDC (London), 1983.)

structure and performance.[1] This, therefore, encompasses chiefly elements 2 and 3 in Figure 2.1, viz. policies for the promotion of efficiency, and innovation and new technology in industry, but also the promotion of competition and the encouragement of new business opportunities.

Since the election victory of the Conservative Government in June 1983, the Department of Industry has been brought together again with the Department of Trade and the work of other Departments has a role in industrial policy. As will be shown, expenditures through the Department of Employment on employment measures constitute a large and growing proportion of spending in this overall area and there is merit in questioning whether this should be included as an element of industrial policy. Some of this spending clearly meets the objective of promoting human skills, but much is used for temporary, job-supporting schemes and is, therefore, outside the scope of industrial policy. Because of the importance of the unemployment issue, the topic is pursued in the final chapter of the book, where, however, the requirement for a sustained and coordinated international programme of demand expansion is seen as the major potential contributor to employment levels. The issue of whether or not expenditure is efficiency-promoting and therefore within the scope of industrial policy arises again in relation to the Department of the Environment's activities including the Urban Programme, Inner City Partnerships and Enterprise Zones.

Before concluding these introductory comments on the nature of industrial strategy, it is necessary to make some remarks on the position of regional policy, since this has been a crucial element of policy in a Scottish context. As Figure 2.1 indicates, the achievement of the efficiency objective is seen as requiring, *inter alia*, a 'reduction of UK regional disparities in resource utilisation through industrial adaptation'. Following this approach, regional policy is regarded as a component of industrial policy in this book. It must be accepted, nevertheless, that many are still in accordance with the view expressed in 1969 that 'the case cannot be made without reference to political and social factors'.[2] Indeed some would regard the social case for regional policy as even more compelling at present because of the widening of regional disparities with high unemployment spreading throughout the country.[3]

Given the meaning of industrial policy and the brief comments above on the Government departments involved in policy formulation and implementation, it must be questioned whether or not the concept of 'a Scottish industrial policy', independent from that of the UK, is possible. Scotland is a regional economy, and, as with other regions of the UK, lacks sovereign power over the choice of economic policies. The openness of the Scottish economy and its strong linkages with the rest of the UK have also been highlighted in Chapter 1. Notwithstanding these observations, there is the potential in Scotland, through bodies such as the Industry Department for Scotland (IDS) and the Scottish Development Agency (SDA) to design Scottish initiatives within the framework of existing guidelines and policies. Through innovative thinking and the scope for flexibility around national guidelines, it may be valid to think of a secondary tier of industrial policy which gives specific attention to the problems of industry in Scotland. It is this tier of industrial strategy, rather than that of 'a Scottish industrial policy', with which this book is concerned.

Industrial Policy in the United Kingdom

The aims of the UK industrial strategy as outlined above have been fairly stable since the 1960s with the emphasis on efficiency improvement and the promotion of technological development. Despite this, the British record on industrial policy has been unfavourably compared with that of some of its competitor nations. There are perhaps three features of policy formulation since the 1960s which have been most frequently criticised. The first concerns the tendency to derive policies which are 'slogan-oriented', relating to rather vague concepts such as planning, restructuring, industrial democracy and so on. The second relates to the frequency of policy changes, varying according to the party in power and to the state of the national economy. The way to consensus in British industrial policy has rarely been sought and never found in the post-war period. Thirdly, the policies which have existed have often been *ad hoc* as Governments responded to some short-term or local problem under specific pressures. This particular aspect has led to discrimination by sector and, more controversially, by firm within a sector – a substantial proportion of actual expenditure falling into this latter category.

Instruments. Many of the instruments of policy operated in Britain are similar to those elsewhere in the world. These include monopolies and restrictive practices policies; the use of tax allowances and investment grants to influence capital investment in industry; labour policy measures relating to labour mobility, industrial training and market clearing; and policies on industrial innovation – the latter being heavily oriented to aerospace and nuclear power industries. Some of the distinctive features of British policy have, however, arisen from the importance of public ownership since World War II. Arguably, the extent of the nationalised sector has absorbed much of the energy and finance which could have been available for industrial policy in other areas.

It is not the intention of this section to undertake a comprehensive review of the types and evolution of British industrial policy instruments, but rather to focus on the major categories of instrument and those with particular relevance to Scotland. These are regional policy, selective assistance, innovation policy, company taxation and nationalised industries' policy.[4]

Regional policy in the UK has a long history, dating back to the Special Areas Act of 1934. Policy has operated with the objective of alleviating the worst excesses of unemployment in certain regions of the country by diverting growth in the demand for labour from the prosperous and allegedly congested areas of southern Britain. A variety of instruments – grants, loans, employment subsidies, infrastructure programmes and limitations on investment in prosperous areas – have been employed since that time. In more recent years, following rationalisation of the programme in the Industry Act 1972 (now incorporated into the Industrial Development Act 1982), a hierarchy of Assisted Areas has existed in which Regional Development Grants (RDGs) have been payable almost automatically on investment in land, buildings and plant in manufacturing industry and, in addition, Selective Financial Assistance (Section 7) has been available. The coverage of the areas and rates of grant assistance have varied; and the negative controls through Industrial Development Certificates (IDCs – required for development in prosperous areas) have been applied with differing intensity. Regional policy measures have been radically cut back in the last few years: from 1982 large parts of formerly Assisted Areas were descheduled and regional aid concentrated in regions of greater need, while IDCs were suspended in 1981. Another instrument of regional policy which was introduced in 1967 was the Regional Employment Premium; this was a labour subsidy to manufacturing firms in Assisted Areas, which was eventually abolished in 1977.

More will be said on the impact of regional policy in the following section relating to Scotland. What is important to note is that the writing of this book was taking place during a period when a fundamental review of regional policy was under way in Government, culminating in the publication of a White Paper at the very end of 1983.[5] While studies of the impact of regional policy measures have indicated that substantial employment opportunities have been created in depressed areas, there has been mounting concern over the payment of grants to large, highly capital-intensive projects where the question of cost per job looms large; over the focus on manufacturing and the exclusion of construction and services; and over the designation of Assisted Areas in a period when high unemployment has spread to formerly prosperous regions such as the West Midlands. All these issues are to be tackled by legislation during 1984–85. Apart from the need for more selectivity, the main general lesson of the operation of policy between 1960 and 1975 has been that 'regional policy can be expected to divert substantial numbers of jobs only in the context of national economic expansion'.[6]

The legislative basis for the second major instrument of industrial policy – selective assistance – is contained in Sections 7 and 8 of the 1972

Industry Act. The three main uses of the Act are in selective assistance to the regions (Section 7) as noted previously, plus the development of sectoral aid and *ad hoc* investment schemes and major interventions or 'rescues'. The first sectoral investment scheme – that for the wool textile industry – was initiated in 1973 and this was followed by sixteen other schemes, representing a mixture of overcapacity sectors (e.g. machine tools), newer developing technologies (microelectronics), those suffering from import penetration (e.g. footwear) and so on. In association with the work of NEDO, the aim has been to identify homogeneous industrial sectors, diagnose problems and devise investment schemes to scrap surplus capacity, encourage new product development and investment in contemporary technology. For companies complying with the established conditions, fixed levels of support, representing generally around twenty to twenty-five per cent of eligible expenditure, were available. There is an absence of research on the impact of the schemes: some benefits seem to have been recorded, but aid has been spread too thinly on occasion and the sectoral schemes may have suffered from being 'one-off' approaches. The Conservative Government virtually ended new schemes in 1979, while allowing the original schemes (all of which had been introduced for a limited time duration) to run their course. The only additions since then have been the private sector steel and coal firing schemes, both of which were introduced in 1981. Apart from these, the one scheme still in existence as at 1983 was the Microelectronics Industry Support Programme, introduced in July 1977 with projects to be completed by 31 March 1985. This, however, has now been encompassed within what the Government terms their 'Support for Innovation' programme.

In the period up to March 1982, £197 million had been offered to companies under the terms of the above schemes.[7] This figure pales in comparison with the sum spent on selective assistance for crisis interventions, which have included Rolls Royce (1972), Alfred Herbert (1974), British Leyland (BL) and Chrysler (1975) and ICL (1981). BL alone received £2.3 billion over the eight years to 1982. Closely linked to this strand of industrial policy is a third element, namely that concerned with the nationalised industries. The relative size, economic centrality and levels of investment involved in the publicly owned sector has meant that it has continued to attract much political attention. Issues such as commercial versus social objectives, ministerial control and, since 1979, privatisation have never been far from the headlines. What is necessary to point out is that the nationalised industries have rarely been employed as strategic instruments of industrial policy in Britain.

A fourth category of policy instrument concerns innovation. Support for innovation is very diffuse within Government, but much of the funding has historically been allocated for projects in the space and aircraft, nuclear power and defence industries. As the Conservative

Government allowed the sectoral schemes of assistance to fade out, there has been a concurrent build-up of general schemes of innovation assistance, concerned with improving manufacturing performance (Manufacturing Advisory Service, Design Advisory Service, etc.); developing new products and processes (Support for Innovation Scheme, Software Products Scheme, etc.); and applying new technology (Microelectronics Application Project; Industrial Robots and Flexible Manufacturing; Fibre-Optics Scheme; Computer Aided Design and Manufacture; Computer Aided Design, Manufacture and Test, etc.). As Figure 2.1 shows, the development of standards to raise design and quality in British industry and the systematic use of public purchasing are seen as further means of attaining the innovation objective of industrial strategy.

In concluding this brief and selective description of industrial policy instruments, mention should be made of company taxation and particularly the hundred per cent capital allowances on plant, machinery and research operated from 1972–84. Prior to this (from 1966) an investment grants scheme was operated, at the level of twenty per cent of the cost of plant and machinery; this was scrapped in 1970 with a return to a system of initial allowances, first at a rate of sixty per cent for plant and machinery. The Department of Industry estimated that tax foregone as a result of capital allowances was £2650 million in 1978–79, arguing further that many companies which were expanding and continuing to invest would pay no UK tax at all on their profits for many years. The outcome is that Corporation Tax is well down the league table of company taxes, with national insurance, rates, and taxes on bank and oil profits presently major items. The tax system is also being manipulated to help small firms, through business start-up schemes etc.

The above review does not cover the entire range of measures which would be included within the concept of industrial policy as defined. Excluded are, for example, various manpower policy measures, competition and merger policy, small firms' policies, etc. Some of these deficiencies are remedied in the chapters which follow, although, as will be shown, the five major instruments account for the bulk of spending.

Expenditures. Table 2.1 presents data on expenditure by the Government departments involved in industrial policy in the recent past and spending plans through to 1985–86. Government spending on regional policy was at its peak in 1975–76, before the period covered by the table, at a level of £1380 million (at 1982 prices) and in that year IDC refusals were about one quarter of all applications.[8] Since that time spending on RDGs, and indeed all regional and general industrial support, has dropped sharply in relation to total expenditure on industry, energy, trade and employment, with further cutbacks being planned. Support for the nationalised industries, again a major item of expenditure in the past, is planned to fall dramatically as privatisation measures take effect and

Table 2.1. Expenditure on industry, energy, trade and employment.

Programme	1977–78		1981–82		1983–84 plans		1985–86 plans	
	£m	% of total	£m	% of total	£m	% of total	£m	% of total
Regional and general industrial support:								
Regional development grants	385	17·2	598	11·2	474	8·4	730	13·5
Other[1]	155	6·9	275	5·2	233	4·1		
Scientific and technological assistance[2]	227	10·2	447	8·4	563	10·0	600	11·1
Support for aerospace, shipbuilding, steel and vehicle manufacture	349	15·6	940	17·7	128	2·3	—	—
Support for other nationalised industries (other than transport industries)	100	4·5	392	7·4	691	12·3	310	5·7
Department of Trade[3]	141	6·3	208	3·9	256	4·6	270	5·0
Export Credit Guarantee Department	−146	−6·5	144	2·7	145	2·6	40	0·7
Department of Employment	957	42·8	2244	42·2	3021	53·7	3340	61·7
Central and miscellaneous services and other[4]	64	2·9	69	1·3	109	1·9	120	2·2
Total	2233	100·0	5319	100·0	5622	100·0	5410	100·0

[1] Provision of land & buildings, selective assistance to industry, British Technology Group, etc. Programmes of the Departments of Industry, Energy and Trade.
[2] Programmes of the Departments of Industry and Energy.
[3] Excluding regional and general industrial support.
[4] Other includes Friendly Societies Registry and Office of Fair Trading.
Source: *The Government's Expenditure Plans 1983–84 to 1985–86*, Cmnd 8789-II, HMSO (London), February 1983, Table 2.4.

commercial objectives are pursued. Huge growth, by contrast, has taken place and is foreseen in spending on employment measures. Many of the schemes are *ad hoc*, 'fire-fighting' policies designed to ameliorate the unemployment impact, particularly among school-leavers.

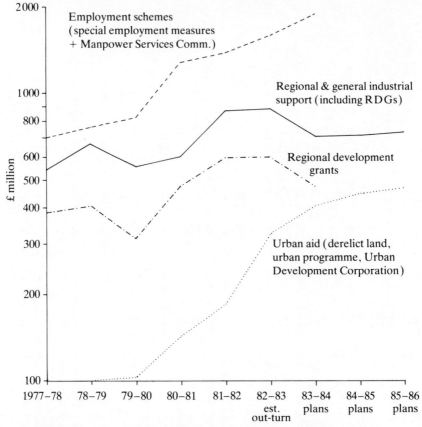

Figure 2.2. Government expenditure plans for selected programmes. (Source: *The Government's Expenditure Plans, 1983–84 to 1985–86*, Cmnd 8789-II, HMSO (London), February 1983.)

The importance of the spending levels on employment lies in its impact on resource allocation within Government, the equivalent of the 'crowding-out' thesis within the public sector. This same point is illustrated even more vividly in Figure 2.2, which looks only at expenditures on selected programmes, specifically those which may be defined as 'money for jobs'.[9] The programmes considered are employment schemes (spending by the Department of Employment on special employment measures and MSC spending); regional and general industrial support (items of conventional industrial policy expenditure); and urban aid (spending by the Department of Environment on derelict land, urban programmes and urban development corporations). The latter is excluded from the items considered in Table 2.1, but a consideration of urban and inner city policy is important because it represents a specific Government policy focus and to some extent an alternative to regional policy. It has been commented that during the 1970s regional policy was in some cases pulling in the opposite direction to inner city policy.[10] The latter was aimed at putting resources into depressed inner cities which were sometimes within the non-assisted areas and thus did not qualify for regional aid. The recent emphasis on urban aid has involved community development projects, educational and social welfare measures and partnership schemes between Central and Local Government and since 1980 a number of Enterprise Zones have been established in selected urban areas; the latter have the aim of stimulating new enterprises and employment by offering financial inducements and fewer controls. With regional policy as the traditional mainstay of industrial policy in Scotland, the change in priorities noted by both Table 2.1 and Figure 2.2 is likely to have quite fundamental implications for this country.

Institutions. The DTI has been the leading department in relation to industrial policy since 1974, with the Secretary of State for Trade and Industry as the chief industrial policy spokesman. Other departments are involved too, however, and, overall, responsibility for industry is divided functionally between various ministries through the principle of 'sponsorship' (for example, the Department of Health and Social Security 'sponsors' drugs and the Department of Energy 'sponsors' oil); and geographically through the regional offices in Scotland, Wales and Northern Ireland. The DTI's control over industrial policy is thus dependent on its ability to handle and coordinate other departments. It is also dependent upon its relationship with the Treasury which is concerned with formulating economic policy and controlling public expenditure, including taxation policy, and financial oversight of the nationalised industries.

Outside of the Government machine, there have existed since the 1960s a number of bodies concerned with national and sectoral planning and the improvement of industrial performance. In 1961, the National Economic Development Council (NEDC) was established, involving high-level representation of Government, management and labour, and the Bank of England, together with an associated Secretariat (NEDO). At the same time as the formation of the NEDC, Economic Development Committees (EDCs) were set up for individual industries with a similar tripartite composition, and in 1976 Sector Working Parties (SWPs) were established under NEDC also to work towards the then industrial strategy. The activities of the (at peak) fifty-seven SWPs and EDCs were closely linked to the sectoral schemes of assistance discussed earlier, and the declining role of the NEDC at least partly parallels the fade-out of these schemes, leaving the institutional mechanism for sectoral planning in skeleton form only.

More ambitiously, the Industrial Reorganisation Corporation (IRC) was introduced in 1966, and survived, with the Labour Government, until 1970 to encourage concentration and rationalisation in industry in order to promote increased efficiency and international competitiveness. A new organisation, the National Enterprise Board (NEB), was brought in by Labour in 1975. Despite the ambitions of its sponsors, the powers granted to the NEB were quite modest and its two-fold role became that of acting as a holding company for a number of publicly-owned firms (particularly BL and Rolls Royce) and stimulating innovative companies in given fields. After the return of the Conservative Government in 1979, its powers were reduced and its role changed to that of a venture capital type of organisation. In this role, its work began to overlap with that of the National Research Development Corporation (NRDC), and this was a major factor leading to the merger of the two into the British Technology Group (BTG) in 1981. The latter had, as at 1983, a limited role in the development of high-technology industry and in providing financial assistance for small firms; and equally limited funding: witness the fact that planned expenditure from Government was £10 million for 1983–84 compared with £41 million in 1981–82.[11]

At the time of the formation of the NEB, the then Labour Government also set up a number of regional development agencies in Scotland, Wales and Northern Ireland. These had broadly complementary objectives to that of the National Enterprise Board, although their establishment should also be seen as a response to regional demands for special treatment within the framework of a unified economy. The role of the SDA in Scottish industrial policy is a constantly recurring theme in this book.

Reviewing the UK institutional framework as a whole, emphasis has been placed upon three features; first, inter-party confrontation, which has produced substantial discontinuities in institutional development and kept industrial policy at the centre of public attention; second, collective decision-making with many decisions being taken through the machinery of Cabinet and Cabinet Committee and meaning, therefore, that such decisions may be heavily influenced by non-industrial and short-term criteria; and third, the role of the Treasury as a sceptical and severely constraining influence on industrial policy.[12]

Industrial Policy in Scotland

Instruments and Expenditures. The major policy instruments outlined above are also those which represent the bulk of spending in Scotland, with regional aid as the principal element of support. Data on identifiable public expenditure in Scotland on industry, energy, trade and employ-

Table 2.2. Identifiable public expenditure in Scotland on industry, energy, trade and employment.[1]

Programme	1977–78		1979–80		1981–82	
	£m	% of total	£m	% of total	£m	% of total
Regional and general industrial support:						
Special assistance for Highland and rural areas	10·4	3·0	17·4	4·7	22·7	4·0
Scottish Development Agency	39·8	11·4	64·5	17·5	75·8	13·2
Other[2]	124·4	35·7	92·8	25·1	177·8	30·8
Scientific and technological assistance	21·5	6·2	31·5	8·5	34·3	6·0
Support for aerospace, ship-building and steel industries	9·1	2·6	7·9	2·1	36·3	6·3
Support for other national-ised industries (other than transport industries)	24·8	7·1	29·7	8·0	25·4	4·4
Regulation of domestic trade	1·7	0·5	2·8	0·8	4·8	0·8
Functioning of labour market	98·2	28·2	112·9	30·6	190·4	33·0
Central and miscellaneous services	5·4	1·6	3·9	1·1	2·2	0·4
Health and safety at work	2·2	0·6	2·5	0·7	3·6	0·6
Shipping services and civil aviation	10·6	3·0	3·9	1·0	2·7	0·5
Total	348·0	100·0	369·4	100·0	576·3	100·0

[1] Current and capital. Expenditure within the responsibility of the Scottish Office and expenditure administered by other departments but which can be identified as having been incurred in Scotland.
[2] RDGs, provision of land and buildings, selective assistance to industry, etc.
Source: *Scottish Abstract of Statistics*, 1983.

ment (IETE) are presented in Table 2.2, with information on regional preferential assistance and selective financial assistance in Tables 2.3 and 2.4 respectively. At the outset it should be noted that the expenditure under IETE is only some ten to fifteen per cent of total gross Central Government expenditure in Scotland; almost three-quarters of the latter is taken up by grants to local authorities and wages and salaries in public administration and defence.

Table 2.3. Expenditure on regional preferential assistance to industry in Scotland (£m, fiscal year).

Programme	1973–74	1974–75	1975–76	1976–77
Local Employment Act				
Government factory building	4·9	5·9	7·8	—
Loans	2·4	—	—	—
Grants	12·1	7·7	6·7	0·7
Scottish Development Agency Act				
Land and factory building	—	—	2·9	9·5
Loans to small tourist enterprises	—	—	—	—
Industry Act 1972				
Selective financial assistance (Section 7)				
Loans[1]	5·9	2·9	19·6	5·6
Grants	0·6	2·3	5·4	6·2
Regional development grants[4]	32·0	61·6	98·5	108·2
Highlands and Islands Development Boards				
Loans[1]	1·8	2·3	2·6	3·1
Grants	1·6	1·6	2·1	2·5
Other Assistance				
Free depreciation	—	—	—	—
Investment grants	6·7	2·7	2·3	0·6
Selective employment tax additional payments	0·1	—	—	—
Regional employment premium	38·7	56·4	78·5	78·8
Department of Employment preferential assistance to industrial training	2·0	2·0	—	—
Tourism	0·5	0·4	0·6	0·7
Small firms employment subsidy	—	—	—	—
Total gross expenditure	109·3	145·7	228·6	216·0
RDGs as % of total gross expenditure	29·3	42·3	43·1	50·1

[1] Includes equity payments.
[2] Excluding estimated non-regionally preferential payments.
[3] Provisional figures.
[4] Scotland's share of RDG payments in Great Britain as follows (%): Cumulative 1972–73 to 1979–80, 26·6; 1979–80, 21·2; 1980–81, 23·1; 1981–82, 23·1.
Source: *Scottish Economic Bulletin*, No. 27, 1983.

1977–78	1978–79	1979–80	1980–81	1981–82	1982–83[3]
—	—	—	—	—	—
—	—	—	—	—	—
0·1	—	—	—	—	—
18·6	27·8	37·8	47·3	55·1	63·7
—	0·1	—	—	—	—
3·9	1·7	0·2	—	—	—
8·1	10·7	14·5	22·6	19·4	20·6
105·0	107·3	70·2	113·3	142·7	287·3
3·8	4·8	6·9	5·0	6·3	6·3
3·1	4·1	4·6	6·4	7·0	8·7
—	—	—	—	—	—
—	—	—	—	—	—
—	—	—	—	—	—
1·5	—	—	—	—	—
—	—	—	—	—	—
1·0	1·3	1·6	1·9	2·0	—
0·7	1·5[2]	7·4[2]	2·0	2·0	—
145·8	159·3	142·6	197·0	232·5	386·6
72·0	67·4	49·2	57·5	61·4	74·3

Table 2.4. Selective financial assistance (Section 7 of the Industry Act 1972): summary[1] of offers and expenditure in Scotland and Great Britain (£m, fiscal year).

	1973–74	1974–75	1975–76	1976–77	1977–78	1978–79	1979–80	1980–81	1981–82	1982–83
Total expenditure (£m)										
Loans:[2] Scotland	5·9	2·9	19·6	5·6	3·9	1·7	0·2	—	—	—
Great Britain	20·4	20·2	41·7	21·5	9·1	6·9	1·5	0·1	—	—
Grants: Scotland	0·6	2·3	5·4	6·2	8·1	10·7	14·5	22·0	19·4	20·6
Great Britain	3·2	14·6	22·8	22·4	34·9	96·6	76·2	73·9	76·3	87·1
Scotland as % of Great Britain (loans & grants)	27·5	14·9	38·8	26·9	27·3	12·0	18·9	29·7	25·4	23·7
Estimated associated employment(000)[3]										
Scotland	14·5	19·8	18·6	17·8	14·0	15·3	18·6	21·2	12·0	18·9
Great Britain	59·5	72·6	64·8	70·0	72·8	86·7	89·2	62·4	48·8	60·7
Scotland as % of Great Britain	8·6	27·3	28·7	25·4	19·2	17·6	20·9	34·0	24·6	31·1

[1] Excludes shipbuilding.
[2] Includes equity payments.
[3] Includes new and safeguarded employment.
Source: *Scottish Economic Bulletin*, No. 27, 1983.

The information presented in Table 2.2 is useful in providing something of a match with the U K expenditures on the various programmes. The two compare relatively closely, especially in regard to the rising share of spending accounted for by programmes relating to the labour market between 1977–78 and 1981–82. The proportion of expenditure on regional and general industrial support, by contrast, fell over this same period and will clearly be subject to further shrinkage if the plans identified earlier come to fruition. Indeed Scotland may be hit disproportionately depending upon the way in which the delineation of Assisted Areas is changed.

The crucial role which regional assistance generally (and RDGs specifically) has played as an instrument of policy in Scotland is only hinted at in Table 2.2, and the following tabulations, therefore, consider spending on the components of regional preferential assistance over a longer time span. RDGs, the major item, are shown to have become more important since the early 1970s, particularly with the abolition of the regional employment premium. On the other hand, Scotland's share of total RDG payments in Great Britain has been declining: between 1972–73 and 1979–80, Scotland received nearly twenty-seven per cent of GB expenditure, falling to twenty-three per cent in 1980–81 and 1981–82. Scotland's share of SFA, a much smaller component of regional aid, has been very volatile: from July 1979, Section 8 expenditures under the 1972 Industry Act were to be for 'viable' projects (specifically those which were either internationally mobile or would lead to substantial improvements in performance) and the 'additionality' criteria under Section 7 were operated more strictly. The latter seems to have been associated with some recovery in the Scottish share of SFA.

The impact of regional aid has been the subject of extensive study in Scotland, as elsewhere in the U K. It has been estimated that in Scotland between 70 000 and 80 000 jobs were created by this policy between 1963 and 1970 alone.[13] Furthermore, manufacturing output in Scotland in 1976 by comparison with 1958 appears to have been about twenty per cent higher than would have been expected in the absence of regional policy; by far the major part of the increase seems to have occurred in the period of strong regional policy since 1965.[14] Regional policy in Scotland has probably had its main impact in the attraction of inward investment, and it is doubtful if the country would have its thriving electronics industry were it not for regional assistance. Although not relating to Scotland alone, what is interesting to observe is that the employment effect of incentives has been very concentrated, with three-quarters of the positive impact on jobs in only twenty out of seventy-eight industries.[15] By contrast, industries such as chemicals, metal manufacture and mechanical engineering which took nearly forty per cent of receipts over the 1966–76 period did not show any net job creation from regional assistance. Ex-

43

cluding these sectors, the estimated exchequer cost per job created was £23 000.

Given that Scotland has fared quite favourably from past policies, with their focus on RDGs, and that the associated expenditures have been fairly effective in creating employment, the question then arises as to whether the changing policy balance will be equally beneficial in its impact on Scotland. Chapter 5 of this book relating to the engineering and metals sector shows low take-up in Scotland for many of the sectoral schemes of assistance and also for certain of the measures designed to promote innovation in industry. The moves towards the greater emphasis on urban policy also have their counterpart in Scotland, and are reflected in the focus of SDA activities on the coordination of major comprehensive urban development programmes. The largest and best known of the latter is the Glasgow Eastern Area Renewal (GEAR) project, but the Agency's activities in this field of industrial and environmental improvement have been expanded to cover a range of programmes in various parts of Scotland. As evidence of the importance of their activity, it has been stated that sixty per cent of the Agency's 'targetable' resources are to be spent in area projects.[16] It is clearly too early to assess the benefit of this, but there have been criticisms of GEAR in that it is alleged to be over-ambitious, integrating social policy with economic and environmental objectives, that its objectives were vague and unquantified, and that its structure was unnecessarily complex.[17]

Despite the inevitable parallels between policy measures in Scotland and in the UK, there is some scope for initiative at Scottish level in connection, for instance, with the promotion of inward investment, stimulating small-firm growth, encouraging the involvement of indigenous companies in subcontracting, assisting the advertising of Scottish products, industrial rationalisation and so forth. In expenditure terms, such industrial policy measures are of relatively minor importance when set against RDG payments and other forms of regional assistance. Detailed work in such areas can, nevertheless, be of major benefit even if it attracts little publicity, and the chapters which follow detail the progress which has sometimes been made along these lines. The ability to operate in these ways is in large part related to the institutional set-up in Scotland and this is now discussed.

Institutions. The institutional network in Scotland is summarised diagrammatically in Figure 2.3. As is indicated, the network revolves around the operations of the Scottish Office, a Government department which has been in existence since the nineteenth century. The Scottish Office, together with similar offices in Wales and Northern Ireland, represent exceptions to the pattern of UK Government in that they are responsible for a range of functions for a single part of the country. The Scottish Office is headed by the Secretary of State for Scotland, a UK

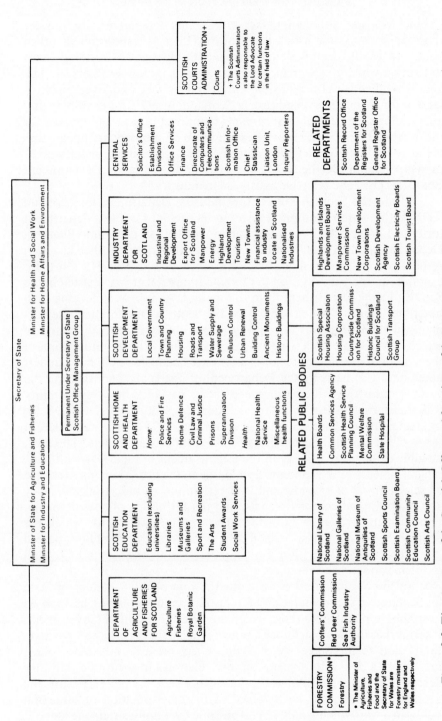

Secretary of State

Minister of State for Agriculture and Fisheries
Minister for Industry and Education

Minister for Health and Social Work
Minister for Home Affairs and Environment

Permanent Under Secretary of State
Scottish Office Management Group

DEPARTMENT OF AGRICULTURE AND FISHERIES FOR SCOTLAND

Agriculture
Fisheries
Royal Botanic Garden

SCOTTISH EDUCATION DEPARTMENT

Education (excluding universities)
Libraries
Museums and Galleries
Sport and Recreation
The Arts
Student Awards
Social Work Services

SCOTTISH HOME AND HEALTH DEPARTMENT

Home:
Police and Fire Services
Home Defence
Civil Law and Criminal Justice
Prisons
Superannuation Division

Health:
National Health Service
Miscellaneous health functions

SCOTTISH DEVELOPMENT DEPARTMENT

Local Government
Town and Country Planning
Housing
Roads and Transport
Water Supply and Sewerage
Pollution Control
Urban Renewal
Building Control
Ancient Monuments
Historic Buildings

INDUSTRY DEPARTMENT FOR SCOTLAND

Industrial and Regional Development
Export Office for Scotland
Manpower
Energy
Highland Development
Tourism
New Towns
Financial assistance to industry
Locate in Scotland
Nationalised Industries

CENTRAL SERVICES

Solicitor's Office
Establishment Divisions
Office Services
Finance
Directorate of Computers and Telecommunications
Scottish Information Office
Chief Statistician
Liaison Unit, London
Inquiry Reporters

SCOTTISH COURTS ADMINISTRATION+

Courts

+ The Scottish Courts Administration is also responsible to the Lord Advocate for certain functions in the field of law

RELATED PUBLIC BODIES

FORESTRY COMMISSION•

Forestry

• The Minister of Agriculture, Fisheries and Food and the Secretary of State for Wales are Forestry ministers for England and Wales respectively

Crofters' Commission
Red Deer Commission
Sea Fish Industry Authority

National Library of Scotland
National Galleries of Scotland
National Museum of Antiquities of Scotland
Scottish Sports Council
Scottish Examination Board
Scottish Community Education Council
Scottish Arts Council

Health Boards
Common Services Agency
Scottish Health Service Planning Council
Mental Welfare Commission
State Hospital

Scottish Special Housing Association
Housing Corporation
Countryside Commission for Scotland
Historic Buildings Council for Scotland
Scottish Transport Group

Highlands and Islands Development Board
Manpower Services Commission
New Town Development Corporations
Scottish Development Agency
Scottish Electricity Boards
Scottish Tourist Board

RELATED DEPARTMENTS

Scottish Record Office
Department of the Registers for Scotland
General Register Office for Scotland

Figure 2.3. The structure of the Scottish Office and functions of departments.

Cabinet Minister, although, in fact, full Cabinet does not usually consider those policy areas for which the Scottish Office is responsible; Scottish issues are usually dealt with at the level of Cabinet and Ministerial Committees on which the Secretary of State and his junior Ministers sit. The Scottish Office is not responsible for all civil service employees in Scotland or for all public expenditure in Scotland; in 1979, for example, only about fifteen per cent of civil servants employed in Scotland worked for the Scottish Office.[18] In terms of expenditure on industry, it appears that about two-fifths is under the Scottish Secretary's control, mainly comprising spending by the SDA, the Highlands & Islands Development Board (HIDB), and selective assistance to industry.[19]

Within the Scottish Office, the Industry Department for Scotland (IDS) is the main economic service. In its present form this department (prior to 1 November 1983 it was called the Scottish Economic Planning Department) only dates from 1973, although the Scottish Office has been responsible for many of its functions since World War II. Thus, for example, an industry division to promote industrial growth existed in the Scottish Home Department from that period. As well as inheriting such functions (many of which came from the Scottish Development Department) in 1973, IDS was later given responsibility for the allocation of selective assistance under the 1972 Industry Act. The administration of the variety of schemes of regional assistance had historically been undertaken on a UK basis by the Department of Trade and Industry and the various ministries which proceeded them. In 1975, this responsibility was transferred to the Secretary of State for Scotland and to IDS for implementation. There is little question that 1975 was a watershed in terms of the Scottish Secretary's powers in industrial matters. The most tangible evidence of this lay in the establishment of the SDA with wide ranging objectives in economic development, the provision, maintenance or safeguarding of employment, the promotion of industrial efficiency and international competitiveness, and the furthering of environmental improvement. However, both the SDA and the HIDB, for which the Scottish Secretary is also responsible, operate under guidelines agreed inter-departmentally within Government, within the limits of overall economic and industrial policy.

An important question concerns the role of the Secretary of State for Scotland in the formulation of industrial policy measures, as opposed to simply implementing those which are agreed by Central Government. It seems that the Scottish Office's role in policy making is largely reactive. In relation to the Secretary of State's effect on UK industrial policy, moreover, a lot will depend on his relationship with the Industry Secretary and his personal and political position. At the very least, the Scottish Secretary will be involved in his determination of industrial policy in a way which would not be possible for a ministerial 'outsider'.

46

Reflecting the number of civil servants in Scotland and the level of expenditures outside the Secretary of State's control, some branches of Central Government departments in Scotland have a responsibility for economic and industrial matters. For instance, the Offshore Supplies Office in Glasgow is sponsored by the Department of Energy; its role in industrial matters concerns *inter alia* help for UK firms in securing orders for North Sea work. Again, and of major importance in the context of the expenditure levels noted previously, there is the Manpower Services Commission. The MSC was set up in the early 1970s to take over the Department of Employment's labour and training services and the Government's special employment creation programmes. In this case there is a more complex intermeshing of Scottish and UK elements; the Scottish Secretary is consulted by the Secretary of State for Employment before the MSC's corporate plan is approved, and within the framework of this plan for Scotland is drawn up. Most of the work of the MSC in Scotland is funded through the Scottish Office vote, but this is not part of an expenditure block over which the Secretary of State has unlimited authority.[20]

The Scottish Development Agency, the second major instrument of industrial policy, was founded by the Labour Government in 1975. A number of bodies were absorbed into the Agency, the Scottish Industrial Estates Corporation, the Small Industries Council for the Rural Areas of Scotland and the section of the Scottish Development Department responsible for administering grants to Local Authorities for derelict land clearance. In fulfilling its objectives of furthering the economic development of Scotland and promoting efficiency and competitiveness, the Agency was also given the role of investment in industry through finance and management services; industrial promotion, particularly the promotion of inward investment; and the coordination of urban development schemes. The resources available to the SDA are quite substantial and as Table 2.5 and earlier tabulations show, its spending represents a relatively important source of industry-related public expenditure in Scotland. As at 31 March 1983, the SDA employed 732 people. Sponsorship of the Agency resides with the Secretary of State through the Industry Department for Scotland.

Although there was speculation that the Conservative Government of 1979 would seek to reduce the role of the SDA, or even wind it up, in fact only limited changes were made. These involved reversing an earlier Labour decision to increase the Agency's funding to £800 million, and a stress on the desirability of the privatisation of the SDA's activity whereever possible by the expeditious sale of its corporate investments to the private sector. With the greater stability and clarity of objectives, the Agency's structure is as shown in Figure 2.4. Planning and Projects Directorate has the key task within this structure of formulating Agency

Table 2.5(a). Trends in Agency spending (selected years; current and capital).

Item	1977–78 %	1979–80 %	Item[1]	1981–82 %
Industry and investments	16·4	7·9	Investment	11·5
			Advisory services	2·4
Small businesses	2·4	2·6	Industrial property	59·2
Factories and industrial estates	49·8	52·1	Land reclamation and environment	
Land renewal	27·9	28·4	improvements	19·9
Urban renewal	1·5	5·3	Promotion	3·3
Research, promotion and information	1·3	3·2	Planning, research and development	3·2
Capital equipment	0·6	0·5	Capital equipment	0·5
Total expenditure (%)	100·0	100·0	Total expenditure (%)	100·0
Total expenditure (£m)	51·8	92·9	Total expenditure (£m)	104·4

[1] Classification of items changed in 1981–82. No equivalent figures published in 1982–83.
Source: Scottish Development Agency, *Annual Reports*.

Table 2.5(b). Source and application of funds for the SDA (year ended 31 March 1983)

Source of funds	£m	Application of funds	£m
UK Government	100·8	Net expenditure	51·2
European Coal & Steel Community	0·6	Property management	3·7
European Investment Bank	0·2	Investment management	1·1
Capital receipts		Promotions	5·3
(properties and investments)	6·0	Planning, research and development	3·8
	107·6	Advisory services	3·6
		Land reclamation and environmental improvements	33·7
		Capital expenditure	65·1
		Repayments	0·8
		Movements in working capital and cash balances and adjustments	–9·5
			107·6

Source: Scottish Development Agency, *Report 83*.

policy and developing a corporate plan within guidelines set by the Secretary of State. The two most recently formed Directorates are Electronics, which was established in 1982 as a spin-off from the multi-sectoral New Ventures Unit; and Area Development, again a 1982 creation, which subsumed the Agency's Urban Renewal Directorate and its Special Development Division. Alongside the Directorate structure is Locate in Scotland, officially an associate organisation concerned with inward investment attraction (see Chapter 4 on the foreign-owned manufacturing sector).

In the early years after the Agency's formation, its role was largely reactive, responding to approaches by firms and Local Authorities as well as carrying on its inherited commitments. It was fortunately able to avoid becoming a pond for 'lame ducks' by resisting pressures to take over companies with no commercial future; by June 1977 it had accepted only four out of thirty-eight rescue proposals. In 1976, however, it was given the task of organising GEAR by the Scottish Office and this to some extent has influenced the direction of policy subsequently, so the co-ordination and management area projects have become the major focus of Agency activity and account for a substantial part of the Agency's financial resources as well as involving all of the SDA's Directorates (see Figure 2.5). In relation to the former, in 1982–83 the Agency's contribution to the Area Development Projects was £32 million but, reflecting the SDA's role as primarily that of a catalyst, total participant budgets for the nine projects in hand was £358 million.

Aside from the area projects, the major activity of the Agency is in sectoral work. Several major research studies have been commissioned with the objective of identifying specific gaps and requirements in the sectors concerned and the formulation of policies to encourage the development of these sectors within the Scottish economy, through the attraction of inward investment and the encouragement of indigenous industry. To date sectors which have been the subject of major enquiry include electronics, health care, biotechnology, forest products, textiles and knitwear, and printing and publishing. The strategy for electronics is furthest advanced, as shown by the emergence of an Electronics Directorate.

Both of the above types of work (which themselves are linked as Figure 2.5 indicates) represent examples of the secondary tier of industrial policy on which Scottish initiatives are required to operate. In a variety of ways, it has been possible for national schemes to be developed further and the emphasis shifted. This is illustrated in the electronics sector work, where a highly visible focus of research and promotional work at Scottish level has gone beyond the objectives of short-term financial schemes at a UK level. As a result, there is at least a Scottish strategy designed to maximise benefits from the electronics industry. In

Figure 2.4. Scottish Development Agency structure.
(Source: SDA, *Report 83.*)

CHIEF EXECUTIVE

Finance and Industry Services
Industry Services: *Interface with larger Scottish companies; investment support and monitoring; advisory services; accounting and industrial relations*
Internal Accounting: *Agency accounting and financial control; computer services, internal audit and management of funds*

Small Business and Electronics
Small Business Division: *Financial assistance and commercial, marketing and technical advice to small businessmen; trade promotion in UK and overseas for small firms; grants and promotional and marketing services to craftsmen*
Electronics Division: *Implementation and co-ordination of Agency programme for the Scottish electronics industry*

Estates and Environment
Factory Policy Division: *Property development and marketing; valuation and estate management*
Building Division: *New building, civil engineering and estate developments; development of St Enoch's complex*
Property Services Division: *Property maintenance, development and refit; engineering services*
Land Renewal Division: *Derelict land and environmental enhancement*

Planning and Projects
Corporate Planning: *Corporate Plan and evaluation of operations*
Economic Services: *Provision of economic advice and information*
Industrial Programme Development: *Formulation of industrial development programmes*
Area Programme Development: *Formulation of area based programmes including integrated area projects*
Industrial Development Projects: *Implementation of industrial projects including the expansion of research and product development*
Health Care and Biotechnology Industries: *Implementation and co-ordination of Agency programmes for the Scottish health care industry*

Area Development
Co-ordination and management of area projects: integrated projects, Task Forces, self help initiatives, Glasgow Eastern Area Renewal Project; preparation of financial programmes and development studies; identification and development of economic initiatives; promotion of private development; programme and performance review

Investment (Scottish Development Finance Limited)
Policy on industrial investment; evaluation of projects, post investment relationships, advice to invested companies; encouraging private sector involvement

Marketing
Industrial promotion; public relations and advertising; information
services; London representation

Secretarial
Board servicing; legal services; staff relations and administration; office
services

Associate Organisation – Locate in Scotland: Attraction of industry to
Scotland from overseas and from other parts of the UK; associated
Industry Act incentives; monitoring existing overseas investment in
Scotland

---

other industries where the SDA has been able to act directly, it is obvious that there is a specific Scottish dimension. So, in the export marketing and promotion of Scottish wool and textiles, it has been possible to complement the work of national agencies. Elsewhere, such as the initiatives to encourage the development of downstream enterprises using wood products, the Agency is acting in areas where there is no policy. In short then, the secondary tier concept has been pioneered by the Agency in a number of areas where there is a specific Scottish interest.

It must be pointed out that while Agency activities and initiatives are to be applauded, there are many of these which would be made more effective if the industries concerned were the subject of UK strategic thinking. Others are so brittle that one major national decision could destroy years of work at SDA level. Energy prices and the aluminium and wood pulp industries; trade policy in the textile and whisky industries; UK steel policy and the Scottish engineering industry are among the examples of this gap between regional action and national inaction. Moreover, there is a grave danger that some commendable regional issues look piecemeal when viewed from a national or international perspective. Alternatively, they may be negated by the growing possibilities of action on the part of other regional agencies throughout the United Kingdom.

A third body concerned with industrial policy in Scotland is the Highlands and Islands Development Board (HIDB). Like the SDA, this organisation is sponsored by the Industry Department for Scotland and was established in 1965 with the general task of 'preparing, concerting, promoting, assisting and undertaking measures for the economic and social development of the Highlands and Islands'. Its potential powers are considerable and, with the approval of the Secretary of State and the Treasury, it can compulsorily acquire land, hold, manage and dispose of it; set up and carry on any business; provide training, management, accountancy and other services; assist in promotional work for the Highlands and Islands area; and give grants and loans. The Board of the HIDB is advised by the Highlands and Islands Development Consultative Council, comprising nominees from Local Authorities and other interests.

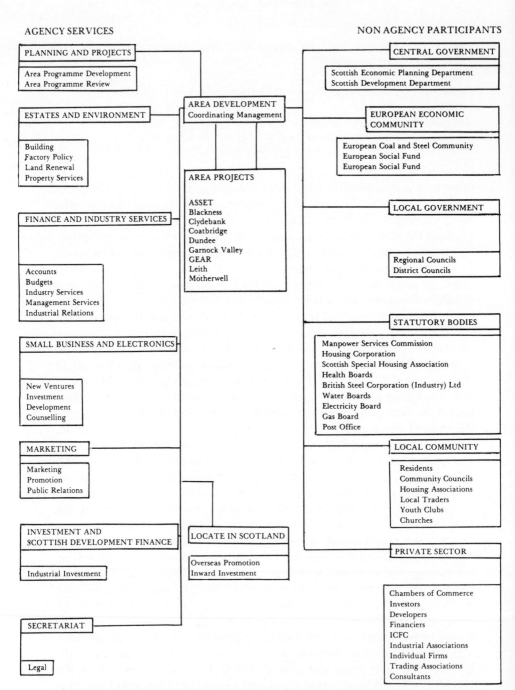

AGENCY SERVICES

PLANNING AND PROJECTS
Area Programme Development
Area Programme Review

ESTATES AND ENVIRONMENT
Building
Factory Policy
Land Renewal
Property Services

FINANCE AND INDUSTRY SERVICES
Accounts
Budgets
Industry Services
Management Services
Industrial Relations

SMALL BUSINESS AND ELECTRONICS
New Ventures
Investment
Development
Counselling

MARKETING
Marketing
Promotion
Public Relations

INVESTMENT AND
SCOTTISH DEVELOPMENT FINANCE
Industrial Investment

SECRETARIAT
Legal

AREA DEVELOPMENT
Coordinating Management

AREA PROJECTS
ASSET
Blackness
Clydebank
Coatbridge
Dundee
Garnock Valley
GEAR
Leith
Motherwell

LOCATE IN SCOTLAND
Overseas Promotion
Inward Investment

NON AGENCY PARTICIPANTS

CENTRAL GOVERNMENT
Scottish Economic Planning Department
Scottish Development Department

EUROPEAN ECONOMIC
COMMUNITY
European Coal and Steel Community
European Social Fund
European Social Fund

LOCAL GOVERNMENT
Regional Councils
District Councils

STATUTORY BODIES
Manpower Services Commission
Housing Corporation
Scottish Special Housing Association
Health Boards
British Steel Corporation (Industry) Ltd
Water Boards
Electricity Board
Gas Board
Post Office

LOCAL COMMUNITY
Residents
Community Councils
Housing Associations
Local Traders
Youth Clubs
Churches

PRIVATE SECTOR
Chambers of Commerce
Investors
Developers
Financiers
ICFC
Industrial Associations
Individual Firms
Trading Associations
Consultants

Figure 2.5. The co-ordination and management of area projects
in the Agency. (Source: SDA, *Report 83*.)

During the 1960s, a major emphasis of HIDB activities was the promotion of large-scale industrial projects based on the growth pole concept (and more will be said on this subject in Chapter 8 on The Natural Resource-Based Sector). Since that time, policy has become more reactive, with the HIDB backing potential developments whether in manufacturing, tourism, agriculture or fisheries. This is in part a reflection of the emergence of new agencies, particularly the Industry Department for Scotland and the SDA, but also the Highlands Regional Council. The Agency and the HIDB have reached agreement covering their respective responsibilities, with the Highlands Board handling industrial estates and small businesses in its area (whereas the Agency is responsible for the same activities elsewhere in Scotland). Considering the HIDB's spending in the form of grants, loans and equity holdings, this amounted to £159 million between 1973 and 1982 (at 1982 prices), of which 44 per cent was grant assistance.[21] Around 13 per cent of assistance went to land development in these ten years, 24 per cent to fisheries, 22 per cent to manufacturing and processing, 4 per cent to construction, 28 per cent to tourism and 9 per cent to other service industries. The major beneficiaries of Board assistance were thus the fishing industry (boats, fish farming, fish processing etc.), hotels and farming. The Board's own figures give a total of 22 000 jobs created or retained over the decade to 1982. Of course, oil development has had a major impact in parts of the Highland area, out of all proportion to any HIDB activity.

The Scottish Council (Development and Industry) is the last major Scottish institution which needs to be mentioned. It differs from the SDA and the HIDB, principally in the fact that it is largely independent of Government. Representation comprises large and small firms, Chambers of Commerce, banks, trades unions and Local Authorities, with the bulk of its funding coming from large companies and Regional Councils. The continuing objective of the Scottish Council is to promote economic and industrial development in Scotland. On the other hand, its functions have altered considerably with time. In its earlier years, the Council was a quasi-Governmental body; it was responsible for the attraction of inward investment, funded both by Government grants and its own resources; and, in addition, trade missions were undertaken backed by the British Overseas Trade Board. It also had a role in industrial and economic planning and was responsible for the production of the 1961 Toothill Report on the Scottish economy.[22] As from 1979, the Agency took over the task formerly handled by the Scottish Council of attracting inward investment, and the Council's export promotion role, as agent for the British Overseas Trade Board, began to shrink. In consequence, the Council has become more of a private body, providing services for its members and lobbying Government for favourable policies. As at the time of writing, it is probably fair to say that the

Council was seeking to re-establish its influence on economic and industrial policy matters. Working parties continue to produce reports on industrial policy issues and the Council has perhaps aspirations as the NEDO of Scotland. In the chapters which follow the potential role of the Scottish Council as such a body should not be forgotten.

Given this background on policy institutions and expenditure in Scotland and the UK, what the rest of this book will attempt to consider is whether the institutional framework in Scotland and the local control of expenditure can be so adapted as to make a significant contribution to industrial and managerial efficiency.

The Limits to Industrial Policy

Before proceeding, it is advisable to sound a cautionary note. There are two broadly contrasting views about the role and effects of industrial policies. The assertive approach lays emphasis on the possible gains arising from a more considered, explicit and ambitious industrial strategy; while the second, equally vigorously affirmed, is that which both emphasises the negative effects associated with particular industrial policies and queries the merit of industrial strategy as a concept. The former school of thought in the UK is largely based on observations about the long-term effects on economic growth and performance arising from the erosion of the industrial base. It is expressed in the view of a former economic director of NEDO that 'only the Government can be relied upon to concern itself with the survival of a modern and relevant industrial base'.[23] From this perspective, industrial policy would become a major element in a programme of UK economic recovery. While many would disagree with the weight placed on industry policy by this view, it is clear that sustained growth will continue to depend on industrial competitiveness and that such an aim must be established at the core of policies towards industry. In essence, industrial policy for the UK and Scotland must be supportive and innovative. To accomplish this, it may also have to be more selective in terms of industries, products and technologies than in the past. Equally necessary is the requirement for continuity and consistency in the pursuit of such selective aims.

Having said all that, the deep-seated nature of the problems of UK industry in general and manufacturing in particular make it naive to claim that UK industry can be transformed by industrial policy. Only gains along a more narrow front can be claimed with credibility. Moreover, the past record of industrial policy in Britain is a forlorn one and gives little encouragement for more of the same in the future. The central premise underlying this work is that selective industrial policy measures have to be pursued alongside expansionist macro-economic policies, which are directed towards the same long-term ends, if industrial recovery is to be generated.

NOTES AND REFERENCES

1. The definition of industrial policy has been the subject of extended debate. See, for example, C.Carter (ed), *Industrial Policy and Innovation*, Heinemann (London), 1981; J.Pinder (ed), *National Industrial Strategies and the World Economy*, Croom Helm (London), 1982.

2. G.McCrone, *Regional Policy in Britain*, George Allen & Unwin (London), 1969, pp. 30–1.

3. This view is expressed in G.Gudgin, B.Moore & J.Rhodes, 'Employment Problems in the Cities and Regions of the UK: Prospects for the 1980s', *Cambridge Economic Policy Review*, vol. 8, no. 2, December 1982, chapter 4.

4. The following discussion draws heavily on W.Grant & S.Wilks, 'British Industrial Policy: Structural Change, Policy Inertia', *Journal of Public Policy*, vol. 3, part 1, 1983, pp. 13–28.

5. *Regional Industrial Development*, Cmnd 9111, HMSO (London), December 1983.

6. Gudgin, Moore & Rhodes, *op. cit.* (n. 3), p. 3.

7. *Industry Act 1972. Annual Report*, HC503, HMSO (London), 1982.

8. Gudgin, Moore & Rhodes, *op. cit.* (n. 3), p. 3.

9. The idea comes from 'Regional Policy Under the Axe', *The Economist*, 19 February 1983.

10. M.Keating, A.Midwinter & P.Taylor, *Enterprise Zones and Area Projects: Small Area Initiatives in Urban Economic Renewal in Scotland*, Department of Administration, University of Strathclyde, August 1983.

11. *The Government's Expenditure Plans 1983–84 to 1985–86*, Cmnd 8789–II, HMSO (London), February 1983.

12. Grant & Wilks, *op. cit.* (n. 4).

13. B.Ashcroft, 'Spatial Policy in Scotland', in M.Cuthbert (ed), *Government Spending in Scotland. A Critical Appraisal*, Paul Harris (Edinburgh), 1982.

14. J.Marquand, *Measuring the Effects and Costs of Regional Incentives*, Government Economic Service Working Paper No. 32, Department of Industry (London), February 1980.

15. P.Tyler, B.Moore & J.Rhodes, *The Impact of Regional Policy on Different Types of Industry and the Implications for Industrial Restructuring*, Department of Land Economy, Cambridge, 1983, quoted in Scottish Council (Development and Industry), *Regional Policy Review: A Consultative Paper* (Edinburgh), October 1983.

16. Quoted in M.Keating & A.Midwinter, *The Government of Scotland*, Mainstream Publishing (Edinburgh), 1983. The section on institutions in Scotland which follows draws substantially on this work.

17. Keating, Midwinter & Taylor, *op. cit.* (n. 10), p. 3.

18. G.Pottinger, *The Secretaries of State for Scotland 1926–76*, Scottish Academic Press (Edinburgh), 1979.

19. House of Commons Committee on Scottish Affairs, *Scottish Aspects of the 1980–84 Public Expenditure White Paper*, Minutes of Evidence 7 July 1980, HC689, HMSO (London), 1980.

20. Keating & Midwinter, *op. cit.* (n. 16), chapter 3.

21. Highlands and Islands Development Board, *17th Annual Report*, 1982.

22. *Inquiry into the Scottish Economy 1960–1961*, Report of a Committee Appointed by the Scottish Council (Development and Industry) under the Chairmanship of J. N. Toothill, Edinburgh, 1962.
23. Cited in D. K. Stout, 'The Case for Government Support of R & D and Innovation' in C. Carter (ed), *Industrial Policy and Innovation*, Heinemann (London), 1981.

3

THE SMALL-FIRM SECTOR

NEIL HOOD

This chapter on small firms and the ensuing one on the foreign-owned sector differ from most of the other essays in the book in that they are not concerned with a single industry but with two areas of considerable cross-industry importance, distinguishable by size or ownership. Moreover, these areas have been, and remain, the focus of particular policy measures, with greater historical emphasis in Scotland having been placed on inward investment. However, given the stress laid on small-firm development in the UK as a whole over the past few years, it is essential to evaluate the characteristics of this sector in Scotland and, where possible, examine the effectiveness of existing policy measures.

The Small-Firm Sector in Scotland

Introduction. Any commentary on 'small firms' has to commence by acknowledging the absence of generally accepted definitions as to what constitutes the small firm. One recent ILO study[1] identified over fifty different statistical definitions in seventy-five countries. In this chapter, British Statistics Office conventions are adopted with small firms in manufacturing employing less than 200, in construction under 25; in other UK sectors, the definition is by turnover size. In reality, however, the majority of policy measures in the UK have been directed towards firms well below the 200 size, several in recent years being focused on new starts or the 'micro' firm. At least in part because of the recent surge of policy interest in small firms in the UK, the statistical base remains weak. Statisticians of small business in the UK were recently compared to 'archaeologists trying to piece together scraps of evidence'.[2] This problem only grows when international comparisons are made of the relative roles of small firms. It is quite clear that the pattern identified by the Bolton Committee is largely unchanged and that, compared with the major Western countries, the UK small firms sector still makes a smaller contribution to manufacturing employment. This is borne out by the available, albeit patchy, data in Table 3.1. While the UK small establishments' share (of manufacturing employment) has risen from 27 per cent in 1973 to 30 per cent in 1979, it remains low compared to Japan's 68 per cent (in 1978) and that of West Germany.[3] Looked at another way, the number of establishments per 100 000 employed in countries like West

Table 3.1. Proportion of manufacturing employment in small establishments in the UK and other countries.[1]

Country	Bolton Committee figures[2]		G. Bannock's figures[2]		Up-dated figures											
	%	Year	%	Year	Pre-1970	1970	1971	1972	1973	1974	1975	1976	1977	1978	1979	1980
UK	31	1963	29	1975					27		29			30	30	
Germany, Fed. Rep.	34	1963	31	1976		30			31		32				31	30
South Africa	n.a.		n.a.		38(1968)							35				
Austria	n.a.		n.a.								35					35
United States	39	1963	38	1972	35(1968)			38					39			
Sweden	53	1965	41	1975		51		50		48	41				41	
Canada	47	1968	44	1975				46			47			48		
Norway	64	1967	58	1975					61		60		60		62	
Spain	n.a.		n.a.											64		
Switzerland	61	1965	64	1975							64					
Italy	66	1961	59	1971			65									
Japan	54	1966	66	1975	64(1965)	62					65			68		
Netherlands	58	1962	58	1962												
France	51	1963	51	1963												
Australia	60	1963	60	1963												
Belgium	51	1962	45	1975												

Netherlands (1962), France (1963), Australia (1963): Up-dated figures for these countries expressed in terms of enterprises

Belgium (1975): No updated figures found

[1] On a similar basis, the Scottish figure was estimated as around 25 per cent in 1977.

[2] Sources as follows: Bolton Committee figures, *Small Firms – Report of the Committee of Inquiry on Small Firms*, Bolton, 1971; G. Bannock's figures, *The Economics of Small Firms*, Bannock, 1981. For non-UK sources see *British Business*.
Source: *British Business*, 19 November 1982.

Germany, UK, Canada and the US varies from 1240 to 1890, whereas in Japan it is around 7000. Examining this data on a firm basis, some 23 per cent of employment in the manufacturing sector in the UK is in enterprises with less than 200, but the figure is as low as seven per cent in the vehicle industry and much higher in, say, leather (61 per cent), and clothing and footwear (38 per cent).

In the context of searching for employment potential in new or small enterprises, some other aspects of the British relative position are noteworthy. The UK has the lowest level of self-employment among the major industrial countries, excluding Sweden.[4] Moreover, UK rates (at 7·8 per cent in 1979) have declined more rapidly than in this group since 1960 with the exception of Belgium. Turning, finally, to the question of births and deaths of firms, the available UK evidence, especially that based on VAT returns, suggests that the two are approximately in balance – the 10000 or so per month representing almost ten per cent of the small firms population.[5] Again, these positions vary by sector, with DoI data showing positive balances in construction, wholesale, finance and other services in 1980.

The preceding paragraphs make disturbing reading. Any strategy which would seek to change the relative position of the small firm in the UK or Scottish economies has an uphill struggle. It requires the reversal of trends and innovative policies. As subsequent sections will show, it has received some of the latter, while it is too early to determine the achievement of the former.

Birth Rates of New Enterprises. While it is relatively easy to demonstrate that small firms play a lesser role in the UK than in other industrialised countries, it is much more difficult to examine differentials between UK regions. There are many reasons for this, chief among which are data inconsistencies arising from definitional questions and inconsistent coverage from one area to another. Having said that, much of the limited evidence about the relative record of Scotland in terms of new company formation points in the same direction, namely, that while there is little difference between Scottish and UK performance, there is no evidence that Scotland is disadvantaged. Based on Record of Openings and Closures (ROC) data, a recent study[6] covering the 1966–75 period showed that the birth rate of enterprises new to manufacturing (ENMs) in Scotland compared reasonably favourably with that in other Standard Regions of Great Britain, with Scotland ranking fourth equal of ten in the 1966–71 period and second equal of ten in the 1972–75 period. The implied improvement is probably strongly related to oil developments. Table 3.2 shows these findings, although the reliability of the interregional comparisons is open to some question and there is a general tendency to under-record in view of the small size of these enterprises. Having said that, this work does suggest that Scotland is above the UK

average for employment in ENMs over this period, though behind East
Anglia, the South East, Northern Ireland and Wales in the 1975 rankings.

Table 3.2. Employment in enterprises new to manufacturing (ENMs)
per thousand of the areas manufacturing employment.

Region	1966–71		1972–75
Northern	5		3
Yorkshire and Humberside	3		4
East Midlands	10		5
South East	11		6
East Anglia	20		8
South West	6		4
Wales	14		5
West Midlands[2]	1		[1]
North West	3		3
Scotland	10		6
Borders	13	Borders	22
Edinburgh	6	Lothian	[1]
Falkirk/Stirling	12	Central	[1]
Glasgow	9	Strathclyde	5
Highlands & Islands	25	Highlands[3]	[1]
North East	14	Grampian	7
South West	[1]	Dumfries and Galloway	[1]
Tayside	15	Tayside	2
		Fife	9

[1] Employment per 1000 less than 0·5 or not disclosed
[2] The low figures for the West Midlands may be misleading since a higher
employment cut-off point for inclusion in the Record of Openings and
Closures (ROC) was used in the West Midlands conurbation than in
other areas.
[3] The three Island Authority areas are omitted because the
manufacturing employment in each one in 1975 was less than 1000.
Source: *Scottish Economic Bulletin*, No. 24, Spring 1982, p.23.

These indications are consistent with other recent evidence, including one study[7] which showed that Scotland's share of all UK ENMs
over the period 1966–75 and which survived to 1975 was around nine per
cent, a figure broadly in line with Scotland's share of the GDP of the UK
over that period. Equally relevant, but applying to an earlier period and
examining the comparative rate of formation of new manufacturing
establishments in the Central Clydeside and West Midlands conurbations, it has been shown that lower birth rates and 1972 employment
were recorded in Clydeside.[8] Earlier evidence in the West Central Scot-

land Plan in 1974 had suggested that Clydeside's record for the generation of new companies was poor. For reasons noted above, all of these pieces of evidence must be regarded with considerable caution. Taken together, however, they do not suggest that Scotland has been worse off than other parts of the U K in the absolute numbers of new manufacturing firms being established. Of course, they say nothing about the relative record in non-manufacturing areas, nor about the type of manufacturing enterprises emerging – although, given the similarity between Scotland's industrial structure and that of the U K, there is no *prima facie* reason to expect major differences in this regard.

Table 3.3. The contribution of small enterprises in Scotland.

	Small enterprises	All enterprises	% contribution of small enterprises
Employment – total	151100	616900	24·5
–ATC[1]	33800	150000	22·5
Net capital expenditure (£m)	84·5	493·3	17·1
Gross value added (£m)	774·3	3707·9	20·9
Net capital expenditure per employee (£)	560	800	
Gross value added per employee (£)	5126	6011	

[1] Administrative, technical and clerical.
Source: *Scottish Economic Bulletin*, No. 23, Summer 1981.

Performance. Of equal importance in the context of this chapter is the record of performance of the small business sector in Scottish industry. Here again, analysis is limited by both data availability and quality, the most recent being that emerging from the 1977 Census of Production and relating only to manufacturing enterprises. From this source, it was estimated that in 1977, some 7000 enterprises employing under 200 people in Scotland accounted for just under one quarter of the total manufacturing employment.[9] As Table 3.3 indicates, both investment and output per employee in the small enterprises was somewhat lower than that for manufacturing as a whole. The best measure of output from this data source is that of gross value added and, in this case, the small firms accounted for twenty-one per cent of the total. These figures are analysed on a sectoral basis in Table 3.4. The contribution of small businesses is seen to be comparatively small in electronics, instrument and electrical engineering, and in chemicals and allied industries. In contrast, it is highest in textiles, leather and clothing and in other manufacturing industries. Such generalisations must, however, be made with caution and take into account the variations in the character of small

Table 3.4. Output, investment and employment in small business in Scotland, 1977.

Size of enterprise	No. of enterprises	No. of establish-ments	Employment Total	Employment ATC¹	Net capital expenditure (£000)	Gross value added (GVA) (£000)	Net capital expenditure per employee (£)	Gross value added per employee (£)	GVA less labour costs per employee (£)	Labour costs per employee (£)
All manufacturing industry (SIC III–XIX)										
20–49	1125	1247	34427	7750	19511	178982	567	5199	1979	3220
50–99	483	578	33918	7980	23262	179871	686	5303	1941	3362
100–199	332	474	46247	10173	25061	225103	542	4867	1654	3213
1–199	7292	7741	151070	33755	84530	774348	560	5126	1927	3198
Food, drink and tobacco (SIC III)										
20–49	195	211	5993	1078	4902	42995	818	7174	4264	2910
50–99	75	96	5109	883	3801	27888	744	5459	2551	2908
100–199	43	64	5903	1018	3986	29200	675	4947	2126	2821
1–199	1061	1131	22980	3932	16880	133173	735	5795	2961	2834
Chemicals and allied industries (SIC V)										
20–49	30	38	943	418	1243	8295	1319	8796	5083	3713
50–99	16	19	1120	418	4409	9352	3937	8350	4150	4200
100–199	11	12	1510	582	1085	8677	719	5746	2102	3644
1–199	206	220	4538	1775	7640	34724	1683	7652	3858	3794

Size band									
20–49	168	188	5132	1449	3059	29415	596	5732	1875	3857
50–99	69	78	4709	1500	4258	32306	904	6861	2869	3992
100–199	43	73	6101	1765	2737	32644	449	5351	1403	3948
1–199	903	973	20666	6005	12109	120234	586	5818	1982	3836

Instrument and electrical engineering (SIC VIII, IX)

Size band									
20–49	44	48	1384	449	503	7263	364	5248	1819	3429
50–99	31	39	2256	862	1234	12518	547	5549	1952	3597
100–199	22	27	3093	891	3766	17812	1217	5759	2393	3366
1–199	403	430	8880	2882	6232	48994	702	5517	2163	3354

Electronics (MLH's 354, 363–367)

Size band									
20–49	15	20	430	162	149	2250	346	5234	1571	3663
50–99	18	21	1336	443	703	6719	526	5029	1512	3517
100–199	12	19	1672	568	3046	10293	1822	6156	2765	3391
1–199	192	209	4409	1502	4261	24937	966	5656	2266	3390

Textiles, leather and clothing (SIC XIII, XIV, XV)

Size band									
20–49	190	203	5921	845	1539	19325	260	3264	885	2379
50–99	91	100	6370	918	1657	22211	260	3487	951	2536
100–199	90	110	12798	1914	5289	46345	413	3621	1076	2545
1–199	902	954	28898	4183	9245	101189	320	3502	1031	2471

Other manufacturing industries (SIC IV, VI, X–XII, XVI–XIX)

Size band									
20–49	498	559	15054	3511	8264	71689	549	4762	1355	3407
50–99	201	246	14354	3399	7904	75549	551	5266	1685	3581
100–199	123	188	16842	4003	8190	90452	487	5369	1843	3526
1–199	3817	4033	65108	14978	32425	336035	498	5161	1776	3385

1 Administrative, technical and clerical staff.
Source: *Scottish Economic Bulletin*, No. 23, Summer 1981.

businesses in these sectors, as well as the relative performance in the various indicators shown in Table 3.4. Thus, for example, while small firms are numerically more important in textiles than in electronics, the gross value added is much higher in the latter. Equally, net capital expenditure per employee is smallest in the two sectors where small firms are relatively more important. It should also be remembered that efforts to generate new enterprises (in areas such as electronics) as well as the differential efforts of recession on sectors has probably considerably changed the mix shown in Table 3.4.

One of the critical performance issues concerns the role of the small firm in job generation, an issue which has been the focus of particular attention in Scotland and elsewhere following the Birch findings for the USA.[10] This study suggested that two thirds of net new jobs over the period 1969–76 were created by firms employing less than twenty people. To date, there has been no directly comparable work in Scotland. The evidence which exists is not entirely encouraging. One recent study has pointed to a much better performance in job generation by large rather than by small firms over the period from the mid-1950s,[11] while another showed (*inter alia*) that a significant proportion of the rapidly growing new manufacturing units in Scotland were of foreign ownership.[12] It is not yet possible to say whether Scotland has been markedly different in job generation rates than the UK as a whole. What is clear is that the considerable expectations placed on the small-firm sector for employment growth are more based on hope than on evidence of past performance. This is not to discount the contribution from the small-firm sector but rather to set it in its proper context.

The process of small-firm growth is complex and it is frequently difficult to isolate the relative significance of different sets of factors which contribute to it. Some recent Scottish work highlights these problems. Examining the 120 small manufacturing units which employed less than 200 in 1954 but whose employment had grown above this figure by 1974, an Industry Department for Scotland (IDS) study attempted to identify some of the important influences on and constraints to the growth of small units.[13] It was shown, as expected, that small firms grew faster in periods of growth in overall manufacturing employment and that the role of major customers in encouraging supplier growth was a key factor in many cases. A number of common constraints emerged including finance for expansion, lack of suitable space at a critical period and lack of access to appropriate advice. Perhaps the most complex influence to determine was the relationship between employment growth and ownership change. Within a sample of these firms, 66 per cent were independent in 1954 but only 18 per cent in 1974. By implication, a number of the growth problems were 'resolved' by changing ownership structures, generally involving takeovers by major competitors, customers or suppliers. While it is not possible to compare Scotland and other UK regions in this regard, there are no *prima facie* reasons for expecting differences. In view of the potentially important findings in this study, a further piece of work was undertaken for the IDS, based on company interviews, concentrating particularly on ownership change.[14] The results did not suggest that the occurrence of takeover was associated either with more rapid employment growth or greater employment stability. It was, however, shown that in the last decade the firms remaining independent had a more consistent pattern of sales growth and employment performance, with a lower propensity to record losses. Of equal importance was the identification of certain development 'thresholds' in these firms, including, for example, that associated with attempts to penetrate the English market for family firms and export markets for firms which were taken over. It is clearly to the identification of these thresholds that external advice should be directed, although not all firms are receptive to the solutions proffered.

As regards the relative technological and innovative capacity in small firms in Scotland, the evidence is sparse and somewhat confusing. There is some general UK evidence to suggest that small independent firms in the South East are almost twice as innovative as are similar firms in the development regions.[15] Yet one recent study comparing small, independent firms in instruments and electronic components in Scotland, the South East and the Bay Area of California, highlighted some positive findings for Scotland.[16] These included a higher incidence of full time Research and Development (R&D) staff, high levels of external R&D links with local universities, and some general evidence of positive effects stemming from SDA support in the encouragement of indigenous high technology.

Entrepreneurs and the New Firm. There is a wide variety of UK evidence both on factors determining the establishment of new enterprises and conditions affecting their growth.[17] While there is no particular reason to believe that Scotland differs from the UK in these matters, little of this work has been directed to the identification of general principles. Entrepreneurs generally establish new businesses close to their home and are induced into this action by a series of push and pull factors. In certain circumstances (e.g. unemployment) the push factor may dominate. In the Scottish context, it has been suggested that the new firms' foundation process is the result of interaction between the local labour market, an individual's prospects with his present employer and a variety of factors affecting that interplay.[18] By extension, therefore, some labour markets containing different combinations of employment opportunities and sectoral mixes have differing numbers of new firms.

Again, there is ample evidence to suggest that a major factor influencing immediate post-formation performance is the educational/

professional background of the founder.[19] This has been re-emphasised in a study applying to Scotland, Ireland and France where the importance of skilled tradesmen as new firm founders was stressed in all cases, although, in this instance, post-formation was not examined.[20] Generally speaking, new business founders are not dynamic entrepreneurs involved with new products, services or technologies, but are rather individuals involved in close replicas of activity known to them and in those which offer a fairly immediate profit opportunity. For this reason, there are invariably strong ties with immediate past employment, both in terms of experience and markets. A recent study of sixty new enterprises in local small business development schemes in Scotland showed that 88 per cent operated in a business area related to the founder's degree, professional and trade/craft qualification.[21] While wholly understandable, this situation poses real problems for any industrial strategy which would seek genuine diversification and innovation through the small-firm sector. This is, therefore, a matter which is directly addressed later in the policy section of this chapter.

There is widespread agreement that small firms, especially those in the early stages of development, have a number of recurrent needs and share common problems. Less agreement can, however, be claimed either for the way in which these needs should be met and the problems solved, or on whom the balance of responsibility should lie to take such action. The small-firm sector in Scotland appears to acknowledge that help is often required. An SDA study drew attention to the fact that over seventy-five per cent of the firms surveyed indicated a need for outside assistance for at least one aspect of their business.[22] In general, the perception of needs increased according to the size of the firm, with those employing less than ten making lighter demands. This latter was correctly attributed to the lack of realisation of difficulties rather than to an absence of problems. Finance and administration together with marketing were regarded as the most important areas for required advice. In terms of recurring difficulties over the previous five years of operation, the SDA study indicated that cash flows and Government and local authority 'red tape' together accounted for some twenty-five per cent of all problems; inflation, recession and lack of skilled labour together amounted to a further twenty-three per cent of them. Results of this type must, of course, be purely regarded as indicative of the characteristic problems of firms of this scale. They inevitably vary with time, circumstance, industry, location and so on. In no way are they peculiarly associated with operation in Scotland.

One recurrent theme concerns the apparently serious communications gap between the small-firm sector and agencies designed to offer help. The complexity of such mechanisms is not helpful, but neither is the low tolerance level of many small enterprises. Thus is is not difficult to record negative reactions from the latter in all parts of the UK and beyond. A recent survey of two hundred UK small firms, including fifty in the Lothian region, is but one example of this.[23] Around one half of the sample had used one or more of the relevant services offered by the SDA, while the other half were critical of their initial contacts and seemed unlikely to make further contacts. Of course, the assistance requirements of small firms are invariably highly specific and very immediate. Both of these features mitigate against ease of matching between the provider and the user. Hence this is an issue for consideration at a policy level in the following section.

Existing Small-Firm Policies

Fired both by the recession conditions of the 1970s and the widely-held view that the relative contribution of small firms to the UK economy must be improved as a basis for economic recovery, the last five years have witnessed an unparalleled effort to aid small firms. While the roots of some of these policies and institutions lie in the Bolton era, a number have been rather hastily conceived. Moreover, the recent date of a number of the national policy initiatives make an accurate evaluation of their effectiveness very difficult; doubly so at Scottish level. Such an assessment is necessary, however tentative. In this section two different perspectives are taken, the one concerned with UK policy initiatives in recent years, setting this in the broad context of policies of some other countries, and the other at the Scottish level. Within the latter, a distinction is subsequently made between regional and local measures.

UK Measures in their International Setting. All the evidence suggests that the problems of small businesses in the UK are shared throughout the world as governments attempt to counteract the rise in bankruptcies during the recession by encouraging entrepreneurship and firms based on new technologies. It is worth noting the policy trends in the major countries which have taken the lead in fostering the small-firm sector. For example, in the USA, the Small Business Administration (SBA) programme has increasingly stressed the need for loan guarantees (of up to 90 per cent) for the small business, $3.4 million being spent in 1980 at rates between the prime lending rate and the prime plus 2·75 per cent.[24] In addition to administering a direct loan programme of around ten per cent of the total guarantee value, the main thrusts of SBA policy have been in large-scale management assistance programmes. These involved assistance for over 300000 enterprises in 1980. There has also been a specific push on trying to achieve a larger share of government contracts for this sector and the SBA had claimed a move from eighteen per cent of all such contracts in 1977 to around twenty-five per cent in 1981. In real terms the main SBA lending schemes have not grown in recent years and the movement has been away from loans and towards guarantees. While the reduction in Federal funding through the SBA has been partly offset by the rapid growth of venture capital in the US since 1979, after a considerable period of relative stagnation, this source is only available to the more glamorous projects. In short, the small-firm sector in the US is increasingly embattled by high capital cost and restrictions on SBA activity, although the very fact that this sector has such tangible representation over a long period is in itself a lesson for the UK.

Recognition at national level is also present in Canada where there has been a Minister of State for small business since 1976 and the Small Business Secretariat, along with the Department of Industry, Trade and Commerce operates regional offices across the country. As elsewhere, however, there are coordination problems in Canada due to the plethora of measures at provincial and municipal level. One of the most interesting Canadian institutions for the small business is the Federal Business Development Bank (FDBD), with over a hundred branches and aimed at businesses of all types which cannot obtain financing otherwise at reasonable cost. The emphasis is on small business, and ninety per cent of loans authorised in 1979 averaged Can $52000 each. Financing is through loans, loan guarantees, leasing or equity which can later be redeemed. In general, the small and medium-sized sector in Canada has been nourished carefully over a long period with a large range of Federal direct aid programmes, including low rates of corporate tax on the first Can $400000 of profits (estimated to benefit the small sector by Can $2 billion per annum), direct subsidies on new product development and export efforts and a low-cost financing programme such as a small business bond scheme operated through the banks. To this is added special Federal and provincial direct aid schemes for small firms in particular high-technology sectors. In spite of all of this, the sector in Canada has suffered very badly in the recession of recent years.

The change of Government in France in 1981 has led to a considerable increase in funds being made available to the smaller sector. The new and enhanced schemes include increased volumes of cheap credits distributed by the Government-backed Caisse d'Equipement des PME (CEPME) which operates as a type of soft loan bank for small companies; advances of 'prêts participatif', a type of semi-equity funding of loans carrying interest payments on a sliding scale related to profits on a project; while funds to ANVAR, the state industrial innovation body have also been doubled, with a particular remit to aid research workers attached to smaller firms. In the French case these policies have to be seen against other less favourable aspects of the current environment for small business including the wealth tax measures, the additional costs of the proposed move to a 35-hour working week and so on. Having said that, the French have had a long history of small-firm support dating back to

World War II and there has been a substantial transfer of resources to this sector, particularly within the last decade.

An equally impressive policy sequence can be detected in the West German case towards the 'mittelstand'[25] and again there are many different types of programme. Among the most prominent is the provision of development credit through the Kreditanstalt für Wiederaufbau (KfW). In 1981, for example, KfW approved subsidised finance of DM 5.2 million for the small and medium company sector as part of its expanded activity in this field over recent years. Equally active has been the Ministry of Research and Technology in the promotion of innovation in the smaller business; while many of the well-endowed Chambers of Commerce have special departments for small business.

In terms of developed economies, the classic example of a durable and consistent small-firm policy is that of Japan. In this case, it has been reinforced both by the power of law and by a well-established and interconnected institutional framework.[26] These are shown in Figure 3.1. Thus, for example, since 1963 there has been a programme to strengthen the finances of small businesses, and aid for access to government procurement on many other schemes coordinated by the Small and Medium Enterprise Agency established within the MITI framework in 1948.

Viewing the British policy position against this background, a number of sharp contrasts emerge. Not only is the time period over which the smaller enterprise has been a substantive policy issue much shorter, it has also consistently featured at a less senior level in Government. Further, the UK approach has only recently become more coordinated and as yet does not match most of the examples given. Of course, it is now possible to trace ingredients of many of these measures within the British system since such technology is readily transferred. In truth, the UK is still experimenting with the components of a small-firm policy and it will take at least a decade before the full effects of many of the measures of the last few years can really be assessed. Much will, even then, depend on the general economic environment during this period, to say nothing of whether this sector will remain of serious interest to successive UK Governments.

From the early 1970s, British policy towards small firms was stimulated by the report of the Bolton Committee. The Committee was of the view that positive discrimination by Government in favour of small business was not justified, although recognising that some unintentional barriers had been placed on their development by Governments. Thus, most subsequent policies were directed to the removal of existing discrimination against the small firm and ensuring that further discrimination was not built into new policies. It was not until the late 1970s that UK policy began to move towards discrimination in favour of small firms, including policies with the specific aim of encouraging their birth.

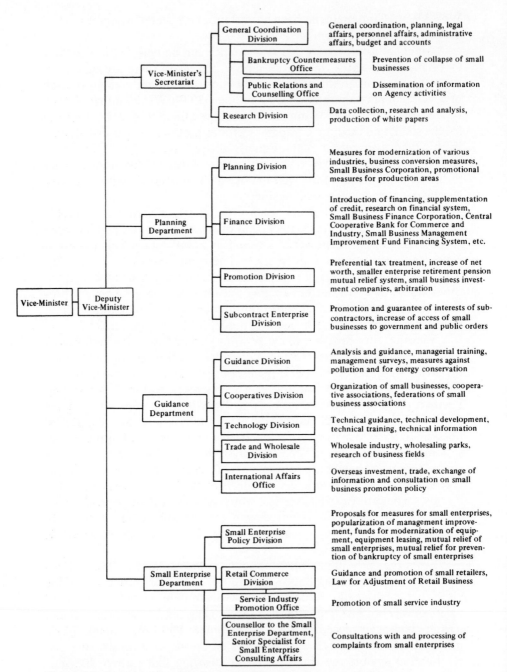

Figure 3.1. Organisation of Japanese small and medium enterprise agency. (Source: JETRO.)

An examination of the measures since the early 1970s categorising them into three groups, viz. indirect assistance, removal of discrimination and direct preferential assistance shows a sharp rise in the latter over recent years.[27]

While U K small-firm policy does not date from 1979, it has received a major stimulus since then. The new national measures designed to specifically assist small firms have perhaps been in four main categories. Each of these constitutes an assault on well-recognised small-firm problems. First, under the taxation and finance heading, there has been the Loan Guarantee Scheme, operating on a pilot basis since June 1981. Designed to improve the flow of commercial funds to projects which would not otherwise be backed, this scheme for eighty per cent Government guarantees was heavily oversubscribed in the first year. As a result, the ceiling was raised from £150 million to £300 million, although it will take at least two to three years to conclude whether this pilot scheme is really effective. The Business Start-up Scheme of 1981 constituted a new tax incentive to attract individual investors to back new enterprises by giving relief against income tax on up to £10000 invested in any one year. Other approaches under this heading have included the Venture Capital Scheme from 1980, more favourable corporation tax arrangements, a Special European Loan Scheme for the Assisted Areas and Northern Ireland and so on.

Secondly, in the context of planning and premises,[28] further measures were taken to encourage more private investment in small factory premises where shortages had been identified. These included reduced planning constraints, joint financing between public and private sector and increasing the thresholds of Industrial Development Certificates.

Thirdly, a series of measures were introduced in the 1980 Employment Act to aid the smaller firm, especially with regard to unfair dismissal claims, length of contracts, and so on. Finally, a miscellaneous group of measures have been brought in aimed at reducing bureaucracy, requiring direct labour organisations in local authorities to put certain contracts out to tender, extending finance for the Small Firms Service and measures to ensure further cooperation between agencies concerned with small firms. In addition, there would seem to be more systematic efforts to obtain co-operation across Government departments in matters relating to the small-firm sector.

As noted, it is too early to judge the effectiveness of these schemes. Such an evaluation will take time and also be conditional on sharp improvements of data sources. If anything, too many schemes have been introduced too quickly (with over seventy measures between 1979 and mid-1983), although this might be justified in the cause of initial experimenting en route to establishing longer-term and simpler support mechanisms. There is little doubt that some of these measures do touch on matters of long-term concern, especially as regards reducing red tape, loan guarantees and sector-specific investment schemes, such as that for small engineering firms. One of the problems which remain for UK Governments is to accept more risk and failure emerging from such measures, learn from them and proceed without being frightened off if a particular measure has undesired effects. Such vagaries can only be effectively handled within a robust, long-term strategy for this sector. The latter has yet to emerge in the UK.

Initiatives at Scottish Level. With businesses employing less than 100 people accounting for around one million jobs in Scotland and given the record of recent years in terms of large-scale closures in areas of special need, it is not surprising to find a wide range of small-firm initiatives in Scotland. It is not the purpose of this section to consider these exhaustively but rather to first draw attention to the spectrum of initiatives and thereafter devote attention to their relative effectiveness, insofar as that can be determined.

For the first of these purposes, Figure 3.2 should be regarded as purely indicative of the types of activity undertaken by differing sponsoring bodies within Scotland. The schemes and projects listed differ vastly in scale; in emphasis as between the provision of items such as finance, advice and premises; and also in terms of their durability. They range from massive area renewal projects, albeit often with a relatively minor small-firm spending component, to self-help programmes run on a shoestring. One particular scheme (Clyde Workshops Ltd) which has attracted attention is the subject of an appendix to this chapter. As a national development body the SDA is by far the most ubiquitous organisation, covering most aspects of small-firm support within a variety of its divisions. Almost equally active in the last five years, albeit on a much smaller financial scale, have been the local authorities operating (with and without SDA support) in a large number of local schemes to set up new businesses and encourage expansion in others. Many of these schemes, as later evidence shows, are directed to the micro-firm, employing ten and under. Even more fashionable now has become the enterprise trust at local level involving the private sector or co-operation between private and public sector interests.

Reviewing the material in Figure 3.2, some important points emerge. First, as is equally true of many UK regions in the early 1980s, almost every possible scheme for small-firm creation and development is being tried somewhere in Scotland. Secondly, not only is it difficult to determine which of these approaches is most effective at solving which problems, it is also true to say that there has been little interest in finding out. Both public and private sector bodies have been striving for visibility in the small-firm sector and in some areas there are more schemes than entrepreneurs. Thirdly, there is inevitably some measure of duplication

Focus	IDS	SDA	Local authority	Private sector	Others	Combinations
			Sponsoring organisation:			
1. National	Administration of UK and EC financing, start-up and allied services	Advisory service of Small Business Division; provision of premises; agency for ECSC funds				
2. Regional		As above in regional offices	NESDA Small Business Enterprise Scheme; SRC		HIDB initiatives	
3. Local		Special Area initiatives (e.g. Dundee, Motherwell, Clydebank, GEAR, Leith, etc.); industrial improvement areas	Local small-firm development schemes; managed workshops, etc. Advisory services	Enterprise Trusts	BSC Industry in steel closure areas; New Towns	Enterprise Trusts (e.g. SDA, private sector, local authorities)
4. Company-specific	Financial and advisory packages	Individual financial, premises and advisory packages	Local small-firm development schemes; managed workshops, etc. Advisory services	Venture capital companies; development depts of banks; 'start-up' funds, etc.	Scottish Producer Co-operative Development project; Community enterprise projects, etc.	Management buy-outs (SDA; private sector)

Figure 3.2. Illustrative groupings of small-firm initiatives in Scotland.

implicit in Figure 3.2. This exists, for instance, between national and regional advisory services, various 'venture' capital organisations, and so on. Fourthly, there has been a distinct trend over recent years to tackle the small firm at a more local level. While in many ways desirable, especially in the stage of new enterprise formation where local markets and suppliers are invariably critical, this trend has occurred underneath an existing national system. Among these local manifestations are special area initiative projects at the one end and community enterprise schemes at the other. In part at least, this trend is associated with the desire for local political visibility in job creation projects. Fifthly, almost all the schemes outlined have either emerged totally or changed very substantially within the last five to seven years. Many are still at an early stage in their evolution and some will have short lives. For these reasons, plus the fact that a number of the bodies involved publish very little data which would enable the testing of effectiveness, critical appraisal is almost impossible.

In an ideal situation, these initiatives would be subject to test in terms of new enterprises encouraged, new jobs created, higher birth rates, survival and growth rates, and so on. In reality, this could not be undertaken on anything approaching a comprehensive basis. Thus, actual EC spending through its various schemes which impinge on smaller firms in Scotland has not been accurately estimated. It is clear, however, that several of the recent EC loan schemes for small business have been very unsuccessful. For example, two such schemes from ECSC and EIB funds managed through branches of a Scottish bank have had very low uptake. In part this is due to the fixed interest charges involved at a time of declining rates, ineffective overall design of schemes and to indifferent marketing. Equally critical is the emergence of better small-firm packages from the SDA. The actual take-up rates of venture capital by the smaller company are not readily estimated, although in recent years it is well known that the dearth has been of available projects rather than of money. No accurate data exists on management buy-outs in recent years, although this form of operation is clearly growing, and preserving some employment in closure situations; nor is it easy to evaluate the effect of advisory services for the smaller firm. For these and other reasons, an assessment of progress in assisting the small-firm sector in Scotland must be a much more modest exercise, concentrating on the limited evidence available. Such an approach is taken in subsequent paragraphs, addressing both the known effects of recent UK schemes and those identifiable within Scotland.

It is not possible to determine with any accuracy whether the small-firm sector in Scotland is receiving more or less funding support in the recent past. Very inadequate proxy statistics are available, most of which show a growing interest in directing modest funds to smaller business but no dramatic shift in uptake. Table 3.5 suggests that a growing number of small-firm (under 100 employees) cases are being supported by the Small Business Division (SBD) of the SDA over the past three years, although clearly the amounts invested are very small. Geographically, the pattern of loans runs broadly in line with population distribution, with 50 per cent in Strathclyde region. In terms of industry spread, between 60 and 70 per cent have gone to manufacturing enterprises, with service operations accounting for between 20 and 30 per cent. The balance goes to 'high technology' firms and in that regard Scotland does not differ from the rest of the UK, in that emergent and supported small firms are not normally at that end of the technology spectrum. Perhaps of greater importance is the growth in equity investments made by the SBD over the past few years. The 1982–83 figures indicate that some forty per cent of the investment money offered was in this category, thus reflecting SDA initiatives both to bridge the 'equity-gap' in firms of this scale and to take greater risk in their small-firm lending.

There is very little evidence to suggest that the plethora of Scottish-based venture capital organisations receive an abundance of applications from supportable projects from Scotland, whatever the size of the firm.[29] Relatively little hard data are available on these issues. Table 3.6 outlines the pattern of ICFC lending in Scotland over the past five years, although information on firm size is not available. The figures suggest that Scotland is marginally below the UK average uptake over this period, but this could be as much a function of the marketing of available funds as anything else.

Another very tentative and recent indicator is provided in Table 3.7 in the context of the national Small Business Loan Guarantee Scheme. The fact that Scotland was somewhat below the expected *pro rata* uptake level in both number and value could be attributed to the recency of the scheme, initial communications difficulties, the existing activities of Scottish financial institutions and so on. In any event, relatively little can be learned from one year's data.

Referring back to Figure 3.2, it is possible to determine the effectiveness of only some of these initiatives. As an example, local small-firm development schemes operated under a variety of sponsors have been the subject of recent study.[30] One of the major experiments of this type, namely Clyde Workshops, is the subject of more extended consideration in the appendix to this chapter. The activities of the Ardrossan, Saltcoats and Stevenston Enterprise Trust (ASSET) are a further example of this type of initiative, in this case involving SDA, Strathclyde Region, Cunninghame District, Shell and ICI. Motivated by a series of disastrous closures in the area and set up in 1981, ASSET provides a one-door appraisal for potential businesses with an interest in starting or expanding in the area. By the end of its first year, forty-two companies had been

Table 3.5. Small Business Division (SDA): investment statistics.

	Investments offered						Investments accepted						Investments made[1]		
	1980–81		1981–82		1982–83		1980–81		1981–82		1982–83		1980–81	1981–82	1982–83
	No.	£000	No.	£000	No.	£000	No.	£000	No.	£000	No.	£000	£000	£000	£000
Apr	7	122	5	76	26	507	5	97	5	76	19	410	106	59	152
May	3	61	8	136	20	301	3	61	4	56	16	236	135	26	147
Jun	12	313	13	299	31	568	7	142	9	239	28	516	187	130	208
July	12	260	15	347	17	284	10	212	13	336	16	279	193	188	467
Aug	6	70	10	85	37	733	4	43	3	29	17	354	138	89	144
Sep	7	117	16	269	29	560	5	67	13	232	12	160	120	126	423
Oct	7	174	11	194	31	441	7	174	9	154	29	395	214	193	315
Nov	11	222	8	155	32	761	10	203	7	135	31	620	132	118	278
Dec	11	239	17	295	35	675	5	95	10	181	28	500	62	305	521
Jan	6	92	20	410	28	351	5	92	16	291	17	291	57	127	253
Feb	5	85	17	286	23	289	4	65	14	221	32	403	186	126	561
Mar	10	151	25	451	32	520	8	151	23	402	11	205	111	195	709
Total	97	1915	165	3003	341	5990	73	1402	126	2352	256	4369	1641	1682	4178

[1] It should be noted that many of the packages involve other financial backers and so the actual sum invested in total would be higher.
Source: Scottish Development Agency.

76

Table 3.6. ICFC lending in Scotland, 1977–82 (£ thousands).

Financial year	Total gross advances[1]	Gross advances in Scotland	Gross advances in Scotland as % of total
1977–78	66·5	5·9	8·9
1978–79	81·4	8·0	9·8
1979–80	101·7	9·1	8·9
1980–81	92·1	11·1	12·1
1981–82	102·5	8·1	7·9

[1] All UK areas: excludes Channel Islands and overseas.
Data on loan size and industry split are not published.
Source: *Investors in Industry* (formerly ICFC).

established in the project area and 165 jobs created or safeguarded. Since that period, the Enterprise Trust model, drawing heavily on private sector support, has expanded dramatically.

Most of the local schemes aimed at generating new small firms are on a smaller scale. They often involve the provision of small premises, usually grouped together in a specific location, and some combine these with various forms of managerial advice and financial assistance. Such 'workshop' models are now present all over Scotland, usually initiated by local authorities. Private sector attempts to get into this small end of the market have often met with difficulties. Reviewing the performance of a sample of five of these schemes and of sixty enterprises within them, it becomes clear that occupancy rates are high but that the demand is for a wide variety of types of small premises available at different cost structures.[31] In spite of a preference for manufacturing, around forty per cent of the sample were found to be in service or distribution activity. Eighty-eight per cent of the sample were totally new enterprises, the entrepreneurs having been in other employment for an average of fifteen years before establishing their business. The scale of these operations is very small, some 456 people being employed in the sample of sixty, although this represented an employment growth of over seventy-five per cent since establishment a few years previously. In short, there is some scope for encouragement in these small-scale ventures, in that they do appear to attract new enterprises. What is not clear is whether they actually generate new initiative by their presence or simply provide more visibility for a process which exists in any event.

Another manifestation of interest in stimulating entrepreneurial initiative, again not by any means distinctive to Scotland, is the growth of the use of management buy-out (MBO) techniques. In truth, this is purely a financial technique to enable managers either to acquire effective control or majority ownership of the companies which they manage, by

Table 3.7. Small Business Loan Guarantee Scheme, 1981–82[1]

	Number	Value (£m)
National		
Guarantees issued	4440	149·1
To new businesses	2214	70·7
To existing businesses	2226	78·4
To manufacturing businesses	2020	76·3
To construction businesses	73	2·3
To retail businesses	639	16·6
To other service businesses	1708	53·9
By region		
England: North-East	150	4·7
North-West	583	19·3
Yorks & Humberside	344	10·3
West Midlands	446	14·7
East Midlands	301	10·0
South-East	1681	61·2
South-West	404	13·3
Scotland	258(5·8%)	7·2(4·8%)
Wales	255	7·7
N. Ireland	18	0·7

[1] Data apply to the first full year of the scheme,
namely 1 June 1981 to 31 May 1982.
Source: Department of Trade and Industry.

enabling the company to operate with excessive debt capital. Invariably, initial financial gearing is, therefore, high (around 5:1 at times) and interest burdens heavy. Although there are no official figures on this phenomenon, it has been increasingly used in the UK with perhaps some two hundred MBO deals being struck in the last decade. Most of these are very recent and little work has been done on the issue in Scotland. In the Scottish context, some fifteen are known to have occurred between 1980 and 1982, with the SDA being involved in at least twelve of these.[32] They constitute a method of enabling a phoenix to emerge from the ashes of a divestment decision, almost always on a much-reduced scale.[33] Again, because of their recent emergence, it is impossible to determine the effectiveness of such deals, although initial signs are encouraging.

Equally difficult to evaluate is the Scottish experience in workers' co-operatives. The Scottish Cooperative Development Committee (SCDC) was recognised in 1977 as an official body under the 1976 Industrial Common Ownership Act. During the time since then, there is some evidence to indicate that such operations have become less

Table 3.8(a). Nature of NVU Cases: business origins.[1]

Structure of Case	No.	%
New starts	19	34
Extension of existing businesses	27	49
Significant development of existing businesses	5	9
Joint ventures	2	4
Rescue/short term assistance	2	4
Total	55	100

Table 3.8(b). Industrial classification of NVU cases.

Classification	No.	%
Data processing of which:	6	11
minicomputers	4	7
peripherals	2	4
Software-related[2]	7	13
Components of which:	7	13
semiconductor	4	7
pcbs[2]	3	5
Consumer products	2	4
Commercial applications	6	11
Industrial applications	8	14
Sub-contract	10	18
Non-electronics	9	16
Total	55	100

[1] Covers fifteen-month period in December 1980.
[2] Includes 'flexible' circuits.
Source: SDA.

involved in 'alternative society' and pump-priming activities, and more in main-line business. In 1977 when SCDC started, there were four workers' co-operatives, while by 1982 there were forty employing 350 people with a combined turnover of £4 million. It is perhaps true to say that this will remain a limited-scale activity at least until it becomes more available as a mode of operation by conventional funding sources. This, in turn, is likely only to follow the establishment of a credible track record by such co-operatives in Scotland.

While many of the initiatives outlined in Figure 3.2 harbour ambitions to encourage higher-technology small enterprises, relatively few succeed. The exercise of identifying the effect of these measures on this aspect of small business is made the more difficult by the private sector financial involvement and the subsequent lack of data. The SDA has, of course, made a considerable commitment to this area initially through its former New Ventures Unit (NVU) and some of the results give limited grounds for encouragement. Some insight into the nature of of this operation is given by the data in Table 3.8, covering the first fifteen months of its activity up to December 1980. This material is interesting on several counts, not least because it provides some indication of the level of activity in higher-technology areas. Of the fifty-five cases, one third were proposed new starts, almost half of which were spin-offs from established 'high-tech' companies. As in all such screening operations, the number of cases surviving external scrutiny is relatively low, with perhaps no more than twenty per cent becoming operable projects.

Turning to records of known new electronics company starts in Scotland, seventeen were recorded during the period 1978–81. Nine of these were established by entrepreneurs emerging out of existing electronics companies in Scotland, including Rodime (from Burroughs) and Subscan (from Fortronic – itself originating in Hewlett-Packard). These seventeen spanned a wide range of products and services, including data processing, medical, software/design consultancies and so on. In total, they employed between 200 and 300 by the end of 1981. Many of these new starts were undoubtedly aided by the improved availability of venture capital in Scotland, through public sector activities such as NVU from the SDA and the Scottish office of NRDC, and the expansion of private sector finance houses in this field. In the electronics context at least, there is no evidence to indicate that the absence of start-up capital has been a constraint on the generation of new companies. It has to be said, however, that most of these indigenous electronics companies (excluding those in sub-contracting) are in specialised low-volume products or offering local design/consultancy services and that in consequence their growth prospects are limited.

A Desired Role for Small Firms in Scotland and Possible Policy Directions

The two previous sections have indicated that Scotland does not differ markedly from the UK as a whole in the role played by small firms, although the dominance of external ownership in some sectors adjusts this picture at times. It has also been shown that the wave of interest in the small firm has broken over Scotland and that there are many schemes aimed at small-firm creation and development. Inevitably, many of these are experimental and lay different emphasis on the resolution of the problems of the small firm. Given the relative position of the small-firm sector in the UK as a whole and the avowed desire to change it, it is difficult to argue against the continuation of such a flexible approach, provided that the effectiveness of different schemes is really being monitored and the necessary lessons absorbed. There is serious doubt over whether this is occurring in Scotland or the UK as a whole. The desire to generate new employment sources and the associated unrealistic expectations placed on this sector has often meant that such issues have had a low priority.

It is quite clear that any significant reorientation of the Scottish economy towards the smaller firm, thus moving in the direction of other developed nations, will be conditioned both by the general health of the UK economy and by the way in which UK policies are developed to radically change the fiscal/legal framework within which they operate. It is as yet too early to say whether there is a long-term commitment to that change at UK level or whether the intensity of small-firm development activity in Scotland could make any more than a marginal difference to the role of small firms in that economy. Yet some lessons could be learned in the meantime.

In contrast with the other chapters in this book, there are a number of rather distinctive problems faced by the policy maker in deriving a meaningful set of small-firm initiatives for Scotland over the next decade. These include:

(a) The plethora of national (UK) measures, many of which are of recent date, few of which have therefore been examined for their effectiveness.

(b) The variety of Scottish and sub-regional initiatives falling into the same category.

(c) The number of statutory bodies and organisations committed to pursuing their own small-firm initiatives in view of the expected employment pay-off. Most of these enter with low-cost, high-visibility local initiatives which will never be readily regulated.

(d) The lack of general agreement that policy approaches coordinated at Scottish level are valid for this sector.

(e) The embryo state of knowledge of the relative merits of micro- versus macro-climate policies to encourage small firms.

(f) The lack of clarity as to what objectives a small-firm policy should pursue.

While it is true to say that a number of these difficulties surround the delineation of all industrial policy in UK (especially those in items d and e) they coincide in a rather unusual way in the small-firm area. Many of the schemes discussed in previous pages emerge out of a desire to be seen to be involved in tackling specific employment problems. Because such involvement can be undertaken at very different levels of resource commitment, it is to be expected that they will continue and in so doing generate an array of activity much of which probably has very little effect in the sector as a whole. Viewed realistically, then, many groups will continue to take small-firm initiatives, but only IDS/SDA are in a position to formulate a small-firm policy for Scotland which is both considered and capable of adding value to that of the UK as a whole. Thereafter the implementation thrust would lie with the SDA.

To date no such policy has emerged. The criteria by which the Small Business Division (SBD) of the SDA has been guided over recent years have been more immediate, with the emphasis on the expansion of existing services in greater depth, extended information support, the establishment of a counsellor network and, alongside other Agency divisions, the provision of additional small factory space. The task facing SBD is a substantial one. In terms of their advisory provision there are many thousands of manufacturing and service enterprises to cover, hence the focus on areas of highest need. Given a resource base of some fifty to sixty field and executive staff, plus part-time counsellors, the coverage is inevitably thin. Around seventy per cent of visits (which currently average about 600 per development officer) are to manufacturing companies, there being no plans to develop extensively into services. Some fifteen per cent of visits made are to new starts. For SBD the dominant operational problems surround client diversity; the need for a meaningful regional presence throughout Scotland; and the development of sufficient specialist skills to enable relevant advice to be given. All of these demands have placed strains on limited SBD resources, additional sources of which have been, on the one hand, the emergence of new UK schemes to be explained to their client group and, on the other, the intense scrutiny at sub-regional level from regions and districts about the effectiveness of their operation. It is perhaps not surprising that longer-term issues have not been examined.

However, the time is ripe for a more considered approach to the future of this sector and for the Agency to take and maintain the initiative. Starting with basics, Figure 3.3 sets out a possible series of short- and long-term strategic objectives for small-firm policy in Scotland. They are not weighted or placed in order of priority in this illustration. A number of items within the table are open to debate; others would meet with ready agreement. For example, item 7 in the short-term list is in the former category. Much of the work associated with the 'incubator' hypothesis has placed emphasis on the importance of the inner urban environment for small-firm creation, hence the view that the small firm is an appropriate vehicle for the regeneration of urban areas.[34] Recent studies have questioned this, including work in Glasgow showing that the birth rate of new firms in the inner city area was some two-thirds of that of the conurbation as a whole.[35] By weighing up the evidence, by planned efforts to

Short term

1 Attainment of a higher level of new firm starts
2 Sustenance of existing small-firm sector
3 Acceleration of growth rates in the sector
4 Provision of advice/support to cross development thresholds
5 Generation of a higher proportion of spin-offs from existing established businesses
6 Increasing proportion of high-technology projects
7 Maximising contribution to inner urban renewal programmes
8 Provision of an adequate spectrum of premises at appropriate size, cost and terms of tenure

Long-term

1 Achievement of levels of small-firm contribution to GDP comparable to those in major developed countries
2 Raising proportion of indigenous ownership and control in key manufacturing sectors
3 Substantial increase in contribution of small firms to offsetting large-scale job-losses in specific geographical areas

Figure 3.3. Possible strategic objectives for small-firm policy in Scotland.

generate new evidence, a series of objectives such as those in Figure 3.3 are an essential starting point to any serious policy framework.

But there are bigger questions to decide first regarding the overall philosophy of the Scottish approach. One of these concerns the balance between firm-specific advisory policies (on technical and managerial issues) and policies concentrating on removing 'environmental' hazards which constrain growth. It is difficult to see the final outcome of a policy based on the former. Such an approach is highly labour-intensive and may not be sustainable by the SDA on a resource cost basis. Arguably, at least as much attention should be given to minimising discrimination against small firms from whatever source, by a vigorous 'troubleshooting' approach towards all the key public and private sector organisations in Scotland who are capable of exerting negative influences on small-firm creation and growth by their practices. In the long run, the dismantling of such institutional barriers would probably be of more direct benefit than an endless proliferation of advisory services.

Another strategic question surrounds the relative attention given to hardware and software. It is probably true to say that the easiest part of small-firm support is the provision of premises. While this has been an essential part of Agency work, the balance will soon have to change towards more creative ways of developing the human resource. Such approaches could lead Scottish initiatives in many new directions placing greater emphasis on training; regional technological signposting services;

schemes to promote research and development in smaller firms; collective approaches to subcontracting; mobilising resources from other providers (e.g. in education) towards aiding the smaller firm; and so on. Should the balance be tilted towards both more software and more environmental troubleshooting, such as is suggested above, there would be a genuine possibility of some rather forceful new policies emerging at Scottish level. More importantly, they would be going in directions which have paid dividends elsewhere. Such an approach could lead to some key areas such as the small firm and public purchasing being tackled seriously in this country, as they are increasingly elsewhere. This might on the one hand involve the emergence of guidelines leading to the breaking up of public contracts in order to aid small-firm tenders, while on the other, require new forms of co-operation between small firms to gain tenders. Whether the approach suggested in these paragraphs is adopted or not is a matter of debate. The essential exercise is to decide on strategic directions and avoid the trap of undertaking more of the same policies without questioning where the most effective long-term contribution might be made.

The next stage is to ask whether and in what way existing initiatives are capable of attaining objectives to a measurable degree within an agreed time scale. Such an approach immediately begins to provide a benchmark for existing efforts. Assuming the adoption of the short-term list in Figure 3.3 this can be readily illustrated. Many resources are already devoted to achieving objectives 4 and 8. If, however, objective 1 was a prime aim there would be a real need to consider whether existing support policies are not perhaps too geared to an idealised entrepreneur. This person could readily be styled as the 'entrepreneurial, management trained graduate engineer' (or an equivalent) and is obviously in the minority. To target more directly on the working-class entrepreneur would require some radical reappraisal of the relationship between unemployment and self-employment. Such initiatives might include provision of guaranteed benefit for up to one year for a formerly unemployed entrepreneur. This is not to advocate a non-commercial approach which would falsely increase the number of new starts, but rather to draw lessons from the galaxy of routes by which new firms actually do start without external intervention. In the absence of a more open approach, there is a danger of directing too many resources away from groups in society who traditionally have generated a considerable proportion of small businesses. Of course, items 5 and 6 (Figure 3.3) both remain important. They are areas which feature in most lists of desirable objectives, but are not readily achieved. Here too, radical measures are required involving the co-operation of the private sector.

Very few companies actually encourage spin-offs although most large businesses have the capability to do so. It requires detailed analysis of their purchasing patterns and product development with their co-operation. Too often such exercises are only undertaken with the threat of closure on the horizon in a belated attempt to maintain some economic activity in an area. In effect, if item 5 was raised in public sector priorities with some imaginative funding schemes, some positive benefits might accrue. After all, there are already some excellent Scottish precedents.

Taking Figure 3.3 as a whole, it has been suggested that only IDS/ SDA are in a position to establish an overall philosophy, set objectives, attribute weight to each of them and re-appraise Scottish initiatives in total to determine where progress has been and can be made. Such an approach would inevitably confront several questions about the relative role of different bodies involved in supporting small firms, as illustrated below.

Consider first the effectiveness of existing arrangements for advisory services. While there are considerable resources devoted to this in Scotland, they do not yet reflect the scale of the need. There is ample evidence in the UK and elsewhere that the development of managerial skills is a critical variable for the determination of survival and growth. As noted earlier, there are, however, different ways by which to tackle this need. Moreover, in the Scottish context, it is one of the areas where the potential for overlap and duplication appears to be greatest. Many local authorities are becoming involved in advisory provision alongside the national service offered by the SDA and there is scope for re-appraisal. A more efficient use of resources might well be achieved by centralising the planning-oriented activities and those for which a national perspective is desirable in the hands of the Agency, while leaving day-to-day operational services to be handled locally. More general advice (on grants, premises, assistance with loan applications, etc.) could be given by local coordinators related to district, regional and other authorities; while more specialist information as regards managerial functions and industry-specific knowledge could be managed by the Agency. In addition, the local tier could be greatly helped by managerial assistance flowing through enterprise trusts and allied sources. Whenever possible, only a single body should be responsible for any one activity. Such an approach is consistent with the earlier view that there are other roles in small business development which only SDA can play, including a programme of measures to ensure positive discrimination in favour of the small firm in Scotland.

Clarification of roles is perhaps most obviously required in the provision of 'public sector' factory space for small firms. At the time of writing, the whole of this area was undergoing radical re-appraisal within the SDA. The major activities involved under this heading include the planning of requirements, building/conversion, letting and management. The first of these stages involves the auditing of small-firm space provision, the identification of gaps in the provision and constraints to expansion. At this level, the lead organisation should be the SDA. Given agreement by all parties, the question of which public (or private) sector organisation has responsibility for building/conversion in any area is of a second order of importance. What is necessary is that there should be interchangeability of industrial estates such that, for example, a District Council could build on a Regional Council estate and vice versa. The third stage, and the one which impinges most on the small firm, is that of letting and management. It would be highly desirable to have single-organisational responsibility for letting and management of all public sector premises in a given area, perhaps at District level. Such a role, combined with that of the troubleshooting of all attendant problems associated with small firms, could tackle a problem area within which tales of excessive bureaucracy still abound.

Concluding Remarks. Looking to the future, where should the operational priorities be placed within the SDA? The highest priority should be given to taking stock of where small-firm initiatives in Scotland are going. This should lead to some basic decisions on the shape of the SBD, its resource base and where its contribution really lies. The second priority should be to ensure that Scotland has an effective conduit through which information and interpretation flows on UK small business schemes. Since these are likely to continue to grow in number and probably in complexity, a real contribution would lie in making these comprehensible as well as in lobbying for their simplification. The third area in which value could be added by the SDA to the benefit of this sector is in effective guidance and coordination of Scottish efforts along lines such as those suggested in this chapter. This undoubtedly includes responsibilities for monitoring the effectiveness of various experimental schemes of whatever origin as well as using that knowledge to guide others at more local levels. The fourth priority is the development of a high-quality advisory resource. Given the need for its availability throughout Scotland and a better UK support environment for the smaller firms, such a policy would require the SBD to attempt to do less, effectively delegate some activity to others and concentrate on achieving excellence in selected key areas.

Appendix: Clyde Workshops Ltd

This case has been chosen for a number of reasons. Not only has it been among the most successful schemes designed to create and develop small enterprises on a specific location in Scotland, it has also been widely used as a model for other organisations with similar intentions. Such copying has not always been based either on a full understanding of the scheme or on a critical appraisal of this approach. The scheme is interesting for another reason, namely that BSC (Industry) Ltd are committed to bowing out of such direct regional involvements by 1984. Having found an appropriate way into such action it will be crucial to pass its continuation to another party.

Background. The immediate context of this particular initiative on the part of BSC (Industry) Ltd was the closure of the Clydebridge and Clyde Iron Works in 1977. Following a feasibility study in 1978, the scheme became operational in November 1978 with building works and letting of units commencing early in 1979. It involved the re-use of some twenty buildings on a sixteen-acre site. The underlying principle leading to the establishment of the workshops was the statutory obligation placed on BSC to try to alleviate the effects of closure. The form in which this was expressed was regarded as very experimental, the aim being to generate some 250 jobs on the site over the ensuing two years at a cost of some £0.25 million. This finance was given as a cash allocation for both revenue and capital expenditure. In effect, it worked as a notional overdraft upon which the BSC Industry executives drew.

Clyde Workshops Ltd is in effect a property-development and management company, its initial immediate task being the conversion and division of redundant industrial and office buildings in order to lease these on fully commercial terms to small businesses. Subsequent conversion work had made available some fifty-two units (total area 63000 ft²) by early 1982. From the outset, the philosophy was not to offer subsidies or allied support to its client firms. Thus, rent-free periods, subsidised rentals, loans, grants or equity finance were specifically excluded. On the positive side, the philosophy has been to attempt to remove as many of the disincentives to establishing small businesses as possible, by applying a simple formula to both screening and scheme management.

Basic Characteristics. On the surface, the BSC formula consists of two essential elements, namely, adapting redundant buildings and leasing these on the basis of a simplified short-term licensing arrangement. The so called 'licence' is on a continuing three-month basis, the payment including the cost of insuring the premises, maintenance and all service charges with the exception of rates. Tied up closely with these, however, was an overall plan for the development of an integrated business community involving the workshop occupants, although the evidence suggests that this did not materialise. On the face of it the lettings policy seems to have been highly selective. The other components of this scheme consist of a variety of central services ranging from managerial advice (essentially from the scheme manager) and access to common services such as exhibition, conference, training and catering facilities. These latter also include typing, photocopying, VAT and PAYE assistance at a cost.

Since its inception the Workshops scheme has been managed by a full-time manager whose activities have combined the estate management and entrepreneur support roles. The reporting links to BSC Industry were originally fairly informal and subject to frequent change.

Application Screening. Application is made to the scheme on a very simplified form which is designed not to intimidate. The application is, however, allied closely with the preparation of a business plan for the applying enterprise by a firm of external advisors and paid for by Clyde Workshops. Verbal referees' reports are sought from the applicants' professional advisors. Thereafter, the aim is to give a 24-hour decision on an application. In all these matters there is an accent on a fairly strict adherence to the ground rules and a strong emphasis on the establishment of commercially sound ventures.

As regards overall priorities in applications, there is a preference for manufacturing although the needs of both pragmatism and complementarity have required the acceptance of a number of service and commercial operations. A guideline density of employment relative to the area leased of around 250 ft² per job is employed and, of course, there is a declared preference for applicants who will offer employment to ex-steelworkers. While there are no accurate figures available on this latter element, it is thought to be very small. Specifically excluded are branches and subsidiaries of larger companies, freight, storage or vehicle repairing operations. The emphasis is thus on small, local enterprises which are either starting up or relocating for good cause. It is interesting to note that by early 1982, thirty-four of the sixty-one tenants had started up as new businesses. The total on-site employment at that time was just over 300.[36]

Operational Experience. It is perhaps inevitable that different criteria have been applied with differing degrees of rigour to assessing the effectiveness of Clyde Workshops. Enthusiasm has, however, occasionally led to claims being made about it which are difficult to justify in objective terms. Having said that, the early evidence did point to a considerable latent demand for premises under these conditions and applications were reportedly at a level of 250–300 per annum. Around sixty tenants came on-site within the first nine months of 1979, with low applicant-rejection rates. Thus, when letting started in January 1979 there were some fifty applicants, only two of whom did not finally become tenants. The volume of applicants dropped off substantially towards the end of 1980, due in part to the economic climate and space limitations. In common with many of the other schemes, the grounds for rejection include space limitation and physical unsuitability of many of the projects. Absence of credible references, competition from other small-firm factory sites and complementarity of tenancies also feature, although the latter has probably not been a major discriminator in this scheme.

There has been no analysis of the industry mix within the scheme. The actual number of jobs created in the Workshops is not readily determined and has been variously quoted as between 300 and 600. A more accurate and official estimate as at January 1982 was 316, although there may be a few more off-site. Given the high proportion of new ventures within the scheme, this is a substantial addition to local employment by any standards. In these terms, the initial objective for job creation was probably exceeded within the two-year period.

Although not undertaken on a comprehensive basis, a sample of twenty enterprises in Clyde Workshops was examined in September 1981.[37] 80 per cent of the entrepreneurs had not previously owned a business; 75 per cent were unemployed prior to set-up; 60 per cent were in the 36–45 age group; and 50 per cent had no formal education. Some 51 per cent of their sales (by value) were within ten miles of the site, with a further 22 per cent between eleven and fifty miles; only one of the sample did any inter-trading with other enterprises in the scheme. As is common in such situations, around one-third of total sales went to the largest single customer. Supplies were from a wider geographical area, with over forty per cent from the UK outside Scotland. All of these units were leased on a three-month basis and the majority of firms recognised that the total rental payments in the scheme were higher than comparable premises in the local area, with quality being somewhat lower. For the tenant, however, the dominant motivation was undoubtedly short lease and speed of entry. There are many of these features which are common to all such schemes, although the proportions of people formerly un-employed appear to be relatively higher than in other similar Scottish initiatives. Turning to broader questions of experience, some aspects of the scheme have been subject to a little change over the past three years. Thus, while the basic package of premises, common services, information and operational advice remains, some leasing of equipment has been added on a selective basis. As regards the dozen or so firms developing out of the scheme, a few have moved to SDA premises, the rest to private landlords. While there are no accurate details around, between eight and ten are believed to have failed on the site. Encouragement is given to enterprises to re-site as close to the scheme as possible for inter-trading reasons, but in general enterprises which move quickly become disassoci-ated with the common services offered.

Financing the Scheme. The gross cost of Clyde Workshops to BSC Industry has been around £340000, a figure which represents a very low cost per job. The intention was that the scheme should be commercially based, but it is very doubtful whether this scheme can be finally profit-able, taking all costs into account. Other factors are also involved. For example, the estimated loss of rent from on-going conversion work in 1981–82 was some £40000. In effect, therefore, BSC Industry has continued to have to pay a premium to stay in this type of business, a matter of considerable importance in the context of potential disengagement. On the mechanics of the financing of the Workshops, the BSC management have proclaimed their belief that this approach can be economically viable. The initial cost of conversion in this scheme was around £4 per ft², although it is now evident that the standard to which they were working was probably too low – hence the upgrading. A nominal ground rent of 30p per ft² is paid to BSC for the site. On this basis, BSC estimate that their rentals will give some 14 per cent return.

An Overview of the Scheme. There would seem to be little doubt that this operation, which commenced in the context of considerable scepticism on the part of some BSC management, has been made to work, and that to a large degree by the energies put into it by BSC Industry. One of the important lessons here is the requirement for a catalyst. The management regard the concurrent build and let policy as a further general lesson, together with their aim of avoiding the creation of an uncommercial environment. While this latter has been achieved, as a managed scheme, the environment is a sheltered one which appears to have created some of the conditions for incubating new businesses. The typical enterprises in this scheme are of two types. One consists of tradesmen with over ten years' experience, often working as sales or works managers in smaller businesses. They often have enough ready contacts to find a market niche, providing their own fail-safe system for the first period of operation. The second group, accounting for over one third of the enterprises, are under 25. They are invariably professionally qualified and/or are in higher technologies, with a few years of industrial experience. They have entered business on their own account before either enjoying the benefits of employment in a large enterprise or having high domestic overheads. Both these groups seem to have been effectively attracted by this scheme in considerable numbers, although before drawing wider conclusions, the size, variety and industrial structure of the catchment area (broadly a ten-mile radius) would have to be noted. In short, there are some important lessons to be learned from this activity, notwithstanding the uncertainty about its future ownership.

Conclusions. As noted, several attempts have been made to transfer this scheme to other parts of Scotland. It does have merits, provided it is recognised that it succeeded in a large catchment area at a time when appropriate small premises were at a premium. Ease of entry, insistence on commercial criteria for the projects, relatively high cost (when initial quality was considered), general efforts to remove other barriers to growth, and a committed scheme manager were all ingredients for the success of this project.

NOTES AND REFERENCES
1. P.A.Neck (ed), *Small Enterprise Development: Policies and Programmes*, Management Development Series, no.14, ILO (Geneva), 1977.
2. G.Bannock, *Financial Times*, 22 June 1982.

3. For a useful consideration of the definitional problems associated with these comparisons, see 'Small Firms Survey: The International Scene', *British Business*, 19 November 1982 and G. Bannock, *The Economics of Small Firms*, Basil Blackwell (Oxford), 1981.
4. The percentage of total civilian employment which is in self-employment in industries and services, excluding agriculture.
5. *British Business*, 29 January 1982; data split by region in publication of 2 April 1982.
6. R. Pounce, *Industrial Movement in the United Kingdom 1966–75*, HMSO (London), 1981.
7. S. Nunn, *The Opening and Closure of Manufacturing Units in the UK 1966–75*, Government Economic Service Working Paper no.36, Department of Industry (London), 1980.
8. J. Firn & K. Swales, 'The Formation of New Manufacturing Establishments in the Central Clydeside and West Midlands Conurbations 1963–72', *Regional Studies*, vol. 12, 1978. In Scotland, as elsewhere, it has long been recognised that the rate of new business foundation responds positively to industry growth. This was most recently demonstrated by R. Hamilton, *Measures and Determinants of Entry and Exit Rates of Businesses in Scotland*, unpublished PhD dissertation, University of London, 1982. Hamilton also showed that higher proportions of independent businesses were associated with sectors where there were already a high proportion of small businesses.
9. 'Small manufacturing business in Scotland: output, investment and employment', *Scottish Economic Bulletin*, no.23, Summer 1981. The above figures overstate the small business share because some larger businesses which employ less than 200 people in Scotland are included. For some impression of the effect of the latter see 'Small Units in Scottish Manufacturing', *Scottish Economic Bulletin*, no.20, Spring 1980.
10. D. L. Birch, *The Job Generation Process*, MIT Programme on Neighborhood and Regional Change (Cambridge, Mass.), 1979.
11. J. Hamilton, L. Moar & I. Orton, *Job Generation in Scottish Manufacturing Industry*, Fraser of Allander Institute, University of Strathclyde, February 1981.
12. *Scottish Economic Bulletin*, no.20, 1980, *op. cit.* (n.9).
13. R. Whyte, *Employment Growth in Small Successful Manufacturing Units 1954–74*, ESU Discussion Paper, no.14, May 1982.
14. N. Hood, M. Milner & S. Young, *Growth and Development in Small Successful Manufacturing Firms in Scotland*, Report prepared by Strathclyde Business School for Scottish Economic Planning Department, September 1982.
15. R. P. Oakey, A. T. Thwaites & P. A. Nash, 'The Regional Distribution of Innovative Manufacturing Establishments in Britain', *Regional Studies*, vol. 14, no.3, 1980.
16. R. P. Oakey, *Research and Development Cycles, Investment Cycles and Regional Growth in British and American Small High Technology Firms*, Discussion Paper no.48, CURDS (Newcastle), August 1983.
17. Much of this evidence is summarised in *The Role of Small Firms in Employment Generation: A Review of Recent Work*, Department of Industry (London), 1981.
18. M. Cross, *New Firm Foundation and Regional Development*, Gower Press (Farnborough), 1981.

19. For example, in the context of the East Midlands, see S.Fothergill & G.Gudgin, *The Job Generation Process in Britain*, Centre for Environmental Studies (London), 1979.

20. D.Hunt, J.Jackson & J.Marceau, *Small Independent Enterprises and their Environment: Factors Affecting the Maintenance and Growth of Employment among Small Independent Enterprises*, Report of Study 78/13 for the Commission of European Communities, November 1979.

21. N.Hood & S.Young, *Local Small Business Development Schemes in Scotland*, Phase II of a report prepared for the Scottish Development Agency, October 1981.

22. *Small Manufacturing Firms in Scotland: A Survey of their Problems and Needs*, Scottish Development Agency, 1978.

23. *Information and the Small Manufacturing Firm*, Capital Planning Information Ltd. (Edinburgh), 1982. (This report was funded by the British Library Research & Development Department).

24. In this case, small business in manufacturing includes all firms under 500 employees. The US has, of course, a long tradition of legislation sympathetic to independent business; for example, S.W.Bruchey (ed), *Small Business in American Life*, Columbia University Press (New York), 1980.

25. Estimated to account for some two-thirds of West German GDP in firms under 500.

26. For a useful summary of Japanese policy, see 'Promotion of Small and Medium Enterprises in Japan', *New in Japan*, no.31, JETRO, 1980.

27. This is usefully considered in M.Beesley & P.Wilson, 'Government Aid to the Small Firm since Bolton', in J.Stanworth *et al.* (eds), *Perspectives on a Decade of Small Business Research*, Gower (London), 1982.

28. Motivated, for example, by a study by Coopers & Lybrand with Drivers Jonas, *Provision of Small Industrial Premises*, Department of Industry (London), 1980. For a recent examination of the role of premises see N.Falk, 'Premises and the development of small firms', in D.Watkins *et al.* (eds), *Stimulating Small Firms*, Gower (London), 1982.

29. M.Williamson, *Scottish Venture Capital Companies*, unpublished MBA dissertation, University of Strathclyde, 1982.

30. Hood & Young, *op. cit.* (n.21).

31. As operated by Glasgow and Falkirk Districts; Central and Lothian Regions; BSC Industry.

32. One recent project considered ten of these. See C.Johnson, *The MBO Concept and its Characteristics in Central Scotland*, unpublished MBA dissertation, University of Strathclyde, 1981.

33. In the Johnson study, around fifty per cent of the jobs (some 950) in the ten firms were maintained by the initial MBO transformation.

34. See, for example, N.Falk, *Think Small*, Fabian Society Tract no.453 (London), 1978.

35. Illustrated by B.Nicolson, I.Brinkley & A.W.Evans, 'The Role of the Inner City in the Development of Manufacturing Industry', *Urban Studies*, no.18, 1981; G.C.Cameron, 'The Inner City: New Plant Incubator?', in A.W.Evans & D.Eversley, *The Inner City: Employment and Industry*, Heinemann (London), 1980.

36. *Starting from Cold: a Report on BSC Industry Small Enterprise Workshops*, BSC Industry (London), 1982.

37. Hood & Young, *op. cit.* (n.21).

4

THE FOREIGN-OWNED MANUFACTURING SECTOR

STEPHEN YOUNG

This chapter studies the foreign-owned manufacturing sector. The justification for considering foreign direct investment (fdi) as a topic on its own derives from the well-accepted fact that foreign ownership raises a number of issues, e.g. external control and decision-making, the internationally mobile nature of investment projects, technology transfer and diffusion, etc., which are both quite distinct from those involving domestic companies and sometimes highly controversial. Furthermore, in the organisation and implementation of policy, particularly from a promotional perspective, the foreign-owned sector has been treated separately; some might argue, indeed, that excessive attention has been paid to multinational firms (MNEs) to the detriment of indigenous companies.

Given the employment concentration in a narrow range of sectors, there are, inevitably, close links between this chapter and some of the industry chapters, especially engineering but also the section on new, high-technology industries in Scotland.

The Nature of Foreign Ownership in Scottish Manufacturing Industry

Extent and Characteristics. Not too much is known about the early growth of foreign direct investment, although Scotland was host to the first foreign manufacturing subsidiary of the first truly multinational business – the Singer Company, which commenced assembling sewing machines in Glasgow in 1867. In general multinationality has, nevertheless, been a post-World War II phenomenon, and the number of US-owned manufacturing units, which totalled only six in 1945, had risen to 178 by 1981; by this time there were, in addition, 138 units from other sources, with Canada (as represented principally by Hiram Walker and Seagrams) and the Netherlands (with Philips as the major investor) being the two main investing countries. The small Japanese presence was represented by four companies – Nippon Electric Co., Mitsubishi Electric, Daiwa Sports and Teresaki Europe. In total, therefore, there were just over 80000 people employed in overseas-owned units in 1981; this represented seventeen per cent of employment in all manufacturing industry, but with the penetration level rising to over forty per cent in the engineering sectors (see Tables 4.1 and 4.2). In addition to the employment effect, foreign investment has undeniably been a major contributor to capital formation, technology, new products and exports in Scotland, although various academic studies during the 1970s did point out potential problems associated with the inward investment inflow.[1]

Table 4.1. Overseas-owned units and associated employment by country of ownership, 1981.[1]

Country	No. of units	% of units	Employment (000)	% of employment
USA	178	56	57	71
Canada	29	9	6	7
Netherlands	25	8	4	5
Other Europe	63	20	11	14
Other	21	7	2	3
Total	316	100	80	100

[1] Complete ownership breakdown not available for earlier years, but in 1975 employment in US-owned units was 86 400 (79% of the total) and in other foreign-owned units 21 800 (21%).
Source: SEPD, *Overseas Ownership in Scottish Manufacturing Industry: A Statistical Note*, September 1982.

Since the mid-1970s, employment in American-owned companies has slumped sharply – from 86 400 in 1975 to 57 000 in 1981. This decline has been faster than that in manufacturing industry as a whole, with closures or job rundowns in some of the largest and most well-known names, including Singer, Monsanto, Goodyear, Honeywell and STC. Although accompanied in the early 1980s by some large non-American firms such as Massey-Ferguson (Canada) and Talbot Scotland (owned by Peugeot S.A. of France), the overall employment loss in the multinational sector was no greater than that in manufacturing industry as a whole. The end result was that MNEs accounted for a stable seventeen per cent of jobs in both 1975 and 1981, albeit seventeen per cent of a sharply declining employment base.

Multinationals have not, thus, contributed disproportionately to unemployment problems. There have admittedly been special difficulties associated with the decline in employment in long-established, American mechanical engineering enterprises, in MNEs in Strathclyde Region and to a lesser extent in Tayside and in the largest size group of foreign-owned units.[2] These very real problems have been discussed fully elsewhere, highlighting the major MNE-induced unemployment problems which have arisen in localities such as Clydebank, Cambuslang, Linwood,

Table 4.2. Overseas-owned units live in Scotland: breakdown by industry, 1981.

Order	Industry	Overseas-owned units				Employment in overseas-owned units
		Units		Employment		as % of total industry employment
		No.	% of total in Scotland	No.	% of total in Scotland	
3	Food, drink, tobacco	47	15	8195	10	11
4–5	Chemicals, coal and petroleum products	26	8	6030	8	22
6	Metal manufacture	7	2	1233	2	5
7	Mechanical engineering	67	21	18634	23	32
8	Instrument engineering	16	5	8555	11	62
9	Electrical engineering	49	16	19662	25	45
10–12	Shipbuilding, vehicles, metal goods n.e.s.	25	8	3580	4	5
13–15	Textiles, leather, clothing	25	8	3927	5	6
16–17	Bricks, pottery, glass, timber, furniture	14	4	1217	2	4
18–19	Paper, printing and publishing, other manufacturing	40	13	9047	11	18
	Total	316	100	80080	100	17

Source: As Table 4.1.

Uddingston/Newhouse, Kilmarnock and most recently Dundee.[3] The high foreign employment penetration in some of the New Towns, particularly Livingston, Cumbernauld and Glenrothes, is a potential cause for concern for the future, although the enterprise concentration is not so great as in some of the aforementioned areas.[4]

More optimistically, when consideration is given only to the overseas-owned manufacturing units opening in Scotland after 1954, the employment performance of the MNEs is seen to be uniformly superior to that of other manufacturing openings in the same period.[5] And even over the recession years 1973–81, the overseas units (which had set up in Scotland since 1954) recorded in aggregate a smaller rate of net employment loss than UK-owned units. Especially important in this more encouraging picture has been the build-up of foreign direct investment in the electronics industry in Scotland, which has created 19000 or so jobs in recent years (see Chapters 5 and 9). Apart from its importance in giving Scotland a major presence in a high-technology and fast-growing sector, it has produced some diffusion of industry regionally into areas such as the Borders, through Exacta Circuits and BEPI, and Ayrshire, with Digital Equipment Corporation, etc.

Aggregate Performance. In terms of overall performance, Table 4.3 shows that foreign firms' share of net output in Scotland fluctuated quite considerably over the period 1971–79, but net output per head has been considerably higher in the overseas-owned than in the indigenous sector; in 1979 the difference in net output per head was almost twenty-four per cent. This would be expected, given presumed higher technology, larger size meaning greater opportunities for exploiting scale economies and more up-to-date facilities, as well as differences in industry mix. Despite this, in 1979 net output per head in foreign firms in Scotland was sixteen per cent below the figure for the UK foreign sector as a whole and also below all other assisted areas except Northern Ireland.

Table 4.3. Employment, net output and net capital expenditure.

	Scotland				UK
	1973	1975	1977	1979	1979
Employment (000):					
Overseas-owned	97·6	101·2	101·3	95·7	974·2
Scotland total	636·3	638·8	616·9	576·4	6925·6
Overseas as % of total	15·3	15·8	16·4	16·6	14·1
Net capital expenditure (£m):					
Overseas-owned	39·2	54·1	81·7	112·6	1490·5
Scotland total	229·8	425·6	493·3	596·6	6946·4
Overseas as % of total	17·1	12·7	16·6	18·9	21·5
Net output (£m):					
Overseas-owned	434·1	584·4	797·5	1104·6	13436·5
Scotland total	2263·2	3075·1	4261·7	5379·3	66351·4
Overseas as % of total	15·6	15·4	13·6	20·5	20·2
Net output per head (£):					
Overseas-owned	4448·0	5775·0	7873·0	11542·0	13792·0
Scotland total	3557·0	4814·0	6908·0	9333·0	9580·0
Overseas as % of total	123·7	118·0	114·0	123·7	144·0

Source: Annual Census of Production, *Business Monitor* PA1002, various issues.

Scotland and Other UK Assisted Areas. The comment in the previous sentence touches upon another standard for assessing the performance of foreign companies in Scotland, namely the comparison of their activities with those of overseas subsidiaries located elsewhere in the UK.

Scotland still accounts for a much higher proportion of foreign-owned than of all manufacturing industry in the UK, although Northern Ireland, Wales and the South East are ranked above it in these location quotient terms. And the rate of new openings in Scotland has continued to be quite healthy: for the 1972–77 period, for instance, out of the 230 new openings in the UK, employing 16 000 people at the latest date, Scotland's share was 18 per cent and 36 per cent in terms of number of units and employment respectively (Table 4.4). For a slightly more recent period, 1976–80, the overall position was much less buoyant and within this Scotland accounted for 14 per cent of units opened and 16 per cent of employment.

Table 4.4. Openings of foreign-owned manufacturing units by region, 1972–77 and 1976–80.

	1972–77		1976–80	
Region[1]	No. of units	Employment[2] (000)	No. of units	Employment[2] (000)
UK	230	16·0	102	6·4
Scotland	41	5·7	14	1·0
N. Ireland	7	0·4	10	1·4
Wales	23	1·6	22	1·7
North	21	1·4	16	0·8
North-West	19	0·8	15	0·6
South-East	60	4·0	8	0·3
Scotland as % of UK total	17·8	35·6	13·7	15·6

[1] Selected regions only.
[2] Employment at end of period.
Sources: *Regional Trends*, 1981, HMSO (London), Table 10.5;
T. Killick, 'Manufacturing Plant Openings, 1976–80 Analysis of Transfer and Branches', *British Business*, 17 June 1983, Table 3.

Where Scotland has fared relatively less well is in closures among the existing stock. Taking 1978–1981 figures for a sample of foreign-owned plants, Table 4.5 shows that employment contraction in Scotland was less than in Great Britain as a whole and below that of most individual regions. In terms of closures the two main exceptions to the Great Britain norm were Wales and Scotland: in Wales surviving foreign-owned operations declined much less than average, whereas in Scotland the reverse was true. Once again, nevertheless, the Scottish picture is distorted by a few exceptionally large closures – Singer and Talbot principally.

Turning briefly to the characteristics of foreign ownership, Scotland matches the UK average almost exactly in terms of the breakdown

Table 4.5. Employment change 1978 to 1981 by region.

Region[1]	Percentage change in employment in expansions and contractions		Employment lost in closures as percentage of 1978 employment		Percentage of all employment in foreign-owned plants in 1978
	Foreign-owned	All units	Foreign-owned	All units	
Great Britain	−14·6	−16·7	7	6	13·3
Scotland	−10	−13	20	9	16·8
Wales	−14	−22	3	2	17·6
North	−14	−13	10	8	11·3
North-West	−15	−15	3	5	13·2
South-East	−16	−16	8	8	18·9

[1] Selected regions only.
Source: T. Killick, 'Employment in foreign-owned manufacturing plants', *British Business*, 26 November 1982.

between American and non-American sources. If there is a deficiency in the non-US sector it is that Scotland does not seem to have attracted a sufficient number of firms of a single nationality in a locality; this can prove important from an attractional viewpoint as the Welsh have found in relation to Japanese and German MNEs. On an industry basis, the reliance on mechanical, instrument and electrical engineering is higher than elsewhere, with a weak representation in sectors such as chemicals; metal goods; and paper, printing and publishing.

Impact Issues in Foreign Direct Investment in Scotland

Up to this point, an attempt has been made to summarise the available statistics on foreign investment in Scotland. Clearly there are policy questions which arise from this discussion. These particularly concern the need to stem the job loss in existing foreign-owned subsidiaries while maintaining the high level of new openings and project announcements, which have recently included Rockwell Valves, Burr-Brown Corp., NEC and Wang Laboratories. Devising policy on these and other issues requires a much more detailed understanding of the motives for investment and divestment as well as in-depth consideration of the multinational impact in Scotland. Information is far from complete on such questions but some of the major issues are highlighted briefly in the following paragraphs.

The Attraction of Foreign Direct Investment in Scotland. As noted above, Scotland has continued to be successful in attracting new foreign enterprises. Although the average size of new entrants is a good deal smaller than in the past, and changing technology has meant a reduction in optimal plant size, on past evidence there is every reason to expect fairly rapid employment growth after entry (assuming a revival of the level of international economic activity). Studies of locational determinants have shown that the dominant reason for foreign investment in the UK was British or European market size and growth, with Government financial aids being important in the actual choice of location and being considered of greater significance, not unexpectedly, the higher they are within the British Isles.[6] In such circumstances, then, the actual flow of new investment into Scotland will be partly a function of the overall level of foreign direct investment into Europe and Scotland's relative attractiveness as a manufacturing base, which in turn is related to the financial assistance available here and elsewhere and factors such as Scotland's ability to market itself as a desirable location. All of these questions require consideration in this chapter, since they impinge very directly on policies pursued in Scotland as present.

The Foreign Direct Investment Environment. Global trends in foreign direct investment in manufacturing industry reveal that real growth, in flow terms, slowed sharply in the late 1970s, although continuing to outpace domestic investment. Within the total, the US share of outward investment flows dropped sharply in the 1970s. Japan, West Germany and the Netherlands, by contrast, accounted for substantially increased shares, and, while very small in world terms, it is possible to observe a widening of the sources of fdi to include a number of firms based in the newly-industrialised countries, in OPEC states and in state-trading nations.[7] Considering the UK as a host country for United States investment, there is clear evidence of a diversion of fdi from Britain to the Common Market in the years following the establishment of the Community; the low point seemed to be reached in 1976 and since then some improvement in the relative British position has occurred. While some European countries, such as Germany, have become much more important as sources, there is not much evidence that the UK has been or will be a major host country target for these investors. Of the other major source nations, Japan is clearly the most significant: of the small amount of Japanese fdi in Europe, the United Kingdom has picked up a high proportion of this. Protectionist pressures are building up in Europe; a strengthening of the yen on the foreign exchanges might well be sufficient to bring about a substantial inflow of Japanese fdi. But Japanese firms have tended to make investment approaches through governments and conduct negotiations with governments; at the very least this has implications for promotional methods.

Such trends must have an important bearing on attraction policies. What is also relevant is that international investment has become more heterogeneous in terms of entry methods used, in terms of sector – with service industry investment growing rapidly, and in terms of ownership,

99

management and control – with joint venture and non-equity arrangements becoming very much more important.

Competition for Foreign Direct Investment in Scotland. Given the international investment environment and fdi flows into Europe, Scotland's share will be determined by its competitive position *vis-à-vis* other locations. Much has been made of the emergence of the Republic of Ireland as a competitor to Scotland, and the raw figures of projects approved by the Industrial Development Authority (IDA) are quite striking; these indicate 216 overseas projects (excluding projects originating in Great Britain) approved in 1980 and 1981 alone, whereas between 1972 and 1981 there were 99 Section 7 offers to non-UK companies for the establishment of new plants in Scotland.[8] Despite the fact that there was little foreign investment in Ireland until the 1970s, by 1980 there were 80000 jobs in overseas-owned manufacturing companies, or one-third of the Irish manufacturing workforce.[9] The number of projects in which Scotland was considered as a genuine alternative to investment in Ireland is not known, nor is it known how many of the projects would actually have been welcomed in or beneficial to Scotland. Evidence is available on the importance of the Irish inducement package, which is more attractive financially than that available in Scotland; and the efforts of the IDA have been important in marketing this package. In appraising policy in Scotland and suggesting possible new policy initiatives, it is important that the Irish success should be borne very clearly in mind.

The Retention and Development of MNEs in Scotland. Analysis of the existing stock of fdi with a view to assessing factors which are significant in the maintenance and development of a Scottish presence is very complex. At one level the overall competitiveness of the global corporation will clearly impact upon the Scottish subsidiary: rapid growth in some of the electronics subsidiaries in Scotland is a reflection of the success of the multinational parent in technological innovation, marketing and so on; conversely some of the recent, highly publicised divestments in Scotland have been matched by large-scale job losses throughout the corporate networks. Commonly, nevertheless, expansion or contraction at one location, particularly within Europe, will take place at the expense of or to the benefit of other European subsidiaries of the corporation. This production switching emerges forcefully in the Timex case at the end of this chapter; and the strategic dimensions of US multinational activity have been the focus of some of the present editors' previous work on MNEs in Scotland.[10] The policy issues which arise concern the need to try to direct new investment projects towards Scotland (as with the IBM personal computer) and/or to attempt to minimise the disadvantageous effects on Scottish operations when companies are rationalising within a European framework. This links back again to the significance of Government financial assistance. Recent research has suggested that regional incentives may be nearly as important in reinvestment (capital replacement or expansion) decisions as in the initial investment choice. Moreover, in a reasonable minority of cases, regional assistance may impact upon the scale and capital intensity of the investment, and perhaps on the timing of technology introduction.[11] In addition, there is no doubt that Scottish subsidiary performance plays an important part in such decisions; and it has been concluded that where divestment or rationalisation has been involved, then low productivity, overmanning, restrictive practices or poor labour relations are commonly alleged. Other issues which may figure in such decisions include the size of subsidiary, whether or not the facility represents a unique source for a particular product or component and the existence or otherwise of a research capability.

Technology Transfer and Development. One of the major contributions derived from multinational firms is technology, arising from the concentration of these companies in technologically advanced sectors and their large size and research and development (R&D) resources. The extent of technology transfer from parent to subsidiary is, however, not known nor are the processes by which transfer takes place fully understood. Because of this, great emphasis is placed on autonomous technology creation through R&D at subsidiary level. Evidence suggests limited R&D among US plants in Scotland and, even where present, little of the R&D undertaken could ever be regarded as contributing anything to fundamental product and process innovation (but see Chapter 9 for a different view).[12] Even the existence of R&D is thus no guarantee of an innovative capability at plant level; nor is there any guarantee that any products or processes developed will be manufactured by the same subsidiary, although recent research on R&D in electronics MNEs in Scotland saw benefits in both of these and other areas (such as graduate employment).[13] There clearly must be some substance to the strong policy emphasis in countries such as France and Canada on subsidiary R&D. It may not be possible or desirable to stress indigenous R&D as a precondition of entry to Scotland. Even so, encouragement to establish even a technical service function may be useful given the evidence which reveals that such activities may well evolve into R&D centres over time. In the Scottish case, if the example of Hewlett-Packard is anything to go on, then subsidiary R&D can be of major benefit. Within Hewlett-Packard, the South Queensferry operation in Scotland has sole R&D and manufacturing responsibility for communications instrumentation for worldwide markets. It may be relevant that the Canadians see the allocation of global product franchises to subsidiaries in that country as a means of stimulating R&D.[14]

Management and Linkages in Branch Plants. Closely linked to the issue of R&D is the more general question concerning autonomy and decision-making in MNE affiliates in Scotland. Within large multi-national firms with a number of production facilities in Europe, Scottish plants will tend to operate as limited-activity production units, with headquarters and marketing functions elsewhere. The same type of problem emerges in multi-plant UK enterprises and has been seen as a serious deterrent to the development of entrepreneurial management in Scotland as in other assisted areas. Some have gone further to argue that fdi has led to a dual economy problem: the indigenous sector within a regional economy is seen as being locally-oriented in markets, suppliers and managerial outlook, while the externally-controlled (mainly foreign-controlled) sector maintains its existing backward linkages, meaning supply, administrative and financial ties outside the region.

A limited amount of evidence exists on the issue of foreign/indigenous sector linkages (a more detailed discussion relating to electronics specifically is in Chapter 9). One study of the electronics industry drew attention 'to the very limited impact which the multinational presence has had upon the indigenous sector, . . . and to the satellite role that the few indigenous firms in the industry tend to play'.[15] An SDA-commissioned study on sub-contracting in this same industry identified specific problems in the indigenous sector, including the absence of companies sufficiently large to serve volume feeder plants; and a lack of willingness to engage in speculative efforts to demonstrate their ability as potential suppliers together with weaknesses in technical specialisation and marketing.[16] Quantifying the position for a small sample of MNE affiliates in the mechanical and electrical engineering and chemical sectors in Scotland in 1980, it was estimated that around one fifth of the total value of inputs were obtained in the country, with a further 50 per cent being derived from other parts of the UK; in terms of local purchasing, the Scottish position was similar to that recorded for MNE subsidiaries in the North West and North of England but the proportion of inputs obtained locally was much lower in Wales and Northern Ireland.[17] Although speculative, it is likely that the changing structure of the MNE sector in Scotland has reduced the extent of linkage between the multinational and indigenous sectors.

Trade and the Balance of Payments. Aside from the positive employment and technology effects, it is likely that the major contribution of MNEs derives from their export performance, even though this may be chiefly a function of their size and sectoral distribution. The study quoted in n.17 above indicated around 37 per cent of output exported in 1980, albeit with a large difference between American and Continental European-owned companies – the export proportion was 57 per cent for US MNEs but only 10 per cent for their European counterparts; and the latter were more UK-market-oriented than European MNEs with affiliates in assisted areas elsewhere in the United Kingdom. Overall, the net export position of MNEs in this sample was strongly positive, and the balance of payments contribution may also be judged to be positive, despite outflows of dividends, management fees, royalties, etc. and the high level of local borrowing. Once again, changes in the sector in the last few years are likely to have reduced this contribution, without showing any signs of adjusting the overall position of gain.

Foreign Firms' Entry Methods and Relationships between Nationality of Ownership and Performance. As the balance of sources of investment into Scotland has changed, increasing attention has been given to the methods of entry used by multinational companies, with a particular focus on the differential impact of acquisition entry on the benefits and costs of fdi for the Scottish economy. While the overwhelming proportion of American MNEs in Scotland have been established as greenfield ventures, around one-half of European entrants have come into operation through the acquisition of domestic enterprises. From the country perspective, there is every reason to look closely at the behaviour of acquisition entrants, as no employment gain is likely to be involved at time of setting up; indeed rationalisation is perhaps more plausible. Based on a fairly large sample of MNE affiliates in the UK as a whole, a recent study identified lower levels of technology and integration in acquisitions; a greater UK orientation of sales than among MNEs formed as greenfield ventures and, despite stronger input linkages with the local economy, a poorer net export position; higher levels of unionisation in acquisitions; and a lower incidence of target attainment.[18] These differences perhaps derive largely from the former UK origins of the enterprises, and many were quite recent, but even so relatively little seemed to have been done to reorganise and reorient the enterprises. In a study of takeovers in European companies in Scotland, specifically, acquisitions did not show up in such a poor light, and most involved small firms with an emphasis on the food, drink and tobacco industry.[19] Important policy questions are, nevertheless, raised when foreign-owned (or even UK-headquartered) firms are involved in takeover bids for Scottish companies as a number of recent cases referred to the Monopolies and Mergers Commission (MMC) have shown. In addition, there are implications for the targeting and promotion of inward direct investment, as it has been shown that greenfield investors tend to begin as exporters to the UK, whereas acquiring companies have frequently had no former supply links with the market.

Some of the same types of issues arise in comparisons between American and Continental European MNEs. Given that the latter group may be more likely to use the acquisition entry route which will thus condition their behaviour patterns, the research quoted above showed much higher net exports from American affiliates in the UK; in addition, there was a greater likelihood of R&D in the US sample, higher levels of technology, higher proportions of managerial and professional personnel in the workforce and lower levels of unionisation. Once again such dimensions are relevant to the formulation of policy.

Existing Policies Towards Foreign-Owned Firms

In introducing this review of the policy environment, it is necessary, initially, to consider the possibility and desirability of policy measures applying exclusively to multinational companies as opposed to all large companies or all industrial concerns. It is important to note additionally that policy formulation in a Scottish or UK context is not unconstrained, but must comply with UK commitments to international organisations and the policies of the latter. From an EC perspective, the most important constraint to date derives from Community action to coordinate regional policies and to establish aid ceilings varying with the type and severity of regional problems.

In considering policy within the United Kingdom, it is helpful to distinguish between policies pursued at national and regional (Scottish) levels, and between policies of attraction and of evaluation and control. The former in turn comprise promotional activity and the financial and fiscal incentives provided by Government.

In terms of attraction, the main UK agency is the Invest in Britain Bureau (IBB) which is involved in the promotion of investment into the UK as a whole. Based in the Department of Trade and Industry, the IBB emerged in 1977 from a variety of individuals and groups in different ministries already involved in inward investment attraction. In builds on initial contacts from consular officials and others overseas, arranges international seminars and missions and operates generally in an information provision role. The IBB is not involved in negotiations concerning financial packages, nor in the detailed site selection process within the UK. Nevertheless, its activities are relevant to Scotland since in 1979 (admittedly before new organisational arrangements came into effect in Scotland), the IBB were apparently involved in nine out of every ten projects placed in this country.[20] Associated with this national-level attraction activity is the Foreign and Commonwealth Office (FCO), whose consular staff at posts overseas are engaged for part of their time in making contacts and providing information designed to attract inward investment to the UK.

In relation to evaluation and control, the UK has, at least in theory, a number of mechanisms for regulating foreign direct investment through the Industry Act 1975 and the Inland Revenue; while the Monopolies and Mergers Commission (MMC), which is concerned with anti-competitive activity irrespective of company nationality, has handled two references with Scottish dimensions involving foreign multinational companies in recent years – the bid of Hiram Walker for Highland Distillers and the bids of the Standard Chartered Bank and the Hong Kong and Shanghai

Bank for the Royal Bank of Scotland. Attitudes towards foreign firms have, in reality, been very relaxed, reflecting Britain's stake in maintaining access to foreign countries for its own outward investing multinationals, the conclusions of net benefit to the economy from the foreign presence and the highly competitive environment within Europe for the attraction of internationally mobile investment projects.

When attraction and evaluation/control policies are taken together, and account is also taken of the range of financial incentives provided by Government, it is clear that all major Government departments have some involvement in this field. Equally, there is no unified approach to MNEs, which, some might argue, rather epitomises industrial policy as a whole in the UK.

Policy in Scotland on Foreign Direct Investment. Unlike the situation in most of the industry sectors which are studied in this book, it is possible to identify a distinctly Scottish approach to the issue of policy on inward direct investment. This focuses on the attraction of foreign firms, an activity which has been given added focus and momentum recently through the establishment of an attraction agency, Locate in Scotland.

By way of background, widespread criticism was voiced in Scotland in the late 1970s about the ineffectiveness of inward investment promotional efforts, first because of the 'number of separate but ill-defined authorities who seemed to have an interest'[21], implying substantial duplication of effort, and secondly, because of the lack of planning and targeting in this activity. As implied, much of this activity, through advertising and promotions, seminars and missions abroad, was aimed at potential foreign investors, broadly defined, without too much attention being given to desired sectors or firms, Scotland's existing presence in the sector or sub-sector and so on. By comparison with Scotland's alleged amateurish approach, the professional marketing efforts of other regional development agencies such as the IDA were held up as a model. In the latter regard, too, Ireland's 'single-door' for foreign investors was compared with the separation of function in Scotland, as between promotions, negotiations with investors over financial packages (the responsibility of the IDS), factory building and letting, etc.

The outcome of these criticisms was that the Committee on Scottish Affairs was given the task late in 1979 of studying various aspects of the attraction of overseas investment to Scotland. The Committee recommended that the IBB should be the main attraction agency in the UK, with the overseas promotion of Scotland, therefore, being handled through a Scottish input of personnel into the Invest in Britain Bureau. Under this scheme the SDA's promotional offices in the United States and Continental Europe would be disbanded. Within Scotland itself, the SDA was seen as the 'umbrella' body in the area of inward investment attraction, but the main Agency role envisaged was that of improving the investment climate and of providing an environment within which foreign investors could flourish. There was a considerable amount of criticism of these proposals in the press and elsewhere in Scotland, the feeling being that the Committee's recommendations had been strongly influenced by the political make-up of its membership. The proposals were in fact rejected, and the Government response in 1981 was to create a Locate in Scotland (LIS) group, bringing together the functions until then exercised by the IDS and the SDA, under a single director and in a single building. The aim was to develop a structure in Scotland 'which can give a strong lead to and provide a focus for other promotional bodies such as the local authorities and the New Towns; which can develop good working relationships and standing with . . . IBB, the Diplomatic Service and its Posts overseas in the presentation of Scotland as a distinctive location for investment; (and) which is clearly identifiable to prospective investors abroad . . .'.[22]

The Activities of Locate in Scotland

Locate in Scotland was set up in April 1981 as a joint venture of the IDS and the SDA operating from the Agency's offices. The Director of LIS, at present an official with relevant experience from the IDS, is responsible to a Steering Group chaired by the Secretary of State and comprising both IDS and Agency representatives. The broad outlines of the LIS operation are given in Figure 4.1. It is not possible to make any ex-post appraisal of LIS because of the recency of its formation; in fact, some of its overseas activities are even more recent than April 1981. Thus, while the SDA has had offices abroad in New York, San Francisco and Brussels since 1979, it was agreed that the position would be reviewed after two years. The Select Committee recommended that these offices would be phased out, with all overseas representation being handled by the Diplomatic Service, and there was pressure against retention from regions elsewhere in the UK. The announcement that the offices had been saved did not come until February 1982, with the overseas presence being expanded in October 1982 (Houston) and November 1982 (Chicago). It should be stressed that these are SDA offices, although most activity is concerned with inward investment attraction. All are quite small, employing at most two executives plus support staff. Outside the United States, there is an office in Brussels which is in the process of being re-organised, and consultants operate on behalf of LIS elsewhere, most notably in Japan.

Despite the fact that it is not possible to evaluate LIS in terms, say, of its success in attracting new foreign investors to Scotland (given that the lead time for a project decision is of the order of twelve to eighteen months and probably longer in present recession conditions), it is feasible

Figure 4.1. The operations of LIS.

Staffing	Total 32, of which 19 at level of Development Executive or above (including posts abroad)
Expenditure[1]	General £1 529 000; operating and management expenses £634 000 in year to 31 March 1983
Major Functions	
Marketing	direct selling to potential firms, advertising at home and abroad, overseas missions and seminars
Casework	initial discussions with potential investors, provision of literature, assistance with site search
Finance and negotiation	detailed negotiations over selective financial assistance etc.
Overseas offices (New York, San Francisco, Houston, Chicago Brussels)	direct selling, contact with potential investors, provision of literature, liaison with American PR consultants and US advertising agency
Links with Other Organisations/Divisions	
Other SDA Divisions	e.g. Electronics Division and Health Care and Bio-technology Division for targeted promotional activity, Planning and Projects Directorate for marketing research, Agency's London office for commercial intelligence, links with business community etc.
IDS	important links over SFA, project appraisal etc. LIS Director (Finance) is located in the SDA offices, but is one of the IDS personnel in the unit. SFA applications are approved by the Scottish Industrial Development Advisory Board (SIDAB), an advisory body to the IDS
IBB and Diplomatic Service staff abroad	cooperation on promotions, company contacts
Local Authorities and New Towns in Scotland	consultation, exchange of information on promotional activities; coordination of promotions by LIS; Local Authorities or New Towns may act as lead organisation in certain circumstances

[1] Excludes domestic expenditures and all spending on SFA.
Sources: Scottish Development Agency, *Report 83*; LIS.

to make some remarks about its performance in terms of the objectives set for it by Government.

Coordinated approach to potential investors. It has been accepted that a 'single-door' for potential foreign investors is probably not achievable in Scotland, given that financial responsibility for payment of regional aids rests with Government. Having said that, so far as the potential investor is concerned, LIS is an all-embracing organisation. So, while it may be an official of the IDS who negotiates financial terms, he is acting as a LIS representative. Similarly when an SDA executive puts together an advertising campaign, he is wearing a LIS hat. In reality the need for a one-stop agency, and the advantages accruing to the IDA in Ireland as such a body, may be exaggerated. MNEs have experience of negotiating with multiple agencies in some countries and with a variety of institutions empowered to grant incentives – regional development agencies, states, even municipalities. It is true that in the early stages of discussions with firms or perhaps with consultants undertaking initial site search on behalf of MNEs, LIS may not be able to exactly establish the amount of selective financial assistance which could be offered. But, given the competitive situation, the likely offer is going to be set within fairly narrow limits in most instances. The further relevant point is that the assistance package cannot be exactly established until the company has firmed up on its own business plans.

LIS as an umbrella organisation in Scottish promotional efforts. It was noted previously that Scotland's marketing efforts have suffered historically because of overlap and diffusion of effort as between the local authorities, New Towns and so forth. There are legislative powers concerning coordination in the Local Government and Planning (Scotland) Act 1982, Section 7, but effective improvements in overall marketing are largely dependent upon persuasion; this in turn means that benefits must be shown to accrue to the regional organisations from acting in concert. From the viewpoint of the smaller authorities, there are cost savings in 'piggy-backing' upon LIS marketing efforts and substantial efficiency gains. And because of the Secretary of State's control over posts in the New Town Development Corporations, persuasion to act through LIS is presumably possible. To date, bi-monthly meetings are held between LIS and the regional organisations, with the aim of providing information on advertising and marketing plans, preventing duplication in promotions, seminars, visits to companies etc.

Effective marketing. By far the major task of LIS is not concerned with organisational questions, but rather with making the Scottish marketing effort effective and competitive. The present editors are on record as suggesting that effective marketing involves the efficient implementation of a series of related activities – information, planning and strategy, promotion, negotiation and settlement.[23] However, this only brings the new project into Scotland and, thereafter, there are a further series of marketing operations involved in encouraging re-investment and expansion, viz. monitoring, promotion, negotiation and settlement.

Very substantial resources have been pumped into the information generation activity in the Agency, mainly through the Planning and Projects Directorate. A series of large-scale industry studies have been commissioned and the results of these have been used *inter alia* by LIS in planning and targeting its marketing campaigns. Thus, the American market is the focus of the main effort at present, with target market segments being identified within the electronics, energy and health care sectors of industry. Questions might be raised about whether or not these sectors are 'over-subscribed' in terms of the attention being paid to them by regional development agencies throughout the world, but in general the approach is to be welcomed. As to the promotional campaigns and marketing-mix methods used, a criticism which was levelled formerly concerned the excessive use of large-scale seminars because of their generalist nature. The importance attached to this activity has now been reduced in favour of direct firm-specific approaches, using the Agency's investment and property functions to add new dimensions to the LIS operation. Little can be said on advertising. A major aim is to stand out in an overcrowded market and by the level of expenditure, at least, the SDA and the IDA are way ahead in the field.

The financial package. As noted earlier, in the actual project decision, the financial package offered may be rated quite highly as an investment determinant. Considerable importance, therefore, attaches to the negotiation stage of the marketing process. Selective assistance is individually negotiated with the prospective investor. The aim in such negotiations is to attract the project, while ensuring that net benefit will accrue to the Scottish economy by some criteria. Details of the mechanics of undertaking such calculations would not be disclosed, but factors to be taken into consideration will include the desirability of the project in terms of activity; level of capital investment; import saving and export potential; and employment creation. It is stated that formal cost-benefit analysis is undertaken in some cases, particularly where it is felt that the EC Commission may take an interest or in cases where the EC is involved financially through European Investment Bank or European Coal and Steel Community loans. Otherwise it seems likely that in reality the possibility of losing the project to another European location will weigh heavily in the internal review process. When the negotiations have been completed, the final package is submitted to the monthly meetings of the Scottish Industrial Development Advisory Board (SIDAB), whose membership comprises businessmen, financiers and union officials. It is suggested that formal 'go-ahead' is granted in the overwhelming majority of cases, but very little is known about the conditions which may be tied to SFA grants or whether or not these are implemented subsequently. This would be the only area of policy where it could be said that there is an evaluation/control element involved in Scotland.

Data are available on offers of Selective Financial Assistance (Table 4.6), which show that since inception in 1972 over forty per cent of SFA has gone to overseas-owned firms, and the proportion rose to 51 per cent in the period from 1 January 1980 to 31 July 1982. Average offer value to foreign-owned companies has been about three and a half times as great as that to indigenous companies, partly because of the larger average size of the project; also because of the high incentive value loading in investments for which there may be competitive bids from other locations in Europe. Information is not available on the percentage level of assistance, but the SDA Report for 1982 indicates SFA offers of £21 million against total planned investment of £234 million.

Table 4.6. Offers of Section 7 assistance to overseas firms, 1972 to 31 July 1982.

Category	Offers		Offer value		Average offer value £000
	No.	%	£m	%	
New (including training grants)	106	37	57·0	49	538
Expansion	164	58	50·7	44	309
Safeguarding	15	5	8·3	7	553
Total (to overseas-owned firms)	285	100	116·0	100	407
Total (to UK-owned firms)	1411	—	159·8	—	113
Overseas-owned as % of all-firm total	17	—	42	—	—

Source: IDS.

Reinvestment and Expansionary Projects and the Role of LIS. Table 4.6 shows that projects involving expansions or the safeguarding of jobs have accounted for one half of total SFA offers, by value, to foreign companies. Expansion projects, moreover, have become relatively more numerous in recent years, and safeguarding offers are very much a phenomenon of the period from the late 1970s. The question arises, therefore, as to the role of LIS in attracting such projects, some of which, once again, could be internationally mobile. This seems to be regarded within LIS as 'company friend' or 'after-sales' type activity, rather than a major focus of operation. Certainly LIS has had an important role in the recent expansionary investment announcements of Gray Tool, IBM, General Instrument, Motorola, Levi Strauss, Caberboard, Mitsubishi Electric, etc.; these are instances where efforts have been required to support the Scottish plant's case against other divisions within a company and even the MNE's home base and corporate board. In general, however, the Agency's role in this area of activity still seems to be under debate. Some of the same issues of expansion/rationalisation arise with large indigenous companies in which case the SDA's Industry Services Division would have an input. Given the statistics on job loss versus job creation, formal monitoring should be given high priority and the necessary resources to fulfil this admittedly very time-consuming task.

A Desired Role for Foreign-Owned Firms in Scotland
and Possible Policy Initiatives

The conclusions which emerge from the review of foreign ownership in Scottish manufacturing industry are, first, that the contribution of multinational firms is positive, and, therefore, that every means possible should be used to try to maintain existing job levels in the sector. It is a rather depressing fact that the present editors made much the same comment only a few years ago – at that time there were 100 000 direct jobs in foreign-owned companies. Secondly, efforts should be made to raise the 'status' of multinational affiliates in Scotland so as to improve the security and expansion prospects of the firms, as well as to develop the pool of indigenous management. Thirdly, attempts should be made to use international firms as a vehicle for promoting indigenous industry, through purchasing linkages but also by emphasising other forms of arrangement than the traditional wholly-owned American subsidiary.

Maintenance of Employment Levels. Moving from the general to the specific, Figure 4.2 considers some of the policy questions concerning the foreign-owned sector in Scotland and the adequacy of the response. Looking at the issue of maintaining a certain level of jobs in the sector, from an attraction viewpoint there is merit in questioning the desirability of the strong focus on the United States. As the figure shows, Scotland does seem to have a comparative advantage in that country and the subsequent performance of US MNEs in Scotland has been favourable. The danger with such a heavy US/electronics emphasis is that of concentration. A broader targeting strategy based on pinpointing companies which are presently exporters but non-investors in the UK might help to widen the activity mix. In any event, a clearer strategy to counter the success of the IDA is necessary. More might be done to promote the relative attributes of Scotland – the existence of local supplier industries, for example.

In addition to the USA there is a good deal of interest in Japan as an investing country. There are problems in trying to attract Japanese firms, since to date the companies have generally found it more profitable to export, and an overt presence through LIS might not be useful when Japanese MNEs are used to negotiating with governments. There are also criticisms of the assembly-type activity (with low local content levels) associated with Japanese subsidiary operations abroad. High-level approaches to the Japanese suppliers of Nippon Electric and Mitsubishi, etc., with a view to attracting them as suppliers to these same companies already in Scotland, have been made, with, to date, no effect. Nevertheless, the possibility of a cluster of Japanese firms in Livingston or Haddington, say, remains very attractive.

Maintenance of the foreign sector at something like its present size

111

Figure 4.2.   Policy dimensions and the Scottish response.

The Attraction of International Investment

Slowdown in growth of fdi flows worldwide and in US share – but US MNEs strong in fast-growing sectors e.g. electronics, and Scotland[1] (along with Eire) favoured location.	Major focus of attraction efforts in US. Need to consider competitive strategy v. Eire.
Expansion in fdi from other developed countries.	Little focus on Germany, but complicated by variety of entry routes. Also evidence of greater net benefits from US MNEs. Low profile approach in Japan – approaches by Japanese MNEs direct to host governments create difficulties.
New sources of fdi – OPEC states, Third World MNEs, Eastern Bloc. Growth of MNEs in service industries. New forms of multinationality – joint ventures, licensing, management contracts, co-operation agreements.	Limited response.
Growth in acquisition entry-methods.	No response, but evidence indicates net benefits from greenfield ventures much greater.
Consequences of past and present attraction policies in terms of sectoral concentration of investment, regional concentration within Scotland etc.	No response.
Importance of regional financial assistance in investment decision-making.	High level of SFA offers to MNEs.

Reorganisation, Expansion and Affiliate Development

Continuing high level of job losses.	SFA offers for expansion/safeguarding projects much increased. But policy reactive rather than pro-active; no formal monitoring.
Technology transfer and development of R&D;[2] introduction and development of management functions; linkages with local economy; trade effects.	Import substitution and level of exports may figure in negotiations over SFA. SDA efforts to stimulate local sub-contracting.
Importance of regional financial assistance in investment decision-making.	As above. Some evidence that project shape can be affected by regional aids, but limited attempt to utilise this fact in design of package.

[1] A report by the consultants Electronics Location File indicated that the UK was the most favoured location for expanding US electronics companies, with about half of those expressing a regional preference selecting Scotland. West Germany was ranked second and Eire, significantly, third. Source: *Glasgow Herald*, 5 February 1983.

also requires a policy towards acquisitions. At present there is no mechanism for selectivity[24] or indeed requirement for filing details of most takeover applications. Within the existing Scottish policy framework, therefore, the only option at point of entry is whether to promote or not. Promotion of Scotland as a location for acquisition entrants is not desirable, nor would it be politically acceptable. There could, nevertheless, be value in discreet, selective promotional activity through the overseas offices of the SDA; this would be designed to draw potential investors' attention to specific takeover targets in Scotland. Lists of the latter would be drawn up within the Agency as part of its on-going investment and advisory activity within Scotland and after consultations with local management, shareholders, etc. The alternative to this approach is to take a more active and interventionist role in the management of indigenous companies in Scotland.

Monitoring and Affiliate Development. Despite the gloss, glamour and visibility of new, greenfield projects, the evidence of this chapter is that the job payoff from trying to maintain and develop what is already in existence in Scotland may be equally significant. Monitoring will, thus, have a crucial role to play. If it is to be effective, monitoring should involve discussions at both corporate and affiliate levels on a regular basis. The objectives would be to identify possible changes in corporate strategy which may have an impact on the future operations of the Scottish affiliate, to identify new investment projects which are at an early stage of discussion within the MNE, to identify needs for new products and processes at plant level in Scotland, to obtain early warning of possible production switching which may adversely affect the Scottish operation, etc. The arguments raised against this form of activity are that it is high cost, that outsiders cannot get sufficiently close to decision-makers within MNEs to obtain corporate strategy details, and that even with evidence of, for example, production switching, policy makers in Scotland may be impotent as regards changing the course of events. On occasion, such allegations may be true, but, equally, contrary examples can be given; and adequate forewarning would be a major benefit from a monitoring programme. In addition, is it worth thinking about the possibility of an organisation such as the SDA taking small equity stakes in such enterprises with a view to improving access and information? What is then required, particularly where potential job losses are involved, is high-level Government and Ministerial backing: this perhaps has been lacking on occasions in the past.

---

[2] Discussions with LIS officials indicate that R & D possibilities sometimes raised in negotiations. But usual entry method involves establishment of assembly and test facilities before proceeding to manufacture and therefore no place for R & D.

Closely associated with the issue of monitoring is that of raising the status of MNE subsidiaries in Scotland. It may be argued that this is more a question of the age and experience of the affiliate and of its performance, and certainly these factors will be considered. On the other hand, there might be opportunities to accelerate the process by incorporating new conditions into SFA offers, and/or to ensure that programme objectives associated with SFA offers at present are adhered to. The issue of raising plant status may be even more basic than that of obtaining more managerial activities for the affiliate; rather it may be a question of moving from assembly to manufacture, and certainly this must be insisted upon. Interesting suggestions have been made inferring a relationship between the market area for plant output, the plant's sourcing role for that market and affiliate status. While such detailed issues could be the subject of negotiation either at entry or at times of expansion, obviously detailed knowledge would be required of corporate activities, indicating once again a substantial role for monitoring.

Another important area concerns possibilities for increasing local linkages. The SDA should have a role here in working intensively with individual MNEs and potential suppliers with a view to matching the two, bringing potential suppliers up to satisfactory technical levels, etc., and some success has already been made in this area.

MNEs as Vehicles for Promoting Indigenous Industry. Aside from the role of sub-contracting in developing indigenous enterprises, there may be other ways of harnessing MNE technology for the benefit of Scottish industry. The promotion of joint ventures represents one such possibility. It has already been shown that potential investors may be identified from present exporters to the UK: the reluctance of some of these foreign companies to engage in fdi may be related to their small size and inadequate resources, and they may, therefore, be amenable to approaches for joint ventures. Identification of both the targets in foreign countries – with Europe perhaps a better possibility than the USA, given the greater reluctance of the latter to engage in joint ventures – and potential partners in Scotland would be a responsibility of the Agency. A different approach might be to start with some of the larger Scottish enterprises, assess prospects/requirements for joint venture co-operation and then approach specific target companies abroad. Questions concerning the performance of joint ventures will, however, need further investigation.[25]

Increasing interest has also been expressed in licensing possibilities for raising technology levels in Scottish enterprises. From an MNE perspective, licensing has generally been seen as a way of obtaining residual returns from technologies that are no longer unique, and is most commonly used by small firms or widely diversified firms or where market entry is difficult. Criticisms have been frequently levelled at the terms of licensing agreements because they normally incorporate export prohibition clauses and because of 'tie-in' arrangements, which require materials to be purchased from the technology supplier. In a situation where many Scottish firms may be adjudged to be backward technologically, this is the price which may have to be paid. In its post-war development, Japan relied heavily on licensing, using MITI and JETRO as bargaining agents in negotiations. There is now in existence within the SDA a technology transfer unit to undertake this function. This is located within the Industry Services Division of the Agency, but its activities are still small-scale and experimental.

Organisational Questions. Implementation of any of the suggestions above would require organisational change. Locate in Scotland, irrespective of its brief, seems, to outside observers at least, principally a promotional body for inward direct investment. Consideration would need to be given to whether it is a suitable organisation to undertake monitoring and affiliate development. As indicated earlier, these activities are not confined to foreign-owned firms and there could be advantages in centralising responsibility within a separate 'enterprise development unit'. In the same way a technology transfer unit would have to be operated separately.

The broader question, which also has organisational implications, is whether the entire internationalisation process, including, for instance, exporting from Scotland, should not be considered as a whole. This then brings in not only LIS and the Agency, but also the Scottish Council which is largely responsible for export promotion at present.

Concluding Remarks

This chapter has tried to show that the foreign sector does warrant a distinct policy focus, and has then attempted to indicate some possible approaches to the sector based on an assessment of trends in inward direct investment and the performance of overseas-owned firms and taking into consideration the existing policy response. It should be stressed that the conclusions are interim, and must be seen in the context of overall industrial policy in Scotland. So strategy for the foreign-owned sector needs to be considered alongside policies relating to sectors, area development and so on. Unless this is done, not only will the internal consistency of the policies be questioned but effort will be diffused by a plethora of initiatives. The assumption underlying all of this discussion is that the European legislative framework is unchanged: ideally, it could be argued that if EC legislation would permit combinations of incentives and performance requirements, e.g. specification of minimum local content requirements against certain incentive levels, then improving net benefit in Scotland would be a good deal easier. But clearly in the competitive situation which exists in Europe, the UK could not act independently in this direction without frightening off potential investors. Nevertheless it is important to emphasise that alongside any changes in policy at a Scottish level, continuing efforts should be made within an EC context to reduce the regional aid ceilings and introduce greater transparency in aid schemes as well as arguing the case for linking incentives and perform- ance requirements.

Within the environment as presently exists, there is merit in questioning whether the existing level of financial assistance is necessary to attract foreign firms to Scotland. Within the manufacturing sector, for projects which are EC-market-oriented, the evidence would seem to be that it is. But the trend in UK Government policy towards requiring greater justification for levels of aid offered is undoubtedly desirable. It is also true, nevertheless, that not enough has been done to consider how trade and exchange-rate factors, protectionism, etc., impact upon the fdi decision and the level of aid required to obtain a particular project.

Given that policy is severely constrained, the next question is whether excessive resources are being devoted to foreign firms. It has been shown in this chapter that the employment performance of these companies has been generally better than that of indigenous enterprises and that in terms of technology and trade there are additional benefits from the foreign presence. The latter are not costless, of course, and apart from points raised earlier there are, in addition, 'controversy costs' to be borne; that is, because the companies are multinational, events will continue to arise which cause problems and embarrassment for policy- makers. During the period when this chapter was in preparation alone, issues which have arisen in this vein include:

Production switching at Timex.

The thirteen per cent reduction in wages and fringe benefits for the workers at Hyster's Irvine fork lift truck plant, with the possibility of closure of the factory if the pay cut was not accepted, but the offer of 1000 new jobs if it was (including jobs associated with the transfer of manufacture from Continental factories).[26]

The international row over the supply of equipment for the Soviet gas pipeline, involving General Electric and its licensee John Brown (see Chapter 5).

The Court ruling in the Netherlands that the transfer of production from Hyster's Nijmegen to Irvine plants could not go ahead.[27]

Allegations that Hoffmann-La Roche was receiving £350000 of public money for every permanent job created at its Vitamin C plant in Dalry, Ayrshire.[28]

EC Commission investigations of aid payments to Timex in France and Scotland, and to Hyster in Irvine.

These are the perhaps unavoidable problems of multinational industrial development, and it is not suggested that they are a reason for reorienting industrial policy priorities. Rather, what has been suggested in this chapter is that the balance of effort requires to be reoriented, to give greater attention to the stock of MNEs presently existing in Scotland and their links with indigenous companies. Even this has implications for the focus of financial assistance and the operations of LIS in terms of advertising policy, the nature and purpose of firm-specific approaches and so on. If inward direct investment is seen as only one of a variety of forms of internationalisation, all of which may produce benefits for the Scottish economy, then the organisational implications are much more radical.

Appendix: Timex and IBM

This final section includes two company cases – Timex and IBM – to illustrate something of the contrasting nature of multinational operations in Scotland and to give some indications of how industrial policy has or could have an impact upon the nature of corporate activity.

Timex Corporation, Dundee

In assessing the activities of Timex Corporation, it is interesting to observe initially that even very basic financial data for the British subsidiary and its Scottish operations are unavailable because Timex in the UK is operated as a branch of Timex Corporation, incorporated in the USA, which itself is an obsessively private company; and Timex shares are traded only as a unit with those of Bermuda-based TMX Ltd, which builds watches and parts for Timex and runs some Timex operations abroad. Timex, the largest watch company in the world but with a variety of additional interests, cannot, moreover, be considered separately from the overall holdings of the Norwegian Olsen family. These include Nimslo International, Flawhurst Ltd (a London-based holding company), Norwegian operations with interests in rigs, shipping, oil and gas and a large estate in Galloway (Figure 4.3). These relationships are important in understanding the events of 1982 and 1983 at Timex Dundee.

The Growth of Timex Corporation. The forerunner of Timex was an American enterprise called the Waterbury Watch Company, which produced its first watch in 1878. A Norwegian named Lehmkuhl acquired a majority interest in the virtually bankrupt Waterbury Watch Company during World War II and after the war the company set about designing a quality watch which could be truly mass-produced. Backed by Olsen finance, the first Timex was introduced in 1950.

The company grew rapidly both in the US and abroad and by the early 1960s employed about 7000 people in three US and six European plants located in England, Scotland, West Germany and France. Dundee was the first overseas facility of Timex, being opened in 1946, within months of NCR also coming to the city; the reasons for establishing this plant were the same as those which have continued to have a major

117

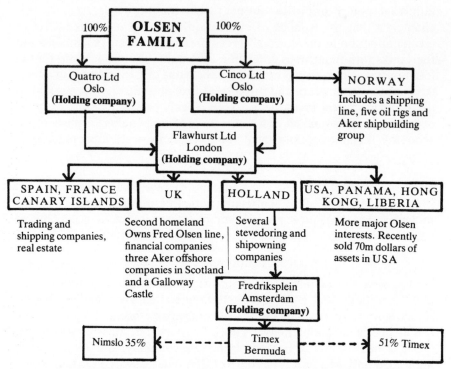

Figure 4.3. Olsen family holdings. (Source: *Sunday Standard*, 16 January 1983.)

influence on strategy, namely cost reduction and the availability of a skilled female labour pool. The company started with an assembly operation in Dundee employing 100 people, but with increased demand and the gradual introduction of more complex sub-assembly work, additional factories were opened in 1947 and 1949. By 1966, Timex employed 3 500 people in Dundee, as part of a substantially self-contained UK operation.

Timex market share for watches continued to rise but, like equally famous names such as Singer and NCR, the firm was electro-mechanically myopic. The belated decision to introduce digitals posed major difficulties and after several years of heavy investment in the 1970s, the company was still struggling with the new technology. The outcome of these events was that the company probably turned in a loss in 1979, net income of $175 000 on sales of $500 million for Timex Corporation being offset by losses of $4.9 million on sales of $256 million for TMX Ltd. Whilst maintaining its commitment to the watch business such problems stimulated a variety of non-watch diversification moves, including the signing of an agreement to manufacture cameras for Nimslo Technology Inc.[29]

Timex Internationalisation Strategy in the 1970s and the Effects on Dundee. As the effects of changing technology started to become apparent, Timex commenced a worldwide search for low-labour-cost assembly points. Countries such as Malta, Taiwan, the Philippines and Portugal were all on the short-list and operations were set up in two of these locations in 1972–73. The intention was understood to be to expand Portugal and run down Dundee in parallel, chiefly because of labour unrest in Scotland. The culmination of these problems was the walkout of 5200 of the 6000 Dundee employees in February 1974, and the management threat that they were prepared to close down in the city. In the event, only around 400 redundancies were announced in Dundee, the turning point in favour of Scotland being the Portuguese revolution.

The Dundee operation was further aided by growth in its non-watch activities. The company had been active in looking for sub-contract assembly, and work for Polaroid led to the manufacture of around 14 million cameras between 1952 and 1979; while in the late 1970s Timex started to undertake sub-contract work for IBM and efforts were made to sell the company's precision engineering expertise to firms in the oil industry. With the sharp decline in the mechanical watch share of the total market between 1978 and 1980, Dundee's stability was, however, seen to be illusory. 600 redundancies were announced in September 1979 due to falling world demand and industrial trouble at home. Further redundancies were announced a year later. The strength of sterling and a switch of business from Dundee to the company's manufacturing division in the Philippines was given this time as the reason for the job loss.[30]

Events at Dundee in the 1980s. Despite the employment reduction on the watch side of the business, there was some room for optimism at the start of the 1980s because of two separate events. The first was the announcement in March 1980 that the revolutionary Nimslo 3-D camera was to be produced in Scotland.[31] The work was forecast to bring 100 jobs in 1981 rising to 860 by 1985. The project was backed by Government assistance of £2.7 million, although it has been reported that SIDAB advised that £2.1 million of the aid should only be given in tranches triggered by rising production.[32] Just under one year later, Sinclair Research announced a deal with Timex, whereby the ZX81 and, later, Spectrum personal computers would be assembled at Dundee. This time job forecasts were 250 by 1982 with a potential of 1000 in five years. Aid to Sinclair Research was estimated as £1.1 million in RDGs and £1.5 million SFA out of a capital cost of £5 million. In both instances, the employment created by the projects was seen largely as transfers, enabling the Dundee factories to sustain 4000 workers.

Both of these projects were surrounded in controversy from their initiation: in the Nimslo case, controversy surrounded the hazy circumstances in which the company came into being; the involvement of Olsen

119

with Nimslo; the extent of development work still to be undertaken on the camera at Dundee to turn an experimental prototype into a device capable of being mass-produced; whether Dundee was ever seen as a long-term manufacturing rather than as a short-term development base for the camera; and whether, finally, the world market share forecasts for the camera (five per cent) were attainable. In the case of Sinclair, the security of the work was questioned, not helped by threats of production switching after industrial action in October 1982, and a decision to second-source manufacture at a factory in the south of England in November 1982.

Rumours that all was not well on the Nimslo project began to leak out early in 1982. Production quotations were obtained from two Japanese vendors, and with output at Dundee still only one-third of target, the decision was taken to switch manufacture of the camera to Japan. By the time of this announcement, no UK regional assistance had been allocated to the company, as output had not risen high enough to trigger off payment of the cash. The loss of employment on the Nimslo project more or less coincided with the announcement early in 1983 that watch-making was largely to cease in Dundee, meaning that in total 1900 jobs were to disappear out of a workforce totalling around 4200. Timex was left with some limited assembly of mechanical and quartz watches for the UK market only along with flat part manufacture, and sub-contract work for Sinclair Research and for IBM. Early in 1983, 600 Timex employees were believed to be working on Sinclair projects, making the future of the plant very dependent on retaining existing Sinclair business (ZX81 and Spectrum computers) and being chosen as a production base for new products (flat-screen mini TV). This was placed in jeopardy when a five-week sit-in took place at the Milton plant to protest against management insistence on achieving its target redundancy level – through compulsory redundancies if necessary. The occupation delayed the launch of Sinclair's flat screen pocket TV until mid-September 1983, and showed that bitterness and suspicion still remains to be overcome if a new era at Timex Dundee is to dawn.

Issues Raised by the Timex Case

Corporate Secrecy. Timex represents an extreme case from the perspective of being able to understand and therefore respond to multinational corporate strategy. The secrecy of the owner, the complex network of privately-owned companies involved in the affair and Dundee's 'branch' status combine to create great informational problems for policy makers. In that sense, getting close to the corporation and understanding corporate strategy is a good deal more difficult than with most other MNEs.

Changing Technology and Job Losses. Despite the above, Timex's core business was watchmaking, and, like a number of other major multinational companies in Scotland, Dundee's problems stem fundamentally from slow and inadequate parent MNE response to technological change. It is arguable that a good deal more could have been done to push for the introduction of electronics watchmaking to Dundee. This might not have saved any jobs but would certainly have provided more security for the enterprise than the reliance on sub-contract work.

Project Announcements and Employment Forecasts. It is surely time to stop quoting potential job targets for up to five-year periods ahead when investment projects are announced in Scotland. This issue arises in the Timex case with both the Nimslo and Sinclair Research projects. In the Nimslo case, for example, jobs were being forecast for five years hence, before a new camera had even reached the market. Apart from the matter of raising false hopes, there are two other points which are worth making. The first concerns LIS corporate plan objectives. Obviously these need to be expressed in job terms, but they also need to be time-related and in the latter respect it is necessary to be very careful in quoting future employment levels. The second point concerns the job targets associated with SFA offers. Would there be merit in quoting these so that failure to meet targets is publicly known?

Production Switching. This issue came to the forefront of attention early in 1983, with the transfer of Nimslo manufacture to Japan and with alleged production switching to France. The latter is particularly interesting but the facts are difficult to establish. It seems that rights have been obtained to manufacture and distribute the 3-D camera in Belgium and France.[33] In addition, the French put together an attractive financial package to bring new products to the plant at Besançon and compensate for the rundown in mechanical watchmaking: while some watchmaking will continue, the company will also manufacture home computers under licence from Sinclair and other types of electronic products, as well as the Nimslo camera. It is interesting to note one observation that 'whereas the British Government only stepped in when redundancies were announced, the French had already spent a year putting together a package to encourage the company to make new investments in its country'.[34]

The disturbing facts surrounding the switch of manufacture to Japan derive from the point that Dundee seems to have had a major role in turning what was an experimental prototype into a device capable of being run off the production line. This seems to have involved a great deal more than simply normal debugging, and loss of the contract after this innovative work was a bitter blow.

Regional Policy and Production Switching. Considerable concern – up to Prime Ministerial level – was expressed over the financial package offered to Olsen by France, and the EC Commission was ordered to examine this with a view to ascertaining whether or not rules on net grant equivalent were being contravened. Irrespective of the outcome of these investigations, important EC-level questions over competitive bidding for investment are raised. Multinationals have always had the ability to play off one country against another, but the problem has become much more serious in times of high unemployment. Coordinated reductions in aid and greater transparency in aid should still be close to the top of the policy agenda in the EC.

From the comments made above, it is obvious that Timex would always have been a difficult case to handle from a policy perspective. But closer involvement with the company at corporate and affiliate levels over a longer period of time might have yielded benefits, and there seem to be lessons to be learned from the French experience. Well before this, however, the decision to give the go-ahead to Nimslo needs to be questioned, given the background of the company, the risks in the project and so forth. Even in a situation of desperately high employment, the issue of 'what jobs and at what cost?' should still be in the forefront of attention.

IBM, Greenock[35]

In a number of ways Timex shares the characteristics of a number of other US MNEs, originally electro-mechanically based, which contributed substantially to job losses in the multinational sector in the latter half of the 1970s. IBM, on the other hand, while almost as long-established in Greenock, has remained as a solid, steadily expanding contributor to the Scottish economy. The purpose of this case is thus to present the other side of multinationalism in Scotland, while still illustrating areas where benefits to the Scottish economy could be improved.

IBM, as one of the world's largest multinationals, is truly global in terms of its operations. In Europe alone the company has manufacturing plants in seven countries, two of these factories being in the United Kingdom (Greenock and Havant, near Portsmouth) as part of a large UK operation of 13 000 people, including research and development facilities and sales and service support units. Manufacture commenced in a rented, unoccupied torpedo factory in Greenock in 1951, with a workforce of approximately 250. Somewhat unusually, IBM did not commence its European manufacture from a UK base, and production facilities had existed in France and Germany since 1924. At least part of the explanation lies in an agreement between IBM and British Tabulating Machinery stating that as long as the British company bought IBM machinery and sold it under their own name, the US MNE would not enter the UK market. This agreement was terminated in 1949 and IBM set up in Scotland, attracted by Government assistance, labour availability and the support of the Scottish Industrial Estates Corporation (SIEC). In 1954, the Greenock manufacturing operation was moved to its present Spango Valley site; this was constructed by the SIEC and then purchased by IBM in 1959.

IBM at Greenock is undoubtedly one of the success stories of multi-nationals in Scotland. From its initial employment, the workforce grew rapidly to around 1600 in the mid-1960s, then stabilised at 2000 employees in the 1970s before expanding again into the 1980s to the present figure of approximately 2500 (between one-quarter and one-third of these being graduates). Factory space grew commensurately from 50000 m² at date of initial occupancy to 500000 m² in the mid-seventies. When the plant was established initially, it manufactured a wide range of IBM equipment, mainly for the UK market. With the divisionalisation of the corporation in the 1970s, the Greenock plant was included within the Systems and Communications Division (SCD), being responsible for the manufacture of a more limited range of products (communications systems, terminals, keyboards etc.) for the European market. This re-organisation, bringing with it increased plant specialisation, has been observed among many US MNEs operating in Europe, mainly as a response to British entry into the European Community. For the Greenock plant the change in market area responsibility has meant a big growth in exports, which accounted for nearly fifty per cent of plant turnover in 1980, making the company certainly one of Scotland's largest exporters.

The Greenock facility is a production unit only. IBM Europe SA in Paris coordinates IBM facilities and interfaces with marketing (which in the UK is based in London) to establish sales requirements and determine the manufacturing plant capable of meeting these demands. Thus IBM Greenock produces in response to Paris instructions and transfers its output direct to marketing distributors or the country as required. The Greenock plant does not have an R&D function and is only responsible for some process engineering. There is an R&D lab associated with the SCD in the UK, at Hursley, and although the IBM philosophy is to separate manufacturing from research and development, there is some support for Greenock's activities from Hursley.

Changes have taken place in production operations in Greenock so that the plant now undertakes no basic manufacture. According to the factory's procurement manager, 'at one time we had a sizeable machine shop here, but we are evolving towards the situation where Greenock is completely a final assembly and test plant'.[36] Thus everything from metal and plastic cabinets, cathode ray tubes and cable harnesses to the printed instructions accompanying finished products are bought in from outside. Even some stages of intermediate assembly are carried out by sub-contractors. This is an important feature of IBM policy, being designed to support their full employment programme for Greenock. Sub-contracting is undertaken where the company has no capacity or where capacity is limited by policy, but there appear to be strict control rules over the amount of work which IBM will sub-contract to individual vendors. It seems that sub-contractors will not receive work from IBM which will account for more than thirty per cent of their turnover or employ more than thirty per cent of their labour. Again, IBM do not give suppliers sub-contracts for extended periods ahead. The objective of both of these policies is to maintain stable supplies, while avoiding over-influencing indigenous firms. From a Scottish perspective the fact that Greenock is an assembly plant would be relatively unimportant, if these sub-contractors were located within this country. It is not known precisely what percentage of sub-contract work is handled within Scotland, but press reports indicate expenditure of £60 million in 1981 on bought-in parts and services, with forty per cent of this outside Scotland.[37] The same source indicates 120 suppliers in Scotland, with considerable stability in the IBM association, most of these firms having been doing business with Greenock for over five years. It is important to note too that some of these sub-contractors in Scotland are themselves MNEs, including, as noted earlier, Timex.

Reports have indicated that Greenock's productivity record is rated extremely highly within the corporation in Europe. This factor and the support of Locate in Scotland undoubtedly had a bearing on the decision announced in January 1983 that Greenock would assemble the prestigious IBM personal computer for European, Middle Eastern and African markets.[38] £8 million investment was believed to be involved, including Government financial assistance of £2.5 million, with a potential job creation of 400 (120 at the plant, 280 with sub-contractors). Although competing within a highly competitive market segment, allocation of the product to Greenock will clearly facilitate the continued growth of the Scottish operation and further its reputation and that of Scotland within the corporation as a whole.

Issues Raised by the IBM Case

On the face of things, IBM seems to have been relatively free from the controversies which have surrounded many other MNEs in Scotland. There have, however, been a number of issues which are worth noting.

IBM and Unionisation. IBM has followed a staunchly non-union policy in its operations around the world. The unions accused the company of prevaricating over their demands for recognition in Britain; and eventually there was an ACAS enquiry in 1977 under the terms of the Employment Protection Act after an application by four unions for recognition at the Greenock plant. Further debate ensued over whether the results should apply on a plant-by-plant basis or for the company as a whole. In the event this mattered little, for 96 per cent of workers responded that they did not wish to have their pay and conditions settled through union regulations; the proportion was only slightly lower at

Greenock (90.2 per cent).

IBM and Public Purchasing. The multinational computer companies in Britain have frequently complained about discrimination in public sector contracts in favour of the indigenous company ICL. IBM has, in fact, made less of an issue of this than Honeywell, but it has been alleged (although denied by IBM) that the company offered to set up the personal computer operation in Greenock on condition that they were allowed to bid for the new vehicle licensing computer in Swansea.[39] Coincidentally or not, IBM won the contract.

IBM and Technology. On a related issue to the above is the UK Government £350 million programme to support the development of 'fifth-generation' computer systems on the recommendations of the Alvey Committee. IBM and the other US companies are to be permitted to participate only if they can guarantee that the work will be exploited entirely in this country and that technical information will not leak overseas to the benefit of Britain's competitors. The technology question has also arisen recently in the other direction as part of the Reagan Administration's attempts to stop high-tech exports to the Soviet Union. British customers for certain IBM computers require American export licences, while large leasing customers need US Government permission before any change of location, ownership or use.[40] IBM is only complying with US legislation but the extra-territoriality provisions involved have caused inter-governmental problems on other occasions. IBM's Greenock plant is, of course, not directly involved in the above.

The 'Status' of the Greenock Plant. The branch-plant nature of multinational operations in Scotland has elicited a good deal of comment, and IBM at Greenock would seem to fit almost exactly into this mould. Discussion of this case shows, however, that such simple categorisations can be misleading: it is true that IBM is an assembly facility with no marketing or R & D, nor is there much likelihood of these functions being allocated to plant level given corporate policy, yet its 'status' in terms of graduate employment is very high and its long-term employment, trade and technology contribution to the Scottish economy cannot be denied.

IBM and Scottish Suppliers. Despite the above, the overall contribution of this Greenock assembly plant is also highly dependent on levels of inputs supplied from outside vendors and from a Scottish perspective there is substantial room for improvement. It has been estimated that between 1970 and 1980, the value of IBM purchases from Scottish companies increased by around twenty per cent per annum, but local suppliers are still in the minority. The SDA has been of help to the company in finding vendors and in giving assistance for specific requirements, and efforts in this direction must continue. Because of its visibility, IBM is probably well-served by support from public bodies. The argument presented earlier in this chapter was that such support should be applied across the board within the MNE sector.

Financial Assistance to IBM. Given the expansion record of IBM at Greenock, it is inevitable that the company has received substantial sums of Government assistance. For RDGs alone, IBM at Greenock received £2.8 million between 1975 and 1980, representing nearly thirty per cent of the total obtained by US electronics companies in Scotland in that period.[41] Inevitably the question arises as to whether or not RDGs and/or SFA had a tipping effect in any of the investment decisions involved. The IBM view appears to be that financial assistance simply reduces the capital cost of projects once these have been justified financially. But clearly there is no way of knowing if similar attitudes would prevail in the absence of financial assistance.

NOTES AND REFERENCES

1. Among these early studies were J.R.Firn, 'External Control and Regional Development: The Case of Scotland', *Environment and Planning A*, vol.7, 1975, pp.393–414; N.Hood & S.Young, 'US Investment in Scotland – Aspects of the Branch Factory Syndrome', *Scottish Journal of Political Economy*, vol.23, no.3, 1976, pp. 279–94.

2. Employment concentration is still very high. In 1981, just over a hundred overseas units, employing on average 630 people, accounted for 84 per cent of employment in the foreign sector. Four enterprises made up 20 per cent of employment in foreign-owned units in 1975 and 15 per cent in 1981; in 1975, three of these four had more than 5000 employees, in 1981 none had more than 4000 workers.

3. N.Hood & S.Young, *Multinationals in Retreat: The Scottish Experience*, Edinburgh University Press, 1982.

4. N.Hood & S.Young, 'Industrial Structure and Ownership in the Scottish New Towns', *Town and Country Planning*, vol.46, no.2, 1978, pp.69–72.

5. SEPD, 'Employment Performance of Overseas-Owned Manufacturing Units Opening in Scotland 1954–77', *Statistical Bulletin*, no.A1.1, May 1983.

6. N.Hood & S.Young, *Multinational Investment Strategies in the British Isles: A Study of MNEs in the Assisted Areas & in the Republic of Ireland*, HMSO (London), 1983, Part 4.

7. *Ibid.*, Part 1.

8. SEPD, *Overseas Ownership in Scottish Manufacturing Industry: A Statistical Note*, September 1982.

9. J.Fitzpatrick, 'Foreign Investment in Ireland in the 1980's', *Multinational Business*, no.4, 1982, pp.1–10.

10. Especially N.Hood & S.Young, *European Development Strategies of US Owned Manufacturing Companies Located in Scotland*, HMSO (Edinburgh), 1980.

11. Hood & Young, 1983 (n.6), Part 4.

12. Hood & Young, 1976 (n.1), p.285; Hood & Young, 1980 (n.10), chapter 4.

13. P.Haug, N.Hood & S.Young, 'R&D Intensity in the Affiliates of US Electronics Companies Manufacturing in Scotland', *Regional Studies*, vol.17, no.6, 1983. See also P.A.A.Scrimgeour, 'Employment in Industrial Research and Development in Scotland', *Scottish Economic Bulletin*, no.27, 1983, pp.13–15.

14. N.Hood & S.Young, 'US Multinational R&D: Corporate Strategies and

Policy Implications for the U K', *Multinational Business*, no.2, 1982, pp. 10–23.

15. P.J.McDermott, 'Multinational Firms and Regional Development', *Scottish Journal of Political Economy*, vol.26, no.3, 1979, pp.287–306.
16. *Scottish Electronics Subcontracting and Components Manufacturing Industries*, study undertaken by Makrotest (London) for the Scottish Development Agency, February 1981, section 6, pp.67 *et seq*. See also M.Lamont & M.Cox, 'Sales and Purchases Patterns in the Scottish Manufacturing Industries', *Scottish Economic Bulletin*, no.27, 1983, pp.6–12.
17. Hood & Young, 1983 (n.6), p.215.
18. *Ibid.*, Part 4, chapter 2.
19. N.Hood, A.Reeves & S.Young, 'Foreign Direct Investment in Scotland: The European Dimension', *Scottish Journal of Political Economy*, vol.28, no.2, 1981, pp.165–185.
20. Second Report from the Committee on Scottish Affairs, Session 1979–80, *Inward Investment*, HC 769–I, HMSO (London), 1980.
21. *Ibid.*, para. 1.1.
22. First Special Report from the Committee on Scottish Affairs, Session 1980–1981, *Inward Investment: The Government's Reply . . .*, HC 205, HMSO (London), 1981.
23. N.Hood & S.Young, 'British Policy and Inward Direct Investment', *Journal of World Trade Law*, vol.15, no.3, 1981, pp.231–250.
24. For some suggestions as to the types of acquisitions likely to produce net benefits to the economy, see Hood, Reeves & Young, 1981 (n.19), p.182.
25. Existing research evidence is reviewed in N.Hood & S.Young, *The Economics of Multinational Enterprise*, Longman (London), 1979, p.260.
26. *Sunday Standard*, 17 July 1983.
27. *Glasgow Herald*, 9 September 1983.
28. *Sunday Standard*, 27 February 1983.
29. *Financial Times*, 12 January 1983.
30. *Glasgow Herald*, 15 September 1979; *Scotsman*, 20 June 1980.
31. *Glasgow Herald*, 11 March 1980.
32. *Sunday Standard*, 23 January 1983.
33. *Economist*, 15 January 1983.
34. *Observer*, 13 February 1983.
35. Apart from other references, this case study draws on P.Haug, *R&D Intensity in the Affiliates of US-Owned Electronics Companies Manufacturing in Scotland*, MPhil thesis, University of Edinburgh, 1981.
36. *Sunday Standard*, 31 January 1982.
37. *Ibid.*
38. *Scotsman Magazine*, September 1983.
39. *Ibid.*
40. *Sunday Times, Business News,* 8 January 1984.
41. *Trade and Industry* and *British Business*, various issues.

5

THE ENGINEERING AND METALS SECTOR

STEPHEN YOUNG AND ALAN REEVES

The engineering and metals sector comprises SIC (Standard Industrial Classification) Orders VI to XII, viz. metal manufacture (VI); mechanical, instrument and electrical engineering (VII, VIII & IX); shipbuilding and marine engineering (X); vehicles (XI) and metal goods not elsewhere specified (XII). This diverse sector thus incorporates a number of the traditional trades which helped to create prosperity during the industrial revolution and into the nineteenth and early twentieth centuries. Engineering, especially heavy engineering, was inextricably linked to iron and steel, shipbuilding, locomotives and textiles in the manufacture, repair and installation of all kinds of machinery and equipment. Equally, in the years up to World War II, Scotland's heavier commitment to such industries, a number of which were depressed or stagnating, was an important factor in the relative decline in the country's economic prosperity.[1] In the post-war period, the difficulties of the staple trades have continued but the 'heavy' emphasis of the engineering industry has changed with the expansion of light engineering and electronics and the growth (and subsequent decline) of the vehicle sector. To complete the picture, most recently the industry has been significantly affected by North Sea oil developments. As at 1981, there were an estimated 230000 people employed in engineering in Scotland, 46 per cent of the total in manufacturing industry. This was slightly below the share of manufacturing employment in engineering in the UK (50·7 per cent). Engineering and allied industries accounted for 42·5 per cent of GDP in manufacturing in Scotland in 1963, a figure which had fallen to 36·9 per cent by 1978.[2]

The diversity of the industry and the varying experience of the sectors within it create major problems for analysis and policy assessment. Difficulties are, fortunately, reduced by the fact that other chapters in this book are dealing directly or indirectly with certain of these sectors: foreign ownership is concentrated in engineering and so the multinational dimensions were handled in Chapter 4, while Chapter 9 focuses on high-technology sectors such as electronics. Moreover, the nationalised industries – British Steel and British Shipbuilders – have been excluded from the scope of the book. The main emphasis in this chapter is, therefore, on the traditional face of Scottish engineering. Following a brief overview of the characteristics of the engineering industry as a whole in Scotland, a number of the major sectors are pinpointed for more detailed analysis, before the discussion is further narrowed to look at the activities of six major companies in the heavy mechanical and electrical field. The chapter, finally, reviews some of the policy areas which impinge on the engineering industry and makes various suggestions regarding the future direction of policy.

Characteristics and Development of the Engineering and Metals Sector in Scotland

The Overall Position. Considering the position of the industry over the last twenty-five years or so, the immediate impression is that, with respect to Scotland's traditional engineering sectors at least, relatively little has changed. As Tables 5.1 and 5.2 show, employment in metal manufacture (iron and steel to miscellaneous base metals) and in shipbuilding and marine engineering declined throughout the period from 1958 to 1981, while mechanical engineering employment, after some build-up to 1965, then fell by forty-five per cent to 1981. The index of industrial production for shipbuilding followed a similar downward trend, and output in metals (SICs VI and XII) and mechanical engineering was only marginally higher than it had been in 1958. Of the newer industries, employment in vehicles built up rapidly in the early 1960s with the establishment of BMC at Bathgate and Rootes at Linwood but then fell steadily; the major decline, of course, came after the end of the period covered by the statistics with the closure of Linwood. Only in instrument and electrical engineering, therefore, was employment higher in 1981 than in 1958, with output volume substantially up over the period. In both of these industries, furthermore, output has increased at a substantially faster rate than in the UK as a whole, the only engineering sectors (except metal manufacture) in which this pattern was apparent. Evidence suggests that Scotland increased her specialisation in shipbuilding and marine engineering and metal manufacture relative to Great Britain throughout the period from 1881 to 1951.[3] Since these industries were in long-term structural decline, the impact in the more recent period would be expected to be felt most severely in Scotland, although clearly there are other factors to be considered.

The data in Tables 5.1 and 5.2 do not show productivity changes directly, but drawing on these figures and other sources it is clear that output per worker has risen most rapidly in electrical engineering: between 1963 and 1978, for example, output per worker rose by 15·1 per cent annually in SIC IX compared with increases ranging from 0·3 per cent in shipbuilding and marine engineering and vehicles to 3·7 per cent per annum in mechanical and instrument engineering.[4] Making com-

Table 5.1. Index of industrial production: engineering and allied industries (index 1975=100).

SIC Order		Scotland					UK	
		1958	1965	1970	1975	1981	1958	1981
VI	Metal manufacture	102	125	126	100	102	97	79
VII	Mechanical engineering	66	84	111	100	73[1]	57	77
VIII	Instrument engineering	27	56	97	100	158[1]	33	101
IX	Electrical engineering	20	48	77	100	151	44	109
X	Shipbuilding & marine engineering	153	143	117	100	62	118	69
XI	Vehicles	75	99	108	100	76[1]	84	85
XII	Metal goods n.e.s.	48	66	80	100	54	83	73
Total eng. & allied industries[2]		58	76	98	100	89	64	85

[1] 1980 figures.
[2] Excluding metal manufacture; the 1982 index for Scotland was 95, and for the UK 86.
Source: *Scottish Abstract of Statistics*, No.11, 1982 & No.12, 1983; *Digest of Scottish Statistics*, various issues; *Scottish Economic Bulletin*, No.27, 1983; *Annual Abstract of Statistics*, various issues.

parisons between Scotland and the UK indicates that the relative growth in output per worker has been a good deal more rapid in Scotland in electrical engineering; in other sectors, output per worker in Scotland has been below that in the UK since 1963 at least, with some deterioration in the Scottish relative position since then in shipbuilding.

The Major Sectors. Given the diverse nature of engineering and the range of specialities within the industry, it is necessary to try to take a more detailed approach to the analysis. In the discussion which follows, therefore, consideration is given to various characteristics of the industry and the firms within it at the MLH level. Most of the data are derived from SCOMER and relate to employment and/or units, a fact which indicates caution in interpretation.

Table 5.3 presents data on recent employment trends at MLH level, excluding only those MLHs where employment in Scotland was 2000 or less in 1981. Reflecting the huge loss of jobs in manufacturing industry as a whole in the United Kingdom during the late 1970s and early 1980s, employment declined in all engineering Orders in Scotland between 1971 and 1981 and in nineteen of the twenty-five MLHs covered by the table. Moreover, among the expanding groups – aluminium and aluminium alloys; other mechanical engineering n.e.s.; radio and electronic components; computers; radio, radar and electronic capital goods and aerospace equipment – employment gains were quite small, amounting to

Table 5.2. Employees in employment:[1] engineering and allied industries (thousands).

SIC Order		1958	1965	1970	1975	1981[2]	1982[2]
VI	Metal manufacture	59·8	53·3	46·7	43·8	26·0	25·0
VII	Mechanical engineering	110·4	118·0	109·2	96·2	65·0	
VIII	Instrument engineering	10·7	13·5	17·9	17·5	15·0	
IX	Electrical engineering	22·6	39·6	52·5	51·3	43·0	
X	Shipbuilding & marine engineering	72·6	51·2	44·7	42·9	34·0	195·0
XI	Vehicles	42·2	41·7	40·8	35·9	26·0	
XII	Metal goods n.e.s.	27·6	30·3	30·9	28·7	21·0	
Total eng. & allied industries		345·9	347·6	342·7	316·3	230·0	220·0

[1] Data for 1970 and earlier derived from IDS estimates designed to produce a consistent employment series by SIC Order.
[2] Figures are published to the nearest thousand. 1982 data are provisional.
Sources: IDS; *Scottish Economic Bulletin*, No.27, 1983.

4 200 jobs in all. And the data do not take into account the recent closure of the Invergordon aluminium smelter. Even in electronics (MLH 354, plus 363–367) there was no overall increase in jobs, with rapidly rising demand being offset by productivity growth. NEDO, in relation to electronic components, for example, estimated output growth of between 14 and 17 per cent per annum at current prices during this period and productivity growth rates of around 15 per cent per annum.[5] Nevertheless, against the backcloth of a 28 per cent fall in employment in engineering, the electronics sector's share of employment rose from 11·6 to 16·1 per cent. It should be noted, furthermore, that 1983 data based on an SDA survey indicated quite a marked growth in electronics employment after 1981, and certainly a number of expansions and new projects were recorded in these years (see Table 9.1, below). Not all the increases in employment share were in instrument and electrical engineering. Within mechanical engineering, nearly all the MLH groups included in the table recorded gains in share. MLH 341, industrial plant and steelwork, employs the largest number of people and its share of employment rose slightly to 8·7 per cent. The demand for industrial plant and steelwork is generated by the oil refining industry, the chemical industry, steel and power plant. Despite the long-term loss of competitive advantage, the proportion of employment in shipbuilding and marine engineering rose slightly up to 1981, although the naval yards plus Rosyth now constitute a significant element of this sector.

Some interest attaches to industry sectors which are not included in

Table 5.3. Employment trends by minimum list heading.[1]

MLH/SIC	No. of employees			% of employees		
	1971	1976	1981	1971	1976	1981
311 Iron & steel (general)	23652	20300	12000	7·4	6·8	5·2
312 Steel tubes	6822	5660	4000	2·1	1·9	1·7
313 Iron castings etc.	9943	7949	4000	3·1	2·7	1·7
321 Aluminium & alum. alloys	3478	3763	4000	1·1	1·3	1·7
Total SIC VI Metal manufacture	45900	39093	26000	14·3	13·1	11·3
333 Pumps, valves & compressors	9342	12097	8000	2·9	4·1	3·5
336 Construction & earth moving equipment	5824	6132	5000	1·8	2·1	2·2
337 Mechanical handling equipment	4642	5237	4000	1·4	1·8	1·7
339 Other machinery	23024	17351	10000	7·2	5·8	4·3
341 Ind. plant & steelwork	24523	27153	20000	7·6	9·1	8·7
349 Other mech. eng. n.e.s.	9722	9790	10000	3·0	3·3	4·3
Total SIC VII Mechanical eng.	96072	91704	65000	29·9	30·8	28·3
352 Watches & clocks	7259	7019	5000	2·3	2·4	2·2
354 Scientific & ind. inst. & systems	8915	7650	8000	2·8	2·6	3·5
Total SIC VIII Instrument eng.	18552	16233	15000	5·8	5·5	6·5
361 Electrical machinery	8554	7023	6000	2·7	2·4	2·6
363 Telegraph & telephone app. & equipment	4354	3477	2000	1·4	1·2	0·9
364 Radio & electronic components	8329	12132	9000	2·6	4·1	3·9
365 Broadcast rec. & sound repr. equipment	293	409	—	0·1	0·1	—
336 Electronic computers	8214	6328	9000	2·6	2·1	3·9
367 Radio, radar & elec. capital goods	7062	6502	9000	2·2	2·2	3·9
368 Electrical appl. primarily for domestic use	5345	6679	4000	1·7	2·2	1·7
369 Other electrical goods	6298	4956	3000	2·0	1·7	1·3
Total SIC IX Electrical eng.	49563	48571	43000	15·4	16·3	18·7

Table 5.3.—*continued.*

MLH/SIC	No. of employees			% of employees		
	1971	1976	1981	1971	1976	1981
Total SIC X Ship-building & marine eng.	45212	42302	34000	14·1	14·2	14·8
381 Motor vehicle manufacture	21248	18315	11000	6·6	6·2	4·8
383 Aerospace equip. manufacture & repair	11876	11192	12000	3·7	3·8	5·2
Total SIC XI Vehicles	36698	32210	26000	11·4	10·8	11·3
390 Engineers small tools & gauges	3105	2831	3000	1·0	1·0	1·3
394 Wire & wire manufacture	4352	4218	3000	1·4	1·4	1·3
399 Metal industries n.e.s.	16680	16198	13000	5·2	5·4	5·7
Total SIC XII Metal goods n.e.s.	29557	27199	21000	9·2	9·1	9·1
Total (including omitted MLHs)	321554	297312	230000	100·0	100·0	100·0
Electronics (MLH 363–367+354)	37167	36498	37000	11·6	12·3	16·1

[1] Excludes all MLHs where employment 2000 or under in 1981. MLHs
363 and 368 included as this is part of the electronics sector.
Source: Department of Employment.

Table 5.3. One of these includes MLH 332, metalworking machine tools, an industry which has virtually disappeared from Scotland since the turn of the century. The decline commenced just after World War I when the world famous lathe manufacturers Shanks & Co. closed down as a result of heavy taxes. A series of amalgamations followed later, one of which involved James Allan Senior & Son, G.&A.Harvey, Loudoun Bros, Craig & Donald and James Bennie & Son, which together formed the Scottish Machine Tool Corporation. Into the period after World War II, the buoyant market encouraged heavy investment in plant designed for volume production of machine tools. Arguably, this was a mistaken strategy, for one of the strengths of the Scottish machine tool companies was the skill level of their workforce and their flexibility to produce one-off products designed for specific purposes. The latter features seem to characterise the only independent machine tool producer left in Scotland, Clifton & Baird of Johnstone, specialising in metal sawing machines, which, nevertheless, has allied these strengths to the manufacture of products which incorporate the latest in technology and design.

Table 5.4. Components of change, 1970–78.

Minimum list heading	1970 Units	Units (number)				1978 Units
		Openings	Expansion & Static	Contractions	Closures	
311, 312 Iron & steel (general); steel tubes	57	+13	+19	-33	-5	65
333 Pumps, valves & compressors	32	+18	+10	-17	-5	45
339 Other machinery	131	+49	+29	-52	-50	130
341 Ind. plant & steelwork	131	+46	+31	-54	-39	124
354 Scientific & ind. inst. & systems	32	+21	+17	-7	-8	45
361, 368 Electrical machinery; electrical appl. prim. for dom. use	57	+20	+16	-21	-20	57
363, 364 & 365 Telegraph & telephone app. & equip.; radio & electronic components; broadcast rec. & sound repr. equip.	47	+25	+18	-13	-16	56
366, 367 Electronic computers; radio, radar & elect. capital goods	33	+19	+12	-15	-6	46
370 Shipbuilding & marine eng.	132	+23	+32	-56	-44	111
381 & 383 Motor vehicle manufacture; aerospace equip. manuf. & repair	100	+29	+23	-33	-44	85
399 Metal industries n.e.s.	218	+90	+67	-87	-64	244
Total	979	+357	+279	-393	-307	1029
Electronics (MLH 363–367+354)	112	+65	+47	-35	-30	147

134

Minimum list heading	1970 Employment	Employment (number of employees)				1978 Employment
		Openings	Expansions	Contractions	Closures	
311, 312 Iron & steel (general); steel tubes	27935	+343	+2866	-6927	-1131	23086
333 Pumps, valves & compressors	11691	+850	+807	-2619	-1126	9603
339 Other machinery	25277	+1131	+1201	-5138	-5058	17413
341 Ind. plant & steelwork	24183	+7621	+1152	-4576	-4444	23936
354 Scientific & ind. inst. & systems	11206	+1134	+532	-1543	-2754	8575
361, 368 Electrical machinery; electrical appl. prim. for dom. use	15876	+1017	+2172	-1354	-2843	14868
363, 364 & 365 Telegraph & telephone app. & equip.; radio & electronic components; broadcast rec. & sound repr. equip.	15565	+2522	+3430	-4490	-2268	14759
366, 367 Electronic computers; radio, radar & elect. capital goods	21487	+1001	+3275	-8503	-768	16492
370 Shipbuilding & marine eng.	41161	+2402	+6738	-3868	-9915	36518
381 & 383 Motor vehicle manufacture; aerospace equip. manuf. & repair	34582	+1054	+2235	-3503	-3083	31285
399 Metal industries n.e.s.	15580	+2247	+1545	-2403	-1944	15025
Total	244543	+21322	+25953	-44924	-35334	211560
Electronics (MLH 363–367+354)	48258	+4657	+7237	-14536	-5790	39826

Source: SCOMER.

Components of Change in the Engineering Industry. Despite the almost universally dismal employment performance, it is, nevertheless, important to establish the potential for growth in the system as represented, for example, by the rate of new firm formation and expansion as compared with contraction and closure. This analysis of components of change for a smaller group of the major MLHs is presented in Table 5.4. Taking these major MLHs together, the number of units increased by around five per cent between 1970 and 1978, with openings and expansions representing 36 per cent and 28 per cent respectively of the number of units in 1970.

Within minimum list headings, the most dynamic sectors were the electronic groups, with openings representing 58 per cent and expansions 42 per cent of the 1970 stock of units. Closures and contractions were also below average, leaving the number of units nearly one-third up over the period. Despite this buoyancy, the job total in electronics still fell by 17 per cent, although this is perhaps mainly accounted for by the replacement of electromechanical by electronics technology by some of the firms categorised in this sector (see Table 5.5 for details of major companies).

Leaving electronics aside, openings and expansions were very buoyant in the pumps, valves and compressors sector (333), and, although the number of units involved is quite small, the size of the sector increased by over forty per cent (in terms of units) over the period. The products of this industry segment are very heterogeneous and serve a wide variety of industries and services, but the opportunities created by North Sea oil are clearly important in the trend observed. Outside the pumps and valves sector and that of miscellaneous metal goods (399), the picture is not optimistic. In fact, the only other MLHs recording net increases in the number of units were iron and steel (general) and steel tubes (311 and 312).

The Leading Companies Within Sectors and Overseas Ownership. The comments on sectoral employment performance cannot be dissociated from the behaviour of the companies in the engineering industry, and Table 5.5 notes the major firms within the main MLHs. What is especially noteworthy is the large number of overseas firms represented; and when the nationalised bodies – British Steel (MLH 311 and 312) and British Shipbuilders (MLH 370) – are excluded, domestic companies appear as leading employers in eight of the seventeen MLH categories. Of these eight, seven are based outside Scotland – Barr and Stroud, a subsidiary of Pilkington Bros since 1977; John Brown Engineering, part of the London-based John Brown Group; Anderson Strathclyde, owned by Charter Consolidated – although in 1981 Anderson Strathclyde was an independent, Scottish-headquartered company; a GEC division – GEC Telecommunications (GEC is also represented through Marconi Space); Ferranti; British Leyland, and Rolls Royce. This leaves one Scottish-

Table 5.5. Major companies within selected minimum list headings.[1]

Minimum list heading	Major company(ies)[2]
311, Iron & steel (general); 312 steel tubes	British Steel
333 Pumps, valves & compressors	Weir Pumps, Howden Compressors
339 Other machinery	Anderson Strathclyde, Consolidated Pneumatic[3]
341 Ind. plant & steelwork	Babcock International, Brown & Root Wimpey,[3] McDermott,[3] James Howden, Motherwell Bridge
354 Scientific & ind. inst. & systems	Barr & Stroud, Honeywell,[3] Veeder Root[3]
361 Electrical machinery	John Brown Engineering, Parsons Peebles
363 Telegraph & telephone app. & equip.	GEC Telecommunications, Pye[3]
364 Radio & electronic components	Motorola,[3] National Semiconductor,[3] Philips[3]
365 Broadcast rec. & sound repr. equip.	Mitsubishi Electric[3]
366 Electronic computers	IBM,[3] Burroughs,[3] NCR[3]
367 Radio, radar & elect. capital goods	Ferranti, Marconi Space
368 Electrical appl. prim. for dom. use	Hoover,[3] Sunbeam Electric[3]
370 Shipbuilding & marine eng.	British Shipbuilders
381 Motor vehicle manufacture	British Leyland, Talbot,[3] Volvo[3]
383 Aerospace equip. manuf. & repair	Rolls-Royce, Scottish Aviation
399 Metal industries n.e.s.	United Glass Closures & Plastics[3]

[1] Relates to the position as at 1981 to ensure compatibility with other statistics in this section. Since 1981 a number of the companies above have closed plants in Scotland or have severely reduced employment including Talbot, Consolidated Pneumatic, Sunbeam Electric & others.
[2] In some cases only the division operating in Scotland is referred to. For example, Howden Compressors is part of the Howden Group. The company mentioned first in each MLH category is the largest employer.
[3] Overseas-owned. Note, however, Distillers Co. have a significant interest in United Glass and Brown & Root Wimpey is also a joint venture.
Sources: Scottish Council (Development & Industry); company accounts.

headquartered company, Weir Pumps (part of the Weir Group), with factories in Glasgow and Alloa. A number of other Scottish firms are included in Table 5.5 as among the largest in their sector – James Howden and Motherwell Bridge – reinforcing the point that the Scottish enterprises are clustered within the heavy mechanical engineering industry.

Extending from this latter point, Table 5.6 is presented to illustrate the importance of overseas as distinct from UK ownership within the main engineering sectors. In terms of number of units, multinational

Table 5.6. Share of employment and units in non-overseas-owned companies, 1981.[1]

Minimum list heading	% in non-overseas-owned companies Units	Employment
311 Iron & steel (general)	97·4	n.a.
312 Steel tubes	88·9	n.a.
333 Pumps, valves & compressors	70·7	72·6
339 Other machinery	92·2	87·2
341 Ind. plant & steelwork	93·3	73·7
354 Scientific & ind. inst. & systems	78·6	48·8
361 Electrical machinery	90·4	87·5
363 Telegraph & telephone app. & equip.	60·0	61·8
364 Radio & electronic components	56·4	21·9
365 Broadcast rec. & sound repr. equip.	85·7	n.a.
366 Electronic computers	50·0	6·0
367 Radio, radar & elect. capital goods	83·3	96·9
368 Electrical appl. prim. for dom. use	84·6	n.a.
370 Shipbuilding & marine eng.	97·1	96·8
381 Motor vehicle manufacture	97·1	n.a.
383 Aerospace equip. manuf. & repair	100·0	100·0
399 Metal industries n.e.s.	95·2	95·1
Total of above	89·6	79·9
Electronics (MLH 363–367+354)[2]	70·0	52·1

[1] Or latest available
[2] Excludes employment data for MLH 365
Source: SCOMER.

corporations account for a small minority of units in most sectors, but are the major employers in computers (MLH 366), radio and electronic components (364), scientific and industrial instruments (354) and probably also in MLHs 365 and 368; almost all, noticeably, are electronics MLHs.

Employment Size Bands and the Role of Small Firms in Engineering. While the comments above have mostly been concerned with large engineering enterprises, Table 5.7 indicates that over one-third of units within the major MLHs employ between 11 and 24 people, with a further 35 per cent of units within the 25–99 employment size bands. Small units dominate in metal industries n.e.s. (MLH 399), motor vehicle manufacture (381), and electrical and other machinery (361, 339). In all these minimum list headings, moreover, there is a much greater concentration of small units than is the case in the UK as a whole.[6]

Table 5.7. Share of units (%) by employment size band, 1977.

Minimum list heading	Employment size band					Total	
	11–24	25–49	50–99	100–199	200+	%	No.
311 Iron & steel (general)	12·2	9·8	14·6	24·3	39·0	100·0	41
312 Steel tubes	16·0	16·0	24·0	20·0	24·0	100·0	25
333 Pumps, valves & compressors	26·1	19·6	19·6	13·0	21·7	100·0	46
339 Other machinery	39·4	21·2	13·6	15·2	10·6	100·0	132
341 Ind. plant & steelwork	25·8	28·0	14·4	11·4	20·5	100·0	132
354 Scientific & ind. inst. & systems	30·2	18·6	18·6	14·0	18·6	100·0	43
361 Electrical machinery	42·6	14·8	13·0	11·1	18·5	100·0	54
363 Telegraph & telephone app. & equip.	n.a.	n.a.	n.a.	n.a.	n.a.	100·0	11
364 Radio & electronic components	n.a.	n.a.	n.a.	n.a.	n.a.	100·0	40
365 Broadcast rec. & sound repr. equip.	n.a.	n.a.	n.a.	n.a.	n.a.	100·0	6
366 Electronic computers	n.a.	n.a.	n.a.	n.a.	n.a.	100·0	14
367 Radio, radar & elect. capital goods	13·3	33·3	16·7	10·0	26·7	100·0	30
368 Electrical appl. prim. for dom. use	n.a.	n.a.	n.a.	n.a.	n.a.	100·0	14
370 Shipbuilding & marine eng.	32·4	19·4	13·9	11·1	23·1	100·0	108
381 Motor vehicle manufacture	51·9	28·5	7·8	5·2	6·5	100·0	77
383 Aerospace equip. manuf. & repair	n.a.	n.a.	n.a.	n.a.	n.a.	100·0	7
399 Metal industries n.e.s.	53·0	20·0	15·7	3·9	7·4	100·0	230
Total of above	36·3	20·4	14·9	10·8	17·6	100·0	1010
Electronics (MLH 363–367+354)	25·0	15·3	17·4	13·9	28·5	100·0	144

Source: SCOMER.

The role of small firms in engineering is closely linked to the issue of sub-contracting, since many of the enterprises in the smaller size categories will be reliant on supplying other companies for a large part of their business. A recent SDA study on the sub-contract and component supply industry in Scottish engineering (excluding electronics) estimated that Scotland obtained only one-quarter of the value of purchases made by the 100 top purchasers.[7] Of the £323 million spent by these sample purchasers, companies located in the rest of the UK accounted for 62 per cent of supplies and imports for the remaining 14 per cent. Forgings were the major item purchased, followed by fabrications and castings; in the former category, 15 per cent of purchases were sourced in Scotland, rising to one-third for fabrications and castings. The survey of users indicated that Scottish suppliers were not considered inferior in terms of price, quality and delivery, but that their sales and marketing efforts were generally weak. By this view the changes required to increase the Scottish share of the sub-contract market included greater professionalism and aggressiveness in sales and marketing; more rigorous quality control procedures; a move into other product areas where necessary; and a more market-oriented approach to investment. The suppliers' views on this same issue stressed, conversely, the difficulty of breaking into the large users' market, because of lack of size and experience, not helped by the location of central purchasing departments outside Scotland in many branch operations.

Sub-contracting is clearly an important issue in relation to the development of the Scottish engineering industry. On the other hand, there is evidence within Scotland that the growth of some firms is, in fact, inhibited by an excessive sub-contracting focus.[8] Shielded by the 'umbrella' of large enterprises, small firms in this category may become lethargic and complacent. For such companies, what is required is the encouragement of diversification into final product, or, at least, component manufacture. From a policy perspective, both questions need to be addressed. It should be added that there is no reason to expect the issues posed by sub-contracting in Scotland to be particularly different from those of other regional economies within the UK.

Other Performance Measures. Most of the information presented in this section has related, of necessity, to employment. It is possible, nevertheless, to consider various other performance measures and to look at Scotland in relation to the UK as a whole, as is done in Table 5.8. What is particularly interesting is to compare relative productivity at the sectoral level. What emerges is that net output per worker in Scotland is above the UK figure in only a small number of sectors – valves, compressors and fluid power equipment, radio and electronic components (and electronics as a whole) together with engineers' small tools and gauges and miscellaneous metal manufacture. The former three are sectors where employment in Scotland represents an above-average share of the UK total, but in some other MLH's where Scotland is strongly represented, productivity is well below the UK level; these include, most obviously, industrial plant and steelwork, pumps, and steel tubes.

Considering recent investment trends, the same pattern does not necessarily apply, since capital spending in industrial plant has been very buoyant, along with that in valves, electronic components and computers. Generalising at the Order level, and taking a longer time period, net capital expenditure in Scotland has been fairly healthy in relation to that of the UK, except for shipbuilding and metal goods n.e.s., while investment in mechanical engineering was much firmer in the early seventies than in the period covered by Table 5.8;[9] these investment trends are relevant to the later evaluation of the impact of regional policy measures. What is also clear is that the optimistic trend in investment has yet to show up in productivity, levels of which, in some sectors, are low by UK standards.

It would be desirable to utilise other performance measures, including, for instance, overseas trade patterns, innovation, the characteristics of manpower in the industry etc. In relation to the latter, the heavily male-oriented nature of the industry as a whole is of significance (over 80 per cent of employees being male). For electronics, the equivalent figure for male employment was 57 per cent in 1978, and all the occupations employing a majority of females are concentrated in this sector. The issues raised may be important in areas of the country where declining male employment opportunities are being partially offset by an increased demand for female labour. Associated with these changes brought about by the evolving structure of industry, are changes in skill demands, problems in retraining and the reorientation of attitudes, etc., although these do not alter the general conclusion of engineering as an industry characterised by its high skill requirements.

Data are inadequate to build up a satisfactory picture of overseas trade performance, since most of the information relates to trade through Scottish ports which accounts for only about half of exports from Scotland. This is a large omission. With the declining domestic market base for many engineering enterprises, arising from the fall in user demand from the coal, shipbuilding, marine and locomotive industries, for example, prosperity of the supplier firms is likely to have become increasingly dependent on other industries, e.g. the oil and oil-related market and/or external markets. The newer engineering industries have always had a small market base in Scotland, with exports representing a high proportion of output. Sample data for 1979 relating to large establishments indicate that for all engineering industry Orders, exports abroad represented a higher proportion of sales than was the case for all manufacturing industry.[10] The most strongly export-oriented sectors were

Table 5.8. Employment, capital expenditure and net output in Scotland and U K, 1979.

MLH/SIC	Scottish employment (% of U K) 1979	Scottish capital expenditure (% of U K) 1977–79	1979	Net output per head, 1979 Scotland £	(% of U K)
312 Steel tubes	11·8	12·8	7·6	6800	86·5
Total SIC VI Metal manufacture	7·7	14·0	10·0	4740	60·4
333 Pumps[1]	19·8	18·5	13·8	8204	88·8
333 Valves[1]	11·6	18·2	27·6	15207	163·6
333 Compressors & fluid power equipment[1]	5·7	6·5	5·9	11048	120·0
339 Misc. machinery[1]	7·4	13·1	4·1	6404	69·7
341 Ind. plant & steelwork	11·8	17·9	16·1	10552	86·6
349 Precision chains & other mech. eng.[1]	4·7	5·3	5·4	7879	100·0
Total SIC VII Mechanical engineering	8·0	9·2	8·3	9305	98·1
354 Scientific & ind. inst. & systems	8·2	10·1	9·7	8000	96·3
Total SIC VIII Instrument engineering	11·1	10·1	9·6	7132	91·7
361 Electrical machinery	6·9	5·6	3·0	6490	86·5
364 Radio & electronic components	9·9	14·8	17·7	8962	117·8
366 Electronic computers	22·9	38·2	39·4	22220	95·0
367 Radio, radar & elec. capital goods	8·6	7·9	8·7	9055	99·4
368 Electrical appl. primarily for domestic use	7·6	7·2	5·6	6905	86·9
369 Electric lamps, electric light fittings etc.[1]	5·8	6·6	6·5	6385	88·5
Total SIC IX Electrical engineering	7·1	10·1	10·6	9719	111·8

Table 5.8.—*continued.*

MLH/SIC	Scottish employment (% of UK) 1979	Scottish capital expenditure (% of UK) 1977–79	1979	Net output per head, 1979 Scotland £	(% of UK)
370 Shipbuilding & marine eng.	22·7	20·0	15·2	6677	97·3
381 Motor vehicle manufacturing[1]	4·7	3·5	2·4	6018	65·3
Total SIC X & XI Shipbuilding & marine eng. and vehicles	7·8	5·3	3·9	6563	77·6
390 Engineers small tools & gauges	5·0	5·7	6·1	8600	113·1
394 Wire & wire manufacture	10·5	6·0	4·7	8027	90·0
339 Misc. metal manufacture[1]	5·3	6·0	6·0	8168	104·7
Total SIC XII Metal goods n.e.s.	5·2	5·4	5·3	8043	98·4
Total (including omitted MLHs)	7·5	8·9	7·2	7822	90·8
Electronics (MLH 363–367+354)[2]	9·8	15·5	16·9	11050	114·8

[1] Part of MLH only.
[2] Excludes MLH 363 and part of 365.
Source: *Business Monitor*, PA1002, 1977, 1978 & 1979.

mechanical (48·4 per cent of sales outside the UK), instrument (70·0 per cent) and electrical (42·8 per cent) engineering; the average export proportion for all manufacturing industry was 26·1 per cent. While exports from small establishments generally represented a smaller proportion of sales, broadly similar conclusions apply as between sectors.

The Impact of North Sea Oil on the Engineering Industry. Although the oil and oil-related sector is the subject of a separate chapter in this volume, there is merit in making some brief observations on the impact of North Sea oil specifically on the engineering industry at this juncture. Data from SEPD indicate that employment associated with North Sea oil in engineering and allied industries represented 6·0 per cent of total employment in these industries in 1974 and 8·5 per cent in 1976 but fell to 6·5 per cent in 1978. The decline between the latter two years has been at the expense of activities such as technical, scientific and financial services. It is only natural that as exploration diminished and production stabilised, the demand for platforms and equipment would decline. This happened especially in these years, with employment in enterprises producing concrete and steel platforms and modules falling by more than one half. Employment figures can be misleading in the sense that they do not convey the net output or wage levels of the activity. In this regard, there is evidence that the demands of the North Sea industry have provided a boost to productivity for some firms, for figures indicate that output per employee is considerably higher in oil-related industry than in Scottish industry as a whole. In general, nevertheless, it would be wrong to place too much emphasis on the impact of North Seas oil on engineering and allied industries, a view which is confirmed in relation to the Scottish economy as a whole in Chapter 10.

The Heavy Mechanical and Electrical Sector – Six Company Cases

Despite the significance of industries such as electronics to Scotland for the future, the data presented here have shown that heavy engineering is still a major contributor to employment and output. It is arguable that the focus of interest on electronics by the SDA, for example, has diverted attention away from the problems and prospects of heavy engineering; this is a cause for concern given the relatively strong position of indigenous companies within the sector and the fact that within some sub-sectors world demand is continuing to grow strongly. Before considering the policy issues, therefore, this section looks at six companies which represent this more traditional face of Scottish heavy industry, especially that of mechanical engineering in Strathclyde Region. All are long-established, and together employed nearly 14 5000 people in Scotland in mid-1983 (Table 5.9). Given that the firms account for between thirty and forty per cent of total employment in their respective sectors (MLHs 333, 339, 341 & 361), they clearly play a pivotal role within the heavy engineering industry in Scotland. This role is further emphasised when set alongside the evidence of Table 5.8 which showed low productivity by UK norms in three of the sectors or sub-sectors (pumps, electrical machinery and industrial plant) and low level of capital investment in the former two of these. Three of the six are headquartered in England – Babcock International, John Brown and, most recently, Anderson Strathclyde – while the other three are Scottish-based enterprises. The aim of this section is to examine a number of key characteristics of these organisations, and in particular their strategy and performance over the recent past. In so doing an opportunity is given to consider some of the dominant issues which may require or be amenable to policy intervention.

Company Backgrounds. As the data in Table 5.10 indicate, the companies concerned date from the turn of the century or earlier.

Table 5.9. Employment in Scotland in six major engineering companies, mid-1983.

Anderson Strathclyde		Babcock International[1]		John Brown[2]		Howden Group[3]		Motherwell Bridge Holdings[4]		Weir Group[5]	
Motherwell	2023	Renfrew	3430	Clydebank	1770	Renfrew	1300	Motherwell	900	Glasgow (Cathcart)	2200
Glasgow (Bridgeton)	666	Dumbarton	207			Glasgow	354			Alloa	900
Glenrothes	327										
East Kilbride	94										
Kirkintilloch	253										
Caley Hydraulics (East Kilbride)	24										
	3387		3637		1770		1654		900		3100

[1] All employees in Scotland are part of Babcock Power. Renfrew employment includes 220 employees at the Renfrew research station. Excludes employment at sites in Scotland.
[2] Represented in Scotland by John Brown Engineering.
[3] Glasgow employment relates to Howden Compressors.
[4] Excludes employment in another group company, John Young, Glasgow.

[5] Alloa employment relates to Weir Pumps; it was announced after the preparation of this table that employment at Alloa was to be reduced to 400 with the transfer of some work to Cathcart. Cathcart employment refers to Weir Group, Weir Pumps and Weir Group Management Systems.
Source: Company data.

Anderson Strathclyde emerged from Anderson Boyes and Company Limited and Mavor and Coulson Limited, both of which had their origins as engineering partnerships in the late nineteenth century. These firms had strong interests in coal cutting and associated equipment, the product area which has remained at the core of Anderson Strathclyde's business. Apart from this firm, all the other five had their origins as suppliers to the shipbuilding industry. The Babcock origins lie in the US-based partnership of Babcock and Wilcox who worked together as boilermakers from 1866. The UK company was formed in 1891 and six years later the firm established at Renfrew the then largest factory in Britain for the construction of water-tube boilers both for marine and land purposes. From the turn of the century the US and UK sides of the business became separate financial operations, although the US corporation had a twenty per cent stake in its UK offshoot until the 1970s.

Table 5.10. Corporate data for the six major engineering companies, 1982

	Registered[1]	Pre-tax profit[2]	Turnover (£m)	Net assets employed (£m)
Anderson Strathclyde	1904	11·5	100·0	51·3
Babcock International	1891	23·6	1002·2	336·2
John Brown	1837	14·2	680·8	203·9
Howden Group	1907	8·7	142·2	53·6
Motherwell Bridge Holdings	1898	0·2	77·1	20·8
Weir Group	1895	7·6	136·9	57·9

[1] In several cases there are considerable differences between registration and establishment dates.
[2] Excluding exceptional items.
Sources: Annual reports; Extel Statistical Services.

The John Brown Group dates from 1837, when John Brown started manufacturing steel in Sheffield. The company's presence in Scotland from 1899 was, however, in shipbuilding, when the Clydebank Engineering and Shipbuilding Works was acquired as an additional outlet for the steel plate and forgings of the group. The current Clydebank specialisation in gas turbines arose from a diversification move in the 1960s in the face of declining shipbuilding demand, as the company became one of the first to implement the proposals of the Geddes Report on shipbuilding. The critical decision, made in May 1965, was to manufacture the General Electric Company's range of industrial gas turbines under licence from the US.

James Howden commenced business as a consulting engineer and designer in 1854, moving from the East Coast to be near the shipyards.

The firm's range of marine products were extended to include high-speed engines and turbines for land use from the early part of the century. From this base Howden continues to be recognised as an important force in the engineering, design and sale of air and gas fluid handling equipment, systems and installations.

Motherwell Bridge has continued to operate as a private company under family ownership since it was founded by a Lanarkshire iron master in 1898. Its original reputation was in bridgebuilding, although from the 1930s it developed as a specialist producer of storage tanks for the oil industry. A wide range of cognate activity has subsequently followed including many types of specialist vessels, spheres and domes for storage and process plant projects; offshore fabrication; heavy structural work; and so on.

Finally, the firm of G. & J. Weir was established by two marine engine consultants in Glasgow in 1870. They patented a boiler feed pump and other auxiliaries and in 1886, dissatisfied with those who were engaged in manufacturing based on their patents, they commenced their own manufacturing in Cathcart. Despite having pursued numerous diversification routes during its history, the Weir Group has remained an important producer of boiler feed pumps for marine and land use as well as having strong interests in desalination and heat-exchange equipment, etc.[11]

The Scottish Operations. In many ways the strengths of all these companies have been based on their emergence as dominant firms within a particular market niche. To varying degrees, they have stayed relatively close to their original source of competitive advantage. The position of Anderson Strathclyde in the longwall mining equipment market in the UK and the export record of John Brown in gas turbines are both tokens of that. Another common factor is the extent to which all the firms have had to diversify away from the original markets within which they established their advantage.

Inevitably, as part of this process of development, the positions of the Scottish operations within the overall groups have changed. Anderson Strathclyde had been least affected until 1983 in that its activities continued to be strongly Scottish-centred, with its main manufacturing unit at Motherwell and smaller plants in four other locations in Scotland. Babcock International, on the other hand, is represented in Scotland only through Babcock Power; its Scottish employment represents less than one quarter of UK employment and little more than one tenth of worldwide employment. In turnover terms, the UK Power Group was the biggest component of the company (21·9 per cent of turnover in 1982), but only marginally larger than the North American Group (21·4 per cent of turnover). As noted previously, the John Brown Group expanded into Scotland through an acquisition and, currently, John Brown Engineering at Clydebank represents the gas turbine manufacturing arm of a widely based engineering company; Scotland accounts for about seventeen per cent of UK employment. Although the company's shipbuilding interests in Clydebank were finally phased out in 1970, John Brown Engineering Offshore was established in 1974 to build modules for offshore oil exploration; lack of orders, failure to meet delivery schedules and a series of damaging strikes led to the 1977 closure of an operation which at peak had employed around 900 workers. The John Brown Group's machine tool factory in Scotland was also closed, with the loss of 235 jobs, in 1979.

The Weir Group is another company where activities in Scotland have become more narrowly focused. The loss-making subsidiary Weir Construction was sold off in 1974, and Weir formerly owned Argus Foundry which made iron and non-ferrous castings at Thornliebank. The requirement for steel castings led to a series of acquisitions in England and subsequently to the closure of Argus. Weir Pumps, with factories at Cathcart and Alloa, is, however, the largest company in the Group and represents about two-thirds of UK employment.[12]

The final two companies – Howden and Motherwell Bridge– are Scottish-headquartered, and while their main lines of activity are represented in Scotland, growth, mostly elsewhere in the UK for Motherwell Bridge and mainly outside the UK for Howden, has inevitably reduced the importance of their Scottish bases. This is illustrated clearly in the review of diversification and internationalisation strategies which follows.

Strategic Directions. In order to illustrate the challenges facing the management teams in the six companies over the last decade, three interrelated themes have been selected, namely, diversification; internationalisation; rationalisation and technological change. These issues have not always featured in each of the companies to the same degree over this period, and the lack of data pertaining to Scottish operations alone makes it difficult sometimes to isolate the specifically local dimensions of the questions.

Diversification. All four of the Scottish-based companies have been under pressure to diversify in customers, markets and to a lesser extent products either as a result of decline in their original markets or because of the potential threats posed by overdependence on certain outlets and products. This is classically illustrated in Anderson Strathclyde (see Table 5.11) where some two-thirds of sales are in the UK, dominantly to the National Coal Board. This relationship has been long-established and very profitable; it is also complemented by the fact that the UK market for coal cutting machinery continued to expand in the last decade. Nevertheless, uncertainties over NCB plans loom large and Anderson Strathclyde remains a relatively undiversified company by measures of product, customer and geographical sales patterns. The Howden Group is in a quite different position: in this case the philosophy over recent years

148

has been to expand through overseas acquisition within its own area of specialisation, resulting in the majority of group sales being outwith the UK. On the question of product diversification, Howden has preferred to stick fairly close to its known area of expertise. As part of its acquisition programme, the company absorbed several potentially new lines, but these were divested in order to concentrate on specialisms in energy efficiency and air and gas handling. A somewhat similar policy has been pursued by Weir, at least in the UK, and in 1978 the company's aircraft equipment division was sold off to concentrate resources in engineering, steel foundries and desalination. In this case the motivation may have been rather different to that of Howden, viz. 'not enough money to develop everything'.[13]

Table 5.11. Geographical analysis of turnover, 1982[1] (per cent).[2]

Company	UK	Rest of Europe	North America	All other	Total
Anderson Strathclyde	66·9	4·6	10·5	18·0	100·0
Babcock International	28·1	10·4	28·4	33·1	100·0
John Brown	40·3	8·2	27·5[3]	24·0	100·0
Howden Group	25·0	7·9	39·4	27·7	100·0
Weir Group[4]	82·5	1·1	13·3	3·1	100·0

[1] Data not disclosed by Motherwell Bridge Holdings.
[2] Taking exports alone as a percentage of turnover, the 1982 figures are as follows: Anderson Strathclyde 18·0%, Babcock International 14·1%, John Brown 23·5%, Howden Group 9·2%, Motherwell Bridge 19·2% (5 year av. to 1981), Weir Group 38·0% (5 year av. to 1981).
[3] Includes S. America.
[4] Data relate to sales by subsidiaries outside UK; excludes direct exports from UK.
Source: Annual reports.

The question of degrees of diversification occurs in a rather different guise in the case of two of the externally-controlled companies. Between its formation in 1966 and 1982, over 95 per cent of the John Brown Engineering power units have been exported to some forty countries. In this case the development thrust has been to convert the operation from a supplier of small gas turbine packaged power plants to being a major international contractor in turnkey energy installations. There is little question that this has been greatly aided by the continued General Electric connection. Diversification has thus been within the company's preferred specialisation as applied to new applications and market areas. The Babcock Power operation at Renfrew is very dependent on power station boiler work with, in the past, about seventy per cent of capacity being devoted to this area of operation. In recent years the parent company's strategy has been to push for increased exports from the plant, from a figure of around ten per cent in the mid-1970s to some fifty per cent in 1982. In addition, the company has been trying to diversify into North Sea oil work.

Internationalisation. Since both John Brown and Babcock already operate on a worldwide scale, this strategic issue only applies directly to the other four Scottish companies. To some degree the future of all these companies lies in their successful penetration of overseas markets using a variety of modes of involvement ranging from exports from the UK, to licensing, joint ventures and direct production in foreign markets. The relative levels of internationalisation have to be examined by a range of measures including geographical sales balance, comparisons of home and overseas employment levels, recent overseas investment patterns and so on. By all these measures the Howden Group is the most international-ised within the four. For Howden, some 46 per cent of employment was in overseas subsidiaries in 1982 (as against 33 per cent in 1977 – see Table 5.12) and only a quarter of total sales are in the UK.

The Motherwell Bridge, Weir Group and Anderson Strathclyde positions are quite different. All three have some 90 per cent of em-ployees in the UK, with Anderson Strathclyde being particularly depen-dent on UK sales. Of these three, Anderson Strathclyde has perhaps been the most active in establishing installation and servicing operations over-seas in recent years and most recently in licensing technical know-how abroad (to the Chinese). Weir, for their part, announced a programme of direct investment in the United States in 1978 in areas other than pumps where they already had a presence through a joint venture with Stude-baker-Worthington; the Group is also active elsewhere in the Americas, especially Mexico. Despite such moves, Weir is still very much a UK-based company; and Motherwell Bridge, with its first European manu-facturing plant acquisition in France in 1981, is still at an early stage of internationalisation too. It has, however, declared that it is pursuing a policy of increasing overseas investments, especially in the field of materials handling and automatic control. In 1981, this was reflected in the fifty per cent purchase of a company in the USA.

It would be over-simplistic to argue that the future health of these companies is solely determined by their relative levels of international activity, any more than by diversification *per se*. Even so, demand trends and the need for a direct presence in foreign markets to exploit these would suggest an expansion of overseas operations. A decline in relative employment levels in Scotland and the UK as a whole may be the price of efficiency and growth.

Rationalisation and Technological Change. The six engineering companies studies in this section have suffered from the performance of the macro-economy in the recent past, including rising real exchange

rates and world and UK recession; the level of investment in the nationalised industries, in turn a function of the demand for energy, and constraints on public sector spending on infrastructure (mainly affecting
Motherwell Bridge and perhaps Weir) have also been important. Rationalisation, enforced by such factors and the application of new technology
to improve competitiveness, has thus been a major theme over the last
decade. The greatest pressures to rationalise, reduce employment and
divest from unprofitable activities have undoubtedly come in the three
largest groups. Table 5.12 illustrates this with reference to the overall
group employment levels in Babcock, John Brown and Weir. In all three
cases this has had a direct impact on the Scottish plants: at Babcock,
employment in Scotland fell from almost 6100 in mid-1976 to 3600 in
mid-1983; including JBE Offshore and the JB Group's former machine
tool factory in Scotland, John Brown has lost over 1400 workers in the
last six years; finally, employment at Weir has declined from nearly 5000
in 1976 to 3100 in 1983, including the closure of the Yoker factory in 1976
which employed 500 people.

Table 5.12. Home and overseas employment, 1973–82.

		Number of Employees			% change 1973–82
		1973	1977	1982	
Anderson Strathclyde	Total	n.a.	4549	4320	−5·0(1977–82)
	UK	4086	4267	3956	−3·2
Babcock International	Total	25865	36948	30116	+16·4
	UK	20716	22521	15188	−26·7
John Brown	UK	13610	14400	10040	−26·2
Howden Group	Total	n.a.	4813	4443	−7·7(1977–82)
	UK	2525	3158	2415	−4·4
Motherwell Bridge Holdings	UK	1462	2935	n.a.	+94·3(1973–81)
Weir Group	Total	13500	10000	n.a.	−29·6(1973–78)
	UK	12856	10095	4709	−73·7

Sources: Annual reports; Extel Statistical Services.

The most public of the rationalisation programmes has perhaps been
that of the Weir Group. Until 1978–79, Weir seemed to have pursued a
successful diversification strategy. Both acquisitions and greenfield
developments had given it a considerable share of the UK foundry
market. Secondly, the pumps business had made some impact in the
North Sea, with an estimated fifty per cent of the 1970s pump installations in that market (but see the comments in Chapter 10 in this regard).
Thirdly, the desalination equipment side had grown particularly fast after

the 1973 oil price shock, with a series of very large orders being won in the Middle East.

In 1979, however, trading conditions in the desalination business deteriorated sharply in the face of extreme price competition from Japan, while elsewhere foundry demand was collapsing. These marketing factors together with management deficiencies in the pumps division, the strong pound and high interest rates pushed the company into a severe cash crisis by the end of 1980, following a year in which net borrowings rose to £43 million against shareholders' funds (before capital reconstruction) of £26 million. The dramatic adjustments in capital structure which followed early in 1981 were matched by major surgery in the pumps company. In the Group as a whole, UK employment halved between 1977 and 1982. It is worth pointing out that virtually alone among the six firms studied here (exluding JBE Offshore), poor labour relations have also bedevilled Weir, and need to be seen alongside some of the other company problems mentioned above.

As a whole, Babcock International has undergone profound changes in size and shape over the past decade. Table 5.12 hints at one of these changes, namely the very rapid rise in overseas employment and the progressive reduction in jobs in the UK from the mid-1970s. The company has been establishing a base in North America, most notably through the acquisition in 1975 of Acco Industries (formerly American Chain and Cable). This and subsequent smaller acquisitions took Babcock's North American turnover from under £18 million in 1974 to nearly £285 million in 1982, representing around one-quarter of total sales. Against this overall picture, the thrust of operational change in Babcock Power's boilermaking plant at Renfrew has been towards achieving major productivity gains in order to remain competitive. The company has experimented with a variety of well-publicised 'action group' schemes combined with heavy investment and labour force reduction in order to achieve these aims.[14] To date, the Babcock operation at Renfrew has made significant progress in being re-oriented from a UK-market to a world-market plant as a result of these changes.[15] This has clearly been critical to its survival given the likelihood that major new UK orders for the replacement of 1950s generating plant will not be placed until the late 1980s.

Rationalisation pressures had been less severe in John Brown Engineering at Clydebank until recently. There were threats to 600 jobs in 1979 because of the strong pound and a levelling-off of world demand for gas turbines as a result of the oil crisis. But these were removed with orders from Latin America, the Middle East, India and the North Sea through lower pricing and delivery dates, and the workforce remained at a level around 1700. Investment in new technology – specifically gas turbine testing facilities – has been substantial and has played its part in the latter.

In late 1983, however, substantial job losses were announced because of lack of orders.

The other three companies have all taken steps to rationalise multi-site operations and reduce personnel to a greater or lesser degree. Howden has invested heavily in new technology, thereby revolutionising design work and costing as well as manufacturing, while in 1982 Anderson Strathclyde announced a £7·5 million programme to install what was claimed as Europe's largest automatic machine tool complex in order to cut costs and boost productivity.[16]

Performance. In this section a number of different performance measures are briefly considered for the six companies, where data are available. In terms of turnover growth, Motherwell Bridge and Anderson Strathclyde have grown most rapidly, with sixfold increases in the 1970s. Howden and Weir have grown around threefold in that period, with expansion in the former being particularly sluggish in the years 1976–79. In terms of profitability, the four Scottish-based companies (including Anderson Strathclyde) have generally achieved a return on capital employed of 10–15 per cent per annum. Howden and Anderson Strathclyde have been the most notable exceptions to these figures, with levels of 20–25 per cent being recorded in some years. Together, these companies have also shown the most consistent profit improvement. In contrast, both Motherwell Bridge and Weir performance deteriorated from 1978, with Weir making a sharp recovery from 1981. Corporate performance data for JBE and Babcock are less relevant in a Scottish context. What is clear from the results is that the UK power group in Babcock made a much better contribution to profit from 1980 than in earlier years. In John Brown the gas turbine (JBE) side was a major contributor to the improved 1978–80 group position. While certain problems were experienced for a time thereafter, by 1983 JBE was viewed as the group's most attractive asset and negotiations were undertaken with Hawker Siddeley to sell off the Clydebank operation to clear the debts of the parent (these fell through in August 1983).

As shown above, all of these companies have placed emphasis on export expansion. The JBE, Babcock and Howden records are particularly outstanding in this regard. By 1982 some 65 per cent of Howden sales were made by overseas subsidiaries. Few of the companies provide data on the relative profitability of their overseas sales, although the evidence of Weir, JBE and Babcock certainly points to considerable pressure on margins since the mid-1970s. An important, though often less quantifiable, feature of performance is the relative position of these companies as innovators within their respective markets. All six have considerable reputations by the standards of this sector, although this is not necessarily identified in R&D expenditure figures. For the companies concerned, available data suggest that this has been around one per cent of turnover per annum at the Weir Group, with an R&D lab being opened in Alloa in 1980 to provide a range of facilities for simulating pump operating conditions; and about three per cent in Anderson Strathclyde in recent years. Babcock Power have had a large research and development centre at Renfrew since 1932 engaged in research into nuclear and fossil-fired power generation plant. Nevertheless, the companies' innovative records have not always been reflected in their marketing performance. Major criticism has been levelled at Weir's failure to exploit their lead in desalination technology in this regard.[17]

In the context of this book, the local linkages associated with these firms is of considerable importance. Such data are most readily available for Anderson Strathclyde.[18] Two-thirds of its component supplies were Scottish in the early 1980s against the Scottish industrial average of just under one quarter. Given the strong local traditions of the other five companies it is highly probable that they are also well above that average.

Viewed as a whole, these companies stand out principally because of their size; and, as such, their problems epitomise those of the sectors in which they operate. The recent financial performance has been mediocre for most of the firms. They remain highly traditional enterprises, which have been managed as such, although at the same time there are some indications of appropriate response to major changes in their trading environment. Strategic planning and marketing functions remain weak in several of them, and improvements in these managerial areas are critical if they are to remain competitive by international standards.

Dominant Issues for the Future. Several of these companies have been in the public eye in recent years for quite different reasons: Anderson Strathclyde in 1982–83 arising from the disputed bid by Charter Consolidated; JBE in 1982 and 1983 because of the threat of US sanctions against the Siberian pipeline, which highlighted its dependence on the GE licensing agreement, and because of the financial difficulties of the John Brown Group; the Weir Group in 1980–81 because of the financial reconstruction of the company; and Babcock International because of the problems of planning in the power plant industry, within the highly uncertain environment in the UK. Each of these experiences is critical to the future direction of the companies. While in some senses quite distinct to the individual firms concerned, they are illustrative of general themes influencing the future of Scottish manufacturing industry. Thus, the consequences of external control for the Scottish economy, the potential disbenefits of certain forms of technology transfer and the inability to finance and control expansion are issues of general relevance. For such reasons these dominant issues are briefly considered.

The Acquisition of Anderson Strathclyde. In May 1982, Charter Consolidated (CC), who already owned 28·4 per cent of Anderson Strathclyde (AS), decided to launch a full bid for the company. CC viewed AS as fitting into their investment plans, and regarded itself as being able to finance more rapid expansion of the company than would be possible if it remained independent. At the time Charter were underinvested, with their last balance sheet before the bid showing assets of £497 million and debt of some £42 million. From the beginning the AS board rejected the bid, vigorously denouncing any of the alleged benefits which might emerge from being a subsidiary of a financial conglomerate. In June 1982, the matter was referred to the Monopolies and Mergers Commission (MMC).

The Charter Consolidated case rested on a number of issues.[19] Weaknesses were alleged in Anderson Strathclyde including inadequate financial resources, which were reflected in insufficient investment in plant and in product development. In the CC view the AS ability to finance the future would diminish because of rising competition, an increasing rate of technical change, the growing need to develop effective overseas marketing and the rising demand for working capital. Anticipating counter-arguments, CC indicated that location, type of manufacture and employment would remain unchanged in the event of a merger. The evidence from informed opinion in Scotland supported the Anderson Strathclyde case, which was based heavily on the record of the company in product development, marketing and servicing, and on the view that none of these areas would benefit from CC control.[20] Adverse effects were rather to be expected in terms of managerial efficiency, the possibilities of rationalising AS activity round new control centres and so on. In addition, AS anticipated considerable damage to the Scottish economy in areas such as maintaining a stock of professional and engineering skills, subcontracting and in career opportunities for senior management.

The MMC were not unanimous in their findings. The majority group found against the merger, laying particular emphasis on its potential adverse effects on managerial effectiveness, labour relations and employment. The minority note of dissent was, however, accepted. The Government decision was based on the significance of the case for competition policy generally rather than with the position of Scottish companies alone. Nevertheless, in allowing Charter to bid, this was the first time the Government had overruled the MMC. This is a formidable precedent given the inadequacy of the rationale profferred for the course of action. Without adjustments in the terms of reference of the MMC, this case poses real problems about how any Scottish company mounts a defence against such a bid in the future. At a corporate level, this incident is crucial to the future of Anderson Strathclyde. Taking stock of the evidence, AS emerges as a company with a good record of performance, but with a need to accelerate away from some of the traditions of the past which lay inadequate stress on marketing, product development and overall strategic planning. Given independence, these issues could perhaps have been tackled from a Scottish base. But the possibilities were not to be: AS failed in the High Court in its bid to challenge the Government decision to permit the takeover proposal to go ahead, and a substantially increased offer price to shareholders was enough to complete the acquisition in May 1983. As Table 5.5 (above) shows, this reduces still further the ever-diminishing stock of indigenous Scottish engineering companies, with no indication that the process is at an end. It is interesting, on a related point, that Howden confirmed its commitment to a Scottish headquarters for the company at the end of 1982, commenting that a move outside Scotland leaves firms 'like gutted fish'.[21]

John Brown Engineering and US Sanctions Against the Soviet Union. An interesting series of questions emerged about some aspects of the future of John Brown Engineering during 1982. The company had a contract to supply twenty-one turbines for the Siberia-West Europe gas pipeline, which immediately came under threat following the ban by the US Reagan administration on the supply of goods and technology to that project. The JBE problem stemmed both from the fact that it manufactured the turbines under licence from General Electric and from its dependence on rotor blades made in the US to fulfil its contract. On the one hand, the company faced commercial pressures and penalties for non-performance on the contract and, on the other, the ultimate challenge to its licensing arrangement. The situation was further complicated by the UK Trade Secretary's invoking of the Protection of Trading Interests Act 1980. This was designed to protect UK companies when demands placed on them by foreign governments are considered to be against the national interest. This course of action set off US reprisals, blocking the export of oil and gas technology to the John Brown Group. In the event, JBE were able to complete the turbine order using some of the spare rotors ordered by the USSR from the only European source of supply, Alsthom Atlantique in France. The US sanctions, after intense international pressure, were ended in November 1982. There is little doubt that this incident drew attention to the vulnerability of the Clydebank operation and caused considerable uncertainty for the workforce.

The links between JBE and GE were also an issue in the negotiations between John Brown and Hawker Siddeley for the sale of the turbine division. It was reported that General Electric was unhappy about the proposed deal, which could have turned Hawker Siddeley into a serious rival.[22]

The Rescue and Reconstruction of the Weir Group. A number of the factors underlying the Weir reconstruction have already been considered. In such cases there is always a question as to the appropriate balance of internal and external factors precipitating the crisis which so damaged its equity base. But the background document detailing the financial rescue gave heavy weight to the former, noting that major deficiencies were uncovered in the estimating and management reporting systems in Weir Pumps, leading to cost overruns on major contracts. The effect of the reconstruction plan early in 1981 was to reduce borrowings by some £16 million and the percentage of net borrowings to shareholders' capital from 168 per cent to 65 per cent. The financial package put together by Finance Corporation for Industry, Equity Capital for Industry, the Royal Bank of Scotland and the SDA, acting as a catalyst, amounted to around $50 million in total. This package, combined with a substantial cost reduction programme and management changes in the pumps division gave the Weir Group another chance. Since these events, the Group has made a remarkable recovery in spite of the recession conditions. Problems of industrial relations perhaps still remain, as indicated by a sit-in which took place late in 1982 to protest about the transfer of various administrative activities from Alloa to Cathcart. The transfer of the company's desalination operation from Cathcart to the South of England has, furthermore, probably weakened the Scottish end of the firm.

There are a number of important lessons from the Weir case. Some of them relate to the level of managerial skills in technically competent companies; others to the long-run effects of recession and undercapitalisation on the ability of formerly sound companies to continue; still more to the ability of the existing financial community to gain access to companies in such difficulties and derive creative strategies for their reconstruction. There is little question that the Scottish engineering industry currently contains many companies with symptoms akin to those shown by the Weir Group before 1981. The challenge to all concerned is to get close enough to help while the operations remain viable. In this instance, the SDA played a valuable and innovative role in the financial support and restructuring, but earlier intervention would clearly have been desirable. The onus is also on company managements to look for assistance and to allow others to help in appropriate circumstances.

Babcock International and Strategy for the UK Power Plant Industry. Several of the companies reviewed in this section are very dependent on public sector purchasing, but none more so than Babcock's Scottish operation in its role as a supplier of power station boilers. From the mid-1970s, there have been frequent discussions at all levels concerning rationalisation of the power plant industry – relating to Babcock and Clarke Chapman in boilers and GEC and Reyrolle Parsons in turbines. A Think Tank report recommended rationalisation so as to create a single UK enterprise in both these lines of activity. Babcock and Clarke Chapman failed to agree on a merger and the latter went ahead with Reyrolle Parsons to form a new company, Northern Engineering. Discussions then extended for a period of eighteen months between Babcock and Northern Engineering, until these were abandoned in summer 1978, in part because of a failure to reach agreement on the means of allocating redundancies between Gateshead (the Northern Engineering boilermaking facility) and Renfrew.

The problems of the power plant industry were first brought into focus when government intervention was required to bring forward the CEGB order for the Drax B power station as a means of preventing large-scale redundancies in Babcock and the other supplying firms. Having obtained the lion's share of boiler orders for Drax B, however, the Renfrew plant was allocated only a small share of contracts for the Torness and Heysham power stations in 1980. It was this setback which forced the company into its reorganisation and re-equipment programme and into a more active search for export orders. The difficulties of the latter seem likely to mean that further pressures to rationalise the whole power plant industry will emerge, well before new UK power station orders are placed at the end of the present decade or later.

Questions such as the need for long-term ordering strategies to smooth out work for the manufacturers without creating excess capacity and on the desirability of a stable home market base to keep down costs arise forcefully in this case; and although the extent of their involvement in power station work cannot be compared with Babcock's, some other companies, such as Howden and Weir, are affected too, while Anderson Strathclyde is highly dependent on the publicly-owned NCB.

The Engineering and Metals Sector and Industrial Policy

Policy Issues in Engineering. The above review has considered the position of the engineering industry in Scotland alone. Yet many of the well-publicised problems of the industry are shared equally by engineering enterprises elsewhere in the UK; these problems and weaknesses, in turn, could almost be applied generally to British manufacturing industry (and in some ways explain why Government measures have tended to be of general application rather than tied to particular sectors). Among the issues highlighted by recent investigations such as the Finniston Report[23] included, at the very fundamental level, the need for enhanced recognition of the nature and importance of engineering; the requirement for a greater commitment to engineering from the school level upwards, derived from present deficiencies in the education and training of engineers; competitive weakness arising from the lack of innovative strategies by engineering firms and antipathy to technology-based change from company employees and trades unions; failure to compensate for deficiences in internal innovation (through R&D) by the purchase of licences and patents; weaknesses in transferring new technology within the engineering dimension, and particularly to smaller firms; problems in companies' market responsiveness and the compartmentalisation of functional activities meaning, for example, research conducted with little or no assessment of market needs, or products designed with insufficient attention to the demands of production; and the hindrances to the production of standardised, internationally-competitive goods arising from the plethora of rival domestic and international technical standards.

Reviewing the detailed work of the NEDO Sector Working Parties (SWPs) in engineering (especially heavy engineering to maintain the focus on this sector of the industry), there are again various common themes which occur. A number of these focus on problems posed by the performance of the macro-economy, but, in addition, industry-level and firm-level issues highlighted include:

> The need for productivity improvements, through the progressive uptake of new technology in manufacturing systems, better labour utilisation (relating to flexibility, commitment, training and participation), and improvements in the utilisation of capacity.

> More generally, a requirement for greater exploitation of computer technology for design, detailing and estimating to improve production and as an aid to better marketing.

> Improvements in marketing effectiveness, covering everything from product standards to the arrangement of inward and outward trade missions.

> Skilled work force recruitment and retention.

> Maker/user relationships – 'poor service' by UK suppliers in terms of price, quality and availability.

> Public purchasing questions – the need to plan the flow of work and orders to individual firms; uncertainties over nationalised industries' plans; preference for UK engineering companies.

> Export performance – identifying opportunities; facilities for testing machinery against foreign specification; supply of free trial installation; need to assist companies not involved in exporting through joint marketing, joint contracting, etc.

> Import penetration from Japanese firms and from foreign companies which have established themselves in the UK and increasingly act as importers (although these imports may be offset by exports in such MNEs).

Some of these points apply quite directly to the heavy engineering industry in Scotland as well as that elsewhere in the UK. For example, the key role of the public sector as buyers of the industry's products emerged very strongly in the case studies. So, too, did the issue of the application of computer technology to improve productivity and competitiveness. The need to compete in world markets and reduce dependency on the UK was an important theme. And internationalisation, whether through a greater export-orientation or direct manufacturing abroad or, indeed, through licensor or licensee activities, was also shown to be of major significance in a Scottish context. In addition, however, a number of issues were raised in the earlier discussion which were of specific relevance to Scotland. The question of external control loomed large throughout; the fact that so few indigenous companies exist as 'sector leaders' places a constraint on the possibilities of using these firms as instruments of industrial policy, but more generally raises question marks over policy towards the engineering industry in Scotland. A second major question which only has its counterpart in other regional economies within the UK is that of sub-contracting, and the potential for stimulating local linkages. The different structure of the engineering industry in Scotland, with its stronger base in heavy engineering, also changes the problem emphasis in this country.

Existing Policies for the Engineering Industry. In considering existing policies, little attention is given to the electronics sector since this is dealt with elsewhere in the book. Outside this sector, nearly all schemes to assist the industry are UK-wide in scope, and the most important of these in financial terms, viz. regional financial assistance, is not even industry-specific. It would be helpful if it could be established whether or not the assistance available has had an impact on helping to overcome the deficiencies of the industry as outlined in the previous paragraphs, but this is not possible. Regional policy measures are not, in fact, directed specifically at issues of industrial efficiency and other industrial problems. Because of data deficiencies, the following section is restricted to a summary of the major schemes which affect engineering firms either exclusively or as part of wider industrial support measures.

Investment Assistance. Included within this heading are the variety of regional incentives available. Comprehensive measures of evaluation are not available for the various forms of assistance, but one possible way ahead is to consider take-up rates by sector.

Detailed data, relating to Scotland alone, are available for offers of selective financial assistance (SFA) within the major MLHs studied previously (Table 5.13). The growing importance of electronics is reflected clearly in the SFA offers, accounting for two-fifths of total offer value in the years 1972–75 but nearly three-fifths in the 1979–82 period. Similarly, within the electronics sector the proportion of offers to foreign as opposed to indigenous firms has been increasing. The other major beneficiaries of SFA offers have been MLHs 333, 339 and 341 (pumps, valves, machinery, plant and steelwork). The share of assistance directed to these sectors reflects their capital spending programmes (see Table 5.8, above) and, to the extent that in certain of these industries productivity is good by UK standards, there is some indication of financial assistance supporting Scottish comparative advantage, which is clearly desirable. On the other hand, a case could also presumably be made out for financial

Table 5.13. SFA offers to engineering firms in Scotland (numbers and value £m).

Minimum list heading	1972–75 No.	Value	1976–78 No.	Value	1979–82 No.	Value	1972–82 No.	% of total	Value	% of total	Share of total value by MLH to non-overseas-owned companies 1972–82	1979–82
311, 312 Iron & steel; steel tubes	7	0·2	13	0·6	12	2·7	32	6·9	3·5	2·5	n.a.	n.a.
333, 339 Pumps, valves, machinery, 341 plant & steelwork etc.	35	7·5	30	4·7	47	17·4	112	24·0	29·7	20·8	51·9	61·4
354 Scientific & industrial instruments & systems	15	3·6	9	2·3	12	3·8	36	7·7	9·7	6·8	39·3	63·3
361, 368 Electrical machinery & appliances	7	0·8	5	1·2	14	5·3	26	5·6	7·2	5·1	n.a.	n.a.
363–367 Telegraph, telephone, radio, electronic components, computers etc.	21	7·8	25	5·1	59	49·9	105	22·5	62·8	44·0	19·2	7·7
370 Shipbuilding & marine engineering	21	8·3	21	5·9	14	3·2	56	12·0	17·4	12·2	n.a.	n.a.
381, 383 Motor vehicles, aerospace equipment, etc.	3	0·5	11	1·5	20	6·7	34	7·3	8·7	6·1	n.a.	n.a.
399 Metal industries n.e.s.	13	0·4	21	1·2	32	2·1	66	14·1	3·7	2·6	n.a.	n.a.
Total of above	122	28·9	135	22·5	210	91·2	467	100·0	142·6	100·0	45·8	36·7
Electronics (MLH 363–367+354)	36	11·4	34	7·4	71	53·7	141	30·2	72·5	50·8	21·9	11·7

Source: SCOMER.

aid to assist industrial restructuring and productivity improvements in weaker sectors.

Sectoral and General Schemes of Assistance under Section 8 of the Industry Act 1972. Sectoral Schemes: these are all to be seen in the context of the widening of the use of 'selective' assistance from the early 1970s in the UK, but they ceased to be a central feature of industrial policy when the Conservative Government came into power in 1979. The general aim of the sectoral schemes was to improve the efficiency and competitiveness of companies by encouraging new product development and investment in contemporary technology.

The range of these schemes in the engineering industry is shown in Table 5.14. Some payments are still being made, but all had closed for offers by end April 1979 and none was open for more than two years. What is very striking is the very low Scottish share of offers and payments: except in the ferrous foundry scheme Scotland did not account for more than 5·5 per cent of assistance offered. Rates of take-up are influenced by industrial structure and there are other part-explanations in the fact that there is some trade-off between assistance obtained under Section 7 as opposed to Section 8 of the Industry Act. On the other hand, Section 8 assistance was designed to be project-specific, whereas Section 7 aid could be granted on a more general basis for expenditures on new plant and equipment and buildings. Even if the option was available to companies, the fact that Section 8 assistance was generally available at higher rates (as low as 15 per cent on buildings for some schemes, but as high as 33·3 per cent in the microelectronics scheme latterly) should have been an incentive for them to use this source of funds. What is perhaps relevant is that Section 7 assistance is administered in Scotland whereas the sectoral schemes were handled through the Department of Trade and Industry in London.

Small Engineering Firms' Investment Scheme (SEFIS): this £30 million scheme (SEFIS I) was introduced in March 1982, being designed to assist firms in the UK engineering industry with fewer than 200 employees. The aim of the scheme was to accelerate investment in new, advanced types of capital equipment, including machine tools operating under NC, CNC or microprocessor control; non-robotic welding equipment; metrology equipment; and laser or plasma technology equipment. While there are no figures on the value of applications, SEFIS I specified a maximum of £200000 and a minimum of £15000 with at most two machines being bought: successful applicants were eligible for a 33·3 per cent grant. Following a very strong response, SEFIS I was closed on May 28, 1982. In terms of number of applications, Scotland was very under-represented, accounting for only 87 out of 1748 (5·0 per cent); by comparison, the South-East accounted for 33 per cent of applications and the West Midlands for 19·3 per cent.[24]

Table 5.14. Sectoral schemes of assistance under Section 8, Industry Act 1972. (offers and payments in Scotland to 31 March 1981).

Scheme	Date of introduction	Closing date for applications	Number of offers	Scottish share of UK total	Assistance offered (£000)	Scottish share of UK total	Payments (£000)	Scottish share of UK total
Ferrous foundry	5/8/75	31/12/76	32	9·1	6182	10·0	4832	10·5
Machine tool	5/8/75	31/12/77	13	4·2	1196	3·5	601	3·0
Non-ferrous foundry	24/1/77	31/7/78	11	4·3	333	1·5	230	2·4
Electronic components	24/1/77	31/12/78	3	3·4	168	0·9	104	1·0
Instrumentation & automation	1/11/77	30/4/79	4	2·4	55	0·6	29	0·6
Drop forging	8/11/77	30/6/79	1	1·1	18	0·3	9	0·4
Printing machinery manufacturers	13/8/76	31/12/77	1	1·7	28	0·2	14	0·2
Textile machinery manufacturers	13/8/76	31/12/77	3	5·6	71	0·6	24	0·4
Microelectronics Industry Support Programme[1]	26/7/78	to be completed by 31/3/85	3	6·8	827	5·5	131	2·1

[1]Date relate to period ending March 31, 1982.
Source: *Industry Act 1972. Annual Report*, HMSO (London), HC460, 1981 and HC503, 1982.

Given that SEFIS I was heavily oversubscribed, a new scheme (SEFIS II) was introduced more recently. The employment limit for applicants was raised to 500, with all businesses, including subsidiaries of foreign firms, being eligible. Moreover, the scheme is no longer restricted to firms in SIC Division 3. Some of the criticisms of the earlier scheme, namely that the size limit of 200 employees was excessively restrictive and that firms outside SIC Division 3, yet employing advanced technology, were excluded, have thus been overcome. Yet such changes will not assist Scotland unless utilisation of the schemes increases substantially. Knowledge of the schemes should be very widespread, for the IDD wrote individually to every small engineering company employing over 10 in Scotland about SEFIS.

General Schemes: under the heading of general schemes in Section 8 come those schemes which are available to engineering enterprises although they are not designed solely for this sector. These include the Energy Conservation Scheme and the Small Firms Loan Guarantee Scheme. The last scheme proved extremely popular following its introduction in June 1981 and the allocation was doubled to £300 million in the 1982 Budget. No analyses by sector for Scotland are available, but overall Scotland received just 211 guarantees valued at £6 million in the period up to March 31, 1982, representing 6·5 per cent of the UK total in terms of guarantees and 5·3 per cent of value.

Innovation Assistance, Export Assistance, etc. Reflecting changing policy philosophy and priorities, a number of schemes have recently been introduced to support industrial innovation. In May 1982, the Department of Industry amalgamated its Product and Process Development Scheme and the assistance available for longer-term R&D from its various Requirements Boards, and increased the maximum level of what is now termed 'Support for Innovation' to one third. Up to November 1982, some £40 million had been offered; no regional breakdown was available but it seems that engineering in general has been the main beneficiary. Then in June 1982, the £60 million Flexible Manufacturing Scheme, designed to assist industry with the cost of adopting more advanced manufacturing technology, was set up. The scheme is designed to aid batch production processes by combining microelectronics and mechanical engineering to bring economies of scale to bear, and it includes the application of robotics. No figures have been published yet.

Other recent schemes include Computer Aided Design and Computer Aided Manufacture – CADCAM; Computer Aided Design, Manufacture and Test – CADMAT; and Computer Aided Design and Test Equipment Support – CADTES. In all these schemes, grants of up to one third are payable.

A number of schemes which have been operating for a longer period of time (since 1978) go under the generic title of the Microelectronics

Application Project (MAP). Under MAP, a variety of activity is promoted, covering awareness, training, feasibility studies (known as MAPCON) and technology application grants. Especial interest attaches to MAPCON because of the analysis of the programme which has been undertaken in Scotland.[25] The industrial distribution of MAPCON applicants was considered and compared with the actual and 'expected' number of applications (on the basis of the ratio of Scottish to UK employment). It emerged that in the mechanical, instrument and electrical engineering Orders, the number of applications was only between one quarter and one half of the expected level. While not broken down on an industry basis, it is also interesting that foreign-owned firms and British headquarters of multi-plant firms were both much more likely than average to apply for MAPCON assistance.

To complete the picture, there are a range of other existing or recently-introduced schemes of advice and assistance which the Government run or have recently run. These are the various export schemes, about which IDD are in regular contact through visiting officers with engineering companies in Scotland. There is the Manufacturing Advisory Service and the Small Firms Technical Enquiry Service; and there are various MSC initiatives.

The Work of the National Economic Development Office. As implied by the descriptive comments above, there has been very little by way of evaluation of this wide range of financial support and other measures; although the DTI has now begun to commission studies of the impact of certain of the schemes on the efficiency, capacity and trading performance of the industries. What can be said is that the schemes only have the potential to impact upon *some* of the industry weaknesses as outlined above. They may be valuable in encouraging and accelerating the use of new technology and effect productivity improvements, but do not directly have an influence upon issues such as marketing effectiveness and more general marketing questions; export performance and import substitution; and shortages of skilled workers. It is in such areas that the activities of NEDO, principally through its Sector Working Parties, should be particularly important. Of course, the work of the SWPs and EDCs cannot be disassociated from the Schemes discussed above, since a number of these have been shaped by both the findings and pressures of the NEDO groups. Nevertheless, one of their main contributions should have derived from tackling other detailed sectoral problems. Thus, for instance, in late 1980 the Pumps and Valves SWP decided to establish an Overseas Trade Committee (OTC) to encourage joint export marketing ventures (noting that in Germany there existed a common marketing company that sells the production of a number of German valve manufacturers), to investigate the possibilities of using export houses, to identify target markets, assist in export missions through the British Valve

Manufacturers Association, etc.[26] The Mining Machinery SWP has been similarly active on the export side:[27] agreement was reached in 1978 with PD/NCB Consultants that it would act on behalf of the sector and attempt to identify potential total export packages in developing countries in order to secure contracts which would be supplied by British mining machinery companies; and the SWP was able to obtain agreement on the establishment of a facility for testing mining machinery in the UK against foreign specifications (a service which is necessary for the American market in particular).

The effectiveness of the different committees has varied, quite apart from problems relating to the implementation of their recommendations, and in any event, the period since 1979 has seen a reduction in the number of EDCs and SWPs as part of the process of disengagement. Nevertheless, the potential for further development of the NEDO work does exist, providing the political climate is right. Reflecting this, the Finniston Report recommended that the role of the NEDC should be enhanced and re-oriented in a number of ways.[28] It was suggested that the NEDC machinery should be used to bring together the relevant bodies to develop a national policy for standards and quality;[29] and, more generally, to incorporate the lessons from a number of joint industry-Government exercises concerning the development of closer liaison between UK purchasing and supplying industries, the role of the design function in manufacturing industry and so forth. The NEDC was seen as adopting the role of catalysts in setting priorities for action at national, sectoral and company level; as part of this, it was recommended that the economic and industrial expertise of the NEDO Office would benefit from the recruitment of staff who could contribute engineering and technological expertise to policy deliberations.

The Engineering and Metals Sector and Policy in Scotland

The Scottish Dimension. It is probably fair to say that while the affairs of the engineering industry have been a major preoccupation of policy makers in Scotland, the activity has mainly been at a corporate-specific level and of a defensive nature. Excluding the SDA electronics initiative, there have been few attempts to devise and implement sectoral policies for engineering as such. This deficiency is only partly explained by the similarity of problems between Scotland and the UK. Recognising the importance of the sector for the Scottish economy, the Agency, through its Small Business Division, has formed a working party to develop sub-contract links. This has the support of some of the major engineering enterprises, including Rolls Royce, the Weir Group, Anderson Strathclyde, and potentially many more. Its success will depend on the flexibility of users in their purchasing behaviour, the degree to which suppliers can respond to the needs of users and on the Agency's ability to assist the process by matching users' needs with suppliers' capabilities. As yet, it is much too early to draw any conclusions on the impact of the project.

The SDA is also involved in engineering through its corporate investment in shares and loans. At the end of March 1982, the SDA had an equity participation in forty-seven companies, of which eleven were in electronics and computers and seventeen were in engineering and allied industries.[30] Of those firms in receipt of large loans (exceeding £50000), engineering was less well represented, although by far the largest loan was to an aero-engineering enterprise – Caledonian Airmotives Ltd (£3.4 million).

Finally, and relevant to engineering and other manufacturing sectors, the work of the Agency's Technology Transfer Unit should be mentioned. The aim of this is to promote joint ventures and licensing arrangements. At present, the main targets as potential licensors are US companies, and certainly the John Brown experience does indicate the potential benefits through such link-ups. The work of the Unit is still at an experimental stage, and there must be some question as to how such an operation should actually operate. Currently, the Unit is engaged in the very time-consuming activity of both identifying potential partners for Scottish firms and then negotiating terms and conditions of licensing agreements. For this same 'hands-on' procedure to be applied on a larger scale would be extremely resource-intensive.

New Approaches in Scotland. The discussion of UK policy measures and their operation in Scotland, and the brief review of Scottish initiatives above, do highlight weaknesses which might be amenable to new policy approaches. This concluding section, therefore, makes some suggestions for change, which are compatible with the existing policy framework and philosophy in the UK. The latter proviso is important: regeneration of the engineering industry, according to the Finniston Report, needs to start in the schools. Some might argue that such an approach would require a comprehensive planning strategy for the UK economy as a whole, which attempts to bring about changes in the educational, social and institutional system to put the emphasis on creating a climate to foster innovation and boost productivity. In terms of the implications for (although not the objectives of) policy, this approach would be at odds with present Government philosophy, although it might be possible to alter educational content and attitudes in other ways, in particular by engendering a change in attitudes to engineering skills. The second point which is relevant is that financial support schemes have been moving away from the regional and sectoral towards the national and issue-oriented (technology applications as an issue, for example).

Notwithstanding these remarks, there are a number of areas where the Scottish Office and the SDA could have an impact on the growth and performance of the engineering industry as follows:

Finance Issues. There is a real need to investigate the reasons for the apparently low take-up in Scotland of the sectoral and general schemes of financial support. It has been remarked in a UK context that despite the huge growth of 'awareness brokers', the current proliferation of programmes 'has lacked impact through a combination of sheer volume, fragmentation, lack of relevance and basic indifference from industrial recipients.'[31] There is only anecdotal evidence in Scotland concerning problems stemming from the proliferation of programmes and there could be merit in initiating formal investigation of this. Further study is also required into the effectiveness of advertising and other promotional material and of the role of the advisory services on the ground. As Chapter 3 on the Small-Firm Sector revealed, the involvement of various public sector bodies in industrial development in Scotland is far from making the best use of resources.

There are two additional points worth making. The first is the very practical one that Scottish take-up might be raised substantially if the schemes were administered in Scotland, as is the case with Section 7 assistance under the Industry Act 1972. It has been argued that even where there is little discretion locally, the mere fact that Government personnel in Scotland talk directly to companies and are implicated in decision-making is just as important. But in terms of flexibility of approach, degree of commitment and speed of processing, the advantages would seem to lie in local administration. Related to this is the fact that there is normally a fixed national budget for each of the Department of Trade and Industry's innovation schemes with no allocation of that budget between regions. If this was changed so that there was a Scottish allocation and Scottish administration, there would at least be pressure on the Scottish Office to spend its budget. There would, of course, be a question as to what the budget should be in each instance: this would have to be related in some way to the Scottish presence within the area being supported. For example, Scotland has obtained a negligible share of expenditure under the Fibre Optics Scheme, because the country is scarcely represented in that sector. The second point is equally important and concerns the types of schemes being promoted. The Scottish Office has probably had a significant influence on the nature of regional policy over the years, to the benefit of Scotland. With the declining importance of regional support measures, there should be a commensurate build-up in Scottish Office expertise relating to general support schemes. In this way, it might be possible to influence the nature of the schemes promoted to the Scottish advantage. Such issues are not unique to engineering, but are bound to impact most on engineering because of its importance within manufacturing industry. The evidence of this chapter has been that the distribution of industry between Scotland and the UK is not outstandingly different at the Order level, but there are important differences in structure and performance within sectors and sub-sectors. Analysis at this level could facilitate identification of industry segments where Scottish advantage lies, information which could then be used in formulating and adapting investment and innovation programmes.

Managerial Issues. A whole range of issues are covered here, including the need to improve innovative capacities, marketing and design, manufacturing management, exporting and other forms of internationalisation, etc. The sympathies of the present authors lie with the NEDO-type approach, involving working intensively with interested parties over specific sectoral problems. But the NEDO approach is most effective where problem themes are identified which are general across the sector; firm-specific problems cannot be tackled in this way, mainly because these are areas which management consider to be solely their own preserve. However, this type of limited sectoral planning is no longer in vogue, and, in any event, some of the SWPs themselves have commented on the lack of awareness of the industrial strategy work within industry and trades unions.

There are various ways in which the NEDO work might be utilised or built upon for the benefit of Scottish engineering. The simplest would be to see that the findings and recommendations of the SWPs are communicated to companies within the particular sectors in Scotland. Another possibility would be to try to obtain Scottish representation on the SWPs: there are already Scottish members in the sense that, for example, a Howden Group executive is a member of the Fluid Power SWP but not as a Scottish representative. More radically, consideration might be given to creating some equivalent forum within Scotland itself. It might be feasible to establish on an experimental basis two or three Engineering Working Groups (EWGs), focusing on those heavy engineering sectors which seem to have potential. Pumps, valves and compressors (MLH 333) represents one possibility where there have been problems, but potential also exists on the basis of the data presented earlier; the number of enterprises in the sector is sufficiently small, furthermore, to permit wide company representation. Incentives would be required to encourage private sector participation: these would be seen in terms of public sector assistance, financial or otherwise, for schemes which could be of benefit to the industry or the individual firm. The work of the EWGs would, therefore, be concerned with identifying issues which are of major concern, perhaps using SDA-commissioned research studies as a starting point; and then making claims on funds, making representations to Government, taking joint company initiatives or whatever was necessary to resolve the problems in the interests of efficiency and competitiveness. Composition of the groups would be seen to consist primarily of company representatives, so that responsibility was placed very firmly on the private sector. The tripartite composition of the NEDO SWPs would be maintained by trades union representation plus a representative from the SDA, SEPD and perhaps the local authorities; the latter would be especially important where there was a particular area concentration of engineering firms and perhaps Area Development initiatives under way.

This still leaves the question of firm-specific policy, which in the form of financial assistance to Weir has already been shown to have had an important bearing on the continuance of the company in its existing shape. The discussion in Chapter 4 on the foreign-owned sector made a strong plea for greater attention to be paid to the development of the existing stock of multinational subsidiaries through a monitoring and enterprise development programme. The inclusion of the large Scottish companies within such a programme would seem logical. The major stumbling-block would seem to relate to company attitudes to any such scheme.

Other Issues. A variety of other issues require comment. First is the question of external control in the engineering industry and its consequences for the economy. This covers both overseas ownership and other UK ownership. Perhaps nothing can or should be done about the increasing level of external control in engineering deriving, say, from take-over bids from English-headquartered companies, and many would argue that it would be quite wrong to try to protect Scottish companies from normal market pressures. Yet the consequences, *inter alia*, in terms of a likely shift in the centre of decision-making are real and undesirable. While resolution of the problem is outwith the scope of any Scottish industrial policy, this is less true of the increasing penetration of overseas-controlled enterprises in the economy. Thus, the latter trend is partly a consequence of a decision to commit resources in this direction, rather than towards indigenous companies. Such questions are discussed more fully elsewhere, but what emerges strongly from this present chapter is the need to support heavy engineering, a sector which, as it happens, contains most domestically-owned enterprises. It must be admitted that desirable trends in the behaviour of indigenous firms, as regards, for example, the need for a greater international orientation, may themselves lead to the transfer out of Scotland of certain decision-making activities, in areas such as marketing. In that sense some of the distinctions between companies on the basis of ownership could be rather artificial. Any policy measures designed to ameliorate the problems associated with a branch economy should be directed at all large, multi-plant enterprises.

A further question to be raised concerns public sector purchasing. This question, which primarily concerns the buying policies and investment programmes of the nationalised industries, is again outside the scope of resolution at a Scottish level. Nevertheless, the implications for major Scottish engineering firms are very significant. Despite the encouragement which needs to be given to market and product diversification in such companies, they are bound to remain for the foreseeable future heavily dependent on the vagaries of Government policy towards the nationalised industries. The fact that Scotland is affected disproportionately as an area within the UK because of the nature of its engineering specialisation, may be a strong argument which can be used in representations to Central Government on this question.

There has been very little comment in this chapter on innovation in Scottish engineering, although many of the Government schemes reviewed earlier are designed to assist the take-up of new technology. As regards the actual creation of such technology, studies have commented adversely on British innovative performance across a wide range of industry[32] and there is no reason to distinguish Scotland from the rest of the UK. Interesting efforts are being made to harness University research efforts for industrial purposes, and Scotland is well placed in this regard. One major resource which is located in Scotland is the National Engineering Laboratory (NEL) at East Kilbride, which is one of six research establishments in the UK for which the Department of Industry is responsible. NEL was established in 1947 in order to conduct R&D in a variety of areas of mechanical engineering. The work of the Laboratory at present falls into two main categories, that paid for by the Government and that undertaken directly for or in collaboration with industry on a repayment basis; in both cases the work covers test, design, simulation, the provision of software consultancy and so forth. As at Autumn 1983, NEL was handling 250 contracts for some 400 clients. Over the period April 1982 to March 1983, Scotland accounted for 35 per cent of these contracts by number but only 6 per cent by value; by comparison, the South-East of England represented 18 per cent of contracts by both number and value.[33] Staffing levels have been reduced over a period from 930 to 650, and on the basis of this and the contract distribution figures, there would seem to be a case for a review of NEL's activities with the objective of raising its contribution to Scottish engineering.

Concluding Remarks

This chapter has focused on the very heterogeneous but also extremely important manufacturing sector of engineering, giving particular attention to the heavy electrical and mechanical industries. On the basis of Scotland's differential presence within various sectors of engineering and very mixed performance, the case has been argued for a number of new or adapted policy approaches. Accepting the existing policy framework, these relate to methods of improving the take-up by Scottish industry of the various schemes of assistance available nationally. With the stronger orientation of policy towards innovation assistance and other general

171

support schemes, there would seem, moreover, to be a need to increase Scottish involvement in the formulation of such schemes: this is related to the whole question of the role of the Scottish Office in an era when regional assistance is no longer the major instrument of policy.

Many of the problems of the engineering industry in Scotland and elsewhere in the UK were shown to derive from weaknesses in marketing and design, manufacturing management, exporting methods and so on, and cannot be remedied through schemes of financial assistance. Controversially, in the light of the moves away from sectoral planning in the UK, what is suggested is the establishment on an experimental basis of a number of Engineering Working Groups (EWGs) in Scotland. Their role would be that of problem identification and the promotion of initiatives to resolve the problem in the interests of efficiency and competitiveness. The EWGs would be composed primarily of private sector members together with representation from trades unions, SDA, SEPD and perhaps the local authorities. This still leaves open the question of firm-specific policy, and in this regard the monitoring and enterprise development programme suggested for the multinational sector (Chapter 4) should probably be extended to include large indigenous enterprises.

The policy issues emerging from the analysis of the industry are extended further to include some discussion of external ownership, public sector purchasing policies and investment programmes, innovation, etc. To many, inevitably, the overriding problem concerns employment levels in the industry and the loss of 100000 jobs in Scottish engineering between 1971 and 1982. It must be admitted that the employment creation impact of the initiatives suggested here is likely to be quite small, with the emphasis being on improving industrial efficiency and competitiveness.

NOTES AND REFERENCES

1. N.K.Buxton, 'Economic Growth in Scotland Between the Wars: The Role of Production Structure and Rationalization', *Economic History Review*, Second Series, vol.34, no.4, 1981, pp.538–55.
2. The sources for the statistics quoted are as follows: *Scottish Economic Bulletin*, no.26, 1983; *Annual Abstract of Statistics*, 1983 edition; C.Lythe & M.Majmudar, *The Renaissance of the Scottish Economy?*, George Allen & Unwin (London), 1982, Table 2.6.
3. *Ibid.*, p.14.
4. Calculated from Lythe & Majmudar (n.2), p.58.
5. NEDC, *Electronic Components SWP* (London), October 1981.
6. *Business Monitor*, PA1002, 1977.
7. Scottish Development Agency, *Scottish Engineering: Subcontract and Component Supply Industry* (Glasgow), n.d.
8. See, for example, the findings of some of the Preparatory Economic Development Studies commissioned by the SDA on an area basis in Scotland.
9. *Scottish Economic Bulletin*, no.26, 1983, p.32.
10. M.Lamont & M.Cox, 'Sales and Purchases Patterns in the Scottish Manufacturing Industries', *ibid.*, pp.6–12.

11. W.J.Reader, *The Weir Group: A Centenary History*, Weidenfeld & Nicolson (London), 1971.
12. Weir Pumps was formed in 1969 to carry out the operations until then undertaken by G.&J.Weir of Cathcart, Drysdale of Yoker, Harland Engineering of Alloa and Weir Drysdale Services of London.
13. *Glasgow Herald*, 12 January 1978 and 18 October 1982.
14. *Financial Times*, 12 May 1981, p.12. See also 'The Babcock Way to higher productivity', *The Production Engineer*, January 1982, pp.29–30. The programme was called 'Exercise 81'.
15. It is reported that Babcock Power won a large order for a power station in Hong Kong in 1981 by quoting at 20 per cent below their then current unit costs, *Glasgow Herald*, 21 February 1982.
16. *Scotsman*, 19 April 1983.
17. *Sunday Standard*, 20 December 1981.
18. Monopolies and Mergers Commission, *Charter Consolidated PLC and Anderson Strathclyde PLC, A Report on the Proposed Merger*, Cmnd 8771, HMSO (London), December 1982.
19. *Ibid.*, chapter 8, pp.50–7.
20. *Ibid.*, pp.58–62.
21. *Glasgow Herald*, 18 October 1982.
22. *Sunday Times*, 24 July 1983.
23. *Engineering Our Future*, report under the Chairmanship of Sir M.Finniston, Cmnd 7794, HMSO (London), 1980.
24. 'Small Engineering Firms Investment Scheme', written answer by the Secretary of State for Industry, *Hansard*, 15 June 1982.
25. S.Hampson & P.McLaren, 'The Microelectronics Application Project: An Analysis of Scottish Applicants', *Scottish Economic Bulletin*, no.26, 1983, pp.7–13.
26. NEDC, *Pumps and Valves SWP* (London), July 1981.
27. NEDC, *Mining Machinery SWP. Progress 1979* (London), 1979.
28. *Engineering Our Future*, 1980 (n.23), p.35–6.
29. On this issue, see Department of Trade, *Standards, Quality and International Competitiveness*, Cmnd 8621, HMSO (London), July 1982.
30. Scottish Development Agency, *Report 82*, accounts p.6.
31. *Engineering Our Future*, 1980 (n.23), p.35.
32. For example, K.Pavitt (ed), *Technical Innovation and British Economic Performance*, Macmillan (London), 1980.
33. Data obtained in private correspondence with NEL.

6

THE FOOD, DRINK, AND TOBACCO SECTORS

DRUMMOND B. SMALL AND LAWRENCE D. SMITH

Within Scotland there is a continuing interest in the current fortunes and future prospects of the food, drink and tobacco sectors.[1] Several reasons can be advanced for this interest, the most significant probably being the relative importance of the food processing sector in Scotland. First, in 1982 around 16·6 per cent of total employment in manufacturing industry in Scotland was in food, drink and tobacco compared with 10·6 per cent in Great Britain in general. Second, the continuing concern with unemployment in Scotland, particularly structural employment in the declining 'traditional' industries, leads people to ask, quite justifiably, whether the food industry is suffering, or will suffer, the same fate as some other sectors. In the last decade the numbers employed have fallen by almost twenty per cent, the trend rate of decline being 1·95 per cent per annum; but employment in Scottish manufacturing industry in general has fallen even faster – by 29 per cent – with a trend rate of decline of 3·14 per cent per annum. As employment in both the food, drink and tobacco sector, and manufacturing industry in general, actually rose between 1972 and 1974, the decline since then has been more marked than the trend figures suggest.

One effect of these trends is that the sector's share of total manufacturing employment has risen over the ten years to 1982 – by 1·9 percentage points. The industry is thus of considerable importance in terms of Scottish manufacturing employment, and of much greater relative importance in Scotland than in Great Britain as a whole.

A further reason for interest in the food and drink sectors in particular is the feeling that considerably more processing could be undertaken on agricultural and fishery raw materials currently produced or potentially produceable within Scotland and frequently 'exported' in an unprocessed or semi-processed state at the moment. In other words, could food and drink processing play a larger role in the Scottish economy in the future?

As is well known, the food, drink and tobacco industry in Scotland is dominated by the whisky sector and this is reflected in the structure of the

The views expressed in this chapter are those of the authors and should not be attributed to the Scottish Development Agency.

Table 6.1. Food, drink and tobacco industry employment[1] in Scotland, 1972–82 (thousands).

Industrial Order (1968 SIC)	1972	1974	1976	1977	1980[2]	1982[2]
III Food, drink and tobacco	94·6	98·7	90·8	90·6	86·0	76·0
III–IX Manufacturing industry	643	676	608	604	550	457
Food, drink and tobacco as % of all manufacturing employment	14·7	14·6	14·9	15·0	15·6	16·6

[1] Full-time and part-time employment, male and female.
[2] Provisional
Sources: Census of Employment and Department of Employment Gazette.

present chapter. After some introductory remarks on the composition of the industry, therefore, some more detailed comments are made on the food sector (drawing on examples from a number of the more important sub-sectors) and this leads on to an assessment of the general problems of the food industry and possible policy initiatives. The main section of the chapter is, however, devoted to the Scotch whisky industry, considering performance, problems and policy. This approach means that little attention is given to the tobacco industry or to the non-whisky component of the drinks industry. No case study is included in this chapter. The Distillers Company plc (DCL) would have been an obvious case example to choose, but its role is so central within the industry as to make a separate study of the firm unnecessary.

The Composition of the Food, Drink and Tobacco Industry

The food, drink and tobacco industry can be separated into several distinct sectors, each with its own characteristic structure, performance and problems. The sectors also vary considerably in terms of relative importance to the Scottish economy, as illustrated by consideration of some of the major parameters.

Employment. Unfortunately, the latest detailed breakdown of employment for the industry by its constituent Minimum List Headings (MLH) is for 1978, and thus an analysis of employment trends by sub-sector is presented for the period 1972–78 only.

The component parts of the industry are ranked in Table 6.2 in terms of total employment in 1972. This clearly shows that spirit distilling and compounding (MLH 239) was the most important sub-sector in terms of employment, followed closely by bacon curing, meat and fish products (MLH 214) and bread and flour confectionery (MLH 212). These three components accounted for 57 per cent of total employment in the industry in 1972, and, perhaps coincidentally, still accounted for almost the

Table 6.2. Employment by components of the Scottish food, drink and tobacco sector, 1972 and 1978.

Minimum list heading	Employment in Scotland (000s)		Scottish employment as % of GB		1978 employment as % of 1972	
	1972	1978	1972	1978	Scotland	GB
239 Spirit distilling and compounding	20·2	23·6	68·5	69·8	116·8	114·6
214 Bacon curing, meat and fish products	18·9	16·9	17·4	16·0	89·4	97·1
212 Bread and flour confectionery	15·3	11·8	12·6	13·1	77·1	74·6
213 Biscuits	6·9	6·3	15·8	14·1	91·3	102·1
215 Milk and milk products	4·8	4·8	7·9	9·3	100·0	84·7
218 Fruit and vegetable products	4·2	5·0	7·7	8·8	119·0	103·8
231 Brewing and malting	4·0	4·6	5·8	7·0	115·0	94·4
229 Starch and miscellaneous foodstuffs	3·3	2·4	9·7	6·6	72·7	107·0
232 Soft drinks	3·4	4·0	11·9	15·0	117·6	93·7
240 Tobacco	(3·9)	(2·8)	(11·4)	(8·8)	(71·8)	93·0
217 Cocoa, chocolate and sugar confectionery	3·0	3·5	4·1	4·7	116·7	101·0
219 Animal and poultry foods	2·8	2·6	10·3	10·4	92·9	92·3
211 Grain milling	2·1	1·2	8·6	5·8	57·1	85·6
216 Sugar	1·1	(0·8)	8·4	(6·8)	(72·7)	90·1
221 Vegetable and animal oils and fats	(0·7)	0·3	(9·1)	4·0	(42·9)	97·4
Order III, MLH 211–240	94·6	90·6	13·0	13·3	93·4	93·4

Source: Census of Employment. Bracketed figures are estimates for data not disclosed in the Census of Employment.

same percentage of total industry employment in 1978. However, over this period, employment in spirit distilling and compounding had actually increased by 3400 or 16·8 per cent with its relative share of industry employment rising from 21 to 26 per cent, whilst employment in bread and flour confectionery had fallen by 3500 or 22·9 per cent. Employment in bacon curing, meat and fish products also declined over this period by just over ten per cent.

In terms of employment there is a substantial difference in the size of the three sub-sectors already discussed and the remainder, none of which employed more than 7000 people in either 1972 or 1978. Of these smaller sub-sectors four – fruit and vegetable products (MLH 218), brewing and malting (MLH 231), soft drinks (MLH 232) and cocoa, chocolate and sugar confectionery (MLH 217) – actually showed increases of fifteen to twenty per cent in employment over the period. Five sectors showed substantial falls in employment, but all of these were small employers of labour.

Table 6.3. Gross value added in the Scottish food, drink and tobacco industry, 1976–79.

	1976	1977	1978	1979
1. GVA (£m)	766·3	840·5	983·8	1042·2
2. GVA as % of all Scottish manufacturing industry GVA	22·7	22·7	24·1	22·6
3. GVA as % of UK food, drink and tobacco industry GVA	15·2	15·0	15·9	15·2
4. GVA per head (£)	7693	8273	10014	11081
5. GVA per head as % of GVA per head in all Scottish manufacturing industry	141·5	137·6	147·1	138·7
6. GVA per head as % of GVA per head in the UK food, drink and tobacco industry	116·5	112·8	120·1	118·4

Source: Annual Census of Production

For most MLH's the direction of Scottish employment trends over this period followed those in Great Britain in general, but employment in brewing and malting (MLH 231) and soft drinks (MLH 232) rose in Scotland whilst falling in Great Britain; the converse occurred for biscuits (MLH 213) and starch and miscellaneous foodstuffs (MLH 229). Table 6.2 also shows the share of Scottish employment in each MLH as a percentage of the Great Britain total. Taking the industry as a whole, Scotland accounted for just over 13 per cent of GB employment in 1978. In general, the most important sub-sectors in Scotland also have the largest shares of GB employment. This is most marked with spirit distilling and compounding where the importance of whisky production is reflected in Scotland's seventy per cent share of GB employment in MLH 239 in 1978. Bacon curing, meat and fish products (MLH 214), bread and flour confectionery (MLH 212) and biscuits (MLH 213) of the larger sub-sectors are also well-represented in Scotland, together with soft drinks (MLH 232) of the smaller sub-sectors.

Table 6.4. Gross value added by components of the Scottish food, drink and tobacco industry, 1976 and 1979.

Minimum list heading	GVA (£m)		% of GVA in Order III	
	1976	1979	1976	1979
239/1 Spirit distilling & compounding	333·9	507·8	43·0	48·7
214 Bacon curing, meat & fish products	65·3	96·8	8·4	9·3
231 Brewing & malting	37·2	85·3	4·8	8·2
212 Bread & flour confectionery	50·1	73·3	6·5	7·0
215 Milk & milk products	42·4	42·2	5·5	4·0
218 Fruit & vegetable products	18·0	30·0	2·3	2·9
213 Biscuits	34·8	27·7	4·5	2·7
232 Soft drinks	18·0	23·7	2·3	2·3
219 Animal & poultry foods	20·6	21·9	2·7	2·1
229/2 Starch & miscellaneous foods	22·9	21·7	2·9	2·1
217 Cocoa, chocolate & sugar confectionery	11·3	16·8	1·5	1·6
211 Grain milling	14·7	14·3	1·9	1·4
229/1 Margarine	⎫	5·8	⎫	0·6
221 Vegetable & animal oils & fats	⎪	2·0	⎪	0·2
239/2 British wines	⎬ 97·1	1·2	⎬ 12·5	0·1
240 Tobacco	⎪	⎫ 71·7	⎪	⎫ 6·9
216 Sugar	⎭	⎭	⎭	⎭
Order III	766·3	1 042·2	100·0	100·0

Sources: Annual Census of Production and Scottish Economic Bulletin.

Gross Value Added. Besides its importance in terms of employment, the performance of the food, drink and tobacco industry can also be assessed in terms of its contribution to the GVA of Scottish manufacturing industry and to the UK food and allied industries.

Using the GVA measure, it can be seen that in recent years the industry has been responsible for over 22 per cent of the GVA generated

Table 6.5. Gross value added per head in components of the Scottish food, drink and tobacco industry, 1976 and 1979.

Minimum list heading		GVA per head in Scotland (£000)		GVA per head in Scotland as % of GVA per head in UK	
		1976	1979	1976	1979
239/1	Spirit distilling & compounding	15·4	21·7	105·9	100·2
231	Brewing & malting	6·8	19·0	60·5	115·9
211	Grain milling	12·3	15·8	131·0	124·7
229/2	Starch & miscellaneous foods	9·2	12·1	124·0	108·6
229/1	Margarine	n.a.	11·6	n.a.	88·8
219	Animal & poultry foods	7·4	10·0	105·0	86·1
215	Milk & milk products	8·8	8·8	n.a.	n.a.
218	Fruit & vegetable products	4·0	7·9	70·4	95·6
232	Soft drinks	5·1	7·6	74·2	59·4
214	Bacon curing, meat & fish products	3·4	5·2	80·3	93·3
217	Cocoa, chocolate & sugar confectionery	3·3	4·8	74·3	64·4
213	Biscuits	4·4	4·8	112·4	77·8
212	Bread & flour confectionery	3·0	4·5	87·2	92·0
221	Vegetable & animal oils & fats	n.a.	3·9	n.a.	118·4
Order III		7·7	11·1	116·5	118·4

Source: Annual Census of Production.

by Scottish manufacturing industry; it is, thus, even more important in GVA than in employment terms. Moreover, in terms of gross value added, Scotland accounted for over 15 per cent of the total UK food, drink and tobacco industry (Table 6.3).

In aggregate, gross value added *per head* is also higher in the Scottish food, drink and tobacco industry than in either Scottish manufacturing industry in general or in the UK food, drink and tobacco industries. Indeed, GVA per head in the Scottish food and allied industries is some forty per cent higher than in Scottish manufacturing industry in general, with only the coal and petroleum and chemical industries being above it. As Table 6.3 also shows, in recent years GVA per head in the Scottish food, drink and tobacco industry has been between 12 and 20 per cent higher than GVA per head in the equivalent sectors in the UK.

When the sub-components of the Scottish food, drink and tobacco industry are studied, the dominant role of spirit distilling and compounding is clearly seen, as in the period 1977–79 this sub-sector accounted for between 44 and 49 per cent of gross value added (Table 6.4). The next largest sectors, bacon curing, meat and fish products (MLH 214), and brewing and malting (MLH 231) normally each account for between 6 and 10 per cent of gross value.

Not only is spirit distilling and compounding the largest sub-sector of the Scottish food, drink and tobacco industry in terms of employment and gross value added, but it also has the highest gross value added per employee (Table 6.5), at a level which is almost twice as high as the Scottish food, drink and tobacco industry as a whole. In the majority of sub-sectors, however, GVA per head in Scotland is lower than in the industry groupings in the UK. In some cases this difference may be attributable to a different mix of activities in the Scottish sector, but in other cases there is a hint, at least, of uncompetitiveness in the Scottish sector. It is also noticeable that several sub-sectors have an extremely low gross value per head eg. £5000 or below at 1979 prices, which implies that these must be relatively low-wage industries.

The Food Sector and Industrial Policy

As this brief description of the components of the food, drink and tobacco industry has shown, the industry is very heterogeneous and comprises firms with widely varying goals, structure and status. The intention in this section is thus to focus on the food industry exclusively, and within this to examine three of the larger sub-sectors, using these to illustrate the problems and potential of the industry as a whole and the scope for policy initiative.

MLH 214: Bacon Curing, Meat and Fish Products. MLH 214 is the second largest sub-sector of the food, drink and tobacco industry in Scotland in terms of employment and gross value added, but it is composed predominantly of extremely small firms. For instance, of the 486 firms identified in 1977, 43 per cent had less than 10 employees and a further 23 per cent had between 10 and 19 employees. Only 40 establishments had more than 100 employees and only one had more then 1000 employees.[2] The main companies are MacFisheries, McKellar Watt, Lawson of Dyce and Halls of Broxburn.

A large proportion of the very small firms together with some of the larger firms are engaged in fish processing activities such as filleting, freezing, smoking, canning and the processing of shellfish. Some discussion on this sub-sector is contained in Chapter 8, and the present comments are confined to bacon curing and meat products only.

Firms in the latter category can themselves be divided into two groups: firms engaged primarily in the slaughtering and primary processing of locally-produced animals, and those which mainly purchase meat for the manufacture of pies and other meat products. The fortunes of the former companies can be influenced by *agricultural* policy as well as industrial policy inasmuch as the supply of locally produced agricultural raw materials is influenced by the relative prices and profitabilities of agricultural enterprises. Thus it could be argued that the tendency of EC agricultural price policy to raise cereal prices relative to livestock prices has discouraged livestock production in Scotland by encouraging farmers, particularly in the east of the country, to plant cereals on land formerly devoted to grass, and by making livestock production less profitable by raising the price of cereal feeding stuffs.[3]

Various other factors have influenced the behaviour and performance of these slaughtering and primary processing firms over the past decade. First, since 1972, local authorities have no longer had an obligation to provide slaughtering facilities and in most areas this had led to the gradual 'privatisation' of slaughtering. Second, EC membership carried with it the promise of new market opportunities in Europe. However, slaughtering and handling of meat for sale in other EC countries could only be undertaken in premises meeting stringent hygiene regulations. Third, the growth of supermarket and catering chains has led to a switch from serving large wholesale markets with complete sides of beef or whole carcasses, to direct selling to supermarkets and other outlets of meat already boned out and cut into primal joints.

These three factors have, collectively, led to a dramatic rationalisation and reconstruction programme by private firms and co-operatives, with the upgrading and expansion of existing plants, the incorporation of cutting and packaging facilities, or the construction of new plants on greenfield sites away from the urban centres which were the traditional location of slaughterhouses. Many of the smaller slaughterhouses, particularly those owned by local authorities, have been closed down, but the net effect has been an expansion in slaughtering capacity at a time when the number of animals to be slaughtered has tended to decline, leading to excess capacity in the industry. It is estimated that there is probably fifty per cent surplus slaughtering capacity in Scotland at the moment. This rationalisation has been aided not only by RDGs and selective assistance, but also to a limited extent by the Red Meat Slaughterhouse Industry Scheme which was in operation from 1976 to 1980.[4] The purpose of this scheme was to raise hygiene standards and improve efficiency of the slaughtering process, though not to the levels required for intra-EC trade.

Aid has also been available through the European Agricultural Guidance and Guarantee Fund (FEOGA) under EC Council Regulation No. 355/77.[5] To qualify for assistance the applicant must show that the project is a component part of a specific programme of development for the processing industry drawn up by the government of the member state. Moreover, it has to be shown that the project must benefit not only the processor, but also the producer whose output is being absorbed and that it should help to guide agricultural production in a direction sought by the Common Agricultural Policy (CAP). Slaughterhouse rationalisation programmes are justified under a scheme encouraging diversification of agricultural output away from milk production.

Whilst entry to the EC generated, initially at least, an air of optimism in the slaughterhouse industry, it created major problems for the bacon curing industry. Pig production has never been particularly important in Scotland, but was important in the Grampian region due to low feed prices. A large proportion of the pigs produced in the region were processed at Lawson of Dyce (a subsidiary of Unilever), which in the early 1970s employed more than 2000 people. However, several years of heavy losses led to the cessation of pig slaughtering in 1979 and a large reduction in employment. The firm now purchases pigmeat mainly from Continental countries for the production of pies, etc.

Another major development over the past two decades has been the growth of a broiler production and processing industry in Scotland, a development which has been aided by RDGs and FEOGA grants.[6]

As noted, the second category of meat processing firms are those which chiefly purchase meat for the production of meat products. These tend to be located mainly in the central belt and their fortunes are mainly affected by Scottish consumer demand for the products they manufacture. Several are medium-sized firms and many have made use of RDGs for improvement of their premises. One recently established enterprise which has reached a medium-firm size is Devro Ltd, a subsidiary of the American MNE Johnson and Johnson, which has specialised in the production of sausage casings. This firm has received considerable sums of money from Government sources.

MLH 212: Bread and Flour Confectionery. In terms of employment and gross value added this is the second largest food sector. There has been intense competition within the overall declining bread market and at the UK level the two surviving major plant bakeries, British Bakeries, a subsidiary of Rank Hovis MacDougall (RHM), and Allied Bakeries, a subsidiary of Associated British Foods (ABF) between them control 54 per cent of the total bread market and 70 per cent of the wrapped bread market.[7] At the same time, in the UK, thirty-five independent plant bakeries accounted for 7 to 8 per cent of bread production, with 5000 master bakers representing 26 per cent of total bread output and the remainder being made up by in-store bakeries, hot bread shops, etc.

In Scotland, market shares would not appear to be too dissimilar, because in 1977 it is estimated that RHM and ABF owned between them sixteen establishments and accounted for around 45 per cent of the total employees in this sector. There were, however, another sixteen establishments, many owned by independent firms, which employed over 100 people. These thirty-two largest establishments accounted for 75 per cent of the total employment of some 12 300 people in this sector in 1977. The other 25 per cent of employment occurred in some two hundred smaller establishments, which indicates the continuation of a strong master baker tradition in Scotland.

There has been further rationalisation in the industry since then because Spillers, who were the third largest plant bakers, withdrew from production in 1978 with the eventual closure of their bakeries. Moreover both major plant bakeries, as well as many of the smaller companies, have engaged in heavy capital investment and rationalisation to increase efficiency both in production and distribution, to modify the types of bread produced to suit consumer wants. This modernisation and rational-isation has been assisted by RDGs to both the major and smaller com-panies. In addition, in April 1982 British Bakeries announced that it was to build an £11.5 million factory in Glasgow to replace its present premises, with financial assistance in the form of RDGs and SFA total-ling £3.5 million. Although the new plant will lead to the reduction of employment from 700 to 500, it will allegedly ensure the survival of the remaining jobs.

Even so, it seems as though severe problems of overcapacity remain in this sector and further rationalisation may be required in the near future.

MLH 215: Milk and Milk Products. The third sub-sector of the food industry to be considered is milk and milk products.

In Scotland all milk produced by farmers is purchased by the three regional Milk Marketing Boards (MMBs) and is then either processed by the Board's own creameries or is sold to private creameries for heat processing and sale as liquid milk or for manufacture into cream, con-densed milk, chocolate crumb, butter or cheese. Many of the larger private creameries are, in fact, branches of the major UK dairy product companies or, in one case at least (Carnation Foods), a subsidiary of a multinational.

The MMBs obtain different prices for milk used for different pro-ducts, the highest price being paid for milk for liquid sale. Butter and skim milk powder can be 'sold into intervention' – i.e. purchased by the EC Intervention Board at a guaranteed price – and this effectively puts a floor price on the price for which milk can be sold for manufacture. Farmers are then paid a 'pool price' that is the weighted average price of the milk sold for different uses. It is this pool price, and this price relative to that of other products, which tends to determine the quantity of milk produced, hence the supply of milk to manufacturers; but the profitability of the creameries depends on the demand for the final products and the price at which they can be sold. However the general European surplus of milk products, caused mainly by the relatively high intervention prices which have suppressed demand and increased production, have created severe marketing problems for the creameries. Reform of the CAP, which is high on the EC agenda, further increases the uncertainties of this sector.

As with slaughterhouses, there was a large amount of investment in new buildings and plant in the 1970s aided by Government and EC funds,[8] with a result that there is surplus capacity of technically efficient manufacturing plant, and severe competition both in the liquid milk and manufactured milk product markets. Unfortunately, very little of this investment represented product diversification, most capacity being devoted to the low-value-added products such as condensed milk, cheddar cheese and butter. However, in the last five years there has been much more awareness, particularly by the Milk Marketing Boards, of the need to diversify into new dairy product lines such as speciality cheeses, flavoured milks, etc. For example, the Scottish Milk Marketing Board recently announced a £1 million investment in the production of Feta cheese primarily for export to the Middle East.

Thus this is another sub-sector more affected by agricultural policy than industrial policy.

The General Problems of the Food Sector. These three food sub-sectors illustrate some of the problems encountered by the food processing sector in Scotland. The vast majority of firms are small or medium-sized, the majority being independent, although a surprising number are subsidiaries or branches of UK or foreign companies. There are several reasons which might explain the generally small size of firms. First, interviews with firms in two regions of Scotland have indicated that many companies have no desire to expand, being perfectly content with their existing size of business.[9] Second, the relatively small size of the consumer market in Scotland tends to restrict the size of those enterprises producing primarily for the domestic market. This is particularly so for the wide range of products where demand is declining or is static. Firms producing goods which either rely on bulky raw materials or which produce bulky end-products are further penalised, in that the location of production facilities in Scotland makes it difficult for such firms to be competitive in 'exporting' large quantities of produce to England because of the transport on-costs. Even firms located in the Grampian region find it difficult to service the Central Belt without a distribution depot in the area for bulk breaking. Furthermore, those firms which rely on Scottish-produced raw materials are frequently constrained by the limited availability of raw materials and their geographical spread, together with the number of firms competing for the available supplies.

Although many owners may be content to manage a small firm, limited size does create disadvantages for the industry in general. First, many companies are too small to act as suppliers to the major multiple food stores, whose centralised buyers prefer to buy large volumes of

standardised produce. Even firms which could supply a reasonable proportion of Scottish demand may find themselves too small by U K market
standards to obtain contracts with the larger supermarket chains. With
the multiples' share of the food trade continuing to expand, Scottish
companies may find themselves servicing the contracting smaller outlets'
segment. Second, the small size frequently precludes firms from engaging
in effective marketing strategies, such as the promotion of their products
and the penetration of export markets. The cost of these operations is
frequently excessive in relation to current throughput. In addition, many
firms are too small to engage in effective product development and the
testing and launching of new products, particularly those which would
require high volume output to be economic. These two factors have
resulted in a situation in which many Scottish food processing companies
(but by no means all) tend to be limited to producing 'traditional' products, very often for declining markets. A noticeable feature of the branch
firms in Scotland is that a large proportion are engaged in simple processing activities, or the production of low-value-added products. Few
conduct any research and development activities in Scotland or have
located new plants in Scotland for the production of high-volume new
products or convenience foods.

Although Scottish firms may not be in the forefront of developing
new products, this has not precluded a large number from investing
capital in modernising and expanding their capacity to produce 'traditional' products to extend their product range using existing technologies. As a result, a number of sub-sectors currently experience excess
capacity and extreme competition. Much of this capital investment has
been assisted by a variety of Government or EC schemes. Whether this
approach constitutes a rational industrial policy is extremely debatable.
Product-differentiation strategies have, however, proved to be successful
for some companies, with Baxters of Fochabers and Hudsons Pantry
being two notable examples, both of which rely on these 'traditional'
products.

Some Possible Policy Initiatives. In attempting to formulate possible
industrial policy initiatives for the Scottish food processing industry, two
considerations have to be faced. The first is where one draws the line
between 'industrial policy' and other policies. For instance, the varying
problems of the meat and dairy sector both stem in large part from the
EC *agricultural* policy. Furthermore, many existing firms are placed at a
competitive disadvantage by their present location and the consequent
transport on-costs which they encounter. A possible remedy might lie in
specific transport subsidies, but this is more in the nature of a *transport*
policy or a *regional* policy than industrial policy *per se*.

The second consideration is to decide which parameters are, in
effect, fixed, and which are open to manipulation through appropriate

policy instruments. For instance, should industrial policy attempt to rationalise the structure of the food processing sector in Scotland, encouraging the growth of larger companies, or should the small size of firms be accepted and policy initiatives concentrated on making these small businesses more effective? The latter approach is adopted here as being the more realistic. Within this framework, a major element of an industrial policy for the food sector is the provision of those elements of infrastructure which smaller firms find difficulty in providing for themselves.

One example is the recent decision by the Scottish Development Agency to promote a Food Park at Motherwell as part of the Motherwell Project.[10] This entails creating, on a 26-acre estate, an industrial environment tailored specifically to the needs of food companies, with premises designed to meet their hygiene and other requirements, and with a range of public and private sector services to assist them.

The health and hygiene requirements should be met partly by the specialised nature of the estate, and partly by the construction of factories specifically designed to meet the requirements of food manufacturers with special materials for floors and walls, and sloping floors and internal drains for ease of washing down equipment.

But of perhaps more benefit to small and medium-sized companies will be the proposed provision of on-site marketing services such as:

the availability of large cold storage facilities for raw materials and finished products and of the refrigerated distribution service to retailers;

advice and assistance to individual firms in areas where they cannot afford to employ full-time sepcialists (for example advice on packaging and market research) from the SDA's Small Business and Electronics Divisions;

the possibility of cooperative selling and distribution activities on behalf of groups of firms with complementary products. This may overcome the handicap of small size, helping these firms to penetrate the UK and overseas grocery markets. Such a scheme could obviously extend to firms outwith the Park, but it is envisaged that the Food Park offers an excellent base for such operations;

the provision of training and technical assistance from the Glasgow College of Food and Technology and the University of Strathclyde's food science specialists.

The creation of a single Food Park will only be of direct benefit to a very limited number of firms who start a business there or decide to relocate in the Park. Whether such a policy is readily replicable to create, say, ten Food Parks in different areas of Scotland is doubtful. However, many of the benefits of the food park concept can be obtained without the physical grouping of firms. For instance, there seems to be considerable scope for regional marketing strategies embracing firms producing different products from local raw materials emphasising local characteristics and using a local brand name or image. Co-operation between firms might be extended to shared facilities such as transport pooling, etc. The initiative for creating some form of regional consortium of independent producers might well come from Regional Councils rather than Central Government, but specialist assistance from organisations such as the Scottish Development Agency might also be required. The recently launched 'Food from Britain' initiative charged with the responsibility of improving the marketing of food, drink and agricultural produce grown or processed in the United Kingdom might perhaps provide a platform from which effective collaborative marketing strategies by Scottish-based food companies can be launched.

The Scotch Whisky Industry

While spirits other than whisky contribute to the output of the spirit distilling sector, whisky is by far the most predominant product. An analysis of the whisky industry's recent performance and the impact of past policies both at EC and national levels must therefore form a major part of this chapter. Reflecting this importance of the whisky sector, suggestions for future action and policy will be made separately from those more appropriate for the balance of the food, drink and tobacco industry in Scotland.

To most observers, the importance of whisky distilling, blending, bottling and selling to the Scottish economy will be self-evident. Nevertheless, it is useful briefly to review the significance of the sector in the context of the United Kingdom as a whole. Traditionally between 80 and 85 per cent of Scotch whisky production has been exported, an achievement which no other major industry in the United Kingdom has been able to match consistently throughout this century. In 1980, the latest year for which full figures are available, exports of Scotch whisky were valued at £746 million while industry estimates for 1982 put this figure at £871 million. In addition, sales of Scotch whisky in the domestic market contributed £590 million in excise duty in 1981. This total is equal to 22·6 per cent of total excise duty raised from alcoholic drinks and approximately three per cent of all Customs and Excise revenue. Since VAT is payable on excise duty and the original cost of the whisky plus any mark-up, the overall contribution of Scotch whisky to the United Kingdom Treasury is in reality even greater.

Industry Background and Performance. Two main categories of Scotch whisky are produced (grain and malt), each having different raw materials, production methods and characteristics. Produced solely from malted barley and yeast using the batch production, pot-still method, malt whisky can vary between production runs within a single distillery and, more importantly, each distillery produces its own unique malt whisky with a pronounced flavour and 'aroma'. Since the characteristics of any malt whisky are largely a result of the location of the distillery, a further grouping of malt whisky types by geographical location is used. The heavier Highland malts, for example, are made by distilleries lying north of a line extending from Greenock to Dundee and are generally very highly regarded for use as single malts and in blending.

Grain whisky is the product of a mixture of maize, malted barley and yeast, with maize being the main raw material, accounting for around 85 per cent of the ingredients of the 'recipe'. Grain whisky production is a continuous, large-scale process using the 'Coffey' Still and is more akin to an industrial production process. With little variation in characteristics or quality between distilleries, grain whisky lends itself admirably to its role as the base for blended whisky. The continuous production process of grain whisky has resulted in the typical grain distillery being much larger (average capacity 32 million litres of pure alcohol – LPA – per year) than malt distilleries where the average annual capacity is around 2 million LPA.

Table 6.6. Employment figures in the scotch whisky industry, 1978.

Nature of employment	Malt distilleries	Grain distilleries	Malt & Grain distilleries located together	Other operations	Total
Maltings	216	79	205	—	500
Distilling	3068	2021	—	—	5089
Maturation/ warehousing	515	451	325	84	1375
Blending & bottling plants	3426	32	9893	1570	14921
By-products plants	192	134	33	—	359
Management, sales & administrative staff	1336	160	1424	152	3072
Total	8753	2877	11880	1806	25316

Source: Scotch Whisky Association.

Employment. The most recently available Census of Employment figures for 1978 place total employment in spirit distilling and compounding at some 23600 persons. More recent estimates have been provided in response to Parliamentary questions which quote employment levels of 23400 and 21000 in May 1979 and September 1981 respectively. These figures exclude workers involved in some blending, bottling and broking activities, and do not, in any event, provide an accurate picture so far as purely whisky-related employment is concerned. For the latter, industry estimates are the best source. A survey carried out by the Scotch Whisky Association provided a reliable picture of employment within the various functional areas of the industry in 1978, and the results are shown in Table 6.6. Given the shedding of capacity which has typified the sector since 1978, the current trade association estimate of 20000 persons directly employed by the industry is likely to be accurate. Industry sources also suggest a proportionately larger reduction in employment in the whisky industry than in the distilling sector as a whole.

Although whisky distilling *per se* is not a particularly labour-intensive operation, the differences in the production processes between malt distilling and grain distilling result in the latter having an average volume of output per employee some three times greater than the comparative figure for malt distilleries.[11] The most labour-intensive area of whisky production is, not surprisingly, in bottling and packaging, which requires a high level of relatively unskilled and predominately female labour to service the bottling lines. Output per employee in bottling was on average 60 per cent of that achieved in malt distilling and only 18 per cent of the level for grain distilling.

The whisky industry also generates indirect employment, principally in the packaging and printing, glass manufacturing, coopering and transport industries. It is far from easy to quantify the level of indirect job creation, but, as a guide, indirect whisky-related employment in Grampian Region was estimated to be about 500 in 1981.[12]

Industry Location and Structure. There are presently 101 malt distilleries operating or which have ceased production only recently, plus an additional ten grain distilleries. Of the total, 85 may be classified as Highland Malts, of which the majority are located in Grampian Region, with a particularly heavy concentration in Moray District; here approximately thirty per cent of manufacturing employment is provided by the whisky industry. Since quality of water plays such an important role in the production of malt whisky the reason for the locational pattern of malt distilleries is not difficult to deduce. By comparison grain whisky distilling is not so dependent on environmental or geographical factors and as a result most of the distilleries currently in operation are situated in the central belt of Scotland.

Because of the need for high labour inputs, and to minimise transport costs, blending and bottling plants also tend to be concentrated in the central belt and the decade to 1981 saw an expansion and modernisation of such units, frequently on greenfield sites close to major centres of population.

Traditionally the whisky industry has been divided into the two main groupings of, on one hand, distilling, and, on the other, blending, bottling and marketing. For practical purposes this distinction is no longer valid since the vast majority of distilleries are now in the hands of organisations having blending and bottling interests of their own. This trend towards vertical integration within the whisky industry plus horizontal integration into distilling and marketing of other spirits (whether for human or industrial consumption) has been continuing for at least the past fifty years.

By whatever measure one cares to use, the level of concentration of ownership within the whisky industry is high. The Distillers Company plc (DCL) is by far the most important single organisation in the industry, owning some thirty-four malt and four grain distilleries currently operating, and accounting for an estimated 38 per cent of total sales in the world market for Scotch whisky. The current ownership pattern of distilleries is illustrated in Table 6.7.

Ownership of malt distilling capacity, in particular, has become increasingly concentrated over the past twenty years, in part as a result of the nature of Scotch whisky. Blenders of whisky need to be able to guarantee the long-term stability of their blends and this in turn means a reluctance to purchase the output of new malt distilleries with little or no track record for quality. It is hardly surprising therefore that mergers and acquisitions have been an important factor in the industry's development. As an example, over the period 1970 to 1980 the number of companies involved in the malt side of the industry declined from 40 to 31, while the number of operating malt distilleries rose from 109 to 117.

Whilst ownership of distilleries reveals a highly concentrated industry structure, the percentage of industry distilling capacity owned by the major companies reinforces this picture. Not taking into account those distilleries which have been temporarily shut down, an estimated maximum annual production capacity for all types of malt whisky of approximately 248 million litres of pure alcohol is generally accepted. Of this total some 33 per cent is owned by DCL with a further 17 per cent in the hands of foreign companies. So far as grain whisky distilling capacity is concerned roughly 17 per cent is in foreign ownership and 40 per cent under the control of DCL.

Considering overseas ownership specifically, in the twenty years from 1960 to 1980 foreign penetration of malt distilleries rose from 14·4 per cent of the total to 20·5 per cent.[13] With the acquisition by Amalgamated Distilled Products of the Barton Brands distilleries plus the divestment programme of Publiker of its Inverhouse interests, 1982 saw a slight fall back in foreign ownership to 19·5 per cent. However, the closure of eleven malt distilleries by DCL in 1983 has raised the foreign ownership of operating malt distilleries to 22·7 per cent. Cointreau, in addition, has acquired the Glenturret distillery. Foreign companies with interests in

Table 6.7. Estimated ownership of
operating distilleries, 1983.

	Malt	Grain
DCL	34	4
Seagram	9	—
Hiram Walker	9	1
Highland Distilleries	5	—
Arthur Bell	5	—
Invergordon	4	1
IDV (Grand Met)	4	—
Long John (Whitbread)	3	1
Whyte & Mackay (Lonrho)	3	—
ADP (Argyll)	3	—
Wm. Grant	2	1
Scottish & Newcastle	2	—
McDonald Martin	2	—
Teachers	2	—
Stanley P. Morrison	2	—
Pernod Ricard	2	—
Cointreau	1	—
Others (UK owned)	9	1
Others (foreign owned)	—	1
Total	101	10

Sources: Campbell, Neill & Co.; SDA.

the Scotch whisky industry are all spirit distillers in their own right which
have followed a strategy of horizontal integration into the production and
marketing of other alcoholic drinks.

The Consumption of Scotch Whisky. Not surprisingly, consumption
of Scotch whisky varies both by product category and by geographical
market and each of these aspects is examined in the following section.

Scotch whisky sales fall into the two broad categories of bottled and
bulk whisky. Within these two classes there are further sub-divisions as
follows (estimates of UK brand leaders from Campbell, Neill & Co. data
are shown in brackets):

Bottled Whisky	*Bulk Whisky*
Bottled blend	Bulk blend
Premium brands (Johnny Walker Black)	Bulk malt
Standard brands (Bells)	Bulk grain
Secondary brands (Claymore)	
Bottled malt (Glenfiddich)	

Bottled whisky, known by convention as 'Bottled in Scotland' (BIS), is sold in both domestic and export markets with the various brand categories reflecting the market positioning of the products. Bottled malt whisky is a high-price product promoted on the basis of extended maturation, which imparts a unique quality to the drink and emphasises the individuality of single malts produced by different distilleries. It is generally sold at around eight years old but often at ten or twelve years or even older.

Bulk whiskies, whether malt, blended or grain, are exclusively for export markets. Distilled, matured and blended in Scotland, bulk blend is shipped at high strength for subsequent dilution and bottling, packaging and distribution in the export market. Bulk malt, however, is used almost exclusively as an 'improving' agent, being admixed with locally produced whiskies to improve quality, palatability and consumer acceptability. By comparison with sales of bulk blend and malt, exports of bulk grain whisky are insignificant.

Exports of Scotch Whisky. The total consumption of Scotch whisky in all export markets, indicating the relative importance of the various categories and illustrating the trends of the past ten years, is shown in Table 6.8.

BIS blended whisky is easily the most important of the product categories, consistently accounting for around 70 per cent of total export sales of Scotch whisky during the decade to 1980. As can be seen from the table there is a slight downward trend in BIS market share over the period. Nevertheless, the compound annual growth rate in volume for BIS blend over the period to 1980 was 3·3 per cent.

BIS malt has shown the most encouraging export trend, with compound growth in export volume of 20 per cent per annum for the period 1971 to 1980. The five-fold rise in volume sales from 1971 is, of course, from a very limited base, and even now BIS malt has captured only a 1·3 per cent share of total Scotch exports. As with BIS blends, bottled malt sales suffer from the tendency of consumers to switch to cheaper whiskies during recessionary periods. 1975 saw a declined in bottled malt volume sales and a similar situation occurred in 1980.

The general industry opinion is that in the longer term the outlook for BIS malt is bright as it becomes an increasingly understood and accepted drink. However, this will require greater promotion of single malt brands by companies in order to differentiate the product. Judging by the increased budgets presently being allocated to promote BIS malt brands, this need has been recognised and is being responded to.

Bulk Whisky Exports. The export of Scotch whisky in bulk is a subject which has generated long and frequently acrimonious discussion both inside and outside the industry, with the protagonists adopting equally entrenched positions. A detailed discussion of the bulk export

Table 6.8. Exports of scotch whisky by category, 1971–81 (million LPA).

	Blended Whisky				Malt Whisky				Grain Whisky		
	Bottle	%	Bulk	%	Bottle	%	Bulk	%	Bottle +Bulk	%	Total
1971	128·42	70·4	44·91	24·6	0·55	0·3	8·49	4·6	0·13	0·1	182·50
1972	125·62	70·4	40·92	23·0	0·90	0·5	10·55	5·9	0·42	0·2	178·41
1973	140·51	59·0	45·40	22·4	10·3	0·5	16·17	7·9	0·47	0·2	203·58
1974	158·19	69·6	48·60	21·4	1·74	0·7	18·38	8·1	0·48	0·2	227·33
1975	155·38	66·3	56·46	24·1	1·28	0·6	20·64	8·8	0·51	0·2	234·27
1976	166·70	70·0	48·25	20·2	1·56	0·7	20·78	8·7	1·01	0·4	238·30
1977	169·23	69·5	49·83	20·4	2·01	0·8	21·84	9·0	0·72	0·3	243·63
1978	189·58	69·2	56·53	20·6	2·39	0·9	24·87	9·1	0·70	0·2	274·07
1979	184·61	70·3	49·46	18·9	3·05	1·2	24·44	9·3	0·86	0·3	262·42
1980	170·90	68·4	51·64	20·6	2·93	1·2	23·22	9·3	1·23	0·5	249·92
1981	160·54	65·7	56·95	23·3	3·08	1·3	22·74	9·3	0·93	0·4	244·25
1982	163·21	64·9	61·28	24·4	3·27	1·3	22·68	9·0	1·08	0·4	251·47

Source: Campbell, Neill & Co., *Scotch Whisky Industry Review* (Glasgow), 1983.

controversy would merit a book in its own right, and consequently only a summary of the main arguments for and against the trade is included here.

The major elements of the bulk whisky export trade are bulk malts and bulk blended whisky. In 1982, 84 million LPA (33 per cent of total Scotch whisky exports) left the country in bulk form. The underlying reasons for the bulk export trade vary between malt and blended whisky. Although the casual observer will probably be more familiar with the controversy surrounding the bulk malt exports, the trade in bulk blend exports is the larger and has to date attracted less attention.

Exports of bulk blended whisky accounted for over 24 per cent of all whisky exports in 1982, with secondary brands accounting for the majority of the trade. Blended whisky shipped in bulk incurs lower transport costs, which are of some significance in specific markets such as Australia. Also the margins charged on secondary brands are smaller than on standard and deluxe brands, therefore it is important to minimise transport costs to maintain the appropriate price levels.

Up to 1980 bulk exports of blended whisky into the USA gained significant tax advantages over its BIS counterpart, since tax was levied on the volume of product as opposed to its alcoholic strength. Bulk blend which is shipped at full strength and diluted later was thereby given an advantage over BIS brands which are diluted to 'drinking strength' prior to export.

In recent years it is disturbing to note that bulk exports of blended whisky have risen substantially to markets where the cost of transportation could not be considered a significant factor, especially France and Western Germany. Trends such as this give credence to the view that, so far as secondary brands are concerned, Scotch whisky is becoming increasingly considered as simply a commodity, an event which surely cannot be regarded as in the long term interests of either the industry or the Scottish economy in general. In support of this view, it is understood that the Scotch Whisky Association has expressed strong reservations about the potentially damaging effects of the increased shipment of blended whisky in bulk, despite the fact that the increase has allowed the industry to sustain its export volume. Whether or not the trade association's view will have any effect upon individual firm's decisions remains to be seen.

Broadly, the arguments in favour of the bulk exporting of blended whisky are based on two main propositions. First, since Scotch whisky has to meet the needs of a variety of consumers it is necessary to offer the cheaper, bulk brands as an alternative to the more expensive BIS brands. Without the availability of bulk brands it is argued that consumers would simply switch to alternative, locally-produced spirits. Similarly it is believed that the cheaper bulk exported brands give consumers the taste for Scotch whisky and that eventually they will trade up-market to the BIS brands. Bulk brands are therefore seen as an important means of opening up a market. Secondly, there is the more simplistic but undoubtedly persuasive short-term argument that business is business and should not be refused. Given the current recession it is not difficult to appreciate the attractions of this approach.

On the other side of the argument, it is frequently alleged that quality standards are likely to suffer through the bulk export of blended whisky, since it is more difficult to supervise the dilution and bottling process when it takes place overseas. Any reduction in the quality standards of Scotch whisky, and therefore its perceived quality image among consumers, will encourage the tendency to consider bulk blended whiskies simply as a commodity spirit rather than a unique product. Again, the lower prices charged for bulk exported blends reduce the foreign exchange income of the UK, whilst the lower margins, it is believed, reduce the profits of the whisky companies. Finally, there is the view that the exporting of whisky in bulk is tantamount to the exporting of jobs since employment opportunities are lost in the bottling and packaging industries. This latter point is one which has been consistently stressed by the trades unions which oppose bulk exporting.[14]

Bulk malt exports are sold almost exclusively for mixing with locally distilled spirits to make the resultant blend more palatable. Sales abroad have grown dramatically, from less than 8·5 million LPA in 1971 to nearly 23 million LPA in 1982. However, the peak level of exports occurred in the late 1970s, since when there has been a modest decline. Whether or not this was due to the efforts of the industry to regulate shipments is difficult to determine.

The most important market is Japan which accounts for over 70 per cent of bulk malt exports. It cannot be denied that the export of bulk malt does help significantly to improve the quality of the Japanese product thereby increasing the competition to Scotch whisky in many markets. The degree of confidence of those who say that Scotch whisky is well able to compete with any non-Scottish whisky, whilst admirable, is open to question and perhaps indicative of a lack of strategic understanding of the nature of competition in the international market for alcoholic beverages.

It has been estimated that in 1982 the five major exporters of bulk malt accounted for 80 per cent of the trade, with two firms, Seagrams and Scottish and Universal Investments (Lonrho) accounting for 9·75 million LPA, 43 per cent, alone. Of the five companies, only one is not a major multinational company, or owned by a major multinational company. It is, of course, difficult to establish what autonomy the Scottish-based management of these companies has in determining policy towards bulk malt exporting, but it is interesting to note that the majority of those companies which do not participate in the trade are those with low levels of corporate internationalisation. Chief among these is The Distillers Company plc which refuses to export malt whisky in bulk, holding that it can only be to the long-term detriment of the Scottish product.

As a finale to this discussion of bulk malt exporting, it is indicative of the progress made by the Japanese whisky industry that the Suntory Company now claims that it has the world's top selling whisky brand in 'Old Suntory' a blend which is thought to contain up to 25 per cent Scotch malt whisky. In addition, Japanese whisky is estimated to have a total market share of 15 per cent of the world consumption of all types of whisky, although Japanese sales are concentrated in the Far East.

Exports by Major Markets. Having examined the performance of Scotch whisky exports by the various product types, a brief review of performance in major export markets will complete the picture. Table 6.9 illustrates the changing pattern of demand for Scotch whisky in the major export markets.

The USA remains the single most important market for Scotch whisky in the world, accounting for 31·3 per cent of total Scotch whisky exports in 1982. In the late sixties, however, over 50 per cent of Scotch whisky exports by volume were destined for this market. Within the USA beverage market, non-economic factors have begun to play an increasingly important role in determining consumer demand for spirits in general. It is becoming socially less acceptable to consume heavy spirits and the trend is clearly towards light drinks such as vodka, gin and white rums and, to a greater extent, wines and beer. The pre-occupation with health has reinforced this trend. For example, in 1971 Scotch whisky held a 14 per cent share of the USA spirits market which by 1980 had declined to 10 per cent, and, whilst the influence of the recession has been significant, changing consumer preferences have also been an important factor.

Table 6.9. Exports of scotch whisky to major overseas markets (million LPA, selected years).

	1970	% of total exports	1980	% of total exports	1982	% of total exports
USA	86·68	53·9	74·97	30·0	78·82	31·3
Japan	2·93	2·2	27·96	11·2	25·78	10·25
France	6·43	4·7	15·79	6·3	20·58	8·2
Italy	3·85	2·8	12·07	4·8	11·07	4·4
West Germany	5·09	3·7	8·36	3·4	8·32	3·3
Belgium/Lux.	3·07	2·3	7·54	3·0	5·81	2·3
Other EC	3·02	2·2	7·80	3·1	11·55	4·6
EC Total	21·46	13·1	51·56	20·6	57·33	22·8
Australia	3·53	2·6	7·02	2·8	7·94	3·2
South Africa	2·29	1·7	6·11	2·4	6·56	2·6
Canada	3·22	2·4	5·49	2·2	5·11	2·0
Spain	2·87	2·1	4·59	1·8	6·61	2·6
Sweden	1·73	1·3	3·51	1·4	4·04	1·6
Venezuela	1·95	1·4	8·20	3·3	5·55	2·2

Source: Scotch Whisky Association.

There is also an increasing rise in the proportion of low-margin bulk blends sold in the USA, with the ratio of BIS brand to bulk brand sales approaching the 1:1 point in comparison with the over 2:1 ratio seen in the early seventies. This is of crucial significance to the profitability of the major distillers, since returns on BIS blends can be up to ten times higher than the typical bulk-exported, locally-bottled blend where margins of under £1 per case are not uncommon.[15]

In recognition of the difficulties facing Scotch whisky in the USA market, a major generic promotion has been in operation for the past three years with funds being contributed by the industry as a whole. Given the historical inability of the companies to agree on what is in their long-term interest, the industry is to be congratulated. It is arguable, however, that this agreement should have been reached in the early seventies, and the generic promotion activities will require to be continued for considerably longer than three years for any identifiable impact to be achieved. In addition, the $1·5 million funds committed might be insufficient to influence a market valued in 1982 at $335 million. Compare, for example, the budget of £4 million for the recently announced generic promotion of Spanish sherry in the UK.[16]

Following the USA, Japan is the second largest export market for Scotch whisky with 10·2 per cent of total Scotch whisky exports (25·8 million LPA) in 1982. About two-thirds of Scotch exports to Japan are in the bulk malt segment, which has undoubtedly contributed to the strength of the local competition. BIS brands, though showing growth during the seventies with the removal of import quota restrictions, have suffered badly from the activities of parallel importers, a topic more fully discussed later. To the Japanese consumer, the price of Scotch whisky is a direct reflection of the status of the drink and the drinker. Therefore the appearance of well-known brands at prices significantly lower than those charged by sole agents is undoubtedly damaging to the consumer's image of Scotch as a high-status product. Within the domestic Japanese spirit industry it would appear that there is an unofficial agreement to limit the market share of Scotch whisky to around the 10 per cent level. The Scotch Whisky Association believes that this agreement is actively encouraged by the Japanese government, and as BIS Scotch currently holds about an 8 per cent market share, only a modest improvement is expected in the future. A similar generic promotion campaign to that underway in the USA is being initiated in the Japanese market.

The EC as a whole (excluding the UK) was the destination of approximately 23 per cent of Scotch exports in 1982; 57.33 million LPA by volume. This market as a whole has been relatively stable during the current recession period, although the volume levels have been maintained largely by an increase in bulk blend exports to counteract the decline in BIS sales. Consumers are undoubtedly trading down to cheap bulk blends and it remains to be seen whether the frequently indifferent quality of such products will have a detrimental effect on the long-term demand for Scotch whisky.

Historically, whisky has had a low market penetration in the EC spirits market, and therefore the opportunities existed for the growth rates seen during the 1970s. This growth was aided by the more imaginative marketing and promotional efforts expanded by the industry. Scotch now enjoys a certain *cachet* among consumers in much the same fashion as wine does currently in the UK. An added assistance has been the gradual harmonisation of national duties on local and imported spirits within the EC, where several countries had blatantly discriminatory tariffs to protect their domestic spirits industry. It should be noted that anomalies of this nature still exist despite pressure from the EC Commission and in direct contravention of the Treaty of Rome.

Venezuela provides a good example of the problems which can face the Scotch whisky industry in the developing world. Such emerging markets are typified by unstable economies, which in the case of Venezuela has been severely hit by the slump in world oil prices. In 1970 some 1.95 million LPA of Scotch was imported, with this figure rising rapidly in the wake of the 1973 oil price explosion to reach 8.20 million LPA in 1980. Since then there has been an equally dramatic decline, exports falling by one third between 1980 and 1982 with a further decline of 40 per cent predicted in 1983. To assist the balance of payments, special licenses have been introduced for spirits importers, allied to restricted import quotas and an artifically-inflated exchange rate for foreign currency purchasing. DCL are particularly vulnerable in Venezuela with an 85 per cent market share of the BIS brand-dominated market.

On the domestic front, the UK market for Scotch of 44.8 million LPA in 1982 (14 per cent of total world sales), has seen a volume decline since 1979 of about one sixth. More encouragingly, Scotch has retained its share of the UK spirit market at over 50 per cent. The market was typified by generally steady growth through the seventies aided by price rises which were below the level of inflation. Consumption has naturally been affected by the current recession and by the need for companies to re-establish their margins. This has resulted in price increases in the past few years on average above the rate of inflation. It is expected that as the economy starts to recover from its present recession the Scotch whisky industry will benefit, along with other producers of alcoholic beverages, provided that there are no dramatic price rises by individual companies or excessive duty or VAT increases. It is to be expected, however, that the UK alcoholic beverage market will see the continued increase in the popularity of wines, which must be expected to take some market share from spirits in general, and Scotch in particular.

Stock and Production Levels. Unlike rectified spirits such as gin and vodka, the nature of the Scotch whisky production cycle is heavily determined by the need to mature the spirit for at least three years before consumption. This is the statutory minimum required before the spirit can be called Scotch whisky. Distilling has therefore to take place an average of six years prior to consumption for malt whisky and four years for grain whisky. High reliance is, by necessity, placed on projections of market growth. Given the historical growth rates of the industry's markets, it is not surprising that stocks of maturing spirit held within the industry have displayed a steady upward trend over the past two decades.

Total maturing stocks of both malt and grain whisky stood at 2 900 million LPA in 1982, having reached a high point of 3 070 million LPA in 1980.[17] As an indication of the upward trend in stocks, the 1982 level is

40 per cent higher than that of 1970 and 260 per cent higher than 1960. When viewed as a function of consumption, the present stock levels represent eight years' consumption at current rates. As a consequence, recent years have seen heavy cutbacks in production as the industry tries to bring stock levels more into line with anticipated future demand. This has been typified by long summer closures of distilleries and even the mothballing of some production units. The degree of under-capacity working varies between companies depending on the nature of their individual markets. Tomatin, for example, primarily a supplier of new malt fillings for use by other distillers/blenders, has been utilising only 15 per cent of its capacity recently whilst DCL closed down eleven malt distilleries and one major grain distillery in May 1983. A measure of the significance of these closures is that the malt distilleries represented nearly 14 per cent of DCL's total malt distilling capacity, whilst the Carsebridge grain distillery accounted for 24 per cent of DCL's total grain distilling capacity.

Conclusions. From the preceding examination of the industry's performance it is possible to identify general features which have contributed to the present position facing the industry.

First, at the level of individual firms it would appear that the marketing expertise displayed leaves something to be desired, although there are some notable exceptions to this general statement. It is only really in the past decade that firms have been required to show an imaginative approach to the marketing of Scotch whisky. Prior to the 1970s, whisky, by and large, sold itself, and when sales growth began to slow during the seventies the natural conservatism of the industry resulted in a slow response to the changing nature of the competition in the alcoholic beverages market.

This slowness or, in some cases, failure to respond was typified by a lack of concentration on product development or enhancement within specific markets which could have assisted in the differentiation of brands, making them more pertinent to consumer requirements. Although no criticism is levelled at the apparent lack of new product development, the success of products such as Bailey's Irish Cream suggests that some scope does exist in this area.

The long lead times between distillation and eventual consumption emphasises the need for more convincing strategic planning within individual firms than the evidence suggests exists. In a changing economic and trading environment, close monitoring is a necessity if firms are to be in a position to respond to change. Similarly, organisational structure should display sufficient flexibility to benefit from the monitoring process and the flexibility of response to change has to be guided by a clear set of strategic objectives.

Secondly, at the level of the sector, the lack of consensus within the industry as to what is in its long-term interests has been highlighted by the continuing divisions over the topic of bulk blend and malt exports. Given the apparent reluctance at the level of firm to alienate existing consumers by adjusting brand images and positioning, it is surprising that at industry level there seems to be no such reluctance to avoid long-term damage to the product's quality image by limiting the availability of cheaper, frequently poor-quality blends. Similarly the provision of the means whereby a competitor can improve his own product acceptability with a consequent increase in its competitiveness must call into question the activities of the major exporters of bulk malt whisky.

Finally, at the level of the economic environment we move into an area where the industry in general can exercise a substantial influence but little effective control. Many of the environmental factors stem directly from policy decisions, or indeed lack of policy at national and international level and are fully discussed in the following section.

The Impact of Policy on the Scotch Whisky Industry

Policy measures at both national and international levels can be identified as having had an impact on the industry as a whole, and, to a greater or lesser extent, on specific firms within the industry. Policies will therefore be examined at UK, EC and international levels, although it should be stated that few policies have been introduced which are specifically designed to assist the Scotch whisky industry. Where a particularly Scottish flavour has been imparted to UK policy initiatives or where a specific Scottish policy exists, this will be highlighted.

Legal Definitions of Scotch Whisky. A legal definition of Scotch whisky was incorporated into the Finance Act of 1969 covering the three major elements of what constitutes whisky, what constitutes Scotch whisky and a definition of blended Scotch whisky. The definition has the important effect of laying down a minimum period of maturation of three years in wooden casks; specifies the broad process of production and distillation and allocates the title Scotch whisky a unique geographical meaning, implying that the product was distilled and matured in Scotland. Blended Scotch whisky may only claim that title if each of the individual whiskies in the blend is entitled to be called Scotch whisky in its own right.

Thus, through this legal definition the name and reputation of Scotch whisky can be enforced, albeit only within the UK. The definition also provides the basis for persuading other countries to accept the standards laid down and to incorporate such standards into their own national legislation.

The Scotch Whisky Association has been highly active in this area of 'protection' by litigation where misappropriation of the title 'Scotch whisky' can be identified. The SWA also receives considerable support from various UK Government departments in its monitoring and protection activities.

The recent decision to amend the statutory definition to include a minimum alcoholic strength of 40 per cent of alcohol by volume for Scotch whisky is a much needed step which could provide the basis for action against the growth of low strength whiskies.

In June 1982 the EC published proposals to establish general definitions within the Community to cover various alcoholic beverages. Included in these proposals was the acceptance of the unique nature of various national spirit products such as Scotch whisky and cognac. The proposals also included a definition of Scotch whisky in practice similar to that of the UK and recommended a similar minimum level of alcoholic strength. The Scotch whisky industry welcomed these proposals and requested clarification of various points, e.g. content labelling. At the time of writing these proposals still remain to be finalised. There is no doubt, however, that this further, international definition of Scotch whisky will increase the capacity of the industry to take such legal action as is necessary to protect the name and reputation of its product.

Excise Duty. Within this area of UK policy there are two main features which have affected the industry. First, there is the level of excise duty charged on spirits in general and, secondly, there is the payment mechanism.

Governments throughout history have regarded alcoholic drinks as being an excellent and apparently endless source of revenue through the levying of excise duties. In the introduction to this discussion on the Scotch whisky industry it was pointed out that in 1981 £590 million, almost three per cent of total Customs and Excise revenue, derived from the payment of duty on Scotch whisky and currently some 456 pence of duty is levied on each bottle of Scotch whisky. In addition to this, VAT is charged at each state of the distribution chain from warehouse to final consumer.

The industry argues that successive duty increases are now affecting demand and the pattern of UK consumption would tend to support this contention. It is also argued that the law of diminishing returns is coming into play, thereby restricting both the market demand and the returns to the Exchequer.

It cannot be denied that the current position where possible duty increases are the subject of intense pre-budget speculation and consequent pre-emptive buying causes surges in demand and poses stocking and distribution problems to distributors and retailers alike.

On top of the effects of the high level of duty applied to spirits, there is undoubtedly discrimination in the rate of excise duty when compared with other alcoholic drinks on the basis of alcoholic content. Spirits are charged duty at a higher level per centilitre of alcohol than any other competing alcoholic drink such as beer, fortified wines and table wines. Despite recent increases in the duty on spirits being less in percentage terms than on other alcoholic drinks, a major imbalance still exists, as can be seen from Table 6.10.

Up till February 1983, the excise duty payable on release of spirits from bond had to be paid immediately to the Customs and Excise. The result was that a heavy financial burden was put on the industry since distillers and blenders were not paid by their customers for eight to ten weeks. The grievance was magnified by the fact that the brewing industry received a period of credit on such payments in the UK as did all spirits, wine and beer producers in the EC. Consistent pressure by the SWA on successive Governments brought no respite, until February 1983 when a four-week period of deferment was introduced. This was naturally welcomed by the industry but, according to the SWA, the benefit of this relaxation was largely eliminated by changes in the basis for charging duty introduced in April 1983!

Table 6.10. Comparison of duty charged in pence per centilitre of pure alcohol, 1983.

British fortified wine	8·11
Beer	7·20
Imported table wine	9·42
Imported sherry	7·80
Whisky	15·19

Source: Scotch Whisky Association.

Naturally, those companies with a high proportion of total sales channelled into the domestic market have suffered more from the impact of the policy measures described above than those concentrating on exporting. In particular DCL, Highland Distilleries, Bells and Teachers suffered and, to a lesser extent, Long John, Whyte & Mackay and William Grant.

Competition Policy. Again this is a policy area which has influenced the industry at both UK and EC levels, with the major event in the UK being the decision of the Monopolies and Mergers Commission (MMC) in August 1980 that the proposed merger of Hiram Walker (HW) and Highland Distilleries (HD) should not be allowed to proceed. This decision was welcomed by many in the Scotch whisky industry and Scotland in general and provided the first real opportunity for purely Scottish policy views on the industry to be propounded and recognised in the sphere of UK competition policy.

The main areas of concern expressed by the MMC in its report applied equally to the individual firms involved and the industry in general.[18] Since a large proportion of HW's argument justifying the proposed merger rested on the benefits to HD of access to its international marketing expertise (which would boost the export sales of 'The Famous Grouse' brand), it is of some significance that the Commission felt that an independent Highland Distilleries would be more successful in exporting its brands than one owned by Hiram Walker.

Of broader significance for the industry as a whole was the Commission's concern with the possible effects of still further concentration of ownership and control within the Scotch whisky industry. It was felt that an increase in concentration could lead to a restriction of supply of new, quality malt fillings and the possibility of reduced competition. It is also significant that the Commission accepted the view of the SDA that a distinction had to be made between the attraction of foreign inward investment into those sectors where key technologies or products are not present, and the takeover of existing successful Scottish companies in indigenous industries with the consequent loss of local decision-making and an adverse effect on career opportunities within Scotland.

The Commission also showed a disinclination to accept those undertakings offered by Hiram Walker regarding the continued supply of new fillings after the merger because of the difficulty of enforcing such undertakings and the simple fact that it did not provide sufficient safeguard against a misuse of market power.

Although the findings of the Commission apply to only this one case, the degree to which the workings of the Scotch whisky industry were scrutinised was most welcome, the overall result being to warn against further increases in concentration within the Scotch whisky industry: '... it is our view that if the merger goes ahead it may lead to other mergers which will increase concentration still further'.[19]

Within the realms of EC competition policy, the major impact on the industry involved the Commission's decision on the dual pricing structure operated by The Distillers Company plc within the UK. The primary function of the DCL price structure was to protect its distribution system from the impact of parallel exporting. The distribution of whisky in export markets is normally undertaken by sole agents who are responsible for the marketing and promotion of brands in the particular market. Large margins are therefore required by the sole agent to cover these overheads. Parallel exporters rely on the differential between the net selling price of whisky in bond in the UK and the gross export price charged to the export market. Whisky is purchased, ostensibly for sale in the UK, but is subsequently exported and offered to retailers at substantially below the price charged by legitimate sole agents. DCL attempted to mitigate the worst impact of the parallel exporters by charging the gross UK price to those customers who subsequently exported, effectively creating a dual price structure dependent on where the whisky was destined to be sold.

This practice was referred to the Commission of the EC and in December 1977 it notified DCL that the dual pricing structure was contrary to EC law and must be discontinued, thus implicitly sanctioning the activities of parallel exporters. The EC expected DCL to permit the purchase of whisky at net UK prices but must have been somewhat surprised at the speed and nature of DCL's response. DCL did indeed cease dual pricing in the UK but simultaneously withdrew its best-selling brand, Johnnie Walker Red Label, from the UK market and applied to the Price Commission to raise substantially the price of the remainder of its domestic brands. Subsequently Haig Dimple was also withdrawn from the UK market. By forcing up its UK prices and limiting Johnnie Walker Red Label to an export brand only, DCL protected its overseas distributors at dramatic cost to its UK market share. Competitors such as Bells and Highland Distilleries have naturally benefited from DCL's actions, picking up increased volume and market share for their respective brands.

Subsequent application to the Commission for the re-introduction of a revised dual pricing scheme was agreed on a 'one-off' basis, and this has allowed the relaunch of Johnnie Walker Red Label into the UK market. DCL are permitted to add a Promotion Equalisation Charge to Red Label sold in the UK for export to other EC countries. This charge is based on the average promotion cost of the existing sole agents in those countries but the charge is to be progressively reduced over the next three years.

A somewhat anomalous situation now exists since the Commission insists that its decision applies exclusively to DCL. However, other companies involved in exporting have utilised a similar dual price structure to DCL. The position is patently one which cannot continue without resolution. To date it has caused a major upset to the UK market for Scotch whisky and could in the long run demand a major reappraisal of the sole distributorship system common in the industry or force companies to differentiate previously standard brands between domestic and export markets much more effectively.

The action taken by the EC against DCL suggests that it is easier for the Commission to influence the activities of individual firms which transgress the Community's competition laws than it is to take similar action against national governments. Despite findings against member states, notably France, Italy and Denmark, for various policies designed to protect their own domestic wine or spirit producers, substantial barriers still exist within the EC. These barriers range from differential rates of duty and VAT on imported or cereal-based spirits through import deposits to labelling and customer documentation regulations requiring the use of a specific language. Such practices directly affect intra-community trade and competition in the alcoholic beverages sector and their continued existence despite EC Commission decisions against them does not bode well for the eventual harmonisation of the Community's excise duties for alcholic drinks.

Agricultural Policy. An area of EC policy which has resulted in a more beneficial outcome to the Scotch whisky industry is that of the CAP. Prior to the accession of the UK in 1973, purchases of cereal raw materials were made at the world market price, but after accession the operation of the Cereals Regulation resulted in higher raw material prices. Since other producers of food products using cereal raw materials were allowed a refund of the difference between the EC price and the general world price, the Scotch whisky industry, which did not benefit from the refunds, was at an obvious disadvantage. The SWA argued that the imbalance should be redressed by allowing distillers similar treatment to other cereal users.

Table 6.11. Gross restitution payments
to major distillers (£m).

Amalgamated Distilled Products	0·2
Bells	4·0
Highland	5·0
Invergordon	3·0
Macallan-Glenlivet	1·7
Macdonald-Martin	0·7
Tomatin	2·5
DCL	31·0

Source: Campbell, Neill & Co.

Eventually in mid-1981 an agreement was established that as from 1 January 1981 restitution payments should be made to distillers to compensate for higher EC cereal prices, and back payments for the period 1973–1980 were included. These back payments amount to roughly £80 million and came as a welcome cash injection to the recession-hit industry, especially to the malt distilleries who were the major beneficiaries. The gross amounts of the restitution payments made to various distillers are provided in Table 6.11. Restitution payments are now operating on a regular basis and the industry benefits to the tune of £7 million annually.

Also under the ambit of the CAP, certain aspects of the whisky production process have benefitted from FEOGA grants. Physical improvements only are eligible for grant support, and up to a maximum of 25 per cent of eligible cost may be covered. Up to 1982 a total of eight projects have received capital grants, with the peak year being 1974 when five out of a total of thirteen projects were of direct benefit to the industry. Unfortunately, from the published statistics it is not possible to identify the exact amounts of support involved. FEOGA grants are, nevertheless, discretionary, and therefore a project cannot be guaranteed to receive support.

Trade Promotion. 1982 saw the launch of 'Food from Britain' (FFB) wtih the prime objective 'to help improve the marketing and promotion of British food in such a way as to encourage increased consumption at home and a greater penetration of markets overseas'.[20] With £14 million available over five years the aim is that FFB will become industry-financed by the end of the period of public funding. Of course, it is too soon to judge the likely success of FFB, but certain features are already emerging. First, the concentration on fresh and lightly-processed food indicates that the processed food and drink sector will receive proportionately lower assistance. Secondly, the need for FFB to achieve financial self-sufficiency could distort the organisation's long-term objectives.

Nevertheless, whisky has been designated by FFB as a priority product in two of its major markets, France and Germany, and to that extent the Scotch whisky industry should benefit. However, it is arguable that FFB is likely to gain more from the involvement of the Scotch whisky industry, by way of 'piggy-back' promotions, than vice versa.

General Economic Policy in the UK. Various aspects of economic policy pursued by successive Governments have inevitably influenced the Scotch whisky industry in much the same way as industry in general. Space dictates that only the most recent policy impacts be examined and with some brevity.

Price control during the seventies resulted in a divergence between domestic prices for Scotch whisky and those ruling in the export markets, thereby providing opportunities for parallel exporters with consequent damage to the industry's price structure, distribution system and product image in export markets such as Japan.

The gradual reduction in both interest rates and inflation has been of benefit to the industry in improving the stability of its economic environment and has assisted the industry in controlling the cost factors involved in stock replacement and financing.

Similarly, the gradual reduction in the exchange rate between the pound sterling and the dollar to more realistic levels has improved the returns associated with the US market and allowed companies to maintain acceptable levels of profitability despite virtually stagnant or even reducing volume exports.

The increase in energy prices has inevitably led to increasing production costs in an industry where energy is an important production input. Energy conservation has always been an important aspect of the whisky production process and, in general, the industry has made substantial efforts to ensure a high level of thermal efficiency through the use of conservation techniques. At current capacity utilisation levels the capital investment involved in such projects is unlikely to be worthwhile and where investment has already been undertaken, returns are minimal at best.

From the viewpoint of the Scotch whisky industry itself, the most significant area of policy at the international level remains the high degree of economic nationalism with the resultant reduction of market opportunities. Within the EC the continuing existence of discriminatory barriers to trade has already been highlighted, but on a global basis the SWA estimates that in the region of 350 individual tariff and non-tariff barriers exist which limit the export potential of Scotch whisky.

Suggestions for Future Policy for the Scotch Whisky Industry

In the light of the present Government's commitment to free market operations, the likelihood of direct intervention to regulate the activities of the Scotch whisky industry is low, even where the industry indicates a strong unanimity of purpose. The experience of the Distilling Sector Working Party of the Food and Drink EDC amply illustrates this point.[21] The SWP published detailed policy recommendations following an examination of the Scotch whisky industry but, after five years, action has been taken on only a very limited number of the proposals put forward. A similar approach to that adopted by the Sector Working Party will be used here with recommendations being aimed at both the industry and the Government.

It has been suggested in the past that the Government should introduce measures to control or eliminate the export trade in bulk malt whisky in the face of the continuing failure of the industry to achieve sufficient support to impose voluntary regulation of this trade. The objections to such action, which were fully detailed in the Distilling SWP report on Scotch whisky, still remain valid. The banning or restriction of bulk malt to EC countries would be contrary to the Treaty of Rome (Article 34) whilst restriction on exports to non-EC members would infringe Community regulations. Similarly, any form of quota restriction on bulk malt exports would be contrary to the General Agreement on Tariffs and Trade (GATT). For these reasons alone, excluding the possibility of retaliatory action damaging the Scotch whisky industry if controls were imposed, it is impractical to propose any Government action. The alternative, therefore, is to rely on the industry to police such action as is practicable. Voluntary restrictions are said to be in force by those major participants in the bulk malt trade and indeed the export statistics do show a moderation of exports, but it could be argued that such voluntary restrictions are no more than a reflection of the high stock levels of the principal users of bulk exported malt. Equally, it is possible to channel bulk malt sales via the numerous whisky brokers in the UK, thereby apparently reducing the involvement of major companies in this trade.

Given this situation, which is exacerbated by the current recession, the need for firms to minimise their stocks and the continued divergence of opinion within the industry, the most that can be suggested is an exhortation to those companies participating in bulk malt exporting to reduce the level of their involvement and to urge those companies not participating to maintain the pressure for reduction. The SWA might also like to examine the possibility of incorporating within its current generic activities some programme to highlight single malts, thereby assisting the growth in this expanding market segment and encouraging a possible switch from bulk to bottled malt exports. With the present very limited share of the world market held by bottled malts and its prestige image and price, potential for future growth does exist, but any increased promotional spending by the SWA would be effective only in the long term and would need to be backed by an increase in promotional expenditure at company level.

The problem of bulk blend exports is equally worrying to the industry and it is to be hoped that an improving world economic environment will result in some reduction in this segment as discretionary income rises. It is highly unlikely, however, that individual firms will moderate their activities in this area without continued encouragement and pressure from the Government and the SWA. The SWA, however, is only able to exert such pressure as its members will collectively support and therefore external assistance may be required.

It is suggested that further efforts be made by the SDA to identify some practical means of providing support to the SWA in its pursuit of reducing the levels of bulk malt and blended whisky, for example, by undertaking research to establish the long-term effects of bulk exports.

The UK is presently being pressurised by the EC Commission to reduce the excise duty differentials between beer and wines as this is held to restrict intra-Community trade. The time is therefore ripe for the Government to restructure the levels of excise duty on all alcoholic beverages in a more equitable manner which takes account of alcoholic content. The Government appears to have taken some note of the damaging influence on demand of single, large rises in excise duty, but for the health of the industry it is important that this approach be continued and that the level of economic activity within the industry be considered when further duty increases are proposed.

The growing social awareness of the health aspects of alcohol has been reflected in some markets in a trend towards lower strength products and suggestions have been made that duty should be increased to enforce a more moderate approach to alcohol consumption. The Scotch whisky industry has already displayed a responsible attitude to the damage associated with the abuse of its product. A direct comparison cannot be drawn between the problems associated with smoking and alcohol consumption since responsible and moderate alcohol intake has not been shown to have any serious dangers to health. It would therefore be more appropriate to continue the present method of close liaison between the SWA and the appropriate public and private bodies to ensure a more complete understanding of the extent and nature of the problem. The industry has shown itself to be constructive in its approach where possible solutions have been identified and will undoubtedly continue this policy.[22]

Trade barriers which inhibit the potential export markets for Scotch whisky remain a major area where Central Government has an important role to play. The SWA devotes a large proportion of its resources to the identification and elimination of trade barriers and its impact has been improved by the assistance of various Government departments. It is essential that this assistance be continued and increased. It is particularly important to remove those barriers which remain within the EC since their continued existence can be used to justify similar restrictions by countries in the rest of the world. The complexities involved in negotiating the removal of trade barriers make it impractical to suggest more specific policy initiatives but the problem is undoubtedly long-term in nature and requires continuing vigilance and co-ordinated effort to reduce its worst effects.

The establishment of Food from Britain and its possible benefit to the Scotch whisky industry is mentioned in the preceding section. Trade promotion activities do also offer scope for a more uniquely Scottish initiative. FFB recognises that a generic promotion of British food and drink cannot be mounted because of the lack of an identifiable image within the British industry. However, in a recent study commissioned by the SDA, it was pointed out that Scotland has a strong international image which could be exploited to promote the quality segment of the food and drink industry.[23] Since the political atmosphere appears to be more conducive to the promotion of Scottish food and drink products independently from those activities organised by FFB, the opportunity exists to attempt to create a promotional project from which the Scotch whisky industry could benefit.[24] There is already in existence a body representing the interests of the fresh and lightly-processed food sector in Scotland, The Scottish Farm and Food Group. If a similar organisational grouping of the processed food and drinks industry could be achieved, the two groups could together provide the mechanism for a range of marketing and promotional initiatives of direct relevance to Scotland while also contributing to the overall aims of Food from Britain. The SDA is presently investigating with the Scottish food and drink industry the possibility of creating an appropriate organisation which might allow the eventual development of a promotional body similar in nature to that established with the woollen industry as described by David Crichton in Chapter 7.

Despite the Scotch whisky industry's belief that trade barriers pose the single greatest problem to the continued growth of the world market, arguably the future success of the industry depends largely on its own marketing abilities. The authors can only reiterate the general theme of the report by Wood, Mackenzie & Co. that improved marketing and promotional policies must form the launching pad for 'recovery'. The indications that this message is understood by the industry are already in evidence. The decision to mount generic promotions in both the USA and Japan through the SWA indicates a willingness to fight back on a collective basis, while the increased promotional expenditures devoted to individual brands suggests thtat the determination to preserve Scotch whisky's world market position has worked through to company level.

If Scotch whisky is to continue to enjoy market growth in the future it has to appeal to a wider range of consumers than at present and match in a more specific manner the requirements of consumers in the varying segments of the market. To broaden the market will require a careful mix of strategy designed to attract a range of consumers currently outwith the market profile of the traditional Scotch whisky drinker. This will involve orienting the promotional message towards the younger age group of 25- to 35-year-olds and increasing the proportion of female consumers. At the same time the traditional consumer, the middle-aged upper- and middle-class male, must be retained. Essential too is the need to exploit more effectively the variety of market segments apparently ignored by the industry in the past. Wood, Mackenzie and Co. point, for example, to the prestige gift market. Again, encouraging examples exist to confirm a more vigorous and aware marketing approach; the increased promotion of single malt whiskies, the repackaging and labelling of many brands, the introduction of 'tailor-made' blends to the Japanese market based on extensive consumer research, and the adjustment of advertising themes to project a more pertinent message. The introduction of special blends to individual overseas markets is of particular interest in that it does effectively reduce the opportunities for the parallel trader.

Finally, the slumbering DCL giant appears to be wiping the sleep from its eyes. The reorganisation of the company, after an extended period of critical appraisal by management consultants, confirms the capacity of the Scotch whisky industry to pick up the gauntlet thrown down by its competitors in the world alcoholic drinks market.

Acknowledgements

The authors are indebted to The Scotch Whisky Association, Alan Gray of Campbell, Neill & Co., and Ian McBean of Wood, Mackenzie & Co., for permission to reproduce statistics and tables from their respective publications.

NOTES AND REFERENCES

1. See, for instance, Scottish Council (Development and Industry) *Food Processing Opportunities in Scotland*, Edinburgh, 1971; SC (DI)/ Department of Agriculture and Fisheries for Scotland, *Food Processing Opportunities in Scotland*, Report of the Joint Committee, HMSO (Edinburgh), 1974; 'The Food Processing Industry in Scotland', *Scottish Economic Bulletin*, no.16, Autumn 1978, pp.16–22.

2. F.G.Hay and L.D.Smith, *The Food Processing Sector in Scotland*, a report prepared for the Scottish Development Agency (Glasgow), 1978.

3. See, for instance, W.M.Caldwell, 'Changes in Scottish Agriculture since 1973', *Farm Management Review*, North of Scotland College of Agriculture, no.18, March 1983, pp.15–22.

4. This was one of the sectoral schemes of assistance operated under Section 8 of the Industry Act 1972. See Chapter 2 for details.

5. In the period 1978–82 twelve Scottish applications for FEOGA grants related to slaughtering and meat processing were successful. The total grant awarded for these twelve applicants was £2.4 m. Source: Scottish Office Press Notices.

6. Four Scottish applications for FEOGA grants totalling £167000 were successful over the period 1978–82. Source: Scottish Office Press Notices.

7. Economist Intelligence Unit, *Retail Business*, no. 256, October 1982.

8. In the period 1978–72, nine Scottish applications to FEOGA for grants totalling £879000 have been successful.

9. F.G.Hay & L.D.Smith, *The Food Processing Sector in Dumfries and Galloway Region*, July 1979 and *The Food Processing Sector in Grampian Region*, July 1980, unpublished reports for the SDA (Glasgow).

10. This is one of the Area Projects being coordinated by the SDA. See Chapter 2, Figure 2.5.

11. J.K.Thomson, *Should Scotland Export Bulk Whisky?*, SC(DI) (Edinburgh), December 1979.

12. 'Focus on the Whisky Industry' in Grampian Regional Council, *Quarterly Economic Review*, Autumn 1981.

13. Highlighted in The Monopolies and Mergers Commission, *Hiram Walker – Gooderham and Worts Limited and the Highland Distilleries Company Limited – A Report on the Proposed Merger*, HMSO (London), August 1980.

14. A conference called by the STUC in December 1979 to discuss bulk malt exports provided the forum for many trade union representatives to make this point most forcibly.

15. See, for example, Alan S. Gray, *Scotch Whisky Industry Review*, Campbell, Neill & Co. (Glasgow), December 1983; Ian McBean & Philip Augar, *Scotch Whisky/The Distillers Company. Facing up to the Challenge*, Wood, Mackenzie & Co. (Edinburgh), March 1983.

16. '£4m Generic Company for Sherry', *Harpers Wine and Spirit Gazette*, 29 April 1983.
17. Gray, *Scotch Whisky Industry Review, op. cit.* (n.15).
18. MMC report, *op. cit.* (n.13), pp.47–56.
19. Ibid., p.55.
20. Food from Britain, Food Division, *Outline Operating Plan September 1983–March 1985* (London), July 1983.
21. See Chapter 2 for a discussion of the work of the SWPs and EDCs.
22. Scotch Whisky Association, *Industry Policy on Alcohol Related Problems*, (London), November 1981.
23. A.H.Clarkson and K.Inglis *The Food Industry. French Public Sector Export Marketing Strategies. A Model for Scotland?*, unpublished report prepared for the SDA (Glasgow), 1983.
24. 'Food men urged to go it alone', *Glasgow Herald*, 15 November 1983.

7

THE TEXTILE AND CLOTHING SECTORS

DAVID CRICHTON

Introduction

Of all the manufacturing sectors in Scotland, few fit more neatly into the classic stereotype of a 'traditional, declining industry' than textiles and clothing. The general perception of the industry is of one supplying an at best static domestic and overseas market while at the same time facing growing competition from lower cost producers in the newly industrialising countries (NICs). This perception is a reflection of the rate at which the industry has been shedding enterprises and employment in recent years, in parallel with the expansion of textile industries in Taiwan, Korea and other developing economies. Whilst this same pattern is evident in other traditional Scottish industries such as shipbuilding or engineering, there appears to be a greater willingness to accept the demise of textiles as an inevitable consequence of industrial restructuring at the global and national levels.

It takes only a cursory examination of the industry to demonstrate the two main weaknesses in this view. First, to talk generally of 'the textile industry' is misleading. Sectors classified under textiles use a wide range of raw materials from fine animal hairs to petrochemical-based materials; produce a range of outputs from bulk intermediate products requiring further processing to finely engineered garments for final consumption; and supply a wide range of markets both geographically and in terms of quality. Each of these sectors has its own problems and opportunities, and consequently requires its own responses from industrial policy. Second, many manufacturers in the industry consider their main overseas competition to come not from the NICs but from other developed, high-cost economies such as the United States, West Germany and Italy. This does not suggest that a decline in textiles merely reflects a shift in comparative advantage between developed and developing economies but that there is in fact a contribution still to be made to industrialised economies by sectors of the textile industry, an argument which has recently been made forcefully on behalf of the UK industry by the British Textile Confederation.[1]

The views expressed in this chapter are those of the author and should not be attributed to the Scottish Development Agency.

213

This chapter will therefore concentrate on the diversity of the industry and attempt to demonstrate the long-term contribution it can make to the Scottish economy. It begins with an overview of the industry in Scotland and of the policy environment in which it operates. Three individual sectors of the industry are then examined in some detail, looking at how industrial policy has been applied to them and at how it might be applied in the future to assist in realising their potential. The chapter concludes with a case study which demonstrates the success which one particular indigenous company has had in this industry.

The Contribution of the Industry in Scotland

In 1973, an examination of the textile industry in Scotland concluded: 'In sum, Scottish textiles are a classical case of adaptability in response to market forces and technical change. Many problems have been solved and, whilst many remain, the outlook is brighter than for some years'.[2] How much brighter that outlook really was in employment terms can be judged from Figure 7.1, which shows how the textiles and clothing labour force changed over the period 1972–1981. After two stable years, employment fell dramatically over 1974–75. The next four years were again relatively stable but from 1979 to 1981 a further 20000 jobs were lost. Over the whole ten-year period the industries shed almost 40000 jobs, half of these since 1979, representing a fall of around 35 per cent. This compares to a fall of 24 per cent in manufacturing employment over the same period. The textile and clothing share of manufacturing employment fell from 16·7 per cent in 1972 to 14·5 per cent in 1981.

In spite of these dramatic job losses textiles are still making a crucial contribution to the Scottish manufacturing sector. The absolute level of employment is higher than in newer industries such as electronics or North Sea oil. An examination of other measures of performance supports the view that textiles need not be seen as an industry unable to play a long-term role in the Scottish economy. For example, Figure 7.2 shows how output from the sector has frequently outperformed manufacturing industry as a whole over the last decade, reflecting the increases in productivity which have occurred. Only since 1980 has the index fallen below the manufacturing average, albeit marginally. Looked at another way, textiles and clothing together accounted for 10·3 per cent of gross value added in manufacturing in 1979, a figure that showed an increase over the previous two years. Again, this is a stable share of a declining total but it is another measure of textiles' continuing contribution to manufacturing in Scotland.

Although data on financial performance are limited, there is some evidence to suggest that at least for the larger textile concerns Scottish performance on occasions has been above the UK average. A recent study[3] examined the performance of Scotland's fifty largest manufactur-

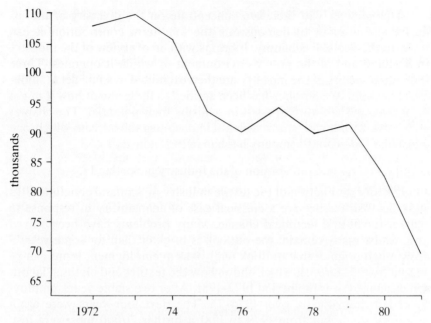

Figure 7.1. Employment in textiles and clothing, 1972–81.
(Source: *Scottish Economic Bulletin.*)

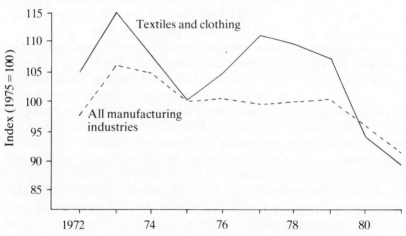

Figure 7.2. Index of industrial production, 1972–81 (1975 index=100).
(Source: *Scottish Economic Bulletin.*)

ing companies against the U K sectoral averages. Nine of these companies were within the textiles sector and six had performed as well as or better than the U K sectoral average. No other Scottish manufacturing sector matched this performance.

A number of the other characteristics of this sector are important in the policy context. Geographically, the textile and clothing industries are heavily concentrated in Strathclyde Region. In textiles, 43 per cent of 1978 employment was in Strathclyde while for clothing the figure was even higher, at 67 per cent. This concentration in an area where regional policy is generally at its most favourable has been an advantage. Unfortunately the higher value added sub-sectors of the industry, particularly wool textiles and fully-fashioned knitwear, are mainly located in the non-supported areas of Borders and Grampian.

As regards its labour force, industrial relations in textiles have traditionally been better than in other sectors. For example, between 1976 and 1980, when textiles and clothing averaged 15·1 per cent of all manufacturing employment in Scotland, the sector accounted for only 3·1 per cent of all manufacturing stoppages.

The figures used so far have covered textiles and clothing in aggregate terms which mask the diversity within the sector. Tables 7.1 and 7.2 give an impression of this diversity and show how the structure of the industry changed between 1968 and 1978.

Table 7.1. Structure of the Scottish textile industry, 1968 and 1978.

Sector	1968		1978	
	Employment	% of total	Employment	% of total
Man-made fibres	1 100	1·2	1 393	2·5
Cotton & flax spinning	8 600	9·5	3 972	7·2
Weaving of cotton, linen & man-made fibres	3 800	4·2	2 415	4·4
Woollen & worsted	17 700	19·5	11 010	19·9
Jute	14 500	16·0	5 749	10·4
Hosiery & knitwear	20 900	23·0	14 419	26·1
Carpets	10 300	11·3	6 084	11·0
Made-up textiles	2 900	3·2	2 519	4·6
Textile finishing	7 200	7·9	5 196	9·4
Others	3 800	4·2	2 581	4·7
Total	90 800	100·0	55 338	100·0

Source: Annual Census of Employment.

Table 7.1 deals with those sectors classified under textiles. Throughout the period, hosiery and knitwear remained the largest single sector and had clearly increased its proportionate contribution by 1978 despite shedding almost 6 000 jobs. Woollen and worsted maintained a stable share of just under twenty per cent and these sectors together accounted for around 45 per cent of total employment by 1978. Of the other sectors, only jute and carpets ever contributed more than ten per cent of the total. Jute, however, showed the most dramatic decline over the period whilst carpets, although its share stayed relatively stable over the period, has in fact experienced a major decline since 1978. Textile finishing increased its share, largely due to its close linkages with the woollen and worsted and knitwear sectors. Apart from the growing share of knitwear and decline of jute, there is little to suggest a substantial restructuring has taken place.

As Table 7.2 shows, clothing maintained its employment level much better than textiles. Within clothing, there has also been a more substantial restructuring than in textiles, with tailored outerwear shedding over twenty per cent of its work force. Overalls, men's shirts, underwear, dresses and lingerie on the other hand have increased both their absolute levels of employment and their shares of the total. Tailored clothing remains by far the largest, however, contributing more than 37 per cent of the total.

Table 7.2. Structure of the Scottish clothing industry, 1968 and 1978.

Sector	1968		1978	
	Employment	% of total	Employment	% of total
Weatherproof outerwear	2100	6·6	2100	6·6
Tailored outerwear, M & F	15400	48·7	12000	37·6
Overalls, men's shirts, underwear	3800	12·0	5800	18·2
Dresses, lingerie	4200	13·3	6900	21·6
Dress industries n.e.s.	3800	12·0	4000	12·5
Others	2300	7·3	1100	3·4
Total	31600	100·0	31900	100·0

Source: Annual Census of Employment.

In terms of the structure of the industry by company, two large groups dominate the sector in Scotland: Coats Paton and Dawson International. The former is one of Scotland's longest-established companies, having been founded in the late eighteenth century. It is also one of Scotland's largest indigenous manufacturing companies, second only to Distillers in turnover terms. Dawson International's history can also be tracked back many years but its major growth and evolution have taken place over the last ten to fifteen years.

Coats Paton had a 1981 turnover of just over £800 million and total employment of 49000. The group has a wide range of textile interests, including threads, woollens and synthetic yarns, garment making and retail. It has also diversified into non-textile products such as diecastings, mouldings and surgical instruments. Coats' most distinctive feature is its geographical diversity. From its early days, it followed a policy of establishing overseas manufacturing operations where high import duties were restricting penetration. Today it has operations in thirty countries and 90 per cent of group profits come from overseas. When this proportion is compared to the 70 per cent of total assets which are employed overseas, it is easy to see why the policy of internationalisation is continuing. Coats Paton activities in the UK have undergone further recent rationalisation and future investment and growth is expected to take place overseas, particularly in the NICs. Diversification out of textiles will also continue, though less than ten per cent of profits currently stem from non-textile activities.

Of the group's total employment of 49000, fewer than 18000 are based in the UK and of these just over 4000 are in Scotland, although the headquarters and registered office remain in Glasgow. The principal operations in Scotland are thread making in Paisley, yarn spinning at Alloa, the Jaeger clothing plant at Alloa, Laird Portch in East Kilbride and the James Renwick knitwear plant in Hawick. There are also smaller units in Campbeltown, Glasgow and Inverness. Despite the small proportion of group activity located in Scotland, its performance and strategy are clearly an important component of the textile industry's total contribution to the Scottish economy.

The Dawson International group is the subject of a case study in an appendix to this chapter and only summary details are given here. Its turnover in 1981–82 was just under £212 million, with employment of over 7000. The group's interests cover woollen and fine hair yarn, woollen fabric manufacture, fully-fashioned knitwear, and garment production. Unlike Coats Paton, it has not diversified internationally to any great extent, though it does have an operation in Hong Kong. Most of its turnover and employment is therefore generated from within Scotland and in turnover terms it is the country's fourth largest indigenous company.

These two firms therefore account between them for over 10000 textile jobs in Scotland. This represents around 14 per cent of textile and clothing employment and such a degree of concentration makes both groups central to the performance of the industry in Scotland.

The Policy Environment

The industrial policy environment in which the textile industry must operate is a complex one, involving separate and potentially conflicting tiers of influence. International trade in textiles is a sensitive issue and has merited separate coverage under the GATT regulations. Within GATT, the importance of textiles to EC member countries has led to trade controls under the Multi Fibre Arrangement (MFA) between the developed economies and lower-cost producers. The EC also exerts an influence through its competition policies with, once again, textiles being considered a particularly sensitive sector. Industrial policy for textiles must therefore be developed against an international background and this undoubtedly creates scope for uncertainty and conflict, since it is unlikely that the interests of all the parties involved will always coincide. Even within the UK, however, the diversity of the industry both in terms of products and of location creates different needs which an all-embracing national policy is unlikely to satisfy.

The EC and Textiles. The textile and clothing industries remain important contributors to the EC economy, accounting for around sixteen per cent of industrial employment in the Community and about eight per cent of industrial output.[4] Thus the EC is still the biggest textile and clothing manufacturing base in the world. The industry has been one of the worst affected by recession with the main difficulties stemming, in the EC's view, from slow internal demand and rapid growth of industrialised textile production in the Third World.[5] The Community accounts for around sixty per cent of the total textile and clothing exports from developing countries to the developed world and it is therefore not surprising that much of the Commission's attention to textiles has been directed at controlling trade with the lower-cost producers.

It must also be recognised, however, that textile trading difficulties lie not only with the Third World. Mediterranean textile producers such as Greece, Spain and Portugal export in considerable quantities to Northern Europe. The United States is another important exporter to the EC, as is the Communist bloc. To see the problem as one of trading relationships between developed and developing countries is thus very much an over-simplification.[6]

For all these reasons it has not been easy for the EC to develop an appropriate textile policy, which for more than a decade has been dominated by MFA issues. Designed with the joint objectives of liberalising trade and protecting individual producers and markets, the MFA I between 1974 and 1977 has aptly been described as 'a disaster for the older established textile industries of the EC'.[7] During that period the Community lost 1.25 million jobs in textiles and clothing, mainly at the cheaper end of the market. By no means all of this was due to low-cost imports since recession and failure to adopt new technologies undoubtedly played a key part. However there were also flaws within the MFA and in the EC's handling of it. For example the Textile Surveillance Board set up under GATT to monitor and adjudicate the agreement proved to be ineffective and was largely ignored. Equally Third World governments found it impossible to control their exports, with goods classed as 'cottage manufactures', and therefore exempt from MFA, often coming from large production units. Another problem was the slowness in application of the 'basket extractor' mechanism. Finally, different member states' policies on participation and the Commission's own slowness in negotiating bilateral agreements compounded the problems. In reality these problems were not resolved by MFA II, established in 1977, with argument centred on issues such as subsidised competition from Italy, outward processing from West Germany and the ineffectiveness of the voluntary agreements with Mediterranean textile producers. In spite of these difficulties, MFA III remains until 1986 with even more restrictions than before.

By the time the new MFA expires, the system will have been in operation for over a decade with no indication that the industry will be in any better position to survive. The lesson which should have been taken from the Long Term Arrangement on Cotton in the early 1960s, namely that trade controls will only delay an inevitable collapse unless they run in parallel with efforts to restructure the protected industries, has still not been learned.

Rather ironically, the reasons why this has not happened during the MFA regime lie to a large extent within the EC's own internal competition regulations. The Treaty of Rome is quite explicit in its position on sectoral aid schemes. Any member states wishing to implement a sectoral scheme must first notify it to the Commission and, if the Commission finds it unacceptable, must agree to withdraw it. These general controls over state aids were supplemented by specific controls over textiles and clothing introduced in 1971 and 1977. The regulations are open to differing interpretations and are regularly the subject of dispute between individual member states or between member states and the Commission. Whether because of this, or because of member states choosing to ignore the regulations, a number of countries have instituted aid schemes for their textile industries.[8]

In Belgium, for example, interest-free loan schemes were introduced in 1976 and 1977 for sectors of textiles and clothing. More recently, commencing in 1982, the Belgian government introduced the CLAES plan aimed at providing support for firms in textiles and clothing which are considered to have long-term viability. In France, the government introduced aid for the wool-spinning and cotton sectors in 1978 and 1979, involving grants of up to eight per cent of the costs of restructuring, and the total costs of both schemes over three years was £2 million. More broadly, textiles and clothing was pronounced a strategic industry in 1980 and in the year to November 1981 this allowed loans and grants of around £230 million to be made available to 105 firms in the industry. These measures were implemented without being notified to the Commission. In Italy, between 1971 and 1973, £95 million was set aside for low-interest loans over fifteen years to assist textile firms in investment and diversification. Evasions of social cost payments have also been cited as prevalent in Italy, particularly among the small wool-textile firms of the Prato area, but these claims have proved difficult to substantiate. The Netherlands have operated a number of sectoral schemes, the most recent involving grants for capital expenditure, rationalisation and export promotion to a total of almost £6 million.

On the basis of this evidence, the Commission has therefore been largely ineffective in controlling instances where member states are committed to providing sectoral aid for their textile industries.

UK Textile Policy. At present, the UK Government's policies towards the textile industry are very much set within the framework of EC trade and competition policy. The UK participates in the MFA through its membership of the EC and, since Britain joined the Community, Governments have only rarely stepped outwith the MFA framework to impose unilateral controls on low-cost imports. Similarly, the Treaty of Rome has been interpreted as precluding textile policies which include the provision of aid to the industry. In recent years, the Government has concentrated its efforts on objecting to support schemes in other member states rather than on offering compensating subsidies to the domestic industry. Whilst this may represent a commendable willingness to fulfil obligations entered into when the Treaty was signed, it poses severe limitations on policy. The classic mistake, of offering an industry protection from lower-cost competition whilst failing to coordinate this with support aimed at removing the long-term need for such protection, is being made. The UK has been in this position before. For example the failure of the 1959 Cotton Industry Act, while attributable to the industry's pessimism about the long term, was not aided by the lack of synchronisation between protection and re-equipment policies.[9]

The wool textile industry did, however, receive support for re-equipment and restructuring under the Wool Textile Industry Scheme, launched in July 1973 under the provisions of the 1972 Industry Act. The components and impact of this Scheme are discussed in the later section on the wool textile sector but for the moment it can be said that, despite some major limitations, this instrument met with more success than the Cotton Industry Act. It was also implemented at a time when wool textiles were one of the products covered by the MFA and so import controls and selective assistance were for once operating in parallel. Unfortunately the UK wool textile industry was not subject to any great threat from low-cost producers, the main competition coming from other developed economies such as Italy and W. Germany.

Another component of UK policy has been the support of research and development. The industry can receive Government support through the Department of Trade and Industry's (DTI) system of Requirements Boards. The Textile and Other Manufacturers Requirements Board (TOMRB) has a very modest annual budget of around £5 million available to support, for example, microprocessor applications, computer-aided design and manufacture and robotics.

The wool-using sector of the industry also had research, development and technical support through the instrument of a statutory levy imposed by the Department of Trade and Industry and used to fund the Wool Industries Research Association, now known simply as WIRA. However the industry voted against continuation of this levy in 1982. The concept of a statutory levy has also been applied to the wool textile sector's marketing effort to fund the National Wool Textile Export Corporation, based in Bradford. The Corporation undertakes corporate promotions and market research for British woollens and, while the sector was rejecting continued payment of the levy to WIRA, it was voting in favour of continuing the NWTEC payments. These two decisions may well reflect the sector's view of the balance between the need to support research and development and marketing, and thus offer a pointer for future policy. They also demonstrate that where a sector feels value for money is being given, the statutory levy, which involves only very limited cost to Government, is accepted as a valid instrument of policy.

Other than these schemes, the textile and clothing industries have received no specific support from Governments although the industries have benefited from more general instruments such as those provided by regional policy. Where the industry is concentrated in an area eligible for support from regional policy, and this is generally the case for the UK industry, there have been benefits. On the other hand, regional policy has tended to provide support for expenditure on new equipment and buildings and this has not always been the need facing the industry. The same limitation applies to the general range of other Government schemes of assistance in that they were never intended to be industry-specific schemes and so any relevance to textiles and clothing firms has been incidental.

In summary then, specific UK Government policy towards textiles and clothing has been limited to participation in the Multi Fibre Arrangements and to schemes of restructuring support limited to two sectors of the industry, cotton and wool textiles. The industry has also shared in the use of Requirements Boards and statutory levies as means of channelling Government support, as well as participating in cross-sectoral initiatives. Whilst this may appear generous by the standards of many other UK industries, it is clear that textiles and clothing as a whole have never been the focus of a policy based on a strategic assessment of needs and opportunities and of development potential. Policy has instead been limited to providing defensive support, and doing so on an *ad hoc* basis with little attention paid to the interaction between the measures used.

Policy in Scotland. The differences between the Scottish and UK textile industries are not reflected in any specifically Scottish policy initiatives. The Scottish industry has been able to participate in UK schemes but, other than through limited support from the Scottish

Development Agency and the Highlands and Islands Development Board, it has had no distinctive treatment from public policy.

Even from the Agency, there has been no coherent strategy for the textile and clothing industry. Selected sectors of the industry have been researched but the output in terms of specific policy initiatives has been limited to the wool textile sector. The Agency's general investment powers have been widely used in the industry, though in its early years these were mainly applied to rescue cases, in particular the investment in Ballantynes, the Peebles-based wool textile manufacturer. This investment has now been returned to the private sector as part of the Dawson International group, as has an investment in MacKinnons, a knitwear manufacturer. More recently, a number of the Agency's textile investments have been made to support management buy-outs reflecting a general trend in its investment activity.

The Agency's Small Business Division has been active in the industry, particularly its marketing section. This reflects what has emerged as a major opportunity for public policy: support for the industry's marketing effort. This was further emphasised by the results of the Agency's review of the wool textile and knitwear sectors. The study is discussed later in this chapter, but its general conclusion was that the most appropriate means for the Agency to provide support for the sectors was to direct it towards marketing and promotions efforts. As a result, a £450000 programme of marketing activity was launched in 1981 for the wool textile sector, although the scheme was subsequently modified to meet EC objections. A similar initiative for the knitwear sector was later proposed, but was felt by Central Government to be incompatible with the Treaty of Rome.

In general the Agency's involvement in textiles and clothing has been reactive rather than initiating. It does, however, provide a further potential instrument of policy for the industry and is currently the only such instrument capable of reflecting the sector's distinctive needs and opportunities.

The Wool Textile Sector in Scotland

Products. This section of the chapter examines the weaving of cloth from yarn spun on the woollen system, though the high degree of integration backwards into spinning and forwards into dyeing and finishing means that the prospects for cloth manufacture will influence to a large extent the prospects for a range of other activities. The Harris Tweed industry is not covered here. Whilst it is an important sector with sound potential, it is basically a cottage industry and thus quite distinctive in production terms from the mainland cloth weavers.

The Scottish wool textile industry is a long established one and is largely concentrated into two geographical pockets: the Borders and the

North-East. Traditionally, around 90 per cent of output has been of woollen as opposed to worsted cloth but there is some evidence of a gradual shift to more worsted production and the woollen share is probably now closer to 85 per cent.[10] At the UK level, woollen production is only around 55 per cent of the total and so the Scottish industry is quite distinctive from the UK as a whole. Its main products are tartans, tweeds, shetlands, saxonies and cheviots with cloth weights generally lying within a range of 350–570 g. Around sixty per cent of output is womenswear fabrics but this proportion can vary widely from season to season and the distinction between menswear and womenswear fabric has in any case become increasingly blurred.

A rough breakdown of the industry's output by end product is presented in Table 7.3. The sector has attempted to diversify away from its its dependence on garment markets and, as the table shows, around fifteen per cent of output goes to the furnishing industry and to the manufacture of accessories, such as hats and scarves. The move into upholstery fabrics came during the 1960s and early 1970s, encouraged by the prospect of long production runs. Despite some success the price pressures in this market are particularly severe and it has room for only a few producers to earn adequate margins. Accessory production is seen as a more direct complement to mainstream cloth weaving and a number of companies are increasingly involved.

Table 7.3. Breakdown of output by end product.

Product	% share
Women's skirts	25
Women's coats and jackets	25
Men's coats and jackets	35
Upholstery	8
Accessories	7
Total	100

Source: SDA.

Natural fibres remain the basis of the sector's output. Wool is by far the major raw material but considerable use is also made of fine hairs such as cashmere, mohair, camel or silk, usually in blends with wool. This allows for a greater diversity in the product range, particularly in cloth weights, though the industry remains generally regarded as a source of heavier fabric for autumn and winter wear. This poses problems which will be discussed in more detail later. The sector has experimented with the use of synthetic fibres but this brings it into more direct competition with lower-cost manufacturers and so concentration on natural fibres and a high-quality product has generally been maintained.

Overall then, the sector produces top-quality cloth aimed at the higher market segments and, whilst each mill has its own particular specialism, or 'handwriting', output is sufficiently homogenous to have allowed the sector to claim a distinctive niche in the market. Scottish cloth is usually recognised by buyers and this offers corporate promotional opportunities which the industry has exploited for many years through the Scottish Woollen Publicity Council (SWPC).

Performance. Table 7.4 gives some indication of the industry's output and sales performance over recent years. Output has clearly suffered over this five-year period but to a lesser extent than experienced in other textile sectors. Further, volumes have held up particularly well when compared to the UK as a whole. In 1972, the Scottish industry contributed eight per cent of total UK woollen cloth production but by 1980 this proportion had risen to twenty per cent. The most striking feature of the table is the growing export-orientation of the industry, with the value of exports increasing from sixty per cent of total turnover in 1977 to 75 per cent in 1981. This reflects a deliberate decision by the industry to increase penetration of export markets to compensate for the decline of the UK as an outlet for high value cloth, a decision which has largely accounted for the sector's relative strength over the period.

Table 7.4. Output, turnover and exports, 1977–81.

Year	1977	1978	1979	1980	1981
Volume of output, m² (million)	15·9	15·2	13·9	14·4	13·7
Turnover, £m	51·7	55·8	54·2	58·0	55·1
Exports, £m	30·6	32·0	34·5	42·5	41·2

Source: National Association of Scottish Woollen Manufacturers (NASWM).

Although year on year export patterns do fluctuate, Table 7.5 gives an indication of the 1981 position. The EC is clearly the major outlet, accounting for sixty per cent of the total. Within the EC, West Germany is by far the largest single market with 25 per cent of exports. This reflects the strength, until recently, of the German garment-manufacturing industry, but is also largely due to the decision of the SWPC to begin overseas corporate promotions in the West German market in 1972. The dangers of this emphasis on a single market has been demonstrated over the last two years as West German demand has slumped dramatically. This has posed a severe problem for Scottish mills particularly when other major non-EC markets, such as the USA and Australia, are heavily protected by import tariffs. It demonstrates the need for the industry to develop a flexibility of response to market changes, as will be discussed later.

225

Table 7.5. Destination of exports,
1981 (% share by value).

Market	% share
West Germany	25
Italy	12
France	3
Other EC	20
Other Europe	8
USA	18
Canada	5
Japan	7
Others	2
Total	100

Source: NASWM.

Turning to other measures of contribution and performance, employment levels in weaving are difficult to identify given the high degree of vertical integration within companies. SDA estimates suggest a current figure of around 4500. Whilst this is a relatively small proportion of total employment in textiles and clothing, a significant number of jobs in spinning and in cloth finishing are dependent on weaving activities and so the wool textile sector actually supports closer to 7000–8000 jobs in Scotland.

The sector has substantially re-equipped since the early 1970s and this process was supported by the Wool Textile Industry Scheme of selective financial assistance. Although the re-equipment has now largely been completed, it has left the industry in a strong position to compete with both developed countries and NICs. The sector in general has therefore performed relatively well. Output and market penetration have been maintained at a stable level and this has been achieved without losing price structure.

Structure. The sector comprises around fifty manufacturing establishments, most of less than 100 employees. Of these, around one-third are vertically integrated mills with spinning facilities supplying yarn to the weaving activity. In volume terms, however, the proportion of output coming from integrated units is in fact much higher than this since most of the larger units produce their own yarn. Much of each mill's distinctive handwriting therefore stems from its own yarns and this can lead to vulnerability to market changes unless yarn is bought in from elsewhere. A recent report on the UK industry[11] considered this a sufficiently serious problem to recommend that the industry reconsider its verticality, especially when compared to the success of the Italian town of Prato where cloth is produced from small, non-integrated units.

226

Most firms in the sector are independently owned but those who are not play a particularly important role. For example, the largest firm, Crombie, is part of the Illingworth Morris group, as is one of the leading firms in terms of design capability, R.G. Neill. One of the most impressive companies in marketing and promotional terms, Reid and Taylor, is part of the Allied Textiles group. Thus important units in the sector are vulnerable not only to the market environment but also to the corporate policies and performance of their parent group.

Comparison with UK Industry. As indicated earlier, the Scottish wool textile sector is more oriented to production on the woollen system than the UK industry as a whole, and also accounts for a disproportionately high share of total UK output. These differences between the Scottish and UK sectors have been examined in more detail in the Rigby report[12] which points out that when the Scottish sector's performance is excluded, the UK industry's susceptibility to imports, its rate of decline in production and its export performance are significantly worse.

The distinctiveness of this Scottish sector in terms of both products and performance creates an opportunity for policy makers to consider it separately from the UK counterpart and develop initiatives aimed specifically at the opportunities and constraints that its distinctiveness creates. This opportunity has not generally been taken, however, as the next section will illustrate.

Policy on Wool Textiles. The Scottish wool textile sector has had only limited specific attention from Government, and policy development rests firmly within the EC and UK framework. Wool textiles are included in the MFA but this offers only limited protection to the sector since the main competition comes from producers in developed countries, particularly Italy and West Germany. The MFA therefore has limited relevance to the sector, though as lower-cost producers improve the quality of their output it will become more important. The EC's restrictions on state aid have been used by the current UK Government to resist calls from the sector for support, but there is one precedent for sectoral initiatives for woollens, the 1973 Wool Textile Industry Scheme.

This scheme was introduced by the Government in July 1973 under the terms of Section 8 of the 1972 Industry Act (see also Chapter 2). It was developed on the basis of a study into the industry's strategic future prepared for the Wool Textiles Economic Development Committee of NEDO in 1969.[13] Its objective was to improve the sector's competitive position by modernising production facilities, improving the industrial structure and eliminating uneconomic excess capacity. It was therefore aimed primarily at supporting fixed capital requirements and the need for this was emphasised by the fact that over 25 per cent of the sector's weaving machinery at that time had been installed prior to 1939. Firms receiving support from the scheme were entitled to grants of up to twenty per cent of the costs of projects undertaken; therefore a considerable burden remained on the industry itself for finding the necessary funds. The scheme was virtually complete by 1977 and over the four years some 300 projects had received support, involving thirty per cent of units in the sector which in turn accounted for sixty per cent of total employment. The eventual cost to the Government was around £16 million in grants and this supported total expenditure by the sector of around £70 million. The scheme was reasonably well taken up by Scottish firms, who received just over 11 per cent of the total support available. Most of the funds, around 85 per cent, went for re-equipment and new buildings and the remainder was spent on rationalisation and on meeting the costs of closures.

The DTI conducted its own assessment of the scheme[14] and this confirmed that from 1973 to 1976 the pattern of investment in the wool textile sector showed a rising trend which ran counter to experience in the rest of the textile industry and indeed to manufacturing industry as a whole. This could not, however, be attributed entirely to the effects of the scheme since a number of other factors played an important role at the time.

In fact, the DTI's survey of thirty-one firms receiving support found that only three would not have made the investment without the scheme. On the other hand, most firms agreed that the availability of grant funding was an important input to their final decision on investment and the industry's view of the scheme was a generally favourable one.

It must be recognised that the scheme played a key role in helping the industry to re-equip at a time when failure to do so would have been disastrous. The positive effects of this are still working through the industry and there is no evidence to suggest that it is any less well equipped than its competitors. It must also be realised, however, that the scheme tackled only one aspect of the sector's problem and that any sectoral policy concentrating solely on the provision of grants for re-investment must have limitations. For example:

The scheme was predominantly used for re-equipment and its other objectives of improving the industrial structure by rationalisation and closures were not well realised. Thus the restructuring required to allow the industry to adjust to lower-cost competition from sources already using the latest equipment was not supported to any significant extent by the scheme.

Many firms in the sector, particularly the smaller ones, specialised in short production runs of quality or high design content fabrics. Grant aid for re-equipment was less valuable to them than to higher-volume weavers and yet their products showed at least as much market potential.

Whilst assistance with fixed capital requirements was obviously welcome, it was not always appropriate for firms in this sector, many of whom would have benefited more from support with their working capital requirements. This is not meant as an argument for a continuous subsidy to loss-making firms but would have applied to situations where, for example, large and expensive stocks of yarn had to be held in order to maintain design flexibility or where the heavy marketing costs of penetrating new areas were proving prohibitive.

During the course of the scheme firms in the industry were debarred from the selective assistance made available under Section 7 of the Industry Act to expanding companies. Thus the scheme could be seen as a defensive one rather than one aimed at supporting the more aggressive, expansionary firms in the industry.

Despite these limitations, the positive impact of the scheme is beyond doubt and recognition of its shortcomings provides pointers to any future policy considerations.

Policy in Scotland. The Scottish industry shares in the albeit limited protection offered by the MFA and as observed also benefited from the Wool Textile Industry Scheme. Within Scotland the only additional source of public support aimed specifically at the sector has come from the SDA.

Most of the Agency's investment activity in the sector is accounted for by the 1973 investment in Henry Ballantyne and Sons Ltd, of Peebles. This was a clear example of an investment made for defensive purposes, since the company would most likely have closed without Agency support. It is one of the few examples of the Agency taking over a company as a fully-owned subsidiary. The investment in fact damaged the SDA's reputation with the rest of the sector, which saw it as a subsidy to a major competitor. This hindered the Agency's ability to develop the type of positive working relationship with the sector on which its potential impact depends. More positively, the SDA's support for Ballantynes kept one of the sector's biggest mills in operation and its judgement in doing so was largely vindicated when the company was returned to the private sector in 1981, when the Dawson Group took it over. The Ballantyne investment was made at a time when the Agency had only limited background knowledge and experience of the wool textile sector. Management of the investment, along with the growing involvement of the Small Business Division in the sector, has allowed a more informed approach to be taken. In addition, a major study of the sector was completed in 1980 which focused primarily on the market opportunities available and the marketing approach required to exploit them.[15]

This study led the SDA into establishing its first ever marketing and promotions project with an industry. The project was agreed with the National Association of Scottish Woollen Manufacturers (NASWM) and the SWPC in 1981, and involves the industry and the Agency jointly funding a £450000, five-year programme. The funds are being used to stimulate increases in individual mills' export marketing activity, to expand the SWPC's corporate promotion efforts and to strengthen the administrative structure of NASWM in order to create a more marketing-oriented organisation. The funds involved are limited but the project does provide a model of a joint initiative by the public and private sectors, tailored to meet specific needs identified during a sectoral research exercise. This model could well be applied in other sectors.

The difficulties of implementing specific policy initiatives within Scotland have, however, been illustrated by this project. After the scheme was introduced, the European Commission took the view that it contravened the Treaty of Rome's competition legislation by providing subsidies to individual firms. The UK Government accepted this view and the Agency and NASWM agreed to exclude EC markets for activities funded by the Agency's contribution. This demonstrates the constraints which the Treaty can apply to new sectoral initiatives, although the schemes quoted earlier in other member states show the latitude with which it has been interpreted.

The Future Contribution of the Sector. The output of the Scottish wool textile sector is insignificant in world terms and its potential to continue contributing to the economy depends on its being able to offer a distinctive selling proposition. It will never be price-competitive with lower-cost producers, nor should it attempt to be so. Its future lies in supplying a top-quality product to high-income markets, and doing so in competition with other high-cost producers. The industry clearly has the potential to do so. The extent to which it realises this is, however, based on exploiting the strengths and minimising the weaknesses summarised in Figure 7.3. Such action will largely have to be taken at the level of the individual company, although there remains an important role for public policy, as the following section suggests.

The Policy Response. Any policy recommendations for Scottish wool textiles must take into account the already existing and complex policy environment. Despite the limitations outlined, there remains scope for initiatives at the Scottish level based, as must always be the case, on an informed and regular monitoring of the sector's needs and opportunities. This requirement must in fact be the first step in undertaking new policy initiatives. The SDA's study of the wool textile sector published in 1980 was limited in depth but did provide a basis for developing a programme of support for the industry. It is vital that reviews of this kind are conducted at regular intervals, say every three years, but they must be more than standard statistical surveys to update employment and turnover data. They must rather concentrate on reviewing the industry's markets and structural characteristics and have as their prime objective the development of specific policy recommendations. Conducted in this

230

way, and involving the industry itself as closely as possible, such studies can themselves become instruments of policy. They remain a legitimate function of the SDA, but their results must incorporate recommendations on how the Agency should co-operate with Central Government, trade bodies and the industry itself in implementing the findings.

Strengths

1. Trading in a relatively stable and premium market segment.
2. Moderately well equipped, with productivity levels comparable to competitors.
3. High-quality product.
4. Tradition of willingness to co-operate in generic promotion of the product.

Weaknesses

1. Facing strong competition, especially from Italy and West Germany.
2. Open to effects of 'trading up' strategies of wool textile producers in Far East and South America.
3. Serious deficiencies in marketing capability.
4. Seasonal orientation to products for autumn and winter season resulting in operations as low as 25–30 per cent of capacity in certain seasons.
5. Structural problems arising from the inflexibility of vertical integration and the vulnerability of some companies to external decision-making.

Figure 7.3. Strengths and weaknesses in the Scottish wool textile sector.

For the wool textile sector, it is clear that the most appropriate area for policy support in Scotland is in marketing and promotion of the Scottish product, and the most likely vehicles of such support are the British Overseas Trade Board (BOTB) and the SDA. As regards the former there might be a case for recognising the distinctive nature of Scottish cloth and promoting this on a sectoral/regional basis. The innovative marketing support scheme being operated by the SDA has already been noted. The sums involved so far are, however, limited and the Agency has experienced some difficulty in securing matching funds from the participating firms. This project should continue to support corporate efforts and extend into further joint market research work, such as has already been undertaken in the French market.[16] The main problems remain those of encouraging marketing initiatives within the companies themselves.

Whilst the emphasis of policy measures should be on marketing support, the sector's structural problems are also an appropriate focus of attention. For example, the traditional seasonality problem could be tackled through a combination of new product development and marketing with support for firms which may have to invest in new machinery to cope with production of lighter fabrics. The problem is sufficiently common to firms in the industry that it may allow scope for a common solution. In particular, a common programme of market research and promotion could help establish the demand for lighter-weight Scottish cloths, and this would be an appropriate initiative for SDA support.

The potential limitations on flexibility imposed by the sector's vertical structure could be tackled in two complementary ways. First, weavers could be assisted to hold larger stocks of yarn bought in from alternative suppliers or even held in a yarn bank accessible to all firms. Second, spinning plants would benefit from support in finding alternative outlets for their yarn. Finally, the prospects for those firms which belong to larger groups should be closely monitored and, if signs of vulnerability to group pressures on the plants are identified, steps should be taken to encourage their independence through, for example, support for management buy-outs.

Provided that such initiatives are effectively coordinated into an overall programme with clear objectives, and that the programme is undertaken with active commitment from the industry, public policy can play an important role in securing the sector's future contribution to the Scottish economy.

The Quality Garments Sector

Table 7.2 showed that the woven outerwear sectors experienced a substantial decline between 1968–78. Yet within this sector, there exists at the top end of the market considerable potential for an important contribution to the Scottish economy. This sub-sector is not defineable in SIC terms, nor does it produce the relatively homogeneous product of the wool textile sector. It does, however, contain some sound companies with good long-term potential and offers opportunities for constructive policy responses.

Products. The sector is heterogeneous in terms of product range, production and design skills. The common denominator that serves to define this sector is its raw material: fabric woven from natural fibres, predominantly wool but also fine animal hairs. The products manufactured may be unstructured, such as skirts and capes, or structured, such as jackets and coats. Some firms also produce accessories such as hats and scarves and there is a growing trend towards buying in coordinated knitwear, shirts and blouses so that the 'total look' can be offered. The largest single product area of the industry is, however, skirts. Most of this sector's output is of classic rather than fashion garments. While this provides some benefit in terms of stability of demand, there is a cost associated with a conservative image in the market place.

A disappointing feature of the sector from the wool textile industry's point of view is the limited trading links between the two. Only around

232

ten per cent of cloth woven in Scotland is actually sold to garment makers in this country, with the main sources of cloth being other U K weavers, Italy, and, for men's suits, Korea. The main exception to this is Kinloch Anderson, who are one of the woollen industry's largest single customers. The reasons for this weak linkage appear to lie in the clothing sector's perceptions of high price and low design capability among Scottish weavers. It is also related to product weight. It is an unfortunate position, since the characteristics of Scottish cloth lend themselves very well to quality garment manufacture. Also, the concept of garments made in Scotland from cloth woven in Scotland could prove to be a valuable marketing proposition which has rarely been tested.

Structure. It is difficult to measure the scale of the sector's employment and output since 'quality clothing' is not a definition used to categorise official statistics. In 1978 (see Table 7.2, above) the woven outerwear sector employed 12000 people but of these only around 7000 will be involved in the production of garments using natural fibres. Table 7.6 categorises some of the key components of this sector.

Table 7.6. Principal structural components of the Scottish woven outerwear sector.

Segment	Type of product	% of output
1. Top quality in U K terms	Branded classics, both for men and women	30
2. Medium to high quality	Mainly womenswear, and kilts. Scottish; sometimes branded	10
3. Value-for-money specification manufacture for large multiple stores such as Marks and Spencer	Large volume mainly womenswear	40
4. Reasonable quality	Small volume, often pleated traditional garments. Often made-to-measure.	5
5. Low quality	Cut, machine, trim (CMT) operations, set up to supply mill shops but now bigger. Skirts and pseudo-classics.	10

Source: SDA.

There are only limited and dated figures on the average size of units in the sector, and these are in any case calculated on a MLH basis and thus not representative of the sub-sector being discussed here. Department of Trade and Industry data for 1977 show the average size of units manufacturing menswear in Scotland to have been 132 employees. The equivalent figure for womenswear units was 83. These sizes were around fifty per cent higher than the U K average though this was probably due to the relative importance in Scotland of a small number of large plants, such as Daks Simpson. Overall, most firms in the Scottish sector are small, with less than 100 employees, though this is in fact large by EC standards.

The majority of companies within the sector are Scottish-owned. Jaeger and Laird Portch are subsidiaries of the Coats Paton group, though Coats' garment-making firms are managed from London. The other major firm, Daks Simpson, is also managed from London.

Performance. The sector's performance has varied widely in recent years, with capacity utilisation rarely higher than seventy per cent. General recession effects have been compounded by recent difficulties in the tourist trade, on which many firms in group 5, and to a lesser extent groups 2 and 4, are very dependent. The strongest performers have been those in group 3, manufacturing almost exclusively for multiple chain stores such as Marks and Spencer, British Home Stores and C & A. A qualification on this must be that although their capacity utilisation has been high, their margins are consistently under pressure from their powerful retail customers. The poorest performance has been in the smaller companies, particularly those in group 4. Their main weakness is the familiar one of marketing, and only the branded names of group 1 are less open to criticism on this. The U K is by far the biggest market for the sector with little exporting being attempted and thus limited options are available when the U K market is less buoyant. Only the larger companies of group 1 are substantial exporters, though even here Kinloch Anderson and Laird Portch are the only ones who could claim less than fifty per cent dependence on the domestic market.

Competition. The biggest competitors in the world market are West Germany and Italy, though their competitive strengths are based on different factors. The Germans lead in womenswear exports while the Italians dominate in menswear. In addition, the German strength lies in tailored, classic garments of top-quality manufacture while the Italians are more oriented to fashion garments, with high design and colour content. The Germans, therefore, are the most direct international competitors for Scottish firms seeking to improve their export performance. This is despite the fact that their labour costs are around sixty per cent higher than our own, thus emphasising their manufacturing efficiency.

Although the main competitive threat is therefore from developed countries, lower-cost producers do have an influence on the world market for quality garments. The effect of Eastern Europe and Far East manufacturers is to depress prices across all product qualities and despite there being little evidence of low-cost producers trading up in quality, except in Hong Kong, they do present a threat to the relative price inelasticity of the top market segments.

Future Contribution. The SDA's study of the sector[17] spent some time on identifying recent market patterns for wool-predominant garments and predicting future trends in demand. The study concluded that over the years 1975–80 there had been only four clear areas of product growth, and these are summarised in Table 7.7, which covers the thirteen largest consuming countries.

The relative growth pattern emerging in recent years fits closely to the product range of the Scottish sector. In aggregate terms at least the industry is not locked into declining markets.

Table 7.7. Wool garment growth (million garments).

Garment	1975 Sales	1980 Sales	% increase
Skirts	49·0	69·9	43
Women's jackets	10·4	20·1	93
Women's suits	17·4	19·7	13
Men's jackets	24·0	25·1	5

Source: SDA.

This encouraging indicator was further enhanced by the appraisal of future trends in the report, which concluded that growth would continue in men's and women's jackets and in skirts, with less promising prospects for women's suits. The main reason for this was the growing fashion trend towards coordinated separates. The pattern of market growth therefore fits very well with the Scottish sector's product capabilities and although competition will be severe, the opportunity does exist for a continued contribution from Scottish-manufactured quality garments. The extent to which industrial policy can assist the industry to realise its potential will now be considered.

The Policy Response. There have been no specific UK initiatives aimed at addressing the needs of the quality clothing sector. More general instruments have of course had an influence. The MFA has imposed controls on the import of a wide range of low-cost garments and, although few of these could be considered as direct competition, their price-depressing effects have been mitigated to some extent. The clothing sector generally is as sensitive in EC policy terms as is textiles, and so the scope for member governments to introduce support schemes is similarly limited.

In the UK, the tools of regional policy have benefited the limited number of new and expanding firms in eligible areas. Other instruments, such as BOTB support, have also been applied. Within Scotland, the SDA's functions have not been focused on the sector in any coordinated way, though the marketing advice available from the Small Business Division has been widely used in the industry. A more radical approach was taken by the Agency in its preparation of a detailed blueprint for the establishment of a new business aimed at exploiting the potential of the market trends identified and discussions are continuing on investment in this opportunity.

In the case of wool textiles, it was concluded that policy would be best directed at identifying and supporting common areas of interest within the sector. Whilst there are such areas within garment making, it is generally a more diverse industry and policy development should recognise this. The needs of the larger firms with strong brand names are very different from those of the volume producers manufacturing for multiple stores, and these are in turn very different from the needs of smaller firms supplying mill shops and the tourist trade.

The limited number of firms operating in the sector provides an opportunity for a 'company-led' policy response. By developing closer links with the sector and developing a better understanding of individual companies' needs, existing public policy instruments in Scotland could be deployed on a company by company basis. It is likely that certain support along the following lines could be appropriate:

It is clear that the Scottish manufacturers who are in direct competition with the West German industry cannot match its productive efficiency, despite having significantly lower labour costs. There is a case, therefore, for selective financial assistance to allow the industry to re-equip. The British Textile Confederation's recent report outlined an interest stabilisation and abatement scheme which could be appropriate for this purpose.[18]

Those firms without marketing skills could benefit from specialist advisory services either supplied directly by the SDA or indirectly through support with professional consultancy fees. These services would be aimed at identifying the company's appropriate marketing strategy.

The concept of some corporate marketing activity, including the promotion of a Made in Scotland label, was tested during the SDA study and was found to be of potential benefit to the smaller companies in the sector which lack their own strong brand. The diversity of qualities within the sector might lead to difficulties over who should be involved in corporate activities but the concept is certainly worth considering in detail, with public funds likely to be necessary on a pump-priming basis.

Co-operation between firms is a possibility without necessarily undertaking an industry-wide corporate programme. It is clear that some firms in the sector have production skills without marketing expertise, while others suffer from the reverse problem. A brokerage function to bring such firms together would be of support.

Linkages between the quality clothing and wool textile sectors are

limited. Whilst garment manufacturers must always retain the flexibility to source fabric wherever appropriate there is little doubt that
improved co-operation, particularly on design and marketing, could
benefit both sectors. There is again a role for industrial policy here
in helping to establish appropriate mechanisms to assist such co-
operation.

In summary, the diversity of the sector does not allow any 'easy
options' for policy. It presents a challenge to adopt existing instruments
to the particular needs of individual firms rather than to rely on industry-
wide projects such as the Wool Textile Industry Scheme or the SDA's
marketing and promotions project for wool textiles. The existing gap
between the sector's clear market potential and its ability to take advantage of it does, however, require this type of response.

The Knitwear Sector

Even excluding the hosiery share of this sector (see Table 7.1, above) and
allowing for the inevitable decline in employment since 1978, knitwear
remains today the largest sector within Scottish textiles and clothing and
by that criterion alone merits a reasoned policy consideration. Its contribution goes further than quantitative measures, however. Other than
whisky, no other industry manufactures a product which is so distinctly
perceived as Scottish in the world market. This perception can be used to
advantage, not just to sell more knitwear but also to increase market
awareness of other Scottish textiles and indeed of other manufactured
products.

Products. The Scottish knitwear industry comprises two quite distinct sub-sectors: fully-fashioned and cut-and-sew. The fully-fashioned
sector uses almost exclusively natural fibres, mainly wool but with an
important cashmere element as well as other fine hairs. It uses straight
bar machinery to produce the components of the garment already knitted
to shape. These are then stitched and linked together to form a garment
designed for durability and retention of shape. The sector's strength has
been built on classically designed knitwear in traditional colours and
most firms have consistently stuck to this pattern in the face of recent
demand shifts to looser fitting knitwear in brighter designs and colours.
Some have however considered this shift firm enough to justify the
necessary investment in new machinery, designs and marketing, offering
a combination of quality output with fashion awareness. There has also
been evidence of a shift to finer wool blends to forestall the possibility of
future constraints on cashmere supply and to the use of cotton fibres to
ease the seasonality problem associated with dependence on wool. The
sector remains, however, predominantly wool- and classics-oriented.

The cut-and-sew sector uses garment blanks knitted on flat-bed or
circular machines. The panels which comprise the finished garment are

then cut to shape and sewn together. The end product is thus of a lower quality than fully-fashioned knitwear, though recent technical developments have reduced the gap. The sector uses mainly synthetic fibres, with wool accounting for only around ten per cent of fibre content. This too differentiates it from the fully-fashioned sector and places it in much more direct competition with the English Midlands and lower-cost producers overseas.

Structure. Available statistics do not allow an accurate estimate for knitwear employment to be made. Data for 1979 suggested that the fully-fashioned sector employed around 8 500 people, and cut-and-sew around 2 000. Both figures have fallen since then, though, for fully-fashioned at least, not to the same extent as for textiles and clothing as a whole. Current employment may well therefore be in the range 9 000–10 000, with around eighty per cent of this in fully-fashioned.

The number of companies in the industry is similarly difficult to identify with any precision, but it has been estimated that there are around eighty units in fully-fashioned knitwear and seventy units in cut-and-sew. These estimates of numbers of units may well have been too high and the membership of the Scottish Knitwear Council (SKC), which claims to represent ninety per cent of the industry, is only between 40 and 50 companies. In any event, both sectors are heavily concentrated into a relatively small number of companies. In fully-fashioned, the largest ten companies account for over sixty per cent of employment and in cut-and-sew the top five companies account for a similar proportion. In both sectors there is therefore a long tail of very small companies, many of them operating as craft enterprises. At this level, costs of entry to the industry are relatively low, and many entrants have short trading lives and are difficult to identify.

Recent changes in the Government's method of collecting output statistics make it virtually impossible to identify the turnover of the Scottish knitwear industry. In the year to September 1980, however, turnover was £94 million. This rose to £97 million in the year to September 1981 and turnover now must be in excess of £100 million per annum. Around 75 per cent of this is in the fully-fashioned sector, which has a much higher unit cost structure than cut-and-sew.

The fully-fashioned industry is heavily concentrated in Hawick and the town accounts for around eighty per cent of the sector's turnover. Other important pockets of the sector are located around Dumfries and in the East Stirlingshire and Clackmannan area. The cut-and-sew sector is predominantly located in the West of Scotland, particularly around the Ayrshire towns of Cumnock and Irvine, and in the Hillfoots area.

The concentration of the industry into a relatively small number of units is reflected in the heavy concentration of ownership. The most striking feature of this is the dominant role of the Dawson International

Group which currently employs around 7000 people, though this includes its substantial spinning and weaving interests as well. Its knitwear employment is probably closer to 4000 but this still represents around 40 per cent of the industry. Dawson's 1982 turnover from knitwear and clothing was over £77 million, and although this again includes a large non-knitwear element it is likely that Dawson companies account for over half of the industry's output in value terms. Many of the other important knitwear firms are part of larger groups. Lyle and Scott and Queen of Scots, for example, are part of the Courtaulds group and James Renwick are part of Coats Paton. Non-UK ownership in the industry has however been fairly limited. An interesting feature of the sector has been that most major job losses in recent years have been from firms within larger groups rather than from independents.

Performance. Across the range of performance measures, the fully-fashioned knitwear sector has consistently produced better results than other textile sectors and in fact than most other manufacturing sectors. This is especially true of the larger companies, particularly Dawson International. It is only in the last year or so that the effects of the current recession have been felt to any extent by the sector, with some short-time working being introduced. Until then, fully-fashioned sales had been increasing at around five per cent per annum, with rationing of sales to retail outlets being a common practice. The sector has consistently resisted increasing capacity to fully meet demand since it was felt this might threaten quality standards. The smaller cut-and-sew sector has been much less successful and there have been a number of substantial closures in recent years.

Much of the sector's success has been due to its strong export-orientation. Export sales account for about seventy per cent of the fully-fashioned sector's output, the largest markets having been West Germany and North America. Japan too has been a successful market for the relatively small number of firms that have tackled it. The sector is stronger in marketing than others in textile and clothing and this is reflected in a well developed branding strategy in the fully-fashioned side. Marketing skills are much less evident in cut-and-sew where exports are only around twenty per cent of the market.

The knitwear sector generally views re-equipment as a continuous process. This has allowed it to take advantage of the productivity improvement generated by knitting technology changes over the last twenty years and to compensate for the shortages of skilled labour which have particularly affected the Hawick trade until recently. The fully-fashioned sector remains much more labour-intensive than cut-and-sew and this is aggravated by the high labour content of some of its auxiliary operations and of the use by some companies of specialist knitting techniques, such as intarsia.

239

Availability of finance has not generally been a problem for the industry, though again a distinction has to be made between the fully-fashioned and knitwear sectors. The industry has a shorter production cycle than, say, wool textiles and this causes fewer working capital problems. There can be problems, however, when companies supply overseas customers from a local stockholding operation, an activity not covered by ECGD support.

Competition. The main competition facing the fully-fashioned sector is from producers in other high-cost countries. The premium market segments to which it is selling tend to be relatively open to importers, even when there are substantial import controls or levies as in the United States. The Italian industry represents the most effective competition and its threat has grown rapidly in recent years. As with fabric and garments, its competitive strength is based on design and colour flair and it has benefited from the growing fashion-orientation of the classic sector. France, West Germany and the United States also present competitive threats and there has been more evidence of trading up by lower-cost producers than in other textile sectors. This is particularly true of Hong Kong, and although other Far East producers are far from achieving premium quality they do bring the usual price-depressing effects.

The cut-and-sew sector is much more exposed to low-cost producers and its continued dependence on the easily penetrated UK market has aggravated this. The maintenance of a strong MFA is seen as vital by cut-and-sew producers but this will not reduce the threat from higher-cost countries, particularly Italy. This sector is extremely vulnerable to competition.

Future Contribution. It is quite clear that the knitwear industry has a continued, and potentially a growing, contribution to make to the Scottish economy. It is to be expected that the greatest proportion of this contribution will continue to come from the fully-fashioned sector. Cut-and-sew producers are likely to continue to be under severe competitive pressures and further rationalisation in the sector seems inevitable.

Considerable potential for further increases in export sales has been suggested and it is clear that the industry has much greater capabilities to realise its potential than the wool textile or garment-making sectors. Its productivity is comparable to its competitors, its access to finance has not been a major constraint and, most important, it has a much more aggressive and professional marketing approach than most Scottish manufacturing industries. There are some areas of concern, however, and these might form a basis for policy consideration. In summary, they are:

> There is a continuing market trend towards fashion-oriented garments. In the past a distinction has tended to be drawn between classic and fashion knitwear with Scottish producers deliberately, and rightly, concentrating on the former. This distinction is be-

coming less clear-cut, with a growing requirement for fashion products and an increasing demand for design and colour innovation in classic garments. Some Scottish knitters have recognised this and acted upon it but there is a need for more intensive qualitative market research to measure the firmess of the trend. If the market is found to be sufficiently strong, investment in increased machinery flexibility may be required. It may also be necessary to review the established industry practice of knitting from stock-dyed yarn. The Italian industry, for example, can react more quickly to colour changes by dyeing yarn and garments.

The industry has made very little use corporately of the Scottish product origin, unlike the fabric weavers. And yet the market's awareness of Scottish origin is much higher for knitwear than for cloth. The industry may therefore be losing an opportunity to consolidate its market position by heavily promoting, on a co-operative basis, a Scottish, quality image.

There has been growing concern over the last five years about the security of cashmere supplies, particularly from China. As cashmere growers instal their own processing facilities up to the finished garment stage, the highest-value and 'flagship' products of the Scottish industry could come under severe pressures. Some firms have begun to anticipate this by developing improved-quality wool blends or even establishing their own cashmere-growing facilities as a long-term option.

Most of the industry's undoubted marketing expertise is concentrated in the larger, dominant companies. The long tail of smaller firms generally do not have the same level of skills and if they are to have a continuing role to play, an improvement in their marketing approach will be necessary.

The industry is heavily dependent on the strength of a limited number of companies, particularly Dawson International. Any difficulties or threats to these companies could have a disastrous effect on the industry's contribution and their performance must therefore be carefully monitored.

Despite these potential problem areas, the industry has shown itself capable of surviving in severe recession and there is every reason to expect a growing role for it as general economic conditions improve.

The Policy Response. There is little to be said about the recent impact of industrial policy on the knitwear industry. It has benefited, particularly in the cut-and-sew sector, from the protection offered by the MFA, and would hope to continue to do so; but at the UK level there have been no specific initiatives aimed at the industry.

At the Scottish level, the SDA has made a number of investments in the industry, most notably in MacKinnons which was returned to the private sector through its sale to Dawson in 1981. Its Small Business Division's marketing activities have been used by the industry, probably disproportionately so since knitwear is one of the few sectors for which SBD have undertaken specific trade promotions.

The Agency also attempted to implement in 1982 a marketing and promotions project with the industry, on similar lines to the one for wool textiles. This scheme would in fact have been a larger one, amounting to £950000 over a three-year period and again jointly funded with the industry itself. It would have enabled the industry to undertake corporate promotional activity for the first time, under the auspices of the SKC. As noted earlier the scheme was not approved by Government since in its original format it was considered likely to be incompatible with EC competition laws, although it had been drafted in such a way as to bear these laws in mind. This was clearly a major disappointment to the industry and may well limit its expectations of future support from public funds in Scotland.

At a UK level, the industry itself sees three main areas where industrial policy would be of benefit. From its perspective these are: more effective controls on low-cost imports; pressures for the reduction of import barriers overseas, especially in the USA; and financial assistance on a scale comparable to that given to other EC producers. In addition the need for marketing support is acknowledged.

These suggestions seem appropriate avenues to pursue with Central Government, but within Scotland, more specific initiatives may be possible:

These should as a priority include further consideration of support for the corporate promotion of the industry. The challenge here will be in devising a mechanism which is acceptable to the EC but this problem is by no means insurmountable. A closer dialogue with the Commission may well lead to an acceptable scheme being developed.

The increased volatility in market tastes which has recently faced the industry also requires more detailed consideration. The problem is sufficiently common to the sector to suggest that a joint market research exercise could be valuable, with the public sector acting as a catalyst.

The marketing constraints on the smaller fully-fashioned companies and on the cut-and-sew industry generally suggest an important role for marketing advice and support, with the SDA being an appropriate vehicle.

Continued penetration of some markets may depend increasingly on holding local stocks to support agents and retailers. Financing of these can prove difficult and an extension of the available financial support to this activity could be a valuable and relatively risk-free instrument.

As with the wool textile and garment sectors, these policy proposals are intended to be as specific and responsive to the industry's needs as possible. Only through a much more detailed awareness of its performance and a closer degree of consultation can such responsiveness be achieved.

Concluding Remarks

The emphasis in this chapter on selecting three particular sectors of the textile and clothing industry in Scotland should not be taken to imply that only these three have a long-term contribution to make. Important sectors such as cotton, jute and carpets have not been discussed, but contain firms with continued development potential. Unlike wool textiles, knitwear and, to a lesser extent, quality garments, however, these sectors are unlikely to provide opportunities for a sector-based policy response. Their future performance will depend largely on the prospects facing a limited number of companies and any role for public policy must be tailored to their individual needs and opportunities. In carpets, for example, the 1968 employment of over 10000 has now fallen dramatically to under one third of this figure and the sector now comprises only a handful of companies. The SDA has played a role in this rationalisation and restructuring process and a similar role may be required in other textile sectors where a company-by-company approach by policy makers will be required.

The three sectors highlighted here do offer scope for a sector-based approach to policy, though it is clear that the priorities will differ. All this emphasises once more the point made in the introduction to this chapter, namely that the diversity of activities within textiles and clothing will limit the effectiveness of any policy measures aimed at assisting the industry as a whole. Policy must be sensitive to each sector's individual opportunities and constraints, and, to allow this, a much clearer and continuing picture of their structure and performance is required.

The other main theme emerging from this chapter is the central influence of the EC on UK and Scottish policy towards textiles and clothing. This is manifested directly by specific measures imposed by the Commission, such as the MFA or limitations on state aid. There can be a less direct manifestation when EC regulations are unclear or where member states apply them differently. A number of member states such as Belgium, France and Italy are operating substantial programmes of aid for their textile industries while at the same time Scottish policy initiatives of a much smaller scale have been disallowed. The UK Government's response to this has been to request that the Commission implement the Treaty of Rome more stringently. The effectiveness of the Commission's response will to a large extent determine the textile and clothing industry's ability to benefit from new policy initiatives in the UK and Scotland.

243

As indicated in the introduction to this chapter, the textile and clothing industry has long been perceived as one of Scotland's declining, traditional sectors. By breaking down the industry into its component parts, it is possible to see the weaknesses in this perception. Textiles and clothing include a number of activities which have considerable potential to continue contributing positively to Scottish economic performance. The recognition of this diversity will assist public policy to effectively assist the industry in achieving its potential.

Appendix: Dawson International plc

The importance of Dawson International to the Scottish textile and clothing industry, particularly in knitwear, has already been outlined. This section looks at the company in more detail, using it as an example of what can be achieved in an industry popularly thought of as in long-term decline. Its relevance in the context of this chapter is heightened by the fact that it operates in all three of the industry sectors chosen for review.

Structure of the Group. Its 1982 accounts show that Dawson International had a turnover of just under £212 million and over 7000 employees. This makes the group not only the largest single textile and clothing operation within Scotland but also one of the country's largest companies. Its headquarters are at Kinross but these are operated with a very small number of staff, considerable autonomy being given to management of the subsidiary companies. Table 7.8 summarises the current structure of the group and its turnover. Spinning and weaving represent the largest single source of turnover with 44 per cent of the total, and companies included under this heading are Laidlaw and Fairgrieve, Leithen Mills, Blackwood Bros, and Todd and Duncan. Knitwear and clothing contribute 36 per cent of the total and comprise Ballantyne Sportswear, Dorward, Barrie, Gladstone, Glenmac, Mackinnon, McGeorge, Pringle and Braemar. The merchanting and processing category largely comprises Joseph Dawson Ltd, the Bradford-based cashmere processors. The group also has subsidiaries in Australia, Hong Kong, South Africa, Switzerland, the USA and West Germany. Most of these are concerned with marketing and distribution but one of the Australian companies is responsible for the breeding of cashmere goats and production of fibre, while the Hong Kong operation is an outward processing plant manufacturing knitwear.

There is considerable trading within the group, with fibres being sold to spinners, and yarn to weavers and knitters. This trade only accounts for 35 per cent of total turnover, however, and so the bulk of business stems from sales outside the group.

Historic Development. The development of Dawson International began in 1946 when the current President of the Group, Sir Alan Smith, joined the Kinross-based cashmere and wool spinners, Todd and Duncan. In 1961, Todd and Duncan purchased the Bradford cashmere processors Joseph Dawson (Holdings), becoming a publicly quoted company in the process and acquiring the Dawson name. In 1974, the group changed its name to Dawson International and over the last ten years it has followed a rapid but controlled policy of acquisition and diversification.

Table 7.8 Dawson International: turnover structure, 1982.

Activity	Turnover (£m)
Knitwear and Clothing	77·3
Spinning and Weaving	92·8
Raw material merchanting and processing	41·8
Total	211·9

Source: Annual Reports.

The group's progress since the early 1960s has gone largely un-checked, with only two bad years causing setbacks. The first was in 1971, when heavy stock losses led to profits falling from £2.74 million to £380000. The second, in 1975, was more serious, with profits falling from £6.24 million to £500000. This was largely due to heavy over-stocking and adverse demand conditions and the response was a radical reformulation of strategy. The group became much more firmly decentralised with headquarters staff kept to a minimum. Each subsidiary was run as a separate profit centre but was instructed not to order raw materials from suppliers until firm orders had been received from customers, either within or outside the group. The likelihood of being burdened by un-wanted and unsaleable stocks is therefore limited, and working capital requirements and interest charges are kept to a minimum. Since that reorganisation, profits have risen in each successive year over the seven-year period.

Business Strategy. This tight stock control has been an important feature of the company's success. So, too, has been the autonomy given to local operations, with board members visiting subsidiaries only around four times a year. Thus each member company is run very much as a separate company though central control is applied if poor performance is sustained over a prolonged period.

The main basis of Dawson International's success has, however, been its marketing strategy. Although 49 per cent of sales in 1982 were within the UK, much of this was to tourists or to other companies in the group. Thus the marketing strategy is very much an export-oriented one. Considerable investment has been made in all aspects of marketing, from market research to consumer advertising. This has been done aggressively and professionally: marketing staff are multi-lingual; regular visits are made to markets; overseas direct marketing operations are established where appropriate and, where not, agents are carefully selected and controlled; and advertising is subtle, of a high quality, and well targeted. Underlying all of this, the design function is given an appropriately high priority and status, allowing Dawson companies to lead or anticipate fashion trends much more successfully than most other companies in Scotland.

The success of the strategy is characterised by some of the more innovative projects undertaken by the group: its outward processing plant in Hong Kong; its establishment of a cashmere breeding herd in Australia to counteract in the very long term any restrictions on cashmere supply; its introduction, through Pringle, of the 'Lamaine' fine wool blend again to anticipate any difficulties with the cashmere trade; and Pringle's ability to switch into more fashion-oriented knitwear as appropriate to meet anticipated market trends. Finally, unlike most textile and clothing companies the group operates its own research and development division which has introduced, for example, new microprocessor applications to the company's operation.

Performance. The obvious success of the group's business strategy over the recent past is summarised in Table 7.9. Turnover has risen at rates of 17·8 per cent, 13·9 per cent and 16·8 per cent over the years 1979–1980, 1981–81 and 1981–82 respectively. Exports have also risen in each of the years under review, as have pre-tax profits.

Table 7.9. Dawson International: performance, 1979–82 (£m).

	1979	1980	1981	1982
Total turnover:	135·1	159·2	181·4	211·9
within group	38·9	46·0	50·4	58·4
outside group	96·2	113·2	131·0	153·5
Exports	40·3	41·4	54·0	65·8
Profit before taxation	16·3	18·2	20·7	23·6
Dividends	3·4	4·1	4·8	5·2
Earnings per share	21·4	26·2	15·0	19·7

Source: Annual Reports.

Table 7.10 shows the geographic distribution of sales to customers outside the group and how it has changed over the period 1980–82. The table reflects a growing shift towards an export-oriented pattern of business, particularly when it is borne in mind that UK sales include a substantial proportion of indirect exports. Sales to Europe and the Americas have comprised a relatively stable share of the business but exports to the Far East and other countries have grown significantly.

Table 7.10. Dawson International: geographic distribution
of external sales (£m).

Destination	1980	1981	1982
UK (including indirect exports)	65	70	75
Other EC	24	32	36
Rest of Europe	9	10	13
North and South America	10	10	14
Far East and others	5	9	16
Total	113	131	154

Source: Annual Reports.

Characteristics of Success. Certain characteristics of Dawson International's business strategy and performance can be used as indicators of where the future success of textile and clothing companies in Scotland might lie. They are:

An effective, aggressive marketing policy, incorporating the whole package of marketing activities from design through to market research, efficient selling and quality promotion and advertising;

within that marketing policy, a strong export-orientation to counter the relative decline of the UK as a market for premium products;

early anticipation of potential problems as part of sound overall corporate planning, for example the maintenance of substantial R & D expenditure, the tackling of the potential cashmere problem;

tight control of financial planning, and particularly of stock-holding, to minimise working capital requirements.

It would be unrealistic and inappropriate to attempt the creation of an industry of mini-Dawson Internationals. But these fundamental characteristics of the group will have to be more widely adopted if textile and clothing firms are to have a future in Scotland.

Policy Relevance. The Dawson group's experience has owed very little to support from industrial policy and its commercial philosophy has always been a strongly non-interventionist one. An appreciation of the factors behind the group's performance can, however, be used as a guide to effective policy making. Whilst there will never be a substitute for effective and innovative management, industrial policy should aim to create the environment in which such management can develop and subsequently operate effectively within the industry. Using Dawson's experience as a guide allows a clearer identification of policy priorities.

NOTES AND REFERENCES

1. British Textile Confederation, *The United Kingdom Textile Industry, A Plan for Action* (London), March 1983.

2. G.T.Murray, *Scotland: The New Future*, STV/Blackie (Glasgow), 1973, p.71.
3. P.E.T.Addison, *The Comparison of the Performance of the 50 Largest Scottish Manufacturing Companies with the UK Sectoral Averages*, unpublished MBA project, University of Strathclyde, 1981. It should be noted that this data is based on SIC Order XIII only.
4. European Communities Commission Background Report, *Textiles and Clothing, General Guidelines for an Industrial Policy*, Brussels, 1979.
5. *Ibid.*
6. For a detailed exposition of the development of international controls on textile trade see V.Cable, *World Textile Trade and Production*, EIU Special Report No.63, Economic Intelligence Unit Ltd (London), 1979.
7. Chris Farrands, 'Textile Diplomacy: The Making and Implementation of European Textile Policy 1974–1978', *Journal of Common Market Studies*, vol.18, no.1, 1979, p.25.
8. NEDO, *Sectoral Aids to the Textile and Clothing Industries Overseas*, unpublished report, London, 1982.
9. D.H.Humphrey, *A Review of Evidence on the Economic Costs and Benefits of Trade Protection*, NEDO Economic Working Paper No.2, September 1981.
10. SDA, *A Quality Garment Manufacturing Industry for Scotland?*, unpublished report, Glasgow, 1982, prepared for the SDA by John Wilcox and David Rigby.
11. David Rigby, *Changing Needs and Relationships in the UK Apparel Fabric Market*, a report prepared for NEDO (London), 1982.
12. *Ibid.*
13. W.S.Atkins and Partners, *The Strategic Future of the Wool Textile Industry* (London), 1969.
14. Department of Industry, *Wool Textile Industry Scheme: An Assessment of the Effects of Selective Assistance under the Industry Act 1972* (London), 1978.
15. SDA, *Opportunities for the Scottish Wool Textile and Knitwear Industries*, Glasgow, 1981.
16. SDA and SWPC, *The Marketing of Scottish Wool Textiles in France*, Glasgow, 1981.
17. SDA, *op. cit.* (n.10), p.10.
18. British Textile Confederation, *op. cit.* (n.1), pp. 22–23.

8

THE NATURAL RESOURCE-BASED SECTOR

DAVID M. HENDERSON

Introduction

This chapter addresses itself to the experiences of a number of Scottish resource-based industries, specifically in the three areas of forest products, fish products and aluminium smelting – with some slight attention to minerals and renewable energy in order to set the latter in context. Particular consideration is given in a case study to the pulp and paper development at Fort William. It is readily admitted that this is not a complete list of resource-based industries – meat and dairy products, other food processing, whisky distilling, oil refinery and petrochemicals, coal-fired electricity generation could all be included in that category. Several of these are, however, sufficiently important to merit separate treatment elsewhere in this volume.

A definitional characteristic of the process industries considered here is that they are based upon an indigenous resource, which means that it is virtually impossible to separate the fortunes of the process industry from those of the primary industry upon which it is umbilically dependent. Thus forest products industries cannot be understood without an appreciation of Scottish forestry, fish processing without studying the fish industry, nor aluminium smelting without looking at electricity supply. The effects of public policy must, therefore, be observed and analysed at two levels – upon the primary industry, and upon the processing industry. Taken together, these primary and processing industries are an important group in their own right, employing about 32000 people in Scotland (two per cent of all employment). Their importance to the fabric of Scottish life is disproportionate to their size, however, because they are for the most part located in the remote rural areas, where whole communities are often dependent upon them. In the Highlands and Islands, for example, they account for about seven per cent of all employment.[1] Their relationship with regional policy is, not surprisingly, a recurring theme in this chapter.

These are not glamorous industries – their technology is mainstream rather than advanced, and they win few Queen's Awards for exports.

The views expressed in this chapter are those of the author
and should not be attributed to the HIDB.

Theirs is a familiarity born of long experience, and quiet acceptance as 'regulars' on the Scottish industrial scene. Yet they have a capacity to capture the headlines (as EC Fisheries Policy negotiations, the Invergordon smelter closure and timber exports to Scandinavia have recently demonstrated) which reveals that when these industries are threatened, Scotland instinctively recognises their importance.

Forestry

Scottish Forests. Forestry is a major natural resource in Scotland. This was the case in medieval times and down to the early industrial revolution, when there were large-scale timber exports and numerous industrial activities based upon the resource. Rapacious extraction in the seventeenth and eighteenth centuries decimated the forests, and, although there was some recovery in Victorian times, the urgent requirements of World War I led to the hurried removal of most of the accessible stands that remained. This acute depletion and the strategic vulnerability revealed in wartime persuaded Parliament of the need for a national forestry policy. The Forestry Act was passed in 1919, which established the Forestry Commission and laid down the public framework to implement a long-term strategy of forest regeneration in the UK. Further depletion of mature forests during World War II resulted in another Forestry Act, which provided the basis for an increase in the rate of afforestation by the Commission, and introduced incentives to encourage the development of private forestry.

The present state of Scotland's forests testifies to the success of these measures. The area under forest is now about 860000 hectares, or 12 per cent of the land surface of Scotland (compared to 3 per cent in 1919), while the average annual increase in planted area during the 1970s was 22000 ha. Wood production (fellings and thinnings) in 1981 was almost 1.5 million m³, about one-third of the total UK production. Approximately 6300 people are directly employed in Scottish forests.

The distribution of Scottish forests is shown in Figure 8.1. Overall, the Forestry Commission at present accounts for about 60 per cent of the planted area and 64 per cent of wood production, and private woodlands the remainder. Private woodland are most significantly concentrated in the Inner Moray Firth/Speyside area, the Southern Uplands, Deeside and Argyll. Table 8.1 sets out estimates of annual production from Commission and private forests in Scotland in the period 1981–96. The data relate to conifers, which dominate Scottish production, and do not include hardwoods, which account for only 13 per cent of Scottish timber output. In round terms, production from Scottish forests will double to the end of the century as post-war plantings nature. By then, Scottish forests will account for about 40 per cent of the UK total, compared to the present 33 per cent. In this period, the greatest growth in output will

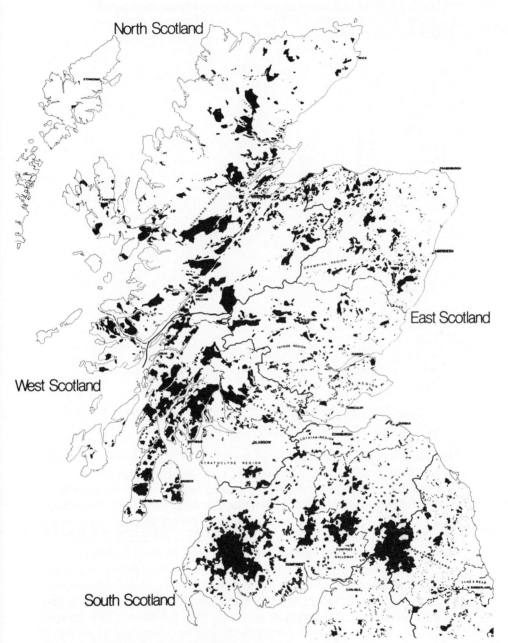

North Scotland

East Scotland

West Scotland

South Scotland

Figure 8.1. Forestry in Scotland, showing conservancy areas.
(Source: *Forestry Commission*, 1978.)

251

Table 8.1. Estimated average annual production of conifer wood in Scotland, by conservancy[1] (000 m³, overbark): Forestry Commission and private forests.

Area	1977–81	1987–91	1992–96	% increase (1977–81 to 1992–96)
Sawlogs				
North	235	285	290	+23
East	230	335	400	+74
South	185	290	365	+97
West	160	300	390	+144
Total	810	1210	1445	+78
Small Round Wood				
North	120	200	290	+142
East	205	325	385	+88
South	205	370	570	+178
West	120	180	290	+142
Total	650	1075	1535	+136
All Timber				
North	355	485	580	+63
East	435	660	785	+80
South	390	660	935	+140
West	280	480	680	+143
Total	1460	2285	2980	+104

[1] Forestry Commission conservancy areas shown on Figure 8.1.
Source: *Forestry and British Timber*, April 1978.

take place in the south and west of Scotland. On these trends, assuming that present policies and planting rates are maintained, output would then double again in the following twenty years. In the international context, however, Scotland will remain a relatively minor producer, accounting for less than one per cent of total European production at the end of the century. Nevertheless, this increase in supply will inevitably have important implications for wood-based industries in Sotland.

Forest Product Industries. The timber resources of Scotland fall into two general categories of use – 'sawlogs' of a size suitable for sawmilling into square-edged timber, and small round wood and residues which may be used to make panel products or wood pulp for paper. The Scottish sawmilling industry is well established, and has a successful record of utilising available sawlog supplies. Since unprocessed timber is a bulky commodity, sawmills have been located near the forest resources to minimise transport costs, and, as a result, are well distributed throughout Scotland. Table 8.2 shows the geographical and size distribution of these sawmills, which collectively employ about 1500 people. Total production of sawn timber in 1981 was 320000 m³ and was mostly directed to the fencing, sheds, packaging/pallets, mining timber and construction sectors of the UK market. Some sawmills are owned by timber merchants, who integrate their domestic production with imported supplies. The largest sawmill is at Kilmallie, near Fort William.

Table 8.2. Size distribution of sawmills by conservancy area, 1981.

Area	\multicolumn{6}{c}{Annual output capacity in 000 m³}
	0–2·5	2·5–5	5–10	10–25	25+	Total
North	4	3	7	1	1	16
East	29	5	6	5	—	45
West	13	4	4	1	—	22
South	27	7	4	4	—	42
Total	73	19	21	11	1	125

Sources: Arthur D. Little; Forestry Commission data.

Scottish sawmills use all of the sawlogs currently available, and account for six per cent of the sawn timber consumed in the UK. The British market is, in fact, heavily dependent upon overseas supplies, with about 86 per cent of sawn timber being imported, especially from Scandinavia, Eastern Europe and North America. As sawlog production in Scotland grows rapidly over the next twenty years and this supply constraint is removed, there will be opportunities for Scottish sawmills to achieve greater penetration of this market. An important factor on their side will be their geographical proximity, which will give a transport cost advantage over importers and permit quick and flexible supply relationships with customers. On the other hand, sawmilling is an industry in which there are considerable production line economies of scale. Mills producing over 100000 m³ per annum are not uncommon in Scandinavia, and even over 200000 m³ in Canada, whereas Table 8.2 shows that the majority of Scottish sawmills have less than 10000 m³ per annum capacity. Many of the potential economies of scale can, however, be realised if mill size is increased to about 35000 m³ per annum, on a double shift basis, and a number of Scottish sawmills (including Kilmallie) have already adapted and modernised their equipment and increased their production to obtain these unit cost reductions. Product quality can be improved by kiln drying and stress grading, while marketing aspects such as brand stamping, technical sales force and active promotion can help the market image of the domestic product. The challenge to Scottish sawmills, individually and collectively, will be to realise these improvements and place the increasingly available volumes of sawlogs into the enormous UK market.

Round wood which is too small to be used economically in a sawmill (generally less than 15 cm diameter) is produced as a result of forest thinning activity and from the tops of sawlogs. Sawmills generate residue products in the form of slabs, chips, sawdust and bark. These lower-value forest products can be used to make a range of composition panels (such as particle board, fibreboard, hardboard, oriented strand board) or as the raw material for wood pulping, which may be integrated with paper manufacture. Productive utilisation of small round wood and residues has an important bearing on the profitability of both forest operations and sawmills.

Recent Scottish experience in this sector has been beset with difficulties which have been well publicised. In 1966, a pulp and paper mill was built by Wiggins Teape at Fort William to utilise the volumes of small round wood becoming available from post-war plantings. This project is considered in detail as a case study at the end of the chapter. The pulp mill closed in 1980 due to a combination of depressed world markets, strong UK currency and superseded technology, making 450 people redundant. Loss of this outlet for small round wood provoked a crisis of considerable magnitude for timber growers, harvesters and transporters in the north and west of Scotland. Some partial relief has been found in timber exports to Scandinavia, but these are less profitable, and unreliable outlets for the longer term.[2] Sawmills in the north have lost their local residue outlets altogether, obliging them to transport these by-products much further in order to secure markets, with serious implications for profitability.

In the mid-1970s, two particle board plants were established by Scottish companies at Cowie, near Stirling, and Irvine. Both of these experienced acute trading difficulties a few years later, due to the world recession and European overcapacity, and were taken over by Bison-werke. This German forest products company appears to have been successful in making the plants competitive and able to survive in the currently depressed market. At Cowie, the original production line makes furniture-grade particle board, while more recently installed plant produces tongue-and-groove flooring material, and medium-density fibreboard. Employment at Cowie is currently around 215. The Irvine factory also produces chipboard and following its recent reorganisation had a workforce of 70.[3]

The decision was taken in 1983 to undertake a £13 million project at Dalcross, near Inverness, to manufacture oriented strand board (OSB) from waferised small round wood. This structural composition board is new to the UK, although it has been used in North America for several years as a substitute for plywood in house construction and packaging. A new company called Highland Forest Products has been set up and it is expected that the factory will employ about 90 people when it opens in

1985. The project will use 160000 m³ of small round wood annually, which will be a welcome outlet for northern growers. Caberboard have also announced an intention to manufacture OSB at Cowie but, at time of writing, their proposals were at a less definite stage of formulation.

Figure 8.2 shows the estimated supply/demand balance for small round wood and residues to 1996. It can be seen that there is an existing large surplus over use which will increase dramatically to the end of the century. A major challenge to the Scottish forest products industry in the next decade will be to find profitable ways of utilising these resources. A study recently carried out for the Scottish Forest Product Development Group suggested that the best opportunities for further development may exist in particle board, oriented strand board, and chemi-thermo-mechanical pulp connected to either tissue or wood-containing paper production.

Although the world supply/demand balance in wood and wood-based products may become tight by the end of the century, the present situation is one of oversupply in a period of major recession. Trade in forest products is international, world markets are highly competitive, and many foreign suppliers are well established in the UK. Opportunities for Scotland will arise from the fact that there will be available rapidly increasing supplies of good quality raw material, in close proximity to the large home market. This opens up the possibility for industrial development in Scotland, founded upon competitively-priced wood-based products.

The Role of the Forestry Commission.[4] The Forestry Commission was established by statute in 1919 and represents the state's first involvement in a productive commercial undertaking. Its form of organisation precedes the public corporation, and the Commission has in fact the status of a Government department, directly accountable to ministers and to Parliament. The responsibilities of the Forestry Commission were consolidated in the Forestry Act of 1967, which sets out the manner in which the Commission is expected to carry out a dual role as both 'Forestry Enterprise' and 'Forestry Authority'.

As a Forestry Enterprise, the Commission has a primary responsibility to develop and manage forests and to produce wood for industrial use. Since 1919, these direct forestry activities in Scotland have grown to a very large scale. The Commission's plantations have increased from 20000 ha in 1930, to 100000 in 1950, to 520000 in 1982, making it by far the largest holder of land in Scotland. It produces over two thirds of Scotland's timber and employs directly 3400 people north of the border. Scotland has always been the region of Britain where the Commission has carried out the largest part of its work. Almost 60 per cent of its planted land is in Scotland, providing 40 per cent of its production at present (a rising proportion as young Scottish forests mature) and about 46 per cent

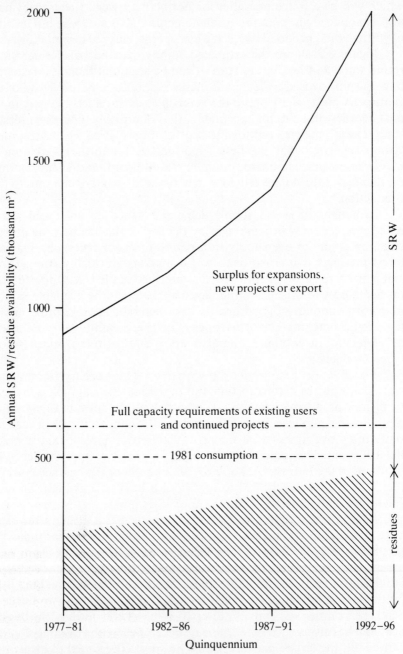

Figure 8.2. Annual availability of small round wood and residues
(1977–81 to 1992–96).

of its employees are in Scotland. The importance of the Scottish dimension is reflected in the fact that the Commission's headquarters are in Edinburgh.

Originally, the Commission's role was seen as that of building up a strategic reserve of timber for the nation, but with that objective realised, in recent years more specific economic and social objectives have been established. The Commission has been set by the Treasury a target rate of return of three per cent in real terms on the assets which it employs. This rate is somewhat less than that which is required of most other public sector trading bodies, in recognition of the strategic and long-term nature of forestry investment, and of the Commission's non-commercial responsibilities (e.g. maintaining employment in areas of rural depopulation, provision of recreational facilities, conservation and amenity activities). The assets of the Commission are revalued every five years, so that performance can be measured against the target rate, and income and expenditure standards set for the next period.

The other aspect of the Commission's work is as the nation's Forest Authority. In this role, it operates closely with private timber growers, timber-using industries, research institutions, and central and local government, to advance knowledge about forestry and to bring about the best overall use of the nation's forest resources. An important role is to administer grant schemes for private forests (£5.5 million in 1982), provide advice to private growers, and to regulate the felling of private forests through a system of licensing. The Commission undertakes research, either at its own hand or by contract, into scientific, technical and management aspects of forestry, and disseminates the findings.

It will be seen, therefore, that in the Forestry Commission, the Government possesses a well-developed instrument through which to implement its policies towards forestry, timber supply and, indirectly, the forest products industries. The first area of policy control is upon the total extent of afforestation. Since 1919, it has been regarded as a desirable strategic goal to increase Britain's forests each year. This has been implemented both by the Forestry Commission and by private growers encouraged by planting grants and tax incentives. In recent years, however, the average annual rate of planting has slowed down, reflecting a shortage of suitable land on the market, the impact of changes in taxation and the requirement that the Commission generate a near-commercial rate of return, none of which may be permanent factors. As it takes a conifer about 50 years to reach maturity, the effect of any sustained reduction in plantings would impact upon timber availability early next century, but present trends and policies indicate a slowing in the rate of growth of the national forest resource, rather than a reduction. It is the size of this available national forest harvest, of course, which will define the scope for forest product industrial development in the future.

The balance of forest ownership and commercial activity between the Forestry Commission and private growers is a sensitive policy issue and one which has some important implications for forest product industries. At present, the Commission accounts for about 64 per cent of timber production in Scotland, which on present trends will increase to 70 per cent by the end of the century. Because it has such a dominant supply position, the Commission has to be careful not to introduce distortions into the market through its selling policies, in spite of the statutory requirement to maximise the return on its assets. In the sawlog market, this is pursued by placing lots of timber for auction, and licensing similar sales from private forests. In the small round wood market, the Commission seeks to encourage industrial investment while preserving competition by a willingness to enter into direct supply for up to 50 per cent of small round wood requirements. These arrangements have the attraction that industrial developers seeking small round wood can negotiate the majority of their requirements with one large and reliable supplier, an advantage which many parts of Europe and North America do not enjoy. Although the private sector comprises a very large number of forest owners, it is not so fragmented in its commercial dealings. Many of the smaller units are collectively run by forest management companies who undertake joint selling as part of their service, and there are various other joint marketing associations. The Commission and the private growers have demonstrated an impressive ability to work co-operatively to ensure suitable supplies of timber for both sawmills and small round wood users.

In July 1981, the Government passed legislation providing powers to sell a proportion of the Commission's forests to the private sector. It was announced that the Commission would be expected to raise £40 million from such sales – £10 million in the first year, and £15 million in each of the following two years. This programme has since been increased by two years and the sales expectation revalued to £82 million. In the first exploratory year of forest sales, a fair degree of interest was revealed by estates and by pension funds and financial institutions, but the market has subsequently proven to be uncertain.

These measures are consistent with the policy stance adopted by the Conservative Government towards other state enterprises such as oil, gas, airways and telecommunications, and predictably have stimulated considerable controversy. Concerns have been expressed that, as there are no restrictions upon the scale of these disposal powers, they could lead to the national forest resource being broken up into numerous small ownings, with harmful consequences for planting rates, management efficiency, employment, and the capability to arrange secure supplies for industrial users. These concerns have been particularly felt in Scotland, where the Commission has always had an important role in the rural economy, in the more remote and economically fragile areas. The Government has issued implementation guidelines requiring the Commission, when selecting areas for disposal, to give consideration to such factors as overall financial implications, effect upon the wood processing industry and impact upon employment (especially in remote areas). Ministers have given verbal assurances that the disposals programme will be a limited one, and that lease-back arrangements will be entered into with purchasers where it is important to maintain continuity of management and wood supply requirements.

Clearly, this legislation marks an important change in public policy towards the forestry industry. The Government has armed itself with powers to reduce the exchequer cost of the Forestry Commission and to break up the concentrated ownership pattern of British forestry. The extent to which these powers are used will reflect the priorities and preferences of subsequent administrations, and the impact upon the cost and security of timber supplies to industry will to some extent depend upon the manner of their implementation, and the commercial intentions of the private interests which acquire the forests.

Other Aspects of Public Policy. The policies and actions of other Government departments and agencies also have a bearing upon the forest products industry. Forest product industries are eligible for both Regional Development Grants (RDGs) and Selective Financial Assistance (SFA), and the availability of these grants can have an important effect upon their growth and development, particularly as many development possibilities will involve potential investors who have more than one location choice internationally. Although almost every forest product operation in Scotland has received assistance from these schemes at one time or another, there are some limitations upon their practical usefulness for the industry. First of all, most forest product developments are capital-intensive, relative to employment creation. This means that although full RDGs may be obtained in Development Areas, SFA (which is subject to a grant cost per job limit) can be restricted to a comparatively small proportion of project costs. For example, new saw-mill developments, which have a relatively favourable capital cost/employment ratio (about £43 000 per direct job), may be able to secure an overall proportion of grant assistance equivalent to that which, say, electronics or mechanical engineering projects might receive. On the other hand, particle board or pulp and paper projects (respectively approximately £115 000 and £375 000 capital cost per direct job) would be likely to receive a significantly lower proportion of aid. This, of course, stems from the employment creation basis upon which SFA is designed to operate, but it can limit the usefulness of these measures to encourage developments to bring about forest resource utilisation, particularly as no account is taken of indirect employment created in the forest and transportation sectors. Against this it should be pointed out that a major pulp and paper project was recently attracted to Shotton, in North Wales, with only these incentives available.

A second problem arises from the fact that the geographical areas of Scotland within which RDGs are available were redefined in 1982 so as to exclude many important areas of afforestation. Thus, many of the areas where small round wood will become abundant in the next twenty years, such as the Borders, Tayside and Grampian, cannot offer RDGs at all, and must rely upon what may be available in SFA to attract timber-using investment. Similarly, while the Highland areas of Scotland, where large volumes of small round wood are already available to support pulp and paper or particle board projects, can offer RDGs at the 15 per cent level, they cannot provide them at the 22 per cent level to match what was available at Shotton. The scope for transporting large volumes of timber into higher grant locations is severely limited by the heavy transport cost penalty involved, and the finely-balanced economics of most forest products industries today.

Some further financial assistance from the public sector may be provided to forest product projects by the Scottish Development Agency or the Highlands and Islands Development Board. Although the SDA is only empowered to assist in the form of equity investment or loans, undertaken on conventional commercial criteria and on commercial terms, this can have an important catalytic effect upon the financing of even a very large project. The HIDB is able to provide discretionary grant and soft loan assistance to a comparatively high proportion of a project's costs, although the absolute amount which it can contribute to a particular development is at present limited to £400 000. Both agencies can, however, make available standard or custom-built factories on attractive terms, and can assist with project research and feasibility study costs. These are measures of support which can have an influence in the development process disproportionate to the sums of money involved. Various training grants can be provided separately by the Industry Department for Scotland (IDS), the development agencies and the Man-power Services Commission.

A negative aspect of public policy towards industry generally, and some forest product industries in particular, are the pricing policies of public authorities providing energy throughout the UK. Prices of electricity, and even of fuels in which Britain is abundant (such as gas, oil and coal), are higher for industry in Britain than in some parts of Europe and in North America, a subject upon which there have been numerous representations to the Government in recent years. The implications of this national energy policy are particularly serious for such operations as pulp and paper making, which rank amongst the most energy-intensive industries and whose main competitors in Scandinavia, Canada and the

USA enjoy very much cheaper power prices. For example, in a UK mechanical pulp mill electricity accounts for over a third of operating costs (a considerably higher proportion than timber supplies). Electricity prices to major users in Sweden and North America are only half of those in the UK.

Another general aspect of public policy which has an important effect upon the forest products industry is the policy adopted by the Government towards the foreign exchange rate. Britain is one of the world's largest importers of every type of timber product, from sawn timber, through panel products to pulp and paper. UK producers have to compete against large and well-established international suppliers, and the exchange rate is an important determinant of the sterling price level of these imported products. In the period 1979–81, when sterling rode high against the dollar, there were several closures of large pulp and paper works (by Wiggins Teape at Fort William, Bowaters at Ellesmere Port and St Annes at Bristol) which could not survive the low prices set by foreign competitors. Since the pound has been allowed to float freely, a new volatility has entered the international business equation, which creates an uncertain environment in which to plan new investment in the forest products sector.

The Scottish Forest Product Development Group. In the painful aftermath of the closure of the Lochaber pulp mill, a group of public and private bodies came together to consider what might be done to encourage the Scottish forest products industry. These were the Forestry Commission, SDA, HIDB, IDS and Timber Growers (Scotland), and the group became known as the Scottish Forest Product Development Group (SFPDG). A major strategic study was commissioned from the international consultants Arthur D. Little, which exhaustively examined the resource base, analysed the scope for attracting new industrial projects and made recommendations for the further research and promotional work of the Group.[5] Since the study was completed in late 1982, the SFPDG has carried out extensive consultation with the wider Scottish forest products community about the study and its recommendations. An agreed programme of promotion and other action is now being pursued by the member bodies of the Group, acting in close coordination. The SFPDG is an interesting example of a number of public bodies coming together in an *ad hoc* manner to integrate better the application of several strands of public policy, and to join with private interests to give focused attention to the special requirements of a particular industrial sector.

Fish Products

The Fishing Industry. The fortunes of the Scottish fish products industry are inextricably bound up with those of the fishing industry itself. Scotland accounts for about half of the UK fishing industry but over the past decade it has been beset by controversy and difficulty. Loss of access to Faroese and Icelandic fishing grounds has brought about a reduction of more than half in the deep sea fleet, which has particularly hit the major East Coast ports. Although the inshore fleet has been less reduced, total employment in fishing declined from 9 500 in 1972 to 8 500 in 1981. Prices rose sharply in the 1970s but since 1978 have declined as abruptly to the same real levels as the 1960s, while profitability has been further squeezed by the rise in fuel and other costs. Total tonnage of fish landed in Scotland peaked in 1973 at about 500 000 tonnes, fell to 370 000 in 1980, but recovered to over 480 000 tonnes in 1982.[6] During this period, the English fishing industry has been rather more seriously affected, particularly its deep-sea operations, with the result that the UK significance of the Scottish industry has increased.

The level and distribution of fishing activity in Scotland in 1981 is shown in Table 8.3. The Grampian/Moray Firth area dominates the Scottish industry with 30 per cent of the tonnage (53 per cent by value) going to ports in that area, 47 per cent of the employment and 30 per cent of the Scottish fleet. The Grampian fleet has wider significance and in fact accounts for 63 per cent of landings (by value) to all Scottish ports. Peterhead and Aberdeen are the primary landing centres, but fishing employment is well distributed along the Moray Firth coast. Ports in the Highlands and Islands account for about half the Scottish fleet and over half the tonnage landed, but only 32 per cent of the employment and 33 per cent of the value of landings. This reflects the importance of smaller, inshore vessels in the area, and the fact that many of the species landed are of lower market value (e.g. sand-eels in Shetland, mackerel in Ullapool). The Forth, Clyde and Solway Firths have about twenty per cent of the boats and employment but only eight per cent of the tonnage landed, which is in the higher-value species. Over the past decade, the distribution of activity between these three geographic groups has remained fairly constant as far as boats, employment and value of landings are concerned. Tonnages landed in the Highlands and Islands increased from 41 to 54 per cent of Scottish landings in this period, but as this increase was mainly in lower-value species, the value of these landings only increased by three per cent of the Scottish total.

Fish farming is a comparatively recent but fast-growing activity in Scotland. Production of salmon and rainbow trout has grown from 1800 tonnes in 1980 to over 3 400 tonnes in 1981 and more than 5 000 tonnes in 1982, and there are now over 170 production units. About 500 people are employed in fish farming in Scotland, the majority of them in fairly remote parts of the Highlands and Islands. A further 1 500 tonnes of these high-value species are caught by estuarial netting and by rod and line.

The Fish Products Industry. The Scottish fish products and ancillary industries employ approximately 12 500 people in total, of whom 57 per cent are male, and 84 per cent full time. The structure and geographic distribution of this sector is shown in Table 8.4. White fish processing and freezing accounts for almost half of this employment, followed by shellfish processing, while herring processing and curing, which was once a huge employer, has now dwindled to small significance. There is a cannery at Fraserburgh and there are fish meal plants in Aberdeen, Shetland, Fraserburgh and Stornoway, although none of these is a major employer. Boat builders and repairers, suppliers of other fishing equipment and harbour, marketing and distribution trades together employ over 4000 people.

In geographical terms, almost two-thirds of the employment is concentrated in the Grampian area, about half of that being in Aberdeen itself. The Lower Clyde has a substantial employment, mainly founded on the prosperous shellfish trade. Relative to the fishing activity in the Highlands and Islands, onshore employment there is low, reflecting the fact that a significant proportion of the landings are transported out of the area unprocessed. Shetland, Stornoway and Campbeltown are the most significant centres of employment in that region. From 1972 to 1982 employment in these activities in Scotland declined from over 19000, a fall of 35 per cent. Most of this reduction occurred in Aberdeen, Fraserburgh, Leith and Shetland.

Public Policy Towards the Fishing and Fish Products Industry. Fishing and fish products together represent a large industry, long-established, widespread in the UK, and populated by fiercely independent people. It is an industry which has been experiencing very serious difficulties in recent years, for which no ready solutions have been found. Various strands of public policy have been involved with the industry, most obviously the UK input to the negotiations towards an EC Common Fisheries Policy (CFP), but for all the industry's size, problems and political sensitivity, these policies have tended to be partial and uncoordinated in their application. A number of Government departments have responsibilities in this area, primarily the Ministry of Agriculture, Fisheries and Food (MAFF), but also the Scottish, Welsh and Northern Ireland Offices and the Department of Trade and Industry.

The Sea Fish Industry Authority (SFIA) was set up by the Fisheries Act, 1982, to incorporate the functions previously exercised by the White Fish Authority (WFA) and the Herring Industry Board (HIB). It has a staff of 250, and its headquarters are located in Edinburgh. The Authority has inherited from the WFA and the HIB responsibilities to administer a Government grant and loan scheme for the purchase and improvement of fishing boats, and in 1981–82 over 800 boats received almost £5.5 million in grants and loans, 54 per cent of that in Scotland.[7] This expenditure is, however, well down on previous years. Throughout the UK, grants for new vessels are awarded by the SFIA up to 25 per cent of purchase cost.

Table 8.3. Fishing activity in Scotland, 1981.

District	Vessels					Employment		Landings			
	over 80 ft.	40–80 ft.	under 40 ft.	Total	% of Scotland	No.¹	% of Scotland	Tonnes	% of Scotland	Value (£000)	% of Scotland
Aberdeen	22	43	28	93	3·9	537	6·3	42029	9·5	18192	14·3
Peterhead	13	86	47	146	6·1	772	9·1	82199	18·6	37619	29·5
Fraserburgh	11	86	42	139	5·9	746	8·8	35341	8·0	7361	5·8
Macduff	10	90	27	127	5·4	677	8·0	4735	1·0	1891	1·5
Buckie	1	105	6	112	4·7	682	8·1	3814	0·8	2095	1·6
Inner Moray Firth	—	89	18	107	4·5	606	7·2	3190	0·7	1136	0·9
Total Grampian/ Moray Firth	57	499	168	724	30·5	4020	47·5	171308	38·6	68294	53·6
Caithness	—	26	75	101	4·3	273	3·2	5166	1·2	2029	1·6
Orkney	1	15	127	143	6·1	291	3·5	905	0·2	580	0·4
Shetland	8	52	95	155	6·5	542	6·4	54567	12·3	4820	3·8
Western Isles	3	53	209	265	11·2	527	6·2	24491	5·5	3579	2·8
W.Ross/Sutherland	—	20	81	101	4·3	206	2·4	109997	24·8	16265	12·8
Mallaig/Skye	2	30	98	130	5·5	300	3·6	27034	6·1	7178	5·6
Oban & Mull	—	10	103	113	4·7	187	2·2	6043	1·4	3212	2·5
Kintyre & Bute	—	60	81	141	5·9	399	4·7	7962	1·8	4424	3·5
Total Highlands & Islands	14	266	869	1149	48·5	2725	32·2	236165	53·3	42087	33·0

	Vessels					Employment		Landings			
District	over 80 ft.	40–80 ft.	under 40 ft.	Total	% of Scotland	No.[1]	% of Scotland	Tonnes	% of Scotland	Value (£000)	% of Scotland
Berwickshire	—	22	31	53	2·2	209	2·5	6466	1·5	3381	2·7
Lothian	1	53	49	103	4·4	374	4·4	1250	0·3	702	0·5
Fife	2	55	65	122	5·1	413	4·9	5968	1·3	2984	2·3
Angus	—	33	50	83	3·5	255	3·0	4794	1·1	1867	1·5
Lower Clyde/Solway	1	79	56	136	5·8	465	5·5	18037	4·1	8164	6·4
Total rest of Scotland	4	242	251	497	21·0	1716	20·3	36515	8·3	17098	13·4
Total Scotland	75	1007	1288	2370	100·0	8461	100·0	443988	100·0	127479	100·0
Total UK	239	1976	4792	7007		23200[1]		745272		229064	
Scotland as % of UK	31	51	27	34		36		60		56	

[1] Includes partially employed.
Source: *Scottish Sea Fisheries Statistical Tables, 1981* (DAFS).

Table 8.4. Employment in fish products and ancillary industries in Scotland, 1982.

District	Fish Products				Ancillaries			Employment total	%
	Herring processors & freezers	White fish processors & freezers	Shell fish processors & freezers	Other freezing & processing, fish meal and oil	Fish traders, transporters, market and harbour staff	Vessel builders, repairers & related trades	Makers of nets, ropes, boxes, ice; fuel suppliers		
Aberdeen	90	2324	46	134	419	226	314	3553	29
Peterhead	61	610	58	28	150	201	119	1227	10
Fraserburgh	75	1159	7	6	122	201	177	1747	15
Macduff	—	117	3	—	30	110	17	277	2
Buckie	—	176	179	—	49	159	38	601	5
Inner Moray Firth	—	23	60	28	28	63	12	214	2
Total Grampian/ Moray Firth	226	4409	353	196	798	960	677	7619	63
Caithness	—	48	8	—	52	21	14	143	1
Orkney	—	—	121	—	6	12	3	142	1
Shetland	11	361	73	27	43	140	37	692	6
Western Isles	—	44	103	17	31	45	9	249	2
W. Ross/Sutherland	2	32	41	—	62	11	14	162	1
Mallaig/Skye	4	7	47	1	36	36	24	155	1
Oban/Mull	—	22	41	—	21	24	10	118	1
Kintyre/Bute	46	2	50	—	36	118	23	275	2
Total Highlands & Islands	63	516	484	45	287	407	134	1936	15

	Fish Products				Ancillaries				
District	Herring processors & freezers	White fish processors & freezers	Shell fish processors & freezers	Other freezing & processing, fish meal and oil	Fish traders, transporters, market and harbour staff	Vessel builders, repairers & related trades	Makers of nets, ropes, boxes, ice; fuel suppliers	Employment total	%
Berwickshire	—	109	181	—	38	43	5	376	3
Lothian	83	163	16	51	59	56	79	507	4
Fife	—	53	12	—	20	61	8	154	1
Angus	—	96	174	—	17	53	10	350	3
Lower Clyde/ Solway	4	310	620	33	197	63	148	1375	11
Total rest of Scotland	87	731	1003	84	331	276	250	2762	22
Total Scotland	376	5656	1840	325	1416	1643	1061	12317	100

Source: DAFS, adjusted.

For its territory the HIDB has powers to provide assistance for the purchase of both new and second-hand vessels, and for small shellfish boats, up to 70 per cent of total cost. In 1981, the HIDB provided almost £2 million in grant, loan or equity for these purposes.[8]

The SFIA is also expected to promote the general interests of the industry, which it seeks to do in a number of ways. The Industrial Development Unit experiments and develops new technologies for catching and handling fish, provides training facilities and carries out management, consultancy and feasibility study work into various aspects of the industry. The Marine Farming Unit operates an experimental hatchery and fish farm, and provides an advisory service to this rapidly expanding branch of the industry. The Market Development Unit undertakes a range of generic promotion work and other activities to revitalise the flagging fortunes of fish in the UK food market, although in February 1983 it was decided that the overseas marketing promotion function would be taken over by the newly-formed 'Food from Britain' organisation.

Finance for the grants and loans which the SFIA disburse of behalf of the Government is provided from MAFF, but the Authority is expected to cover its other operating expenses from a compulsory levy on all fish sales in the UK, as did the HIB and WFA before it. Not surprisingly, this levy is the source of considerable resentment to many in the industry, who argue that as the SFIA is in fact an instrument of public policy, these costs should be borne by Government. Needless to say, questions are frequently raised as to whether the industry receives value for its compulsory levy.

Problems Facing the Fishing Industry. The present crisis in the fishing industry has been brought about by a number of interacting factors and to deal with them there have been a variety of policy responses and initiatives. It is fair to say that until the CFP was agreed early in 1983, there did not exist a fully-integrated UK policy towards the fishing industry, and it is therefore useful in this section to consider separately the policy measures adopted before 1983, and those which are likely to follow its introduction.

The contraction in the fishing grounds accessible to British boats has been a fundamental problem as first Iceland, then the Faroes, extended their limits. The initial policy of the UK Government was to contest these extensions in negotiation, by diplomatic pressure and, finally, by force, but in each case they were eventually obliged to accept accommodations which drastically reduced permissible catches by UK boats in these waters. This hit hard at the deep-sea fleet, particularly the larger trawlers based in the major ports of Aberdeen, Hull, Grimsby and Fleetwood.

Another major problem has been the serious depletion of fish stocks in UK waters and other areas still accessible to British boats. This is due to cumulative overfishing, partly by the UK deep-sea fleet to compensate for the loss of catches elsewhere, partly by the activities of other European fleets, such as the Danes who have a large fish meal industry to sustain, and partly by the former level of Eastern Bloc fishing operations in the area. Herring, once the most abundant species, has been particularly affected. Impartial scientific advice on fish stocks is provided by the International Council for the Exploration of the Sea (ICES), which issues regular reports to guide national governments on the need for, and most appropriate form of, conservation measures. Over the years, scant attention has been paid to this advice as individual boats, fleets and national governments have pursued their own interests. International conventions, guidelines and voluntary discipline have all proven to be inadequate instruments to control this rapacity, and national governments were individually obliged to introduce their own catching controls. Iceland and the Faroes have already been referred to, and Norway, Greenland, Russia and Canada have also set up their limits, controls and quotas. The UK Government introduced a number of such measures in the 1970s, imposing a total ban on herring fishing in the Minches in 1978, and enforcing total allowable catches (TAC) for some other species. In 1978, a crisis was provoked in the EC when the UK claimed exclusive possession of a twelve-mile coastal strip, and preferential possession of fifty miles. This claim was never enforced, and was eventually resolved in the CFP settlement.

Another factor contributing to the crisis in fish stocks has been the growth of the UK fishing fleet in the 1960s and 70s to a size quite inappropriate to present conditions. Many large vessels were built for distant deep-water operations which are now obliged to fish in other waters for which they were not designed and where they cannot be economic. Most of these vessels received public grant and loan assistance from the scheme operated by the WFA, while the HIB and the HIDB handled similar schemes to encourage new vessels for inshore or medium-depth operations. In the later 1970s, these assistance budgets were quite tightly controlled, with the express purpose of limiting additions to the fleet. However, the lack of effective control mechanisms at the Government's disposal was painfully revealed as fleet operators circumvented these curbs by the simple expedient of taking up attractive credit terms offered by foreign shipyards desperate for business. In this way, the Government's policy goals were frustrated and fleet overcapacity perpetuated, while operators became burdened with heavy short-term borrowings which have added to their financial problems in difficult trading times. It is estimated that there is now about twenty per cent overcapacity in the UK fleet of vessels over forty feet long. Purse seine netters are viewed as a particular threat to the mackerel and herring industries, with their enormous catching capacity.

Rising fuel costs since 1973 have imposed heavy additional operating costs upon the fishing fleet. Modern fishing methods are highly machinery-intensive, and fuel can account for as much as half of operating costs. Some countries, such as Norway and France, provide a fuel subsidy for fisherman, but this has never been part of UK policy, in spite of repeated pleas from the UK industry.

The UK market has contracted as an outlet for British fish products in recent years. In the 1970s, UK per capita consumption of fish declined by around one quarter. This is partly explained by the increasing cost and difficulty of obtaining traditionally popular fish such as cod and herring (the price of which increased by about 50 per cent in real terms from 1970 to 1980), but it may also reflect a deeper-rooted change in consumer preferences. The SFIA is addressing itself to the problem of re-stimulating the demand for fish products in the UK. In the period 1980–81, the strength of sterling and a decline in the US as a market for fish exporters resulted in a rapid increase in imports of fish to the UK. In a contracting market, this had the effect of depressing the price of the traded species (mainly frozen white fish), and further lowering the returns to UK fishermen. The situation improved somewhat in 1982, but imports are still at about 30 per cent of the UK market.

In response to the pleas from the fishing industry, the UK Government has been obliged to provide a series of 'temporary supports' to the industry, on a year-by-year basis. In 1981, £25 million was made available to help fishing boats remain operational. There have been complaints that the method of disbursement of these aids has favoured older vessels, purchased at lower original cost and now largely paid-off, more than newer boats carrying heavy borrowing at high interest rates, and larger boats more than the smaller class of vessel.

EC Common Fisheries Policy. When the EC set itself the objective of achieving a CFP, the controversial and hard-fought negotiations inevitably centred upon other nations' access to UK waters, as about two-thirds of the total EC catch comes from the prolific, shallow waters around the UK. Many European fisherman have been fishing here for centuries and important domestic industries in these countries have been based upon these catches. The growing pressure for unilateral protection from the UK fishing industry to compensate for its reversals in other fishing areas met head-on with these traditional interests. Agreement was eventually reached in January 1983, whereby the EC as a whole enforces a 200-mile fishing limit within which the total allowable catch for each species is determined by the EC Commission, and each member state receives a quota. The UK receives the largest overall quota of 37·3 per cent, followed by Denmark with 25·5 per cent, France with 11·6 per cent and West Germany with 11·4 per cent. The agreement also gives special rights for local inshore fisherman. Each country is responsible for enforcing quotas and other conservation measures in its own territorial waters. A price support system will be operated by the Commission, comparable to those evolved for agriculture, and the Commission will also make available about £140 million a year to supplement national aids to assist fleet adaptation and modernisation.

Although it is too early to assess the effects of these policies on U K fishing and fish products industries, some initial observations may be made. The quota of 37·3 per cent represents an improvement on the 31 per cent which was originally offered to the U K, but falls far short of the 45 per cent which U K negotiators sought. Scottish fishermen feel particularly aggrieved about the concessions made to the Danes over mackerel catches for fish meal processing, the reduction of the size of the protected 'Shetland Box' and the relaxation of restrictions within it. Concerns are also expressed about the effect that the entry of Spain and Portugal into the EC will have upon the CFP. The view is widely held that as the overall significance of fishing in the U K economy is relatively small, its interests have been allowed to suffer in order to protect those of agriculture and manufacturing industry.

Crucially important will be the manner in which national governments decide to enforce the CFP. Mechanisms will be required to ensure that each national fleet does not exceed its overall quota, and within that, to allocate the permissible catch between different types of vessel and to determine the basis of national management. There is widespread scepticism over the possibility of controls being implemented which will be both fair and effective. Much will depend on the accurate monitoring of landings or klondyking (the sale and transfer of fish at sea), and there is considerable suspicion that the scope for evasion is great and will prove to be an irresistible temptation to fishermen from all nations.

Control of the size of fishing fleets will also be difficult to achieve. At present, the publicly-funded grant and loan schemes remain in operation and the SFIA and the HIDB have a difficult judgemental responsibility to restrain growth in catching capacity while at the same time permitting desirable modernisation of the fleet to take place, and allowing some flow of orders to enable shipyards and engineers to survive. A more comprehensive policy will be required if the necessary contraction, reconstruction and reorientation is to take place, and if a reasonable reconciliation is to be achieved between the competing sectoral and regional interests. Talks between Government and industry have been initiated, and are likely to continue for some time. The funds identified by the EC will supplement national assistance towards the cost of scrapping and modernising the fleet but the amounts of money available are small relative to the size of the problem. There is little doubt that the U K fishing industry will continue to experience painful contraction and change in the next few years.

Fish Products. The emphasis of discussion in this section has been heavily upon fisheries policy, as this more than anything else defines the scope for the fish products and ancillary industries. If the supplies of fish are there and the price is right, then production activities tend to take care of themselves. However, there are one or two aspects of Government policy which relate directly to these industries.

As manufacturing operations, fish processors, shipbuilders, etc. are entitled to financial assistance under the Industrial Development Act towards the cost of new investment. Regarding access to RDGs, however, they face the same problem as was described in the context of forest products industries, namely that areas of RDG availability do not correspond well with areas of fishing activity. Thus within Grampian area, which dominates the Scottish fishing, fish processing and ancillary industries, no RDGs may be obtained for new manufacturing investment. As these activities already face serious difficulties in that area because of the activity association with North Sea oil operations, this anomaly represents a serious handicap. Another major source of resentment has been that, while over the last few years special 'temporary supports' have been given to fishing boats, no such public assistance has been made available to fish processors, whose problems have been just as acute in that period.

In the Highlands and Islands, on the other hand, RDGs are broadly available and the HIDB deploys a flexible package of supplementary public assistance in support of an explicit policy to encourage fish processing and ancillary industries. In the period 1972–81, the HIDB provided about £5 million at 1981 prices to fish processing, and £2.25 million to boatyards and marine engineering.[9] The Board's aim is to encourage more fish to be landed in its area (to take advantage of shorter steaming distances), and then to encourage as much fish processing and ancillary activity as possible near the point of landing. It has the particular objective to stimulate fishing off the Western Isles and to bring fish processing operations to West Lewis and Barra. These policies pursued by the HIDB, taken in conjunction with its schemes to assist fishing boats, are perhaps the nearest example in the UK to a comprehensive and integrated policy towards the fishing/fish products/ancillary industries sector.

Minerals, Electricity and Aluminium Smelting

Minerals. Scotland, especially the Highlands, is a geologist's paradise which contains virtually every mineral known to man. Unfortunately, very few of these exist in sufficiently concentrated quantities to make them economically extractable with known technology, with the notable exceptions of oil and coal which are excluded from this brief treatment.

The largest single mineral operation in Scotland is a major limestone quarry and cement works near Dunbar which in 1982 employed 450 people. There are numerous sand and gravel quarries distributed throughout Scotland, providing construction aggregate for local markets, and there are active proposals to develop coastal 'superquarries' at Harris and Loch Linnhe, to export aggregates to UK and European markets. Silica sand is mined at Lochaline and in Fife and the Lothians, fireclay near Falkirk for refractory bricks, and talc on the Shetland island of Unst. The famous old lead mines at Strontian (which gave its name to the element strontium) are being worked again to extract and refine barytes, an important ingredient in oilfield drilling fluids. Peat is abundantly available in many parts of the Highlands (especially Caithness, the Western Isles and Yell), the Borders and the Central Belt, but significant production units are so far limited to Falkirk and Aberdeenshire, mainly for distillery and horticultural use. Taken altogether, these various extractive and processing activities in Scotland employ approximately 2 500 people.

During the wars, there was considerable Government encouragement to produce minerals in the UK. Today, the Department of Trade and Industry operates a Mineral Exploration Grant (MEG) scheme, which can make available grants of up to 35 per cent towards mineral exploration activities. These grants are awarded only in respect of non-ferrous metals, fluorspar, barium and potash. Plant and equipment for mineral extraction and processing (except quarries) may be eligible for RDG and SFA support or assistance from the SDA or HIDB. More potent influences on development, however, are international commodity prices, industry demand, and the value of sterling. Public policy towards the discovery, production and processing of minerals other than oil and coal may therefore be described as a realistic one of mild encouragement to the limited number of development opportunities. The Institute of Geological Sciences is publicly funded through the National Environment Research Council to carry out geological surveys, maintain and analyse data, and provide advisory services to Government and the public.

Aluminium Smelting. The reduction of alumina by electrolytic process to produce aluminium has for long been a rather special industry in Scotland, or, more specifically, in the Highlands. Aluminium has been described as 'solidified electricity', as even in a modern plant 15 000 units of electricity are required for every tonne of primary metal, representing about 25 per cent of all production costs. Thus, the aluminium industry has always located where electricity costs are lowest, and originally that meant where hydro power was available.

Britain's first major hydro schemes were privately built for this purpose, the earliest in 1896 when British Aluminium (BACO) opened a small smelter at Foyers, on Loch Ness. This was followed in 1907 by a 10 000 tonne per annum factory at Kinlochleven in Argyll, which is still in operation as the oldest working aluminium smelter in the world. Between the wars, the same company built a 30 000 tonne smelter at Fort William, using the hydro resources of a huge catchment area behind Ben Nevis. Because of the size of the undertakings and the sensitive issues regarding property and amenity in the Highlands, these were controversial developments in their time, requiring special Acts of Parliament.

In 1967, BACO took the decision, fateful in retrospect, to build a 100 000 tonne smelter at Invergordon, a decision which was as much a product of Government policy as it was of commercial judgement.[10] Two strands of policy lay behind the decision – industrial and regional. The Labour Government of the late 1960s was committed to unleashing the 'white-hot heat of the technological revolution' to revive the UK's flagging industrial performance. Earlier investment in Britain's nuclear power industry looked set to pay a handsome dividend through the Advanced Gas-Cooled Reactors (AGRs) which were about to come onstream, with the promise of large supplies of low-cost electricity. The challenge was to find suitable modern industries to utilise this anticipated power bonanza, and aluminium smelting appeared to be perfectly suited. Demand was growing fast, Britain was importing very large quantities of primary metal for her rolling and fabrication industries, and improving the balance of payments was a priority Government policy in the 1960s.

This was also a period when regional development policy was at its popular zenith and was receiving priority commitment from Government. Along with efforts to restructure and revitalise industry went powerful mechanisms and financial incentives to distribute industrial development to the less prosperous parts of Britain. Wherever possible, the Department of Industry used these measures to influence the location of new projects, particularly large ones with important 'linkage' effects on regional economies. A new instrument of regional policy, the HIDB, had been set up only two years previously as Britain's first regional development agency, and the Board had campaigned effectively for a major industrial project to be located on the Cromarty Firth to catalyse that area as a growth pole in the Highland economy.

Thus, in 1968, the Government announced that three 120 000 tonne smelters would be built in Britain. One, at Lynemouth, Northumberland, built by Alcan, would use electric power from a coal-fired station supplied by special contract from the National Coal Board. Another, built by Rio Tinto Zinc at Anglesey, North Wales, would receive power from the electricity grid but contractually allocated from the Dungeness B reactor. The third, at Invergordon, would similarly receive grid electricity, under special contract from the proposed Hunterston B reactor in Ayrshire.

Subsidised Government loans of £29 million were provided to BACO, to enable them to purchase from the South of Scotland Electricity Board (SSEB) a 21 per cent share in the reactor. In return, BACO were to be entitled to an equivalent proportion of the electricity output to be supplied by the North of Scotland Hydro Electric Board (NOSHEB) at a low tariff computed by a complex formula designed to reflect the operating costs of the power station and the cost of replacement fuel. The smelter itself was built at a cost of about £39 million, started production in 1971 and was fully onstream by 1973, employing 900 people directly and perhaps generating as many jobs again indirectly. It was destined to close in 1981, only ten years from opening.

The forces which brought about the crisis for the Invergordon smelter were primarily the disappointing performance of nuclear technology, and the commercial misfortunes of BACO, but the events surrounding the final closure also involved many complicated strands of public policy. The troubles at Invergordon really started with Hunterston B, which was late coming onstream, and then failed to meet its designed power output. To prevent financial burden falling on BACO, the Government passed special legislation in 1976 which allocated the company an extra five per cent share of the power from the station, and compensated NOSHEB annually. Payments of between £8 and £15 million were made under this order, yearly from 1976 to 1981.[11] These provisions did not prevent further serious dispute arising between BACO and NOSHEB regarding power charges under the contract. One major source of disagreement was over operating costs at the power station, which were considerably higher than anticipated. Another was over the issue of the sharing of provision for the eventual decommissioning costs of Hunterston, which has been neglected when the contract was drawn up. And further dispute arose when a disastrous sea-water leak occurred into the station's cooling system, over the additional cost of supplying BACO's electricity needs from fossil-fuelled power stations.

By 1981, the amount claimed by NOSHEB but unpaid by BACO had accumulated to £47 million and the Government's solicitor had advised them that a resolution of the matter could only be obtained in the law courts. Meanwhile, BACO had been experiencing serious trading difficulties. Demand for primary aluminium is a sensitive barometer of the world economy, and it fell sharply as the recession intensified in 1980–81. The problem in Britain was heightened by a strong currency which made imports cheap and exports difficult. BACO had particular difficulties because it was a small operator by world standards, lacked its own alumina supplies (and had made some punitively expensive long-term supply arrangements), was burdened by some inefficient downstream metal processing plant, and was paying more for electricity than most of its international rivals. In the first six months of 1981, BACO made a loss of almost £9 million, and by the end of the year was heading for a loss of £20 million. These trading losses, and the £47 million court action, threatened the financial stability not just of BACO, but of the parent company Tube Investments. During 1981, the Government became alerted to the problem, but early in December BACO made it clear that they had no alternative but to close the loss-making Invergordon smelter and realise a residual value on the power contract (which would expire in the year 2000) to clear its obligations.

The Government tried to find a formula which would keep the smelter open. BACO were offered an additional £8 million on the annual deficit payment for at least three years, but such were the financial pressures on the company that they were unable to accept such an arrangement unless it applied until the year 2000 when the power contract ended. The cost of this long-term doubling of the rate of subsidy was too much for the Government to accept, so in order to preserve BACO's other Scottish operations (especially the Falkirk rolling mill, employing 1200 people) it negotiated a termination settlement. The residual value of the power output of Hunterston B was £79 million, from which NOSHEB deducted the disputed £47 million. BACO also still owed the Government £33.5 million in outstanding loans, of which the Government waived £21 million leaving BACO about £20 million better off from the overall settlement. This amount, equivalent to the 1981 loss, was intended to help BACO maintain their other plants in Scotland. The Invergordon smelter closed on 31 December 1981, making 890 men redundant and delivering a massive blow to the economy of the entire Highlands area.

Subsequently, efforts were made to attract alternative users to purchase the smelter and other power contract formulae were investigated and considered at Cabinet level. But it proved impossible to secure the high level of public subsidy necessary to enable power to be supplied at a tariff which would permit the smelter to operate competitively. In the months following the closure of the smelter, bitter comparisons were made with the situation at the Lynemouth and Anglesey smelters, which continued to operate on power subsidies which were concealed, but almost certainly considerably higher than those offered to Invergordon. The quest for a new operator was complicated by the fact that the closed smelter remained the property of BACO, the assets not having been acquired by Government as part of the settlement. Later in 1982 these and BACO's other assets were taken over by their rivals Alcan, but there is little likelihood that they will wish to reopen the now largely dismantled smelter even in the context of a greatly improved market for aluminium products. The HIDB, which had been so active in promoting the smelter originally, was given an additional allocation of £10 million over three years 'to undertake special measures to create employment in the Invergordon area', but this was widely regarded as a token gesture, and few commentators could see where the development opportunities would come from to meet the employment requirement. In April 1983, male unemployment in Invergordon stood at 20·9 per cent (1250 men), against the Scottish average of 18·3 per cent. In April 1981, the equivalent figures were 7·5 per cent (380 men) and 15 per cent respectively.

The smelters at Kinlochleven and Fort William have not been greatly affected by these events and the change of ownership. The Fort William plant was extensively modernised a few years ago and is now operating at a high level of technical efficiency. With their long-paid-off investments in hydro generating equipment, these smelters enjoy the lowest power costs of any industrial user in Britain.

With a little hindsight, the Invergordon aluminium smelter can be seen as a project which was born out of Government policies towards industrial regeneration, regional development, nuclear power, import substitution, and the balance of payments.[12] Its crisis arose from the disappointing performance of nuclear technology, imperfections in the power contract, and BACO's other commercial difficulties. The project died when Government was no longer prepared to meet the rising cost of subsidy necessary to keep it alive, because the policy goal of Government expenditure control had taken priority over the original public objectives. The tragedy lies in the community of Invergordon, which was raised on one set of policy priorities to be dashed on another, all within the space of a decade.

Electricity. The fortunes of Scotland's energy industries and the complexities of public policy towards them provide the material for a major study in themselves. It will not be possible to pay more than passing attention to these issues here, with some particular reference to those forms of electricity generation which are based upon renewable natural resources.

Table 8.5. Scottish electricity supply, 1982–83 (millions of units).

	SSEB	NOSHEB	Total	%
Thermal	10508	2908	13416	51
Nuclear	8495	—	8495	32
Hydro	334	3651	3985	15
Diesel	—	257	257	1
Total	19337	6816	26153	100

Source: Annual Reports of SSEB and NOSHEB.

The structure of the Scottish electricity supply industry in 1982–83 is shown in Table 8.5. Conventional thermal power stations are the largest source of supply, especially the coal-fired stations at Longannet and Cockenzie which account for about 75 per cent of thermal output.[13] North Sea flare gas is used at Peterhead to provide 21 per cent of the thermal output and only four per cent now comes from the oil-fired station at Inverkip. Flare gas will only be available until 1985, when the Mossmorran petrochemical plant is opened. Nuclear power (Hunterston A and B) represents 24 per cent of output, a proportion which will grow when Torness comes onstream in 1987. Most relevant to this chapter, a significant proportion (15 per cent) of supply comes from hydro-electric installations operated in the Highlands. Most of these were built by NOSHEB, which was set up by Act of Parliament in 1943 with a unique remit to develop the hydro resources of the Highlands and to bring social and economic development to the North of Scotland. During the 1950s and 60s, most of the large hydro schemes were implemented, and today the Hydro Board is able to provide 55 per cent of its area's requirements from hydro sources. The balance was until recently imported from SSEB but is at present being supplied from Peterhead. The actual role of hydro power in the overall Scottish electricity supply system is more important than the figures suggest, however, because both the conventional hydro schemes and the pump storage systems have a particular value as a low-cost 'peak shaving' supply, greatly reducing the requirement to use gas turbines during the brief daily period of maximum electricity demand. There are a small number of new hydro projects in the Highlands which might be carried out in the future, but investment decisions will depend upon overall system requirements, relative generation costs and environmental considerations.

As an instrument of Government policy to bring development to the North of Scotland, NOSHEB has accomplished a great deal in the past forty years. The grid has been extended to the furthest corners of the Highlands (typically through heavily subsidised local connection schemes) and the overwhelming majority of the population is now connected. The hydro schemes brought a great deal of construction employment to the area, albeit temporary, and the Board have an impressive record on environmental and scenic matters. However, while the availability of a reliable grid supply of electricity has removed a constraint to industrial development, consumers in the Highlands do not enjoy any significant price advantage to reflect their low-cost hydro capacity. In that regard, as was clearly demonstrated when the Invergordon smelter closed, the Highlands stand on equal terms with other parts of Scotland. The fact that the Hydro Board offices are located in Edinburgh, well outside its operational area, is widely regarded as inappropriate.

The energy crisis following the 1973 rise in oil prices stimulated a great deal of research effort into other possible means of generating electricity, including wind, wave, peat and tidal power. The Department of Energy set up the Energy Technology Support Unit (ETSU) in 1974 as a channel for public assistance (£15 million in 1981–82) and to provide a coordinating role in this diffuse field of research. So far, none of the technologies has shown a capability to provide power more cheaply than

278

conventional generating methods, and interest in their application is mainly for remote islands not connected to the grid. Scotland has featured prominently in research activity, both as a location of these resources, and as a potential benefactor. Wind power has proceeded furthest, with large-scale demonstration machines installed by NOSHEB on Orkney. Tidal and wave power schemes have great power potential, but appear very expensive so far. Peat power could be attractive on the Western Isles and Shetland, where supplies are abundant, and the Hydro Board are presently considering a peat-fired station on Lewis. Following a recent report to the Department of Energy, however, it has been decided to rationalise considerably ETSU's support activities in these areas of research.[14] Their future will clearly depend upon progress towards lower-cost technology and movements in energy prices generally.

In common with the rest of the UK, Scottish industry has suffered from high energy costs relative to North America and many parts of Europe. There are no indications that the Government is likely to alter the policies of the nationalised power supply industries which have brought that situation about. However, the Energy Act passed in 1983 opens up opportunities for private suppliers to enter what has previously been a virtual monopoly market of the nationalised electricity industries. This will oblige the electricity boards to buy electricity if offered on competitive terms and to afford facilities for power transmission through the grid. It will be interesting to see if any private suppliers are, in fact, able to take advantage of these opportunities, by generating electricity at lower cost.

Conclusions

The natural resource-based industries considered in this chapter are a most heterogenous collection and, it may reasonably be argued, grouped in a somewhat arbitrary manner. However, they represent a distinctive set which do not fit easily into any other categorisation, and, taken together, are an important strand of Scotland's industrial mix. Each of the industries considered has been significantly influenced by public policy, sometimes in a unique fashion, but with several recurring themes of shared experience.

All, by definition, depend upon natural resources, and in each case the Government has applied policies which have influenced the conditions of supply of their raw materials. This is most evident in the case of power for aluminium smelting, which was originally founded upon private hydro schemes, but came to be dependent upon electricity supplied by special arrangements with nationalised energy industries. Similarly, public policy applied through the Forestry Commission has built up the national forest resource, and is the dominant domestic supplier to sawmills and small round wood processors. In fishing, the state is not a direct supplier, but through the highly political process of international fisheries agreement has effectively determined the supply available to British boats and, therefore, British industry. It is an inflexible law of economics that any influence upon supply in a market must also influence price, and it follows that public policy has been, and will continue to be, a great influence upon the development, scope and profitability of all these industries.

Each of the industries discussed operates on a highly dispersed basis, usually in the more peripheral parts of Scotland where alternative forms of economic activity are limited. This has inevitably meant that their fortunes have been closely associated with the development prospects of these areas, and that the industries have therefore become to a greater or lesser extent agents of Government regional policy. The special role of forestry in the Highlands, the Corpach pulp and paper mill, the Invergordon aluminium smelter, the building up of the Shetland fishing fleet and the HIDB's fish processing strategy for the Western Isles are all illustrations of this point. In turn, Government regional policy and the availability of regional investment incentives have been powerful influences upon the development of these industries.

However, regional assistance policies are not at present sensitively attuned to the requirements of resource-based industries, since the policies are more designed to influence mobile investment within the UK, while development opportunities in these industries are quite circumscribed geographically. Thus fish processors in Grampian, heartland of the Scottish fishing industry, may receive no regional development grants while Corpach, at the centre of Scotland's forestry resource, cannot secure the top-level grants with which to attract internationally mobile pulping investments. Public agencies have played a significant role in each of these industries. The Forestry Commission has been a very strong instrument of public involvement, and the electricity boards had a vital part to play in the history of the Invergordon aluminium smelter. The WFA and the HIDB have had an important involvement with the fishing and fish products industries. The SDA and HIDB have a central role in promoting the development of Scottish resource-based industries both in the UK and abroad, and to join with IDS in devising appropriate packages of public grants, loans, equity investments and factory provisions.

A number of other aspects of public policy have also been jointly experienced. Currency fluctuations, for example, following upon the Government's policy to let the pound float to its oil-supported level, have introduced a major uncertainty into the affairs of natural resource-based industries, all of which trade in highly competitive markets open to foreign suppliers. Similarly, the energy policy relating domestic energy prices to the world price for oil has produced public electricity prices which are high relative to those paid by many competitors in these industries, and which constitute a considerable obstacle to the development of energy-intensive industries such as aluminium and wood pulping. It has also pushed up the price of fuel for fishing boats. High interest rates and the prolonged recession may, or may not, be directly attributed to public policy, but they have had a serious effect upon all of the resource-based industries, as upon other sectors of British industry.

. Looking ahead, public policy will continue to have an important bearing on these industries by acts of either commission or omission. The aluminium smelting industry will probably be the least affected, as it experienced its crisis at Invergordon and, having been savagely contracted, is not likely to expand again in Scotland until there occurs another reversal of policy towards power prices for major consumers. The forest products industry, on the other hand, will depend to a degree upon the extent and manner in which the Government implements its policies towards the Forestry Commission. If there is large-scale privatisation of forestry, it could affect the ability to bulk large supplies for industry. Depending on the price at which the assets are sold, it could also influence the selling price of timber. For the fish industry, the volumes and price of fish supplies will depend upon the implementation and evolution of the CFP which, for all its imperfections, is the first coherent policy framework that the industry has known since World War II. Particularly important will be policies towards quota enforcement, fleet reduction and product marketing. The weight attached in the future to regional policy will be another important factor; both in the sense of protecting and preserving the fruits of previous regional investment, and of creating new development opportunities. More geographical flexibility is desirable in regional assistance policy to enable it to support the distinctive requirements of resource-based industries.

Resource-based industries, forest and fish products particularly, have a special place in the spectrum of Scottish industrial activity. They tend to be located in peripheral areas, which depend upon them to an unusual degree. It has been shown that they in turn rely upon public policy to a very considerable extent and are highly vulnerable to sudden changes in policy emphasis. What they and their dependent communities most ask of Government is for policies which are supportive, but above all, policies which are mutually consistent and consistently applied over time.

Appendix: Lochaber Pulp Mill

The decision taken by Wiggins Teape (WT) in 1963 to build a pulp and paper mill at Corpach, near Fort William, was one of the most dramatic industrial developments in Scotland since World War II. A new technology using natural resources, substituting imports, creating a large number of jobs, located in a historically disadvantaged part of the country, involving public assistance – it had all the ingredients to command front-page headlines. When the mill opened in 1966, it was generally regarded as the beginning of a new era for the Highlands, a herald of new industries and new policies which would solve the longstanding difficulties of the area. Even the problems of community growth and social adaptation which the development brought in its train were willingly engaged as 'the problems of life'. Lochaber became a growth centre, a Highland success story. When, in April 1979, WT announced that the pulp mill would close, the impact was equally dramatic. The pains of closure, the commercial, communal and individual loss which were becoming all too familiar throughout Britain, seemed to be particularly poignant in a remote Highland community where expectations had been so recently raised high, and where employment alternatives were virtually non-existent. The Corpach mill has always lived in the spotlight of public attention, but behind the drama there lies an instructive case study in resource-based industrial development and public policy.

Public Policy Background. The foundations of the pulp mill project were laid down many years before it opened, in the afforestation policies pursued by successive Governments before and after World War II. As was discussed earlier, the greater part of this was carried out by the Forestry Commission (some of whose earliest plantations were in the Great Glen and West Highlands), although considerable areas were also planted privately under various grant and taxation schemes. An integral objective of this long-term strategy was to generate a supply of British-grown timber which would support forest products industries in Britain, traditionally a massive importer. WT first discussed a pulp project with the European Commission in 1950, but there was insufficient timber available, and their ambitions had to be postponed until inter-war plantings had matured. From the mid-1960s onwards, a steeply rising supply of small round wood production would become available.

An important strand of public involvement with the project concerned regional development policy, which in the early 1960s was being pursued with determination. The policy was based upon a growth centre philosophy in the belief that if large industrial developments were encouraged (or directed) to areas of unemployment, they would establish economic linkages which would spread employment through multiplier effects. New steel plants were set up at Ravenscraig and Llanwern under this philosophy, and car plants at Linwood and on Merseyside. Awareness and concern was also growing at that time about the problems of the Highlands and Islands, which had experienced depopulation and economic decline for over a century. The Highland Advisory Panel (comprising MPs, local authorities, industry, unions, Government departments, etc.) had been set up in 1947, latterly under the chairmanship of Lord Cameron, and was providing a flow of reports and recommendations about the Highland situation which were eventually to result in the setting-up of the HIDB in 1965.

Another aspect of public policy related to the balance of payments, which, from 1945 until UK oil production built up in the late 1970s, was a major preoccupation of every Government. Britain has always been one of the world's largest importers of forest products, including pulp and paper, and a project which promised to replace significant quantities of these imports was assured of a welcome.

The Project. It was into this policy context that WT brought their project in 1963. The £15 million proposal was for a bleached sulphite mill, producing 80000 tonnes of pulp annually, linked initially to a 40000 tonne per year paper machine producing educational paper and medium/heavyweight printing grades. The project had undergone important changes at the planning stage. The original choice of technology had been a kraft (sulphate) pulping process, which is the most commonly used process in the pulping industry worldwide. Unfortunately, this process results in emission to the atmosphere of unpleasant odours, which were environmentally unacceptable to planning authorities conscious of the need to protect Highland amenity. To reach a viable scale, kraft mills also have a large timber requirement which would have stretched Highland resources to the limit. It was therefore decided to have a medium-sized mill, using a new and relatively untried two-stage, sodium-based sulphite process which had been developed in Sweden. The attractions of this process were that it could accommodate all softwood species (not just spruce), had low environmental impact, gave a high pulp yield from the timber input, and had lower bleaching costs and lower power costs for an integrated paper plant (through the combustion of spent process liquors).

It was realised from the outset that a pulp operation on this scale would not be viable unless it achieved economies of integrated processes with paper production through utilisation of process heat and waste recovery, power generation, site services, etc. The original concept was for two 40000 tonne per year paper machines to use the entire pulp output, but it was decided to build only one in the first instance, and to send the remaining pulp to other mills in the WT group until the second paper machine could be installed at Corpach at a future date. Lochaber was chosen as the location because it was the best collecting centre for the annually required 350000 tonnes of timber. Furthermore, it could readily supply the huge volumes of water required for pulp/paper operations (about 100000 gallons per tonne of pulp). A tidal seaboard location was necessary for effluent disposal and for sea transport and Fort William possessed the road and rail links required for the marketing of products in the UK.

An Act of Parliament was passed in 1963, enabling the Board of

Trade to make available loans of £10 million towards the estimated project cost of £20 million, and to provide grants of up to £1.3 million in relief of interest. In the event, the first phase of the project cost £15 million, receiving £8 million in public loans on virtually interest-free terms for the first three years.

The complex opened in September 1966, to considerable public acclaim. WT employed 700 people initially, rising to 950 by 1979. As expected, the development provided a major boost to other economic activity in the area, both through direct linkages (forest operations, road haulage, the West Highland railway line, support services, etc.) and indirectly through an expanded service sector. About 60 per cent of WT's employees were recruited in Central Scotland and brought their families with them to Lochaber. The population of the Fort William area grew rapidly from 6150 in 1961 to 10250 in 1971, a 60 per cent increase over the decade.

This population growth inevitably brought a number of strains and problems along with the benefits. A crash construction programme was required to provide public housing, and the social infrastructure of Fort William remained under severe pressure for a number of years until the necessary investment was gradually undertaken. Physical constraints on the Fort William site posed real planning difficulties in resolving the often conflicting interests of industry, agriculture, housing, recreation and amenity.

Operational Experience. Several factors contributed to making WT's operating experience at Corpach very different from that envisaged in 1963. A number of serious difficulties arose from the choice of technology, as the two-stage sulphite process proved temperamental in use. In particular, corrosion problems were experienced with the chemicals recovery plant and secondary boilers. Also the strength of the pulp produced was lower than expected, which meant that stronger pulps had to be imported as admixture to the paper finish. Changes in the structure of the paper market exacerbated this problem, as there was a move towards lighter weight, higher specification papers for which sulphite pulp on its own was not particularly suitable. WT were unable to justify investment in the second paper line originally planned. By 1980, only 40 per cent of the requirements of Corpach paper mill were being satisfied from the adjacent pulp mill, and 75 per cent of the pulp was being shipped out to other mills in the UK. This meant that the pulp mill had virtually become a market operation, and had lost most of the original cost advantages of integration to paper-making. Timber supply had posed difficulties too, especially in the early years. Adequate supplies were always secured but haulage distance extended up to 140 miles and, due to this factor and disappointing plant performance at Corpach, WT were faced with higher timber costs per tonne of pulp than they had expected.

By 1979, WT were experiencing annual losses in excess of £2 million per year at Corpach, and were faced with an imminent investment requirement of £10 million to replace parts of the chemical recovery system. These problems were aggravated by the world recession, which led to a slump in world paper sales generally. This was most acutely felt in Britain, where the oil-based strength of sterling made imports cheaper than they had been for many years. As a result of these factors, in April 1979 WT announced their decision to pull out of chemical pulp manufacture at Corpach.

In an effort to preserve the future of pulping operations at the Corpach Mill, WT looked carefully at various alternative pulp and paper-making activities. Contact was established with Consolidated Bathurst (CB), a major Canadian paper company, with a view to CB taking over the mill and converting it to make mechanical pulp for newsprint. Discussions proceeded to an advanced stage, but were ultimately unsuccessful because, it is believed, agreement could not be reached on timber prices, and because of high UK energy costs and the strength of sterling. When, after a year, these efforts to find alternative activities and operators had failed to bear fruit, WT announced in April 1980 that the pulp mill would close in November of that year. In doing so, they gave a firm undertaking to maintain their paper-making operations for at least five years, and to continue to seek an alternative pulp producer for Corpach.

Impact and Response. The immediate impact on Fort William was almost 450 redundancies, with an uncertain additional number to follow through 'knock-on' effects in the local economy. Unemployment in Fort William rose from 685 people in April 1979 (8·7 per cent, as against 7·9 per cent for Scotland as a whole) to 1493 in April 1983 (19·2 per cent, as against 15·1 per cent for Scotland). Employment in forestry operations, the most important dependent group, has to a considerable extent been protected by the success of the Foresty Commission and private growers in finding export markets for small round timber in Scandinavia. These volatile markets cannot be relied upon for the long term, however, and they provide a low return to growers, with minimal value being added to the timber resource. The sawmill at Kilmallie, which is the largest and most modern in Scotland, has been seriously affected by the loss of the adjacent outlet for its residues, upon which the investment was in part based. Fears are also expressed that, without the pulp mill, the future prospects of the paper mill surviving on its own may be in doubt. The economy of Lochaber depends very heavily upon industries based on forestry, which with hydro power (for aluminium) are its only productive resources. In spite of strenuous efforts, the HIDB has been unable to attract alternative major employers to this area.

The interest of Consolidated Bathurst has already been mentioned.

Following the failure of these negotiations, another project was promoted by a company (Lochaber Timber Industries), set up by a former employee at the mill and a local businessman. Their proposal would have led to the recommencement of sulphite pulping, but this did not succeed in securing private financial support. IDS and HIDB were involved in both the CB and LTI proposals and gave them every possible support within the framework of public assistance legislation, while the proposals on wood price and timber supply arrangements were prepared by the Forestry Commission and private growers.

Absent from the public sector response, however, were any special measures to attract inward investment. Although strongly urged to do so, Government did not extend Special Development Area status to Fort William or make available higher level RDGs, even in respect of pulp and paper projects; nor, when Enterprise Zones were introduced, did Fort William receive EZ status. This lack of investment incentives at the level available in some other parts of the UK reflects a further failure of contemporary UK regional policy to take account of the distinctive requirements of resource-based industries. High UK power costs are another discouraging factor, for which no relief is available at Fort William.

In the presently distressed condition of the world pulp and paper industry, it has not yet proved possible to attract an alternative pulp operator to Corpach. However, a major pulp/newsprint project was recently announced for Shotton in North Wales, raising hopes that the next investment may come to Fort William. The Scottish Forest Product Development Group are actively promoting that concept with major companies in the UK and abroad. In the meantime, the HIDB has undertaken a number of measures to improve industrial site availability and to stimulate small business development in Lochaber, but the results of these efforts are too modest to have a large impact on the Lochaber problem.

Conclusion. Although the Fort William pulp and paper investment was carried out on commercial grounds by WT, it was firmly based on public policies towards forestry, regional development and import substitution. The crisis and closure of the pulp mill resulted primarily from difficulties with technology and markets, although the unusual strength of sterling was a contributing factor. In the aftermath of closure, available public instruments have so far proven incapable of stimulating an alternative investment. There are a disturbing number of parallels with the Invergordon smelter crisis, including a new community caught in events which are beyond its control and apparently beyond the effective reach of present public policy.

NOTES AND REFERENCES

1. Valuable information on these industries in the Highlands and Island is contained in the Annual Reports of the Highlands and Islands Development Board.
2. See *Sunday Standard*, 27 September 1981, on this issue. Much was made of the fact that the British paper industry, including Wiggins Teape's paper mill at Fort William, was buying pulp from Swedish mills which process Scottish trees.
3. The Irvine factory of Scotboard Company, a subsidiary of British Plasterboard, was actually closed in 1981, but was later taken over by Bisonwerke. As at 1978, the factory had employed nearly 400 people.
4. This section draws substantially on the Annual Reports of the Forestry Commission.
5. Arthur D. Little, *The Scottish Forest Products Industry: Development Strategy and 1982–1985 Programme*, unpublished report, 1983; see also Scottish Forest Product Development Group, *Forest Products in Scotland: Opportunities for Growth*, Glasgow, 1983. An earlier study covering some of the same issues was Jaakko Poyry, *The Forestry Commission – A Marketing Strategy for Small Roundwood and Sawmill Residues*, London, January 1980.
6. Source: Department of Agriculture and Fisheries for Scotland (DAFS), *Scottish Sea Fisheries Statistical Tables*, 1981.
7. Sea Fish Industry Authority, *Annual Report*, 1983.
8. HIDB, *Annual Report*, 1983.
9. *Ibid.*
10. See G. G. Drummond, *The Invergordon Smelter. A Case Study in Management*, Hutchinson Benham (London), 1977.
11. Hansard, 'Debate on the Closure of the Invergordon Smelter', 21 January 1982.
12. See the *Economist*, 9–15 January 1982.
13. SSEB and NOSHEB, *Annual Reports*, 1983.
14. ETSU, *Strategic Review of Renewable Energy*, R.13, HMSO (London), 1982. See also ETSU, R.14, 1983.

9

HIGH-TECHNOLOGY INDUSTRIES

JOHN R. FIRN AND DAVID ROBERTS

Introduction

It is increasingly clear that for governments the world over the development and deployment of advanced technology has become the dominant industrial policy concern of the 1980s. The United States, for long the acknowledged leader in applied science, has begun to despair of its margin of technological superiority over Japan and Europe, both of which are assumed to depend on heavy government support for unfair technological competition; whilst Japan and Europe are riven with doubts about their ability to match the technological strength and marketing power of the major American multinational corporations. The Communist nations now rate the possession of basic semiconductor skills as an essential component of national security, and the new industrial nations of the Third World prostrate themselves before inward investors in the hope of being allowed to have a small dependent role in the global spread of high-technology industries (HTI). Reflection and research, however, reveal that there is nothing new in the preoccupation with technological strength as a basis for industrial competition, and back through the centuries parallels with the present situation can be found.

Whilst national competition through technology is a well-established feature of the policy environment within which individuals, corporations and governments operate, the role of technology in the growth of sub-national regional economies is an issue of comparatively recent concern. In the 1970s, increasing uncertainty with the then prevalent corpus of regional growth theory, and the growing unease with the apparent results of regional policy, resulted in a more focused and intensive investigation of the determinants of economic and industrial performance in the regions, especially at the level of the individual industrial enterprise. Technology, together with entrepreneurship, corporate ownership and structure and management efficiency, emerged as one of the key factors

The views expressed in this chapter are personal ones and should not be attributed to the Scottish Development Agency. The authors would like to thank colleagues in the Agency for comments and help, and especially Joyce Macdougall and Elaine O'Hara for assembling the material on the word processor – practising what we preach on technology.

affecting the ability of a region to generate its own economic development, and, therefore, as one of the essential bases of inter-regional competition. Whilst this conclusion has become generally accepted, there is much less agreement about the policy implications and the correct policy responses.

The belief that the development of a strong technology base can be a powerful stimulus to the economic growth of a region is encouraged by the amazingly rapid take-off of '. . .the world's most successful economic organization – Bay Area, Inc.',[1] the nine-county region of California more widely known as Silicon Valley. In 1979 the Valley generated a net increase of 90000 manufacturing jobs, almost all in high-technology companies; a further 10000 unfilled vacancies; and residential real estate profits of $30 billion.[2] The desire to emulate this success has made the development or capture of high-technology industry a priority for governments at both national and regional levels.

Scotland, with a long and continuing tradition of excellence in scientific and technical invention and innovation,[3] is one of the comparatively few European regions that can realistically aim to build and sustain an industrial structure with a strong HTI component. If this is to be achieved it will require the continuation and strengthening of the present supportive policy approach which has been pioneered in Scotland. This chapter will first examine the concept of high-technology industries, and the relationship between technology and regional development will then be briefly reviewed. The concern about Scotland's technological strength and its apparent dependence on external sources for new science-based products and industries is explored, and contrasted with what appears to be a stronger technology base than had been generally imagined to exist. The postwar development and performance of Scotland's leading HTI, electronics, is next outlined, together with brief looks at some other high-tech sectors. The policy and institutional framework within which HTI have been encouraged to develop in Scotland is reviewed, and attention focused on the broad policy approach that will require to be pursued in the future. The chapter ends with a case study of Ferranti, a company which, perhaps more than any other enterprise, has played a fundamentally important lead role in post-war technological growth in Scotland.

The Concept of High-Technology Industries

Policy-makers in both the public and private sectors who set out to deploy advanced applied sciences in support of economic growth face a number of real constraints on the formulation and implementation of policies and programmes. First, HTI, while an apparently simple attractive term, in reality embraces a wide range of industries, markets, products and technologies, each of which has distinct policy perspectives and

289

requirements. In a Scottish context this may often mean focusing on a single enterprise. Second, HTI are not a fixed set of industries, but rather an ever-changing collection of enterprises, institutions and individuals which are presently operating at the technological frontier, and which one day will be reclassified into declining, sunset industries.[4] Further, industries which in Scotland are regarded as HTI may well no longer be at the leading edge internationally, while products which are considered dated and low-tech in Scotland may still be viewed as desirable advanced industries in Third World nations – a situation which has interesting policy possibilities for Scotland.

However, the concept of HTI as a useful policy categorisation becomes yet harder to sustain when attention is focused on individual industrial sectors, for an exceedingly complex picture emerges, which can be best illustrated by a number of specific examples:

It is possible to find very advanced products and production processes in industries that are popularly imagined to be firmly disappearing in the sunset. Thus in steel, the introduction of continuous casting has improved the competitive position of the industry in much the same way as float glass revised the fortune of another declining sector. The application of computer-assisted image enhancement (developed for space missions) to digitally recorded X-ray photographs is another example of high-tech reviving an older product.

High-technology materials and products can often be fairly mundane in appearance and function, and thus belie an underlying heavy expenditure on R&D. Two examples of this are the recent development of oriented strand board (OSB) by the forest products industry, which will enable Scotland to utilise indigenous softwoods to compete effectively against imported plywood (see Chapter 8); and the increasing use of carbon fibre in the manufacture of fishing rods, as at Daiwa's factory in Motherwell.

The success of HTI is often more dependent upon the availability and quality of components, sub-contract assembly, and supporting services than on the central high-tech product. So, the competitive production of personal computers is as much determined by the ease in obtaining low-tech plastic components, metal frames, printed circuit boards, cables, keyboards and lead frames as by the central microprocessor chip. Policy for HTI must, therefore, also take account of the efficiency and presence of a number of supporting low-tech industries, including shipping, financial services and even business hotels.

Neither is the success of establishing and attracting HTI conditioned purely by the availability of highly-skilled graduate management and employees. Recent forecasts in the USA have indicated that most new jobs in HTI will not be technical, but rather semi-skilled, clerical and managerial occupations.[5] The same pattern will probably be repeated in Scotland, although it must not be taken to imply that these comparatively low-tech jobs are unimportant, for efficiency, quality and creativity in them will be vital to Scotland's future competitive position, and policy must take account of this.

The long-term switch of the developed nations from manufacturing towards the tertiary sector contains within it an increasing high-tech element complementary to the growth of HTI in manufacturing. Examples are the increasing technological content and sophistication in office occupations and telecommunications; and even the analytical and predictive skills engaged in formulating policy for HTI.

In consequence of the above, considerable disagreement exists as to exactly what economic and industrial features should be used to define an HTI sector. In the US the Bureau of Labor Statistics has recently defined an HTI as one where the expenditure on R&D and the share of technical personnel are twice the average found in manufacturing industry as a whole. On this basis 36 of the 977 US industrial sectors qualify as HTI, including aircraft, computers, drugs, and laboratory equipment, as well as services such as computer programming and research institutions and laboratories. A further 56 industries are included in a second 'high tech intensive' category defined as sectors with R&D expenditure and technical employment above the national average.[6] Unfortunately, for both the UK and Scotland, a similar classification is impossible.[7]

Regular involvement with manufacturing companies in Scotland confirms the inappropriateness of broad industrial sectors as a means of classifying HTI. A more appropriate concept is that of High-Technology Companies (HTCs), as it is within individual enterprises that science and technology are deployed in production.[8] The special characteristics of HTCs appear to be common throughout the industrial nations, and have recently become the subject of growing interest and study. Success is seemingly not solely determined by the development or possession of advanced product or manufacturing technologies, but rather by adoption of a very different corporate culture and lifestyle from that encountered in firms with poor performance records. Apart from the fact that most HTCs are predominantly small, young and fast-growing (companies such as IBM may appear to be exceptions to this), the rationale for their success seems to lie in their dynamic, progressive and relaxed management style, which encourages entrepreneurial behaviour at all levels of a company, and in which risk-taking and success are rewarded.[9] None of the Scottish enterprises which collapsed, often spectacularly, during the 1970s showed the flexibility and resilience of the newer HTCs – but as far as can be judged from the corporate history of Scotland, many of these companies in their formative period in the nineteenth century were

HTCs, and behaved like them. This perspective is important for HTI policies in that it implies for Scotland a return to an earlier pattern of industrial and company behaviour rather than a futile attempt to introduce levels of corporate performance that have never been achieved.

The policy focus on HTCs as well as on HTIs has important implications for Scotland, which need to be borne in mind throughout the remainder of this chapter. First, to support the development of companies that utilise technology in their activities requires the deployment and coordination of policy measures and attitudes across a wide range of activities, including research, teaching and administration in all levels of education; the provision of more flexible and venturesome capital and management assistance from financial institutions; the enhancing of management education and employee training; the continued improvement of the physical environment in which industry operates; and an encouragement of the changing social attitudes that are beginning to appear in Scotland. Second, both HTIs and HTCs are subject to rapid product and technology obsolescence, and there can thus be no assumption of the inevitability of continued growth, nor of any relaxation in the competitive effort that will be required. Companies will be subject to rapid change, and will be part of a constantly shifting population of entrepreneurs and enterprises, requiring flexible and adaptive policy measures. Third, the continuing open nature of the Scottish economy will require of firms, individuals, institutions and Government an outward-looking, international approach to economic and industrial development which will constantly compare competitiveness and performance, and identify rapidly emerging products, markets and technologies offering potential for Scotland.

The involvement of a company in an HTI sector or even its existence as a full-fledged HTC does not guarantee superior economic performance in terms of returns to shareholders and employees that are continually and consistently above average, nor indeed in terms of its net contribution to the local economy, although their management characteristics may well give them a greater chance of survival in harsh economic periods. The evolution of a strong base of HTCs in a region does, however, have one important feature: it signifies the presence of existing and potential entrepreneurs, and thus of a potential capability to generate future growth from internal technological strengths. The principal objective of any attempt to improve comparative regional economic performance depends critically on the ability to encourage, mobilise and expand this capability.

Technology and Regional Economic Development

The causes of differing spatial patterns of economic growth remain little understood, and much policy has been based on intuition rather than on evidence and deduction. Analysis of the usual crop of macro-statistics[10] has taken regional growth theory very little forward, and recent research has shifted to more detailed investigations of corporate growth and change within individual regions, sometimes matched up with parallel investigations of specific industrial sectors or product markets. The initial results of these more industrial and managerial approaches have begun to focus attention on factors such as qualitative differences in the nature and utilisation of capital equipment; labour organisation, performance and training; imperfect information and access to markets and natural resources; and rates of adoption of new technology as explanatory variables in the economic performance of regions. Yet it is also recognised that such issues are merely symptoms of more complex, probably intangible, factors that really shape the economic performance of regions, such as entrepreneurship and other socio-cultural attitudes, all areas where economists fear to tread. This multi-layered concept of economic growth means that policy-makers and implementers are usually operating at two or three stages of remove from the real determining factors, and this may be especially true in relation to technology.

When technology is the objective of regional policy there is still far to go in identifying broad areas for targeting policy measures, and indeed, in even understanding the principal causal mechanisms involved. For instance, there is no known direct way of measuring the absolute, or even comparative, levels and status of technology in any single company, let alone at regional, national or international scale. The best that can be achieved is to rely on a range of indirect indicators, such as patents, graduates in applied sciences, the use of CNC machine tools or robots, and net exports of high-tech products, together with an intuitive judgement on technological status. It is simply impossible, therefore, to rank Scotland against other UK or European regions in terms of technology.

At present a clear consensus exists amongst most regional economists in the UK, and increasingly in Europe and North America, that the ability to shape and utilise advanced science-based technology is a crucial determinant of the long-term comparative economic performance of individual regions, and that major and significant differences in this ability exist between regions. This consensus derives from an increasing base of applied research which has not yet been assembled into a comprehensive, structured and policy-oriented analysis. It is not intended to begin such a major task here, but it is briefly, and very selectively, worth noting some important indicators of inter-regional differences in technological capability, with a principal concentration on the United Kingdom.

It is known that industrial research establishments are clustered in the more affluent and apparently attractive parts of the United Kingdom, with an overwhelming bias towards the South-East, the Thames Valley, and the M4 corridor in particular.[11] Less is known about the determinants of this pattern, and about the means by which the current distribution will influence longer-term economic growth. Evidence is emerging that significant industrial innovations, as measured by the development of new products and publicly-recognised technological achievement, is spatially concentrated in a few regions, again principally the South-East,[12] and it seems likely that this is due to differential long-term changes in the sectoral and organisational structures of the various regions, including the centralising forces of mergers and increasing corporate concentration.[13] Government assistance to industry designed to help firms adopt new technologies and products has also been strongly skewed towards the more affluent areas of Britain,[14] and the flow of capital into new HTCs appears, on the evidence so far, to be far from evenly distributed.[15] The almost complete concurrence of spatial patterns across a range of technology-related factors confirms that the existing and potential technological endowments of individual regions in the UK are very unevenly distributed, and this is a major cause for concern. The growing interest in the relationship between technology and regional development is not confined to Britain, and research and policy debates on this issue are now beginning to surface in individual countries such as the United States, Italy, France and Japan, and within the broader policy deliberations of bodies such as the European Commission.[16] That the topic has finally achieved respectability and influence in government circles can be seen by its adoption as the subject of a major international conference under the aegis of OECD in Paris in October 1983.[17]

It has been argued that the importance of maximising national (UK) economic capability to compete internationally in the high-tech stakes far over-rides any requirement to ensure a national spatial balance in technological capability, with national goals taking precedence over regional ones. It is further suggested that as economic growth is continually imbalanced, spatial concentrations of technological power are essential, and any conscious dispersion of this will affect international competitiveness. An alternative view to this pro-concentration approach does exist, but so far little effort has been made to derive regional policy programmes designed to focus on technological enhancement.

In practice, an optimum policy probably lies somewhere between such extreme positions, with individual regions practising their own variants on the concentration theme. In Britain concern does seem to be developing about the existing technological capability of individual regions now searching for ways to mobilise their local resources of science and technology. The introduction of the HTC element into the regional growth debate has not yet been fully explored, although the postwar experience of Scotland is creating interest, and causing attention to be directed to the corporate component of such growth.

Scotland and Technology

Most outside observers of Scotland's industrial performance seem to be under the misapprehension that the development of a visible corpus of HTCs, especially in the electronics sector, is of comparatively recent origin, and can be credited mainly to the effectiveness of post-war regional policies in attracting HTCs from other parts of the UK and overseas. Whilst there is some truth in this, Scotland's present apparent technological renaissance has much of its base in a long and proud history of discovery, invention and innovation which stretches back for more than two hundred years, and which encompasses an amazingly diverse set of achievements in virtually every major area of the applied sciences and technologies. It is a record about which the average Scot knows little, but one which is slowly becoming internationally recognised as representing a contribution towards human economic, industrial and physical development which is out of all proportion to the absolute and comparative size of the country.[18] The casual factors behind such consistent technological achievement are still little researched, let alone understood, and there are few useful pointers available to assist policy formulation in support of current Scottish industrial growth.

The driving force for Scotland's industrialisation throughout much of the nineteenth century came from the inter-related complex of coal, iron, steel, engineering and shipbuilding companies, which from their base in the west of Scotland provided the capital goods for much of the world. Scotland was truly full of HTCs, and the Clyde Valley in the last quarter of the nineteenth century had almost the same aura and image amongst the industrial nations of the world as Silicon Valley has at present.[19] However, much of the inventiveness and the attendant entrepreneurship had seemingly run its course by the time of World War I, and Scotland then entered a half century when its industrial growth slowed. The reasons cannot be explained by simple references to long waves and Kondratief cycles, but a comparative absence of technological inventiveness does start to appear. In 1932, an Industrial Survey of the South-West of Scotland undertaken for the Board of Trade by Glasgow University economists noted that while 'ingenuity and new ideas are at least as active as they have been at any time in the past, . . . (they appeared to have been) . . . in large measure canalised, having been concentrated on the staple industries.'[20]

The Clyde Valley Plan of 1946 made some telling points about the state of the local economy which hinted at a poor performance in generating and adopting new technology, but never really tracked down the real problem.[21] It was generally assumed that the way forward lay with attracting fast-growing companies and plants from elsewhere in the UK (comparatively easy in the era of IDCs) and from overseas, and through

295

this attracting the new technologies and skills to Scotland.[22] It was the 1974 West Central Scotland Plan, looking in depth at the immense industrial problems of the area, which finally recognised that policy priority should be switched from mobile industry to the existing indigenous sector. The Plan recommended that assistance and advice should be targeted much more directly at individual companies and their specific needs, and to achieve this the team recommended that a new public corporation be established with a range of powers and functions. Amongst its priorities should be the encouragement of local technology.[23] The UK Government rejected the concept of a public corporation specifically for the Strathclyde Region, but accepted the overall logic of the report, and the industrial development recommendations were largely implemented by the establishment of the Scottish Development Agency in 1975 (see also Chapter 2).

Since the Agency was established, it has in its various corporate plans and industrial strategies been gradually evolving an industrial development role for itself in which the encouragement of technology, HTIs and HTCs has come to play a central and important part.[24] Faced with large demands for its limited resources, the Agency has had to establish clear priorities for its involvement in industrial development, and has elected to focus its activities on a relatively small number of inter-related technology-based sectors, namely: electronics; health care and biotechnology; advanced engineering; and energy-related technology; which between them are likely to form the main source of economic and industrial growth during the remaining years of the century.[25] These are now examined, with a particular concentration on the electronics industry.

The Electronics Industry in Scotland

Scotland's evolution into 'Silicon Glen' is a phenomenon of the post-1960 period, but the technological base of this industry goes back much further to the research and discoveries of the universally recognised 'father of modern electronics', James Clerk Maxwell, in the mid-nineteenth century.[26] His influential work was built on by a number of other distinguished Scottish engineers and physicists, including Lord Kelvin, and they were responsible for the development of a strong and widely respected tradition in these disciplines, upon which much of the recent growth of the modern electronics industry has been built.

An initial difficulty in charting the recent evolution of the electronics industry in Scotland is that a degree of disagreement exists about the means used to classify companies to the sector, and consequently as to where the exact boundaries of the industry should be drawn.[27] Obviously there is a great difference between the manufacture of largely mechanical electrical systems, such as time-clocks or electric typewriters, and the 'pure' electronics products such as quartz LCD timepieces and word-processors, which have subsequently displaced older products, often in the same companies and factories. It is generally accepted that there were probably only around 3000 employees engaged in manufacturing products that were recognisably of an electronic nature in Scotland at the end of the war, but in subsequent years the pace of development quickened. The high level of European tariffs and the need to establish a position in a major market area led US electrical and instrument engineering companies to establish manufacturing facilities in Europe, and it was during this time that companies such as IBM, NCR, Burroughs and Honeywell set up their facilities in Scotland. This country's tradition of engineering excellence, its ready supply of skilled labour and attractive industrial property, its English language, its location close to the UK and European markets, and Commonwealth Preference (a factor often forgotten), all ensured that Scotland received a major share of such inward investment from the USA. The arrival of these MNEs, plus the expansion of existing UK and European companies in the sector, resulted in electronics employment in Scotland rising to around 7400 by 1959 (Table 9.1), which still only represented around one per cent of total manufacturing employment.

Employment in electronics in Scotland increased significantly in the 1960s, mainly through further inward investment, principally from the rest of the UK and, after 1965, from the United States, when important corporations such as National Semiconductor, Motorola Semiconductors, General Instrument Microelectronics, Andrew Antennae and W. L. Gore arrived. In the late 1960s the seeds of Scotland's indigenous electronics sector began to be sown; and in the 1970s the sector as a whole showed further substantial growth, at least in terms of the number of companies, to over two hundred firms employing in excess of 34000 by 1978. The last half-decade has seen a further expansion of the industry, through yet further additions to capacity by most of the existing plants; by more arrivals from overseas, including the first major investments by Japanese corporations; by the evolution of a new generation of indigenous electronics companies; and by a move into electronics products and processes by enterprises in other sectors. The result is a strong, diversified sector, in which an estimated 280 plants employ nearly 43000 people, with a substantial additional workforce in companies supplying and servicing requirements of the electronics firms (Table 9.1). Over a relatively short period, therefore, a new industrial sector has emerged in Scotland, accounting for nearly ten per cent of total manufacturing and, at least in employment terms, individually exceeding the shipbuilding (29000), coal (26000), or steel (19500) industries (although the combination of these three older core sectors is still larger despite strange claims to the contrary).

Measuring the structure and growth of employment in electronics is difficult, and similar problems exist in relation to the growth of output in the industry. Using the definitions adopted for the employment estimates shown in Tables 9.1 and 9.2, it appears that output has risen over the recent period from £450 million in 1977 to around £700 million in 1982, but these figures should be treated with some caution. An especially interesting problem is likely to emerge in attempts to value the output of the semiconductor companies, given the tendency for the prices of any integrated circuit to decline in real terms by an order of magnitude every year or so.

Table 9.1. Growth of employment in the Scottish electronics industry, 1959–83.

	1959	1971	1978	1983
Electronics employment in Scotland[1]	7400	37200	34300	42500
Total manufacturing employment in Scotland	698100	669300	603600	431000
Electronics as % of total manufacturing employment	1·1	5·6	5·7	9·9

[1] Data may not be completely comparable due to different definitions. 1981 SCOMER figures indicate electronics employment of 37000 (Table 5.3).
Sources: Electronics employment – 1959: Scottish Council (Development and Industry), quoted in *The Scotsman*, 25 April 1968 (Action 68 Supplement); 1971: SCOMER; 1978: Booz, Allen & Hamilton Survey; 1983: Scottish Development Agency Survey. Total manufacturing employment – 1959: IDS Consistent Series; 1971 and 1978: Census of Employment; 1983: *Department of Employment Gazette*.

Within the Scottish electronics industry, over three-quarters of present employment is concentrated in the four largest product areas, namely industrial products; information systems (including computers); defence and avionics; and electronic components (Table 9.2). The presence of a relatively small number of product areas in Scotland, whilst fortuitous, has helped the industry embed itself in the local economy, and has presented component and sub-contract manufacturers with markets of sufficient scale to be attractive: as will be seen below, these opportunities have only been slowly grasped, and remain an area of policy priority. The electronic components sector of the industry, which currently employs nearly 7500, is in many ways the most important as it contains within it the major semiconductor fabrication plants, which have become the main justification for naming central Scotland 'Silicon Glen'. At present there are four plants operational – Motorola, National Semiconductor, General Instrument and Hughes (all US-owned) – with a further two (NEC from Japan, and Burr Brown from the US) planning to move from assembly to full wafer-fabrication by early 1985. Other integrated circuit production takes place elsewhere in Scotland, in for example the Wolfson Institute in Edinburgh, but is not of a scale to be regarded as manufacturing.

Table 9.2. Scottish electronics industry by product area, 1983.

Main product area[1]	No. of companies	No. of employees	Average size of company	Share of total electronics employment
Industrial products	82	8984	109·6	21·1
Information systems	24	8880	370·0	20·9
Defence and avionics	9	7739	859·9	18·2
Electronic components	52	7406	142·4	17·4
Telecommunications	14	3961	282·9	9·3
Electronic sub-contracting	46	2507	54·5	5·9
Consumer products	11	2048	186·2	4·8
Design and services	17	596	35·1	1·4
Medical electronics	14	402	28·7	1·0
Total electronics	269	42523	158·1	100·0

[1] The product classifications are based on the categories employed by Booz, Allen & Hamilton in their surveys of the Scottish electronics industry. Companies are allocated to a category on the basis of their major product, although many are multi-product firms.
Source: Scottish Development Agency Survey, June 1983.

These semiconductor plants have undertaken a huge investment programme in Scotland since 1980, with over £200 million spent to expand capacity and employment – no mean achievement in the face of a major international recession. The result of this expenditure has been to consolidate Scotland as Europe's leading semiconductor production area, accounting for (in 1983) 79 per cent of the UK's and 21 per cent of Western Europe's integrated circuits, with a special strength in high-density MOS chips.[28] Whilst much of the earlier production of integrated circuits was exported to the Far East for assembly and bonding into chip carriers and lead frames by nimble-fingered Asian girls, future generations of chips, with their high circuit densities, are likely to be packaged and finished with computer-controlled automated assembly facilities in Scotland, and most of the semiconductor plants have invested, or are planning to invest in the necessary equipment. It is also interesting to note that suppliers of materials, components and services (such as mask making) are beginning to develop in Scotland to serve the semiconductor facilities, and that universities and colleges are strengthening their applied research and training efforts in support of company needs. The one missing component for a true Silicon Valley situation is a successful spin-off of a new indigenous semiconductor company, although this may emerge in the near future now that the base of skilled engineers and designers is expanding.

The importance of inward investment by US, English and European companies in the growth of the Scottish electronics industry can be seen in Table 9.3, which shows very clearly the big divide that currently separates the smaller indigenous firms from their much larger multinational brethren. As only 16·5 per cent of employment in the Scottish electronics industry is currently in locally-controlled plants it would appear at first sight that the base of this HTI is not especially deep, but this simple view neglects the interesting fact that many of the larger MNE plants in Scotland, particularly in the more advanced market segments such as semiconductors, systems and industrial products, have begun to increase their potential independence from parent companies through the introduction of their own R&D, design and exporting activities, and as such are becoming less footloose than would be supposed from the history of the industry. Whilst in the final analysis such MNE plants must always be subject to the control of their parent companies, in many cases a strategic decision to encourage greater independence in their overseas facilities has been taken by such parent Boards – an effective vote of confidence in Scotland as an electronics location with long-term prospects.

Table 9.3. Scottish electronics industry by country of ownership, 1983[1].

Ownership	Companies No.	%	Employment No.	%	Average no. of employees
Scotland	178	66·2	7011	16·5	39·4
Rest of UK	49	18·2	17369	40·8	354·5
USA	34	12·6	17386	40·9	511·4
Europe	6	2·2	399	0·9	66·5
Japan	2	0·7	358	0·8	179·0
Total	269	100·0	42523	100·0	158·1

[1] 1981 data, derived from SCOMER, are given in Table 5.6; the associated text presents a rather different view to that expressed in this chapter.
Source: Scottish Development Agency Survey, June 1983.

The geographical destination of the production of the Scottish electronics industry illustrates much of the rationale for the development of the different sources of the industry's growth, as can be seen in Table 9.4. For all plants, irrespective of their locus of control, the Scottish market is

Table 9.4. Market destination for Scottish electronics industry production (%) by ownership, 1978.

	Ownership of company				
Destination	Scotland	Rest of UK	USA	Europe	All
Scotland	18	7	7	7	7
Rest of the UK	47	70	31	86	55
Europe	23	11	46	7	26
USA	6	4	7	—	5
Rest of the World	6	8	9	—	7
Total	100	100	100	100	100
% exported ex-UK	35	23	62	7	38

Source: Booz, Allen & Hamilton Industry Survey, Summer 1978.

of relatively minor importance: even indigenous electronics plants sell less than a fifth of their output into the local market. The Scottish plants of UK companies, many of whom moved to Scotland in the 1950s and 60s through the actions of regional policy, sell over three-quarters of their output in the UK, and might therefore be regarded as virtual non-exporters. The reasons for this are however more complex than might appear: as many English-owned plants make components for incorporation in products made elsewhere in the UK, and/or export Scottish production through agents and distributors in the South-East of England, the real eventual export level may be much higher. It should also be borne in mind that many English-owned plants in Scotland, such as Marconi and Ferranti, are involved in defence-related products which are sold either direct to the UK armed forces or to other British weapons systems manufacturers such as British Aerospace, Dowty or GEC. It is interesting to see, however, the contrast between the sales patterns of the US and European electronics plants in Scotland: the former are very much aimed at producing for the non-UK European market, which takes nearly half of their production (although England will probably remain the largest single national market in Europe), whilst the European plants have moved here simply to supply the UK market, which takes over 90 per cent of their output (see also the discussion in Chapter 4). The fact that Scotland obviously can serve as an efficient and effective 'market base in Europe' (as SDA and LIS marketing proclaims) for US electronics companies has obviously been a principal reason for the recent continued growth of US electronics investment in Scotland by companies such as Wang, and has also been of importance in attracting Japanese companies.

Amongst the more visible indicators of the move by electronics MNEs in Scotland towards more local independence are changes in their

Table 9.5. Technical employment in the
Scottish electronics industry, 1978 and 1981.[1]

Activity	% technical employees 1978	1981
Research and development	4	7
Design engineering	32	28
Production and test	64	65
Total (%)	100	100
Scientists and technologists	50	47
Technicians	50	53

[1] These figures are based on a sample survey covering the 10 largest
electronics plants (all foreign-owned MNEs), which between them
accounted for over 30 per cent of total employment in the sector.
Source: Industry surveys by Booz, Allen & Hamilton, 1978 and 1981.

employment structure, and the growing involvement of these companies
in university and college training in the electronics sciences. The move
towards a higher level of employment skills in larger MNE facilities in
Scotland is apparently of comparatively recent origin; but some indications of it can be seen in Table 9.5, where the proportion of technical
staff involved in design engineering (often adaptation of US models to
European standards and requirements) contracted. By contrast, the proportion of R&D employees rose, an expansion which is all the more
noteworthy given that most of the ten Original Equipment Manufacturers (OEMs) investigated increased their overall level of employment
over the period.[29] One of the fears expressed in the late 1970s was that the
continued expansion of the Scottish electronics industry would be en-
dangered through the inability of such high-tech plants to obtain the
quantity and quality of highly-qualified personnel necessary for their
efficient operation.[30] In 1981 the SDA investigated this particular issue in
detail, and hosted a special Manpower Forum, attended by all the major
electronics companies operating in Scotland. At the (now regular)
Forum, the consensus view emerged that there were no real overall shortages of skilled and highly qualified manpower facing the electronics
industry in Scotland, and where specific shortages did exist they were
typically single-figure requirements for relatively new and esoteric skills
in areas such as wafer fabrication. Subsequent detailed research by the
Scottish Office has confirmed this position,[31] and thus Scotland can
consider continued expansion of the industry with some confidence. The
one confirmed area of shortage is of senior electronic engineers with
perhaps ten years or more of work experience and with management
potential, and to increase the attractiveness and visibility of Scotland

to such people (many of whom are emigré Scots), twenty of the largest electronic companies launched a joint recruitment campaign aimed at attracting high-level engineers (and more importantly their families) to Scotland.[32]

There are three particular policy issues which many consider important to the continued development of the Scottish electronics industry and it is necessary to look at each of these in a little more detail. These concern the real strength of the industry's technological base in Scotland; the ability of Scottish component and sub-contract companies to competitively supply the electronics OEMs; and, perhaps most important of all, the ability of the Scottish economy to develop a strong and internationally recognised collection of indigenous electronics HTCs upon which Scotland's longer-term electronics future will critically depend.

Until comparatively recently it was assumed – perhaps rightly – that the main focus of advanced electronics technology lay overseas in North America, Europe or Japan, and that consequently Scotland could do very little to shape the future of its own development in the industry. When the SDA was considering its first sector initiative in electronics in 1977, the general belief was that the technological power really lay inside a small number of US MNEs, and that little real advanced applied electronics with commercial potential existed in Scotland: the local technological base was therefore weak and ineffective. Subsequent detailed research, observation and actual industrial developments have shown that the real position is far stronger than had been imagined.

The central role in indigenous electronics technology is played by universities and colleges, with Edinburgh, Glasgow, Heriot-Watt and Strathclyde universities having particular strengths. In 1981–82, during the first updating of the SDA-led electronics strategy, Booz, Allen and Hamilton undertook a detailed audit of Scottish electronics technology in universities, colleges and companies, and local strengths were discussed with competing research units overseas and with the R&D directors of leading MNEs. The results were surprising, in that in three critical technologies – VLSI, artificial intelligence and opto-electronics – Scotland had a research capability and capacity that was at the forefront internationally, and which was arousing interest from leading US, Japanese and European electronics companies.[33] What is of even greater importance is that these three technologies lie at the centre of the current effort to build fifth-generation computers, which both Europe and Japan regard as the single most important high-technology project of the present decade. It is crucial in policy terms to engineer the transfer of these research skills in Scottish universities into commercial operations, preferably in Scottish-based enterprises.

Scotland's strengths in electronics technology extend beyond the universities and colleges. A further indication of this is that the local electronics industry is developing a certain technological momentum as seen in the increased R & D activity being undertaken in existing Scottish electronics plants. An interesting and important study recently completed by Oakey alleged that the incidence of full-time R & D activities in small electronics firms in Scotland was higher than in comparable companies in San Francisco's Bay Area (including Silicon Valley). In addition the research indicated that the links between Scottish universities and these small companies featured as the main external R & D links of such enterprises – a situation in sharp contrast to Silicon Valley firms, which evidently regard local universities as mere providers of personnel.[34] Multinational electronics companies operating in Scotland also have begun to enhance their local R & D capability to support growing design strengths. Honeywell Controls has recently introduced a Solid State Applications Centre at its main Scottish facility and is seeking closer involvement with Scottish universities; Hewlett-Packard in its main European telecommunications-test equipment centre near Edinburgh has always fully designed and developed most of their systems locally; and even more advanced R & D capabilities exist in Barr and Stroud, Racal MESL, Ferranti and Marconi.

The second issue of importance to those involved in framing and implementing policy for the industry is the ability of the local industrial base to supply Scottish electronics plants with essential components and services. The picture here is not quite so encouraging, at least on the basis of performance to date, but in examining the supply response of Scottish firms it is necessary to understand the purchasing structures and criteria of the forty or so large electronics OEMs which currently dominate the sector in Scotland. In these plants the level of purchasing autonomy varies substantially, ranging from firms that allow their plants to choose and purchase all their requirements of goods and services (autonomous procurement) through minimum local procurement (where plants assemble centrally supplied components but can buy some services) to full central purchasing, where (especially for components) global searches to achieve the best price, quality and delivery terms are undertaken. In Scotland, electronics OEMs have traditionally had relatively little purchasing autonomy for components (most of which are internationally-traded 'catalogue' items) and only a little greater freedom in their purchasing of services; but over the past few years the level of purchasing authority has risen sharply: by 1980 ninety per cent of the OEM purchases of electronics components and sub-contract services were decided by local management.[35]

The ability of Scottish electronics sub-contracting and components supply (ESCS) companies to sell to local OEMs depends on their satisfying a number of important procurement criteria. The large electronics firms examine potential ESCS suppliers closely to assess their physical, financial and technical ability to supply goods and services, with price, security and speed of supply and the existence of constantly high quality levels being important determinants of companies gaining contracts. The financial credibility of potential suppliers is especially important.

Large electronics firms also try to avoid a single vendor becoming too dependent upon them, and consequently most plants will not purchase more than twenty per cent of a single vendor's sales: only rarely will this be allowed to rise to thirty per cent or more (for an example, refer to the IBM case study in Chapter 4). Most firms are reluctant to single-source even when the above dependency rules are not being broken, and usually seek sourcing security by having more than two suppliers for ESCS goods and services in order to maintain flexibility and competition of supply.

Over the past fifteen years the electronics firms have gradually increased the proportion of mechanical and assembly sub-contract work they are willing to see undertaken outside their own facilities, and (with some exceptions) OEMs now concentrate on direct electronics manufacture and leave most of the sub-contract work, such as machining and plastic moulding, to specialist sub-contractors elsewhere in Scotland and the rest of the UK. This trend is expected to continue. Analysis of the ESCS industry in the USA indicates that over the next decade the changing pattern of sub-contract requirements will demand higher-quality work and the development of an increased design capability within sub-contractors. Components, especially internationally traded items such as capacitors, connectors and switches, are likely to continue to be purchased centrally by electronics companies, and consequently targeted inward investment will be the principal means of expanding this particular part of the industry in Scotland.

It was estimated in 1979 that the forty largest OEMs purchased some £267 million of ESCS goods and services for their Scottish facilities, with the four largest companies being responsible for a remarkable sixty per cent of this total. As can be seen from Table 9.6, most of the purchases were made outside Scotland, especially in components where only twelve per cent were locally sourced. The performance in sub-contract work was much better, with thirty per cent of OEM requirements being met locally, but overall the situation does appear to provide major market opportunities for Scottish ESCS firms, even without allowing for the even larger ESCS markets in the rest of the UK and Europe – with Eire being an especially promising area. Increasing the market share of Scottish ESCS companies will not be easy and will require time and determination but many hundreds of potential jobs are at stake for Scotland. The SDA has established a broad development programme in this particular area, and is working closely with both the OEMs and local ESCSs to help close the main import gaps identified.

Table 9.6. Purchases of components and sub-contract services by Scottish electronics OEMs, 1979.

Origin of supplier	Electronic components		Sub-contract work		Total purchases	
	£m	%	£m	%	£m	%
Scotland	20	12	31	30	51	19
Rest of UK	75	46	57	54	132	49
Europe	36	22	4	3	40	15
USA	21	13	8	8	29	11
Other	10	6	5	5	15	6
Total	162	100	105	100	267	100

Source: Makrotest study interviews, 1980.

The final policy issue of significance concerns Scotland's ability to develop a strong indigenous base of HTCs in the electronics sector. The experience to date has been encouraging, although it is difficult to compare local performance with that elsewhere. Both the existing electronics companies and the universities have produced new entrepeneurs and enterprises, and the result is an indigenous Scottish electronics sector of some 140 companies, many of which are developing and deploying very advanced technologies. The existing electronics companies have spun-off interesting new companies such as Rodime at Glenrothes, which has developed an advanced small Winchester disc-drive system for computers and which has not only achieved a $27 million listing on the US Unlisted Securities Market but has opened a manufacturing facility in Florida;[36] Fortronic near Dunfermline in Fife, which has rapidly become a major force in the banking terminals equipment market; and Prestwick Circuits, which has evolved into one of Europe's leading producers of advanced printed circuit boards and which, like Rodime, also has a United States presence. In the past decade the Scottish Universities have also begun to spawn small electronics HTCs, including Lattice Logic and Walmesley Microcircuits in semiconductor design; Logitech and Intellemetrics in opto-electronics; Edinburgh Instruments in lasers; and M&D Technology in the complex and challenging area of nuclear magnetic resonance (NMR) body-scanning medical systems.

The factors behind the increasing emergence of new Scottish companies in the electronics sector are, as yet, imperfectly understood, but amongst those often quoted are an increased 'venture capital' attitude by Scottish and UK financial institutions; the demonstrative effect of early successful entrepreneurs; changing attitudes towards the private sector; the development of a more understanding and supportive approach to company start-ups by public and private financial institutions;[37] and the increasing base of highly-motivated electronics engineers and managers in Scotland, many of whom have worked for a period in areas such as California or Boston where they imbibed the entrepreneurial spirit that often exists around local HTCs. A key objective for policy for the electronics sector in the future must be to encourage this trend towards new company formation, and to ensure their post-formation growth and success.

The modern electronics industry in Scotland is of comparatively recent origin, but Government attempts to encourage its growth date back to the formation of the Scottish Development Group of electronics companies under the leadership of Ferranti in 1945. In the 1950s and '60s the industry's growth was largely built on inward investment, with the principal Government role being the provision of effective regional policy tools to divert mobile electronics investment to Scotland and to ensure its subsequent expansion – areas in which the Scottish Council (Development and Industry) were also successfully involved. In retrospect, it appears likely that Government purchasing for the UK defence sector also assisted the development of the industry, with Ferranti in particular (profiled in the Appendix) being perhaps the single most influential electronics company operating in Scotland. Yet the policy perspective of the UK Government and the Scottish Office extended little further than regional policy, and certainly little attempt was made to influence the other key sector development issues discussed in this chapter.

The evolution of NEDO, NEB and other public sector initiatives in the 1970s saw a relatively rapid switch towards a more comprehensive policy approach to the UK electronics industry, and in Scotland the newly-established SDA recognised the importance of the electronics industry by selecting it as the first and pre-eminent sector development initiative. The reasons for identifying electronics as the prime future industrial growth sector were a reflection of many of the issues discussed above, together with an element of concern that the rapid pace of technological change in electronics could adversely affect existing operations in Scotland, especially of the MNE-OEMs. The Agency, with the support of the Scottish Office, enlisted the leading management consultants, Booz, Allen and Hamilton, to undertake a comprehensive review of the Scottish and international electronics industries and to develop, jointly with the Agency, a long-term development strategy for the sector in Scotland. The strategy,[38] which was launched in April 1979, has guided the Agency's development activities in the electronics sector since then, and the SDA has in effect assumed responsibility for coordinating public and private assistance to the electronics industry in Scotland through the Agency's Electronics Division, which is staffed by experienced electronics engineers (see, in addition, Chapter 2, Figures 2.4 and 2.5 and the associated text).

The electronics strategy reflected the real opportunities that existed, and therefore it was deemed essential that a regular updating of programmes and policies in the strategy be undertaken, and that progress be monitored. In 1981–82, Booz, Allen and Hamilton therefore assisted the Agency in reviewing progress, and in updating the main operational programmes. The revised strategy was more comprehensive than its predecessor, and contained over fifteen specific recommendations for action by the SDA and others to ensure the continued growth of the electronics industry in Scotland.[39] The action programmes basically aim to build on Scotland's research, entrepreneurial and corporate strengths to ensure a higher level of self-sufficiency in future, especially in the three critical technology sectors.

It is, as yet, too early to fully appraise the results of the Agency's strategy initiatives in electronics, but it is clear that they have provided a coordinated and purposeful development approach that had previously been lacking. The effectiveness of the Electronics Division has been proved in its success in assisting new companies to become established; in providing specialist inputs to the promotional programmes for inward investors; in helping to bridge the university-industry interface; in helping to develop OEM-ESCS linkages; in discussing training needs; and, above all, in aiding the emergence of a recognised 'corporate identity' for the whole Scottish electronics industry.

Other High-Technology Sectors

Electronics is at present the central focus for HTI policy in Scotland, and indeed is likely to remain so because of the growing penetration of that technology into other industrial sectors such as engineering, medicine, and agriculture. There are, however, other industries which display distinct HTI aspects; in which HTCs operate from a Scottish base; and for which specific development programmes have been launched or are under consideration. Some of these – telecommunications, for example – have been the policy responsibility of the UK Government, but in others Scottish initiatives have been introduced, again principally through the SDA. It is not intended here to examine all these HTI sectors on the same basis as the electronics sector, but merely to indicate the main industrial features of some of the more important ones and the policy approaches adopted for each. The ones selected for review here are health care and biotechnology, offshore oil and gas technology, and advanced engineering – all sectors with which the Agency has a growing involvement, and on which there exists a degree of understanding.

Health Care and Biotechnology. Health care is recognised by most developed nations as a key technological sector, capable of generating substantial economic growth through the supply of new products and services all aimed at a common market, namely that of personal health care. It is a very difficult sector to analyse, evaluate and plan, as it is really comprised of an astonishingly diverse set of products including medical electronic equipment (such as lasers, NMR scanners, patient monitoring systems, and bone growth stimulators); drugs and pharmaceutical preparations (from aspirin to sophisticated cardiac drugs); prosthetics and appliances (artificial lenses, bone joint implants, heart valves); wound management products (bandages, sutures and clips, pads); to medical tools (scalpels, needles, life support systems). Each of these products and services have distinct markets on their own, involving unique and often complex technologies and corporations; and strategic analysis of the whole health-care sector presents a major challenge, especially if it is undertaken as a basis for policy programmes.

Scotland has a long and internationally respected tradition and reputation in medicine and the biological sciences, and over the centuries a large number of important medical discoveries, products and technologies have emerged from the medical faculties of universities such as Edinburgh, Glasgow and Aberdeen, and from the many excellent hospitals, clinics and research institutes. As medicine is inherently an area of applied science it would be expected that strengths in it would generate new commercial products and services capable of being manufactured and exported to other markets. Yet despite Scotland's accepted technological strengths – proportionately far stronger than the equivalent electronics base – its health care industry is small, employing only some 6000 people in less than 100 companies in 1981. Output and employment is concentrated in a small number of large MNE plants, and the 24 principal companies account for over 70 per cent of employment, with one US company being responsible for nearly 25 per cent on its own.

In order to try and resolve the wide gap between Scotland's research strengths in health care technology and the small accompanying manufacturing sector, a major strategic review of the sector was undertaken in 1980–81. The assignment was exceptionally complex, and in undertaking it the Agency was assisted by Arthur D. Little, a major industrial consulting corporation, with a strong tradition in the international health care industry. The review had six main components, and it is worth briefly reviewing these, as they give an indication of the scale of investigation involved in major industry initiatives.

A strategic analysis of the world health care industry, concerning 111 competitive arenas in four main areas: ethical pharmaceuticals; medical equipment and devices; clinical laboratory products; and medical supplies. These 111 arenas were then grouped into 25 strategic segments, each of which was examined in relation to its 'fit' with Scotland; its market and technological maturity; and the size and potential growth of the West European market, to identify segments suited to Scotland's strengths.

A detailed review of the existing Scottish health care industry, covering all known companies, facilities and products, and relating these to the results of the international review for their particular market segment.

A comprehensive review of Scottish research activities in medical and other departments of universities, colleges, hospitals, clinics and research institutes, in order to determine areas, projects and products with commercial potential.

An examination of international investment flows in the health care sector, and especially the corporate strategies of leading American and Japanese health care companies.

A comparative review of Scotland's location features from the viewpoint of mobile industry in order to determine issues that might benefit from Agency action.

The development of a comprehensive development strategy for the sector in Scotland.

The Agency, in accepting the strategy and its recommendations,[40] recognised, as with electronics, that it is accepting a long-term, on-going commitment to coordinate the future development of perhaps the most complex industrial sector in existence. To direct this coordination, the SDA has established a specialist Health Care and Biotechnology Division, staffed by executives with appropriate technical qualifications. In the two years that the Division has been operational, it has become involved in a large number of corporate, university and overseas promotional activities. Amongst the most visible of the Division's achievements to date have been the establishment of Drug Development (Scotland) Ltd at Dundee, one of the world's first commercial clinical drug testing facilities; of Bioscot Ltd in Edinburgh, jointly by Edinburgh and Heriot-Watt universities; and of a Medical Laser Development Centre at Heriot-Watt, as well as a growing number of product and corporate development projects. All of these activities have been technologically-based, and thus represent another comprehensive initiative to encourage a complex HTI in Scotland.

Biotechnology, whilst related to the broader health-care sector, is really a distinct industrial sector, and it has been treated as such by the Agency, with responsibility for its development being given to the Health Care Division. Scotland's universities contain a number of individual departments which are comparatively strong in relevant biotechnology skills, and indeed some of the senior professional and executive staff in the first commercial biotechnology companies were trained at Scottish universities. The SDA undertook a detailed review of Scotland's biotechnology activities in the universities and companies in order to determine areas of potential for investment in research and development,[41] and since then has maintained a close relationship with biotechnology activities in Scotland and overseas. The corporate response in Scotland to the opportunities available has been slow to emerge, but some interesting products have been successfully developed, including essential reagents and a new type of 'gene machine'.

Offshore Oil and Gas Technology. Since it became clear in the late 1960s that the North Sea contained substantial reserves of oil, gas and condensates, it has been an important part of industrial policy in Scotland to ensure that Scottish companies take advantage of the opportunities stemming from investment in exploration and exploitation of the reserves. The oil and gas sector has been comprehensively dealt with elsewhere in this book, as have the main features of the engineering response to the challenges of offshore production, but it is clear that in the long term it will be important for Scottish manufacturing and service companies involved in the North Sea to penetrate other markets for their produts as North Sea development changes and slows.[42]

The Offshore Supplies Office has the responsibility for ensuring that UK firms receive full and fair opportunities to participate in the structures, equipment and services purchased by the main operating companies, and can take credit for the level of UK involvement currently achieved (a full discussion and critique is in Chapter 10). However, since the early 1970s a growing range of new offshore technologies in a diverse number of product areas have been developed by Scottish universities, colleges, and companies, and in 1983 the Scottish Development Agency launched a major review of these to determine which of them offered significant industrial opportunities in both the North Sea and other emerging offshore provinces. The review, which was assisted by an industrial advisory group drawn from leading Scottish companies, was not reported until Spring 1984, but already it is clear that there are significant and internationally competitive strengths in technologies such as remote control and automation; subsea inspection, maintenance and repair; and downhole monitoring and survey. A comprehensive strategy is being formulated to assist Scottish companies take advantage of opportunities, and to enhance existing areas of technological strength (but see Chapter 10).

Advanced Engineering. Finally, a brief note on perhaps the ultimate challenge in terms of attempting a strategic initiative to enhance a Scottish HTI, namely that for the large collection of products and technologies that has been termed 'advanced engineering'. Despite the popular perception of mechanical engineering as being a declining, sunset sector, it is actually a critically important component of any advanced industrial nation, containing new products and processes that are every bit as complex as semiconductors. Within Scotland there are still a comparatively large number of companies producing advanced and internationally competitive engineering goods and services, and consequently the introduction of a coherent strategic development initiative for the engineering sector in Scotland is an issue of high priority.

Policy and High-Technology Industries in Scotland

Attempting to influence technology is extremely difficult, and policy for HTIs is, by definition, a policy for technology. Experience so far is that the challenge of technology is perhaps an order of magnitude harder than capital investment, labour utilisation or international trade, especially as it is hard to distinguish from these other inter-related areas. Technology has also some unique policy features which have to be borne in mind. First, high technology is by definition an international phenomenon, and advances in specific sciences, products and manufacturing methods tend to diffuse rapidly between countries and companies. Consequently, maintaining national, regional or corporate competitive advantage can be both difficult and expensive. Second, much advanced technology with commercial potential is evolved and launched from within MNEs, and informed access to developments in such corporations is virtually impossible, even to well-intentioned Government officials offering various forms of financial inducements and other aids. This means that local spin-off companies are important, as they represent perhaps the best potential for extracting advanced technology and expanding the local technology base. Third, and most daunting, the sheer pace of technological change is increasing, which makes it hard for external policy-makers to have much direct influence, given the substantial lag between their identifying (and perhaps understanding) any new area of potential, the subsequent deployment of policy measures, and the eventual evolution of new products. The principal implication is that direct policy assistance may indeed be best directed at encouraging fundamental and comparatively long-term technological research, probably in universities, colleges and research institutes, and of then trying to build links into the existing industrial base.

These features of modern technology present real and continued policy challenges for national Governments, but their importance is even more marked at the level of individual regions such as Scotland. As other contributors to this book show, Scotland is, in comparative international terms, a very small, open and dependent industrial economy, with a tradition over the last fifty years of being more of a technology-taker than a technology-maker. Whilst reliance on external technology is no barrier in itself to national economic and industrial growth, as the post-war experience of Japan shows quite clearly,[43] it is generally no longer possible for policy to be based on the planned acquisition of research and development from elsewhere, especially with today's national protectionist stance on technology.

Whilst no formal policy for HTIs has yet been adopted for Scotland, nor indeed for the UK as a whole, many of the necessary component industrial policy objectives and programmes have emerged, albeit in serendipitious fashion, and thus there already exists at least a partial framework for an HTI development strategy for Scotland. Much more requires to be done, however, if the full potential existing for high-technology industries and companies is to be achieved.

Policy Objectives for Scotland. As indicated above, it is very difficult to establish precise policy objectives capable of being translated into programmes of specific actions guiding the actual deployment of resources. Indeed, given the rapid rate of change in technologies and the companies involved, it is both sensible and desirable to avoid too high a degree of specification. All that perhaps should be attempted is to provide, via the use of (mainly) national economic and industrial policy measures, a supportive and enabling macro-economic environment that allows HTIs and HTCs to flourish. There are always some areas where direct Government involvement can assist HTIs, as in the funding of basic research; the provision of advice and guidance on the adoption of new technologies; and the judicious use of public-sector purchasing, especially in relation to those technology-based products which are absolutely large (new jet aero engines, civil aircraft, or medical research facilities). In the 1960s there was a move towards a much more direct, and indeed directive, involvement in HTIs by the public sector and Central Government,[44] where policy objectives were quite explicitly stated, but more recently the pendulum has swung strongly back towards general and less explicit approaches to industrial development policy. The situation in Scotland is similar to that for the UK, and no general policy objectives for HTIs such as electronics, or oil and gas technology, have been established. But if the relatively promising HTI and HTC performance of Scotland over the last decade is to continue, a number of broad objectives must be confirmed for Government policy in Scotland. The most important of these are:

The development of greater awareness in Government and industry of current and future areas of scientific and technological advance, and an appreciation of how these may impact on Scottish enterprises and their employees.

Continuation of support for research in key applied sciences by universities, colleges, companies and research institutions, and the development of more effective and rapid bridges between discovery and commercial exploitation.

The encouragement of existing Scottish-based HTCs to evolve and grow, both through the expansion of existing enterprises (indigenous and external), and, more importantly, through the continued formation of new science-based companies by Scottish entrepreneurs.

A change in Scotland's corporate ethos towards more effective competition in international markets, based on an enhanced ability to manufacture and market goods and services profitably in an increasingly harsh competitive environment.[45]

These policy objectives for Scotland may seem so broad as to be operationally irrelevant, but they help establish the broad directions for change which more detailed programmes must support. Indeed, experience shows that such top-down policy formulation is the most coherent, consistent, and effective means of enabling the coordination of operational programmes. However, in order to translate these broad, top-level objectives into operational programmes it is necessary to have a clear understanding of what policy measures or tools are available; where these should be best applied; and who should employ them.

HTI Policy Tools. Whilst it is comparatively simple to identify objectives for specific HTIs, it is far more difficult to introduce policy actions designed to achieve them. There are many reasons for this: industrial change occurs in individual companies and institutions, each of which is unique in its policy needs and response; the causative factors behind change may not be capable of direct influence by policy measures; policy tools may be mutually hampering rather than reinforcing; and, most important of all, policies change from Government to Government – indeed from year to year – as priorities change.

Government both at national and regional levels is also relatively restricted in its choice of measures to influence industry, especially HTIs and HTCs which may be producing goods and making markets in new ways, and which may be entrepreneurial and thus not really influenced by public-sector goals or measures. The dilemmas faced by policy makers are illustrated by a brief review of the measures and tools generally available to influence industrial development. The direct expenditure of public resources (examples being university R&D, manpower training, or prototype development) can be used to promote specific technologies; financial inducements and fiscal rewards can be offered to encourage private sector individuals and companies to initiate and adopt new methods and techniques (investment allowances, grants towards innovation, or tax breaks on HTI venture capital); Government can deploy exhortation and persuasion to demonstrate advantages being spurned by private sector companies (sector and market reviews, publicity and promotion, awards and public recognition); and, finally, it can operate directly in industry through operational companies and institutions in HTIs (public corporations, regional agencies, etc.). In practice, all of these approaches have been, and are being, tried in the United Kingdom, with the overall bias shifting quite strongly towards more indirect methods of encouraging HTI. The principal policy focus at present is towards encouragement and acceptance of more entrepreneurial and risk-confronting forms of business and investment activity, especially in HTI sectors and enterprises, and this approach lies at the centre of the HTI policy approach suggested as being appropriate for Scotland.

One of the major themes of this chapter has been that it is more realistic to focus attention and policy on high-technology companies rather than broad industrial sectors, and this concern with the individual companies should also apply to the deployment of Government support and policy for reasons outlined above. Because of this it is very difficult to outline in a compressed manner precise and effective policies for HTI: requirements for these and the environment within which they operate will change before the ink dries in this book. What does seem important is that a sensible decision-making level is adopted, within which policy innovations can be considered; and in the case of HTIs and HTCs, a sectoral approach at the regional level does appear to offer an operationally effective policy approach. It does, by definition, imply an increased element of selectivity in implementation. This, in turn, requires a much enhanced and expanded understanding of companies, markets, products and technologies, both at a sectoral level and for individual product segments; and further demands a degree of sustained specialism amongst professional staff engaged in strategy formulation and implementation. The Scottish Development Agency's experience with the electronics sector since 1978, and with the health care and biotechnology sectors since 1981, would indicate that an efficient level for industrial policy can exist at a regional level.

A Policy Framework for High-Technology Industries. It will be apparent by this point that the temptation to advance detailed, highly specific policy recommendations for individual HTI sectors in Scotland will be firmly resisted, because such would be beyond the scope of this book, would betray important issues and opportunities which are and must remain commercially confidential and would appear dated in a short space of time. Further, effective strategic initiatives require continual adaptation and adjustment to meet new conditions, and to accommodate the rapidly changing circumstances of individual firms. It must also be remembered that some of the most important HTCs for Scotland's future do not yet exist, and their needs may be very different from those of present firms. In such a situation the best approach is really to identify a number of broad policy areas, which in combination will provide the most supportive environment to encourage the continued development of HTIs and HTCs in Scotland during the remaining years of this century:

> The prior policy requirement is to focus activities on HTIs and HTCs which offer opportunities for growth and development, and this may well encompass many segments in apparently declining or static industrial sectors. A flexible set of evaluative criteria will be

needed to appraise industries and companies, and the ability to combine specific action programmes and projects into sector, and even product-level strategic development initiatives. An essential component of this is to ensure active involvement of the industrial companies and entrepreneurs in the sectors concerned, and to encourage them to adopt a positive and supportive approach to such initiatives.

It is important to increase the linkages between basic and applied R&D, typically in the universities, and industry, both through increasing awareness by both sides, and through the more active and regular interchange of personnel between universities, industry and Government, especially the flow from universities and Government into existing and new companies.[46]

At the level of individual companies, management can, via various means, be encouraged to appreciate and understand the importance of technology to the future of their own companies. Technology must be viewed as a strategic resource and employed by companies as such. This will require a greater top-management commitment to longer-term objectives; improved long-range technology planning and enhanced R&D expenditures; the closer integration of technology into business decisions; and a willingness to acquire technology from outside the company.[47] This in turn means that companies will have to look seriously at how they are organised.

Government, especially at a regional level, should ensure that relevant local firms are fully aware of all the national and international assistance available, and encourage them to use this where appropriate. Selective public-sector purchasing should also be used more supportively, especially for newer HTI companies.

An important role in developing new HTCs is now being played, even in the UK, and particularly in Scotland, by venture capital, and policy measures to expand the tax and other benefits available to potential investors should be considered. Paradoxically, whilst venture-backed HTCs can provide an important source of new indigenous companies at a regional level, their entrepreneurial founders can only benefit by selling their stake and this is usually to another industrial company: hence there is a need to encourage more existing Scottish industrial companies to buy such venture HTCs when their founders decide to exit.[48]

It is necessary, on the basis of Scottish experience, to examine carefully the possible impact on the local technological base of takeovers and mergers involving Scottish HTCs. This is one area where a specific regional policy remit may be important and influential, expecially given that access to competitive technology is often a major reason for such industrial change.

Finally, it is important to ensure that HTCs are provided with an attractive and supportive environment for their growth and development, including efficient industrial and commercial premises; flexible and skilled labour force; and competitive communications and telecommunications. The evidence so far is that Scotland rates well in these respects, which are seen as being important determinants of success in area development.[49]

The indications are that Scotland has most of the conditions necessary for the continued successful development of HTIs and HTCs, and that consequently it will be sensible to focus much of Scotland's future economic and industrial development on such sectors. This approach to industrial policy, both at a national and regional level,[50] is being adopted elsewhere, and in the UK the overall focus of industrial policy is moving towards innovation.[51] The experience of Scotland in the past decade is that technology can help transform the long-term development prospects of individual regions.[52]

Appendix: Ferranti plc

The modern electronics industry in Scotland can trace its origin back to the arrival of Ferranti in Edinburgh in 1942, when a new branch factory was opened to produce gyroscopic gunsights – a product which was both revolutionary and highly secret. From those early beginnings, Ferranti has evolved into the pre-eminent electronics company in Scotland, holding an almost legendary position and having a disproportionate influence on the development of both the electronics industry and the Scottish economy. However, from its very inception, it can be said that the company's technological base was built on Scottish inventiveness. In the early 1880s Sebastian Ziani de Ferranti, the founder of the company, was trying to develop an efficient alternator, but, after much experimentation, he formed a business to produce under licence alternators designed in Glasgow by Lord Kelvin.[53] Since then Scotland and Ferranti have continued their mutually profitable symbiotic relationship.

Ferranti in Scotland. Since Ferranti established its first factory in Edinburgh, it has undergone dramatic expansion and diversification, and the Scottish Group is now the biggest single division within the company, accounting in 1982 for over 40 per cent of Ferranti plc's turnover and nearly 60 per cent of trading profits. The Group has over a dozen manufacturing and research facilities in Scotland, principally in Edinburgh and Dundee, and the 7700 employees, representing over 20 per cent of the Scottish electronics industry employment, make it the largest single company in the sector.

Ferranti have a clearly focused corporate strategy which aims to convert its excellence in R&D into successful products in a carefully chosen set of product markets. The company has largely grown by organic development, rather than by acquisition, and has a reputation in the electronics industry of being an effective, but rather staid, competitor. It prefers to keep much of its manufacturing requirements in-house, and consequently it has proportionately lower levels of linkages to other companies in the industry. The importance of advanced defence work to the company also means that by necessity Ferranti is somewhat secretive, and does not encourage outside interest in its operations, especially in Scotland.

The company's Scottish operations are organised into seven main departments, two in the civil products area and the remainder in defence, with each of the departments focusing on a particular area of technology. Below these departments are some twenty-five product groups, each of which is a separate profit centre with its own management, design, production and sales functions.[54] A further seven Ferranti subsidiaries also report through the Scottish management to the Board of the parent company which is based in Cheadle, Cheshire. In practice, the Scottish Group has a relatively high degree of managerial autonomy, and, this, allied to the Scottish self-sufficiency in product research, development, manufacture and sales, results in Ferranti having a more firmly entrenched Scottish position than many true indigenous companies.

Ferranti's products in Scotland can be grouped into three main categories: defence; civil and commercial systems; and precision components. By far the most important of these are defence and weapons systems which currently account for over sixty per cent of the Scottish Group's turnover, and where the radar, electro-optronic and navigation systems products have an international reputation. An especial excellence has been developed in advanced avionics, and the product range currently includes laser equipment for the Harrier and Jaguar interceptors; weapon aiming systems for the Hawk fighter-trainer; inertial navigation systems for the European Tornado; and the much-praised COMED cockpit displays.

The civil and commercial systems products from the Scottish facilities cover an incredible range, including the CAM-X computer-aided engineering package through the Ferranti-Cetec subsidiary, to comprehensive communications systems for the offshore oil and gas industry. The third product grouping, namely that of precision components, was developed originally to supply Ferranti's own large internal market; but the technological excellence of the products and the associated manufacturing facilities has resulted in Ferranti evolving into an increasingly important supplier to other Scottish electronics companies.

Ferranti and the Scottish Electronics Industry. It is difficult to summarise the many ways in which Ferranti has helped shape the Scottish electronics industry in the post-war period. In 1947, when the Scottish Office took its first active steps to extend the electronics industry in

Scotland, it was centred on the Ferranti factory in Edinburgh. New laboratories were built there and through a (now forgotten) Scottish Development Group led by Ferranti it was hoped to spread this new technology through several Scottish industries.[55] Since then Ferranti has retained its overall leadership position, despite challenges from more recent arrivals such as IBM.

Perhaps the most influential Ferranti impact in the longer term will have been its role, especially in the 1950s and 1960s, of producing the engineers upon whom the subsequent growth of the industry has depended. Many of the multinational electronics companies that chose Scotland as the location for European facilities recruited their core engineering and management staff from Ferranti, and the company produced several entrepreneurial figures who went on to play key roles in the formation and growth of indigenous electronics companies such as Fortronic, MESL (now part of Racal) and Nuclear Enterprises. The company has probably not in fact spun-off as many new companies as would have been expected given its size and technological excellence, but this is probably a reflection of its predominantly defence-oriented product and technology structure rather than any inherent lack of innovative spirit: indeed, it is a moot point whether such a company can foster and encourage the entrepreneurial talent traditionally associated with US electronics OEMs, especially given the attitudes to new ventures by UK financial institutions until recently.

Ferranti's R&D base in Scotland has also helped raise the quality of electronics technology in Scotland, both directly and indirectly. Between 1946 and 1973 Ferranti's Scottish staff took out over three hundred patents for locally-based inventions,[56] and in 1982, in recognition of the success of the Scottish division's exports of COMED cockpit displays to the USA, it was presented with the Queen's Award for both Export and Technological Achievement – a visible and much publicised indicator of Scotland's strengths in electronics technology.

The Scottish electronics industry has now developed to a size where it represents a large (£350 million) market for suppliers of electronic components and sub-contract manufacturing. Ferranti, together with firms such as Marconi, IBM, Burroughs and Honeywell, has provided considerable opportunities and assistance to Scottish companies seeking to exploit these markets, and the high quality standards set for specification and MOD approvals have been a major factor in raising the technological and manufacturing standards of many Scottish engineering and electronics companies. Ferranti itself, principally because of the defence orientation of its business, maintained strong in-house component and sub-contract production facilities, and has, for example, invested heavily in precision machining capabilities, resulting in a tendency for much of its external purchasing to be of raw materials rather than components. It has, nevertheless, had a significant impact on the quality of goods produced by many of its suppliers, and this has helped other Scottish based electronics OEMs to achieve high quality levels for their products.

A further important role that Ferranti has played in the Scottish economy has been that of providing influential, albeit relatively low-key, leadership to the Scottish business community. Senior Ferranti executives serve on nearly all the main industrial bodies, institutions, organisations and societies in Scotland, and thus ensure that the needs of the electronics industry are fully represented to Government, unions and other sectors such as engineering. The impact of Ferranti in this role has been significant and wide ranging, and it is no coincidence that the single most influential investigation of the Scottish economy undertaken since World War II was chaired by Sir John Toothill of Ferranti.[57]

The importance of Ferranti to the Scottish economy was perhaps best demonstrated by the widespread concern expressed in 1980 when the National Enterprise Board announced its intention of selling the fifty per cent of Ferranti's equity acquired in the mid-1970s when the company had run into financial difficulties. Ferranti was known to be a principal acquisition target for other UK companies such as Racal, Hawker-Siddeley, and especially GEC, which was then aggressively expanding its advanced electronics interests, and the UK Government was faced with either selling off its shares to the highest bidder or taking the more difficult route of placing them with financial institutions.

The Scottish Office, which normally would not seek active involvement in UK industrial policy matters of this nature, was greatly concerned over the potential impact on Scotland if Ferranti were acquired by another UK electronics company (especially in the defence sector), as it felt that rationalisation and job losses would inevitably follow. Scottish Ministers argued instead that Ferranti should be allowed to complete its corporate recovery and establish its independence before having to fight off a takeover bid. In July 1980, the Department of Industry acceded to this view and announced that Ferranti's shares would be placed with institutions, with a two-year restrictive covenant on their being traded. Provision was also made for four per cent of the NEB shares to be made available to Ferranti employees. The decision was seen as a victory for the Scottish Office Ministers and as confirming Ferranti's continuing independence. The success was tempered, however, by the fact that the Scottish financial institutions only bought about twenty per cent of the shares on offer (about ten per cent of total Ferranti equity), mainly, it was claimed, because of the price asked.[58] In the two years following the bid, Ferranti shares doubled in price, valuing the company at over £300 million and thus effectively making its purchase a very expensive proposition for other firms.

Policy Implications. Ferranti remains one of the key core companies in the Scottish industrial structure, and, as such, its continued growth and profitability is of great policy concern. Its position as a leading defence electronics supplier is both a source of strength and weakness. The defence market is typically cyclical and subject to unforeseeable policy shifts by UK and foreign Governments. The NATO budget commitments for the next few years which have been accepted by the UK Government offer steady growth prospects for Ferranti, but the company's continued reliance on that market does lend urgency to the need to speed up diversification. The company recognises this, and has recently pursued several essentially civil markets. These include computer systems, and a highly successful involvement in manufacturing large-scale integrated circuits (in Lancashire) which led the firm in 1982 to make the somewhat startling claim that it was the world's fastest growing semiconductor company. Abroad, it has expanded sales through subsidiaries, joint ventures and direct marketing, and it has begun to develop strong links into other electronics companies. Ferranti's future remains based on an increasing commitment to technological leadership and superiority, primarily as a defence electronics contractor, a sector which fortunately is likely to remain the single strongest component of the UK indigenous electronics industry. Policy makers would do well to ask themselves, on viewing Ferranti's evolution, whether a similarly successful indigenous information and communications technology industry could have been encouraged had even a small percentage of the active concern and support given to defence electronics been extended to participating UK companies.

Ferranti, the earlier financial difficulties erased by several years of growth and profitability, seems set to evolve into a major international electronics company, selling high-quality, high-technology products into an increasing number of market segments. The company's Scottish Group, by far the largest technology-based, semi-indigenous, industrial corporation in Scotland, remains at the core of the electronics sector, and is thus the pre-eminent HTC in policy terms. Whilst the policy lead will rightly remain with the UK Government, it will be important in the future to develop a greater understanding of the market, technology and corporate dynamics of individual companies such as Ferranti, and to evolve an even closer relationship with their local management to ensure their continued success.

NOTES AND REFERENCES

1. R.C.Carlson, 'The Bay Area Success Story', in SRI International, *The Mid-Peninsula in the 1980s: Issues, Options, and Trade-offs*, SRI International (Stanford), 1980, p.3.
2. *Ibid.*, p.3. See also A.L.Saxenian, 'The Urban Contradictions of Silicon Valley: regional growth and the restructuring of the semiconductor industry',

International Journal of Urban and Regional Science, vol.7, no.2, 1983, pp.237–262.

3. A comprehensive listing of the major recognised Scottish technological achievements can be found in: Elspeth Wills, *Scottish Inventors and Innovators*, SDA (Glasgow), 1983, mimeo.

4. 'The epitome of high tech, of course, is the computer. . . . But so once was the automobile, the Bessemer steel furnace, and the physician's leech. All saw a dawn, all saw, or are seeing, a twilight.' The quotation is from International Data Corporation, 'Computer Systems for Business, Industry and the Home', *Fortune*, vol.107, no.10, 16 May 1983, p.26.

5. Data Resources Inc. concluded that of the 690000 new jobs expected in HTI in the USA over the 1980–93 period, only 31 per cent would be for engineers, engineering and science technicians, and other professionals with high-tech skills. Reported in 'America Rushes to High Tech for Growth', *Business Week*, 28 March 1983, p.53.

6. *Business Week*, ibid., p.51.

7. In the UK, R&D expenditure and technical employment figures are only published for 34 broad industrial sectors. See Business Statistics Office, *Industrial and Development Expenditure and Employment*, Business Monitor MO 14, HMSO (Cardiff), 1979.

8. Experience with strategic industrial analysis lends support to the business school adage that there is no such thing as a declining sector, only declining companies.

9. See T.J.Peters and R.H.Waterman, *In Search of Excellence: Lessons from America's Best-Run Companies*, Harper and Row (New York), 1982.

10. People can determine the gaseous and molecular composition of a far-off nebula, but still find it almost impossible to measure even simple economic and industrial facts.

11. R.J.Buswell and E.W.Lewis, 'The Geographic Distribution of Industrial Research Activity in the UK', *Regional Studies*, vol.4, 1970, pp.297–306; and R.P.Oakey, 'The Effects of Technical Contacts with Local Research Establishments on the British Instruments Industry', *Area*, 1979, vol.11, no.2, pp.146–150.

12. R.P.Oakey, 'An analysis of the spatial distribution of significant British industrial innovations', *Discussion Paper No. 25*, Centre for Urban and Regional Development Studies, University of Newcastle, 1979.

13. J.B.Goddard and I.J.Smith, 'Changes in the corporate control in the British urban system, 1972–1977', *Environment and Planning*, vol.10, 1978, pp.1073–1084; and R.Leigh and D.J.North, 'Regional aspects of acquisition activity in British manufacturing industry', *Regional Studies*, vol.12, 1978, pp.227–246.

14. Scotland appears to have done fairly well in terms of the share of assistance offered under various industrial programmes and schemes (8·7 per cent of the UK) in the period up to 31 March 1983. Closer examination reveals that grants under one scheme, the Microelectronics Industry Support Programme, accounted for 68 per cent of total grants to Scotland, and that, excluding this, Scotland's share was only 3·8 per cent. Department of Industry, *Industrial Development Act 1982: Annual Report*, HMSO (London), 1983.

15. Spatial concentrations of both venture capital firms and venture-backed HTCs appear to exist both in the UK and in the USA, according to a number of recent studies. See R.P.Oakey, *Research and Development*

Cycles, Investment Cycles and Regional Growth . . ., Discussion Paper No.48, CURDS, University of Newcastle, 1983; and Venture Economics, *Venture Capital Investment 1982*, Capital Publishing (Wellesley, Mass.), 1983.

16. The European Commission has established a Task Force on Industrial Innovation in DG XIII as an important component of the emerging industrial policy, and much of its initial work has focused on the role venture capital can play in technological development.

17. OECD Workshop on Research, Technology and Regional Policy held in Paris, 24–27 October 1983.

18. In 1983 the SDA launched a major promotional campaign in the United States and Southern England that builds on Scotland's record of discovery, invention and innovation under the theme 'The Great Scots – Purveyors of Fine Technology since 1765'.

19. For a history of this fascinating period, see R.H.Campbell, *The Rise and Fall of Scottish Industry: 1707–1939*, John Donald Publishers (Edinburgh), 1980, especially pp.37–55.

20. Board of Trade, *An Industrial Survey of the South West of Scotland*, HMSO (London), 1932, p.134.

21. For an initial attempt to review the Clyde Valley Plan team's analysis of industry and technology, see J.R.Firn, 'Industry and the Clyde Valley Plan', in U.Wannop and R.Smith, *The Clyde Valley Plan*, forthcoming.

22. D.J.C.Forsyth, *US Investment in Scotland*, Praeger (New York), 1972, especially chapter 6.

23. The West Central Scotland Plan, *Supplementary Report 1: The Regional Economy*, West Central Scotland Plan (Glasgow), 1974, pp.228ff.

24. The basis for choosing these sectors is outlined in J.R.Firn, 'Industrial Regeneration and Regional Policy: The Scottish Perspective and Experience', in L.Collins (Ed), *Industrial Decline and Regeneration: Proceedings of the 1981 Anglo-Canadian Symposium*, Dept. of Geography and Centre for Canadian Studies, University of Edinburgh, 1982, pp.5–19.

25. The SDA has taken a comprehensive approach to the use of technology in industrial development, and in 1982 a strategy for the development of technology in Scotland was adopted to coordinate its various initiatives, programmes and projects in this area. Technology also provided the theme for the Agency's Annual Report for 1983.

26. James Clerk Maxwell (1831–79) is best known for proposing the electromagnetic theory of light. However, his originality was far broader, and amongst other achievements he prepared the first colour photographs; developed the theory of colours in relation to colour-blindness; formulated the theory of feedback; laid the foundations of global analysis; and also began the science of statistical mechanics.

27. The main problem is that present electronics products may only have formed a very small proportion of any firm's output in, say, 1960 when the firm was classified to mechanical engineering, but by 1980, 90 per cent of the output may be electronics and the firm will be classified as such. In these cases none of the electronics production or employment in 1960 would have been counted, either then or now.

28. See K.G.D.Smith, 'Scotland – a success story', in the *IEE News*, September 1983, pp.29–32, for a detailed review of the current Scottish electronics industry.

29. Monitoring of these trends will continue.

30. The personnel problems of the US electronics industry are comprehensively set out in: American Electronics Association, *Technical Employment Projections 1981–1983–1985*, American Electronics Association (Palo Alto, California), 1981.
31. The qualified manpower accounting is set out in S.F.Hampson and A.K.Macleod, *Electronics Manpower Revisited*, Scottish Economic Planning Department, June 1983, mimeo.
32. The *Engineer*, 8 September 1983, p.14.
33. See Scottish Development Agency, *Electronics in Scotland: The Leading Edge*, SDA (Glasgow), 1982.
34. See Oakey, 1983 (n.15).
35. See Scottish Development Agency, *The Scottish Electronics Subcontracting and Components Supply Industries*, SDA (Glasgow), May 1982.
36. G.de Jonquieres, 'Rodime Runs to Stay Ahead', *Financial Times*, 19 September 1983, p.17.
37. The Agency's Electronics Division has, for example, been involved in over thirty HTC start-up situations since its formation, and the flow appears to be steadily increasing.
38. Booz, Allen & Hamilton, *The Electronics Industry in Scotland: A Proposed Strategy*, Scottish Development Agency (Glasgow), 1979.
39. Booz, Allen & Hamilton, *Scotland's Electronics Strategy*, London, 1982, 2 volumes, mimeo. A confidential report to the SDA.
40. A brochure which summarises the main trends in the international health care industry, and Scotland's corresponding university and corporate strengths is Scottish Development Agency, *Health Care in Scotland: The Natural Choice*, Glasgow, 1981.
41. Prospect Associates, *Biotechnology: A Survey of Scottish Experience*, and *Biotechnology: A Review of the Potential*, Scottish Development Agency (Glasgow), 1982.
42. The changes that are likely to have important implications for both Scottish technology and production are the extension of exploration into the deeper, rougher waters west of the Shetlands; an increased interest in exploiting the smaller proven fields; and the introduction of enhanced recovery systems in existing offshore producer fields.
43. See M.J.Peck and S.Tamura, 'Technology', in H.Patrick and H.Rosovsky, *Asia's New Giant: How the Japanese Economy Works*, The Brookings Institution (Washington), 1976, pp.525–586.
44. The height of this intervention was perhaps reached in the National Enterprise Board's operations in the 1977–79 period (see Chapter 2).
45. The importance of technology must, therefore, be seen alongside the need to introduce and develop a major, coordinated export and trade development programme.
46. In late 1983 the Scottish Council (Development and Industry) published the results of a comprehensive study it had undertaken of the relationships between scientific and technical research in Scottish universities and industry. See Scottish Council (Development and Industry), *Profit Through Partnership*, Edinburgh, 1983.
47. To assist and encourage this process, the SDA established a Technology Transfer Unit in late 1982, and it has already assisted a number of Scottish firms to find and license new products and processes.
48. In the United States the acquisition of new HTCs has become an important means for established industrial corporations to enhance their existing

technology and/or diversify into new markets. The classic recent example was perhaps Exxon's purchase of Zilog to enter the semiconductor field, but in Scotland so far only Coats Paton seem to have been actively interested.

49. Both the *Electronics Review* and the *Health Care Review* investigated in detail Scotland's competitive position in these areas of economic infrastructure; both concluded that few real weaknesses existed.
50. In relation to Canada, see Science Council of Canada, *Forging the Links: A Technology Policy for Canada*, Science Council of Canada (Ottawa), 1975, and G.Steed, *Threshold Firms: Backing Canada's Winners*, Science Council of Canada (Ottawa), 1982.
51. J.Lloyd, 'Industrial aid evolves towards innovation', *Financial Times*, 30 September 1983, p.8.
52. S.Hugh-Jones, 'Living by their wits: a survey of the Scottish economy', *Economist*, 10 September 1983.
53. G.Z.de Ferranti and R.Ince, *The Life and Letters of Sebastian Ziani de Ferranti*, Williams and Northgate (London), 1934.
54. Ferranti Company Brochures; *Annual Report 1982*.
55. J.N.Toothill, 'The New Electronics Industry', in, C.A.Oakley (ed), *Scottish Industry: An Account of What Scotland Makes and Where She Makes It*, Scottish Council (Development and Industry) (Edinburgh), 1953, p.99.
56. E.Wills, *op. cit.* (n.3).
57. Scottish Council (Development and Industry), *Inquiry into the Scottish Economy 1960–61*, Edinburgh, 1961.
58. *Financial Times*, 23 June – 1 July 1980, *passim*.

10

THE OIL AND OIL-RELATED SECTOR

TONY MACKAY

Introduction

This chapter differs from most of the others in the book because it concerns a new industry, the North Sea oil and gas industry, which has been one of the few growth sectors of the Scottish economy during the last two decades. As such, the industry has raised important issues of industrial policy, notably how to encourage and sustain the growth and how to establish a strong Scottish presence. The spread of the offshore oil and gas industry throughout the world has created many potential export markets in which Scottish firms, given their North Sea experience, could have a strong competitive advantage. In these markets the policy issues are very different from those facing the shipbuilding, textiles and other traditional industries discussed elsewhere in the book. The chapter therefore addresses itself to the ability of the industrial policy infrastructure in Scotland to cope simultaneously with the problems of declining industries and the opportunities created by the North Sea discoveries.

The title of the chapter is intended to permit a fairly broad definition of the industry. There is a small onshore oil industry in the United Kingdom – coincidentally, the onshore industry has a long history in Scotland, dating back to Paraffin Young and the eighteenth century – but the present concern is with the offshore oil and gas industry in the North Sea and the related onshore developments. There is, of course, a well-established domestic oil refining and distribution industry in Scotland, based mainly on the Grangemouth refinery and petrochemical complex, but this is considered only in the context of the impact on it of the North Sea developments. The definition of the industry includes both offshore gas and oil, and the oil-related sector embraces the wide range of onshore support industries established in Scotland.

The offshore/onshore distinction can be important. For example, for certain statistical purposes the Government has created a separate offshore region for North Sea production, known as the Continental Shelf region. Thus the output and value added generated by offshore oil and gas are assigned to this offshore region; on the other hand, the employment generated offshore is assigned to Scotland or whichever part of the UK is the base for the offshore operations. As a result it is difficult to obtain statistical data for the North Sea on a consistent basis and this chapter therefore relies on a less sound statistical base than most of the others, at least insofar as data for Scotland are concerned.

An issue of interest is the distribution of the economic benefits arising from the production of North Sea oil and gas. The author has discussed these in detail elsewhere,[1] so only a brief summary is necessary here. In simple terms, the gross benefit is the sum of production multiplied by selling prices. As far as oil is concerned there is a world market price, set by OPEC (the Organisation of Petroleum Exporting Countries), which is largely unrelated to the cost of production. Whereas most industries sell on a cost-plus basis, that is not the case with North Sea oil. There have been two major price rises, in 1973 and 1979, and although 1983 has seen a fall in real terms, the current average selling price of crude oil of about US $30 per barrel is well above the production cost. In Saudi Arabia the average cost is around $5 per barrel and in the North Sea around $12, although some of the marginal fields are now approaching $20 per barrel. On the basis of an average cost for a North Sea field of $12, the value added or resource rent is around $18, of which the UK Government through taxes and royalties takes about eighty per cent.

These Government revenues and the savings on the balance of payments through reduced oil imports have been the two major benefits to the UK economy of the North Sea developments. Although Scotland has benefited as part of the UK from these improvements in the UK economy, the major direct benefit here has been the increases in industrial activity and employment. These increases are a function of the production costs, and deducting imports (from other parts of the UK and overseas) would result in expenditure in Scotland equivalent to approximately $3 per barrel. That is a large figure, but only about one-fifth of the $15 revenue accruing to the UK Exchequer. It was this difference which lay behind many of the arguments of the Scottish National Party and the Liberal Party in the 1970s about 'Scottish oil', because the oil industry is very capital-intensive, and in the light of the OPEC price rises the main benefits are undoubtedly the indirect ones. That is not to ignore the direct increases in industrial output and employment, which are the concern of this chapter.

The following section gives a brief history of the North Sea oil and gas developments and this is followed by a description of the onshore industry in Scotland. The next sections discuss industrial policy and the roles of the Government agencies involved. There are then three short case studies of Scottish firms, which are intended to illustrate the policy issues affecting both successful and unsuccessful firms. The seventh section takes a critical look at technological change and export opportunities, and this is followed by the conclusions.

A Brief History

The North Sea oil and gas industry has attracted a great deal of academic attention and many books and papers have been written on the subject.[2] Consequently a detailed history is not needed here. The industry is an ancient one, dating back at least to Old Testament times and the fiery furnace of Shadrach, Meshach and Abednego. The offshore industry itself dates back to the 1920s and Lake Maracaibo in Venezuela, although the main boost came with the post-World War II development of the US Gulf of Mexico. It was not until the early 1960s, however, that exploration began in the North Sea. The precipitant was the discovery in 1959 of natural gas at Slochteren in the Groningen province of the Netherlands. Geological structures similar with Slochteren extended offshore into the North Sea and across to the East Coast of England where there had been some small onshore discoveries of gas. Consequently, great interest was generated in exploring the southern part of the North Sea. Apart from seismic surveying, this had to await agreement on the territorial rights of the various countries surrounding the North Sea. Sufficient agreement was reached on the basis of the 1958 Geneva Convention and exploration drilling began in 1964 following the convention's ratification by the UK.

Table 10.1 shows the pattern of exploration drilling in the UK sector since then. This is broken down by geographical area. The East of England area is also known as the Southern North Sea and the dividing line between the English and Scottish sectors is latitude 55°50′ North. The 'other' area comprises the West Coasts of Scotland, Wales and England, plus the English Channel and the South-West Approaches. To date there has only been one commercial discovery off the West Coast – the Morecambe gas field – and as the table shows most exploration activity has concentrated on the North Sea.

The first commercial discovery in any sector of the North Sea was the West Sole gas field which was found by BP in 1965. Production began via a pipeline to Humberside in 1967. In 1966 three more large gas fields were discovered off the Norfolk coast and the next few years brought additional finds in the Southern North Sea, including the Dutch sector. These discoveries formed the early basis of the natural gas industry in the UK and all the fields are still producing, but the interests of the oil exploration companies were predominantly in oil, which is a more tradeable commodity than gas, and exploration activity in the south began to decline.

The exploration rigs moved steadily north into Scottish waters. A major stimulus to and redirection of effort, came in December 1969 with the discovery in Norwegian waters of the large Ekofisk oil field. This is located just north of the 56° parallel and led to a substantial increase in exploration drilling in the Northern North Sea, as shown by Table 10.1. In

Table 10.1. Wells drilled.

	East England	East Scotland	East Shetland	Other	Total
1964	1	—	—	—	1
1965	10	—	—	—	10
1966	20	—	—	—	20
1967	35	7	—	—	42
1968	30	1	—	—	31
1969	34	8	—	—	42
1970	12	10	—	—	22
1971	7	13	4	—	24
1972	8	16	8	1	33
1973	7	18	16	1	42
1974	4	25	26	12	67
1975	2	49	23	5	79
1976	3	25	25	5	58
1977	5	23	24	15	67
1978	—	20	11	6	37
1979	—	22	4	7	33
1980	—	19	7	6	32
1981	1	37	7	3	48
1982	9	36	11	12	68
Total	188	329	166	73	756

Source: Department of Energy, *Brown Book*[3]

the UK sector the first oil find was made by the Amoco/British Gas Corporation (BGC) group with their Montrose field, also discovered in December 1969 but not announced as commercially exploitable until four years later. In the meantime BP discovered the large Forties oil field in November 1970 and announced its commercial viability in December 1971. Forties and the smaller Argyll field (discovered in October 1971) began production in 1975. Thus, as far as Scotland is concerned, exploration activity dates back sixteen years to 1967 and production eight years, which makes the offshore industry both new and dynamic.

According to the Department of Energy's annual report for 1982 (published in April 1983 and commonly known as the 'Brown Book'), at the end of the year there were twenty producing oil fields in the UK sector of the North Sea and eight others under development. There are also seven gas fields in production and the Morecambe field off the west coast of Cumbria is being developed. The 1983 Brown Book lists over seventy other significant discoveries which may be developed in the future.

In this light, the exploration of the North Sea has undoubtedly been a great success. The drilling success rate (i.e. the proportion of wells finding hydrocarbons) has been much higher than the industry average worldwide and the relatively stable political regimes of Western Europe have meant that the North Sea is regarded as one of the world's most attractive oil provinces for investment and production. The success of the North Sea can probably best be demonstrated by production figures. Within the eight-year oil production period mentioned above, the UK has become self-sufficient in crude oil and now is a net exporter. In 1975 UK production was 1.6 million tonnes, in 1978 54.0 million and in 1982 103.3 million tonnes. Domestic consumption in 1982 was 65.5 million tonnes, resulting in substantial net exports. Gas production in 1982 was 37 million cubic metres or 39.5 million tonnes oil equivalent, itself a substantial contribution to domestic energy needs.

The United Kingdom is now one of the leading oil producers in the world and the second largest offshore producer (after Saudi Arabia). It is also the second largest offshore gas producer (after the United States). In 1982 North Sea oil and gas production accounted for just under five per cent of UK gross national product (GNP), with the industry's net output being valued at £10.7 billion and the gross value of sales and services rendered £15.4 billion. Total Government tax and royalty receipts are estimated at £7.8 billion in the financial year 1982–83. This compares with the estimated yields from VAT and income tax in 1982–83 of £13.9 billion and £30.2 billion respectively. In this light the North Sea oil and gas industry has had a major impact on the UK economy, over a relatively short period.

Current Industry in Scotland

The preceding section has provided a brief macroeconomic overview of the impact of North Sea oil on the UK economy. Scotland, like other parts of the UK, has shared in this impact, which has on the whole been beneficial although there have been negative aspects such as the upward pressure on the sterling exchange rate which has adversely affected exporting industries. However, the main concern of this chapter is with the more direct impacts on industrial activity and employment.

Scotland has experienced the main North Sea impacts because of geographical proximity to the oil and gas fields. Figure 10.1[4] shows the locations of the main fields and it will be seen that virtually all are in Scottish waters, particularly in the East Shetland basin and to the east of Aberdeen. The main exceptions are the Southern North Sea gas fields off the coasts of East Anglia and Yorkshire. Figure 10.2 shows the main onshore facilities and, not surprisingly, many of these are located on the East Coast of Scotland and in the Orkney and Shetland Islands.

In considering the structure of the industry it is useful to distinguish

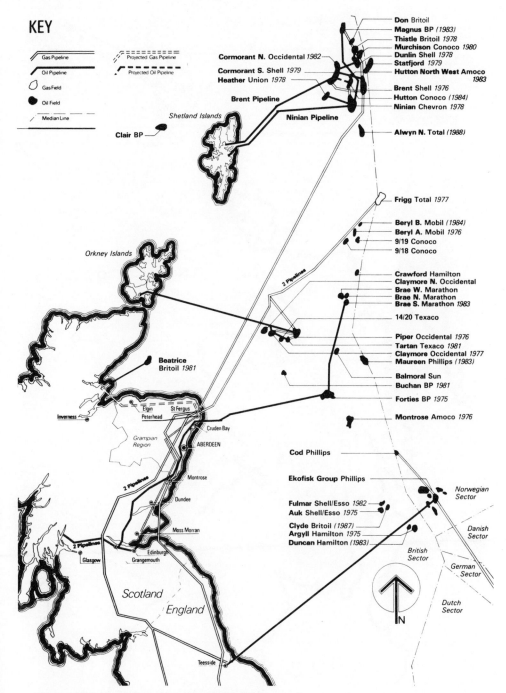

KEY

Gas Pipeline	Projected Gas Pipeline
Oil Pipeline	Projected Oil Pipeline
Gas Field	
Oil Field	
Median Line	

Don Britoil
Magnus BP *(1983)*
Thistle Britoil *1978*
Murchison Conoco *1980*
Dunlin Shell *1978*
Statfjord *1979*
Hutton North West Amoco *1983*
Cormorant N. Occidental *1982*
Cormorant S. Shell *1979*
Heather Union *1978*
Brent Shell *1976*
Hutton Conoco *(1984)*
Ninian Chevron *1978*

Brent Pipeline
Ninian Pipeline

Shetland Islands

Clair BP

Alwyn N. Total *(1988)*

Frigg Total *1977*

Beryl B. Mobil *(1984)*
Beryl A. Mobil *1976*
9/19 Conoco
9/18 Conoco

Orkney Islands

2 Pipelines

Crawford Hamilton
Claymore N. Occidental
Brae W. Marathon
Brae N. Marathon
Brae S. Marathon *1983*

14/20 Texaco

Piper Occidental *1976*
Tartan Texaco *1981*
Claymore Occidental *1977*
Maureen Phillips *(1983)*

Beatrice
Britoil *1981*

Balmoral Sun
Buchan BP *1981*

Forties BP *1975*

Elgin   St Fergus
Peterhead
Inverness

Cruden Bay

Grampian Region
ABERDEEN

Montrose Amoco *1976*

Cod Phillips

Ekofisk Group Phillips

2 Pipelines

Montrose

Dundee

Fulmar Shell/Esso *1982*
Auk Shell/Esso *1975*

Clyde Britoil *(1987)*
Argyll Hamilton *1975*
Duncan Hamilton *(1983)*

Moss Morran

Norwegian Sector

Danish Sector

British Sector

German Sector

2 Pipelines
Edinburgh
Glasgow   Grangemouth

Dutch Sector

N

Scotland
England

Teesside

Figure 10.1. North Sea oil and gas fields (UK sector).

331

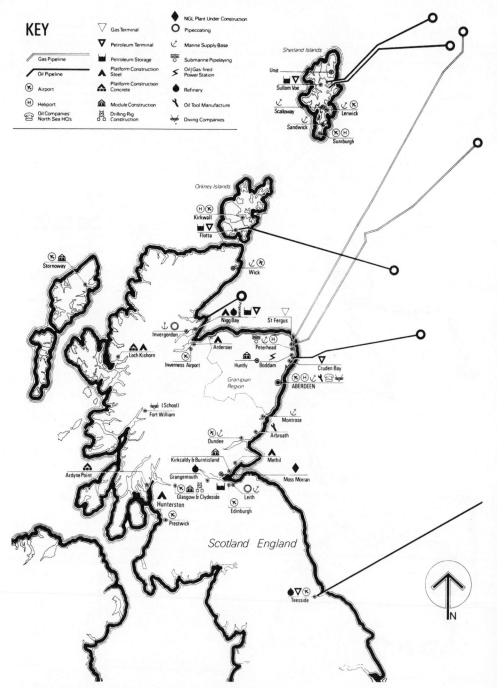

KEY

	Gas Pipeline
	Oil Pipeline
Airport
Heliport
Oil Companies' North Sea HQ's
Gas Terminal
Petroleum Terminal
Petroleum Storage
Platform Construction Steel
Platform Construction Concrete
Module Construction
Drilling Rig Construction
NGL Plant Under Construction
Pipecoating
Marine Supply Base
Submarine Pipelaying
Oil/Gas-fired Power Station
Refinery
Oil Tool Manufacture
Diving Companies

Shetland Islands

Unst
Sullom Voe
Scalloway
Lerwick
Sandwick
Sumburgh

Orkney Islands

Kirkwall
Flotta

Stornoway

Wick

Nigg Bay
St Fergus
Invergordon
Ardersier
Peterhead
Loch Kishorn
Inverness Airport
Huntly
Boddam
Cruden Bay
Grampian Region
ABERDEEN

(School)
Fort William

Montrose
Dundee
Arbroath

Kirkcaldy & Burntisland
Methil
Ardyne Point
Grangemouth
Moss Morran

Glasgow & Clydeside
Leith
Hunterston
Edinburgh

Prestwick

Scotland   England

Teesside

N

Figure 10.2. Onshore developments.

between the three main phases of activity: exploration, development and production. In practice there is some overlap between the phases but the distinction is useful for exposition. During the exploration phase the key function is the drilling of wells to test possible hydrocarbon-bearing structures. Seismic surveying and related tasks precede the actual drilling but the bulk of expenditure goes on the hire of a rig and the drilling of wells. Support services are provided by sea (supply boats) for drill pipe, mud, water and other materials required, and by air (helicopters) for personnel. These services need onshore facilities in the form of supply bases (harbours) and helicopter bases.

It is common for the bases to be located where the transport costs and time will be minimised. Great Yarmouth provides this function in East Anglia. In Scotland at the present time there are eighteen purpose-built bases covering much of the East Coast, ranging from Leith in the south to Lerwick in the north. The three main centres, however, are Aberdeen (where there are eight separate bases), Peterhead and Montrose, and between them these three ports handle about eighty per cent of supply boat traffic for the UK sector of the North Sea. As is evident from the maps, these bases are well located in relation to the fields discovered and the main areas of exploration drilling. Similarly, Aberdeen airport (Dyce) is the main North Sea helicopter and fixed-wing aircraft centre, supported by smaller bases in Shetland and occasionally elsewhere.

The servicing of the exploration rigs is similar to that of the production platforms, so there can be important economies of scale. Other support services have found some of the bases, particularly Aberdeen, good locations for their own activities, although the minimisation of transport costs may not be an important factor for them. Thus around the larger bases has been built up a substantial engineering and oil-related infrastructure.

Nevertheless, the expenditure and employment created during the exploration phase is relatively small. According to the 1983 Brown Book, of total UK North Sea expenditure in 1982 of £3 489 million, only £860.9 million (24·7 per cent) was on exploration and that percentage was in fact the highest for many years. In terms of employment there are currently about 80 000 North Sea-related jobs in Scotland and approximately 7 500 of these are concerned with the exploration phase.

If a successful discovery is made there will be a period of appraisal drilling and if the company or group decides to proceed the development phase will begin. The time profile varies from field to field but on average the exploration/appraisal phase may last three years, the development phase three to five years and the production phase upwards of twenty years. In terms of the direct impact on Scotland the development or construction phase has been the most important. This is the period during which the various production facilities – platforms, modules, pipelines, terminals, etc. – are being constructed. The development of a single field can be extremely expensive: for example, the total cost of the Forties field is estimated at £910 million, Brent £1160 million and the Norwegian/ U K Statfjord field £1850 million.

Of the Department of Energy's estimated 1982 expenditure of £3489 million, £2384 million (68·3 per cent) was attributable to the development phase. Similarly, in terms of employment about 65 per cent of the 80000 jobs in Scotland are concerned with development work. In particular the platform and module yards are large labour employers: in the case of the former, one yard can employ up to 3500 people, although the average is about 1800; with the module yards, average employment is about 1000.

As far as locational factors are concerned, development activities are much more footloose than exploration services, although there are still advantages in being located close to the fields and supply bases. Figure 10.2 shows the locations of the main onshore facilities in Scotland. If we take production platforms as an example, there are five active yards at the present time, three on the East Coast and two on the West Coast. Of the former group, two are located in the Moray Firth area, at Nigg (near Invergordon) and Ardersier (near Inverness), and the third is at Methil in Fife. All three are close to the final destinations of their products. Of the West Coast yards, Kishorn was chosen because of the deep water needed to build concrete platforms and Hunterston because of a combination of deep water, proximity to the Central Belt (for labour and manufacturing sub-contractors) and Government policy. About twenty per cent of all the platforms needed for the U K sector have been built overseas, largely in France and Norway but in the early years also in the United States, so proximity is not necessary.

With modules (the equipment placed on top of the platform jackets) the pattern is more dispersed. In the main, companies have chosen to locate the yards in established centres of industrial activity and labour rather than close to the fields. There are only two specialist module yards currently in operation in Scotland – in Dundee and Stornoway – although the steel platform yards have also diversified into module fabrication. The other seven specialist yards in the U K are all located in England.

Much of the steel needed for the platforms and pipelines has been imported from Japan and West Germany. Moving down the scale to more standard items such as pumps and compressors the supply pattern is very diverse, both in the U K and overseas. For these items Scottish industry has not had a locational advantage and has had to compete with established suppliers to the offshore industry, particularly from the USA. Nevertheless Scotland has obtained a large share of the development phase, notably through platform fabrication and the construction of the landfall oil and gas terminals.

Turning to the third and final phase, the production phase, with oil there is usually a choice between tanker loading at sea or piping the oil to shore. The latter is generally the preferred option but because pipelines are very expensive some of the smaller fields such as Argyll, Auk and Fulmar are using tanker loading. With the pipelines the cost of laying lines offshore is so large that the companies try to minimise the length by choosing the nearest suitable landfall. In one case – the Beatrice field – environmental concerns about the possible risks of offshore loading resulted in a pipeline being used instead.

Figure 10.2 shows the four oil landfall terminals in Scotland: at Sullom Voe in the Shetlands, Flotta in the Orkneys, Nigg Bay on the Cromarty Firth and Cruden Bay/Hound Point on the East Coast. In 1982 these terminals received 85 per cent of total oil production from the UK Continental Shelf. The first three are transhipment terminals whose main functions are to stabilise and store crude oil, prior to its being loaded into tankers for onward transport to refineries on the UK mainland or overseas. BP's Hound Point terminal is connected with the company's nearby Grangemouth refinery (the largest in Scotland) although it is also used for exporting crude oil.

With gas, the offshore loading option is not yet technically feasible so the gas produced is piped to the mainland. There is only one terminal in Scotland, at St Fergus, north of Aberdeen, which currently takes gas from three pipelines – two from the joint UK/Norwegian Frigg field and the other from a number of fields in the East Shetland basin. It is likely that other gas pipelines will be linked to St Fergus in the future.

Only a small proportion of North Sea oil (16 per cent at present) is refined in Scotland and only about forty per cent in the UK as a whole. According to the 1983 Brown Book just over sixty per cent of UK North Sea oil was exported in crude form, with the main markets being the USA, the Netherlands and West Germany.

Downstream production activities based on oil have so far been limited in Scotland to the expansion of the Grangemouth refinery, although there have been recurrent plans for new refineries. At least with gas there has been more production activity related to petrochemicals. The Shell-Esso group are currently constructing a gas separation plant and ethane cracker at Mossmorran in Fife, and there are some processing activities at St Fergus. The Mossmorran plant will constitute about thirty per cent of UK ethylene capacity when it comes onstream. With the conversion of some of the Grangemouth facilities to take ethane Scotland will have about half of the total UK ethylene manufacturing capacity, and this development is solely related to offshore oil and gas production. Large quantities of natural gas liquids are also landed in oil and separated out at the terminals.

Apart from these, the main production phase activities are the operation of the platforms, pipelines and onshore facilities. In the UK as a whole these accounted for an estimated £1338 million expenditure in 1982, 38·3 per cent of the total. In Scotland, about 20000 of the 80000 oil-related jobs are in the production phase and the proportion is rising steadily as more oil and gas fields come onstream. Nevertheless it is important to remember that oil and gas production is a capital-intensive operation: the Sullom Voe terminal, for example, cost £1200 million to construct and had a peak construction labour force of 7500 but the normal operating labour force is only 1100. On the other hand, companies like BP and Shell employ 2300 and 2500 respectively in their Aberdeen office headquarters, although these people cover all three phases of activity.

Table 10.2. North Sea-related employment in Scotland.

	Wholly related	Partially related	Total
1970	2500	500	3000
1971	3500	500	4000
1972	4000	1000	5000
1973	5250	1250	6500
1974	13500	3250	16750
1975	20000	4500	24500
1976	27000	6750	33750
1977	28500	7000	35500
1978	34000	9250	43250
1979	41750	12250	54000
1980	46250	15000	61250
1981	49500	16500	66000
1982	58250	19750	78000
1983	61000	20500	81500

Source: MSC and author's estimates.

The above provides a brief description of North Sea operations and why certain developments have occurred in Scotland. More detailed accounts are available elsewhere.[5] In terms of the economic impact on Scotland, employment creation is probably the best single indicator of what has happened. Unfortunately, it is difficult to produce precise and up-to-date estimates, but reasonably acceptable approximations are possible. A current level of 81500 oil-related jobs was quoted earlier in the chapter. This is comprised of 61000 'wholly involved' jobs and a full-time equivalent of about 20500 'partially involved' jobs. The source of the former data is a regular (now twice yearly, previously monthly) survey of oil-related employment in Scotland, undertaken by the Manpower Services Commission (MSC) in association with Grampian Regional Council's Department of Physical Planning. The 'partially involved' figure is the author's estimate based on additional information on firms involved in the North Sea, but not exclusively so, with the relevant employment data being converted to a full-time equivalent basis comparable with the MSC data.

The increase in oil and gas-related employment over time provides an indication of how activity in Scotland has increased since the early 1970s and this is shown in Table 10.2. There have been two periods of rapid growth. The first, from 1973 to 1976, covered the development phase of the largest oil fields discovered, notably Forties, Ninian and Brent. The second, from 1978–79 to 1981, was a consequence of the oil price rises, new licensing rounds and the development of the East Shetland basin. Further substantial increases in activity and employment are unlikely because most of the major fields are now producing and some will cease by 1990. Also, the employment growth in the last few years is probably overstated because improvements in the coverage of firms, particularly those partially involved, suggest that there were gaps and hence missed employment in the early years.

An interesting perspective on the employment data is given by the geographical breakdown. Table 10.3 is taken from the Scottish Economic Bulletin and divides the 'wholly-related' employment (for June of each year) into the main regions involved. It will be seen that in June 1982 the Grampian region (mainly the Aberdeen area) accounted for 68·6 per cent of the wholly-related total, and the region has had a majority of such employment since 1977. The Highland region (mainly the platform yards and related activities in the Moray Firth area) comes second with 12·7 per cent of the total. The rest of the employment is fairly widely spread throughout Scotland, although it should be pointed out that these figures exclude temporary construction employment and at the peak of construction work on the Sullom Voe terminal in Shetland, for example, the Islands total exceeded 9 500. Consequently, the scale of impact has varied substantially: Shetland, with a permanent population of about 23 000, at one time had over 9 000 oil-related workers; in contrast the 3 800 employed in Strathclyde region represent only 0·4 per cent of the region's labour force.

In broad terms, most of the activity and employment has occurred in the northerly and rural parts of the country. The Central Belt and the industrial heartland have had a relatively small involvement and unfortunately that is where the bulk of Scotland's unemployed live. In contrast, traditional agricultural and fishing areas like the Islands, Highlands and Grampian have experienced a large influx of high-technology, high-profile firms, and there have been consequential social and econ-

Table 10.3. Geographical distribution of North Sea employment (thousands).

		Central and Lothian	Fife	Grampian	Highland	Strathclyde	Tayside	Islands	Scotland
June	1973	—	—	—	—	—	—	—	5·29
	1974	1·07	1·21	4·81	4·86	1·17	0·27	0·09	13·47
	1975	0·42	1·62	8·97	4·45	3·30	1·10	0·21	20·05
	1976	0·69	2·03	11·54	6·78	4·23	1·44	0·40	27·10
	1977	0·62	0·81	15·68	7·09	1·92	1·76	0·77	28·63
	1978	0·55	1·38	22·89	6·00	0·50	2·05	0·63	33·99
	1979	0·62	2·26	28·08	4·81	0·77	2·32	2·92	41·76
	1980	0·86	0·81	32·32	4·35	2·73	1·81	3·46	46·34
	1981	0·99	1·09	33·93	6·01	3·07	1·99	2·53	49·61
December	1981	0·98	1·85	36·35	7·71	3·60	2·11	2·66	55·26
June	1982	1·15	1·25	40·02	7·38	3·80	2·50	2·23	58·32

Source: *Scottish Economic Bulletin*, No.26, 1983, p.27.

omic problems (e.g. for local non-oil firms), particularly in Shetland, the Moray Firth area and Wester Ross.[6]

Finally in this context, it may be worth pointing out that although the 81500 new jobs have been extremely welcome, they account for only four per cent of total employment of 1.9 million in Scotland, and the current number of Scots registered as unemployed is 320000. Including the multiplier effect of the new jobs would not alter the general picture. Over the fourteen-year period shown in Table 10.2 manufacturing employment in Scotland has fallen by over 250000. This is not to belittle the beneficial impact of the North Sea developments, which represent the establishment of a major new industry over a short period, but to place the impact in the context of the severe economic problems which faced Scotland in the 1970s.

Turning to other indicators as a conclusion to this section, Baxter has estimated recently that the North Sea activities probably now account for about ten per cent of Scottish gross domestic product (GDP).[7] No very up-to-date figures are available but there is evidence that the North Sea was the main factor in the relative improvement of the Scottish economy in the 1970s. For example, in 1970 Scotland contributed 8·7 per cent of UK GDP (excluding the Continental Shelf region) and this rose to 9·0 per cent in 1975 and 9·1 per cent in 1976. However, the latest figures for 1980 put the Scottish share at 8·8 per cent, only slightly higher than the level ten years earlier, and the relative decline may reflect the levelling-out of North Sea activity. A similar picture is given by earnings data. In 1971 average male, manual weekly earnings in Scotland were only 97 per cent of the Great Britain level but the figure had risen to 101·8 per cent in 1975 and 100·4 per cent in 1980, and the latest figure for 1982 is 102·3 per cent. These relative improvements may seem small but, bearing in mind the adverse trends in most other sectors of the Scottish economy, in practice they represent a substantial change in the country's fortunes.

The author's conclusion in an earlier (1978) study[8] was that 'the direct impact of North Sea oil activities was not sufficient to transform living standards nor the dominance of the traditional industrial structure' and that it therefore provided 'a welcome relief from short-run difficulties, rather than a solution to the long-run problem of building a more efficient and prosperous economy'. Three years later Baxter[9] endorsed that view: 'Although North Sea oil activities have continued to grow, this growth was apparently insufficient to offset adverse trends reflecting the national and international economic environment. Nor, probably, would it be reasonable to have expected much more.' Nevertheless, there can be no doubt that North Sea oil and gas have become one of the country's leading industries and consequently the role of industrial policy in that growth is of great importance.

Industrial Policy

The second chapter of this book discussed the definitional problems which arise in any work on industrial policy. These concern the North Sea oil and gas industry as well. Many relevant policies are formulated at the UK level, and possibly also at the EC level, but the concern of this chapter is with policy insofar as it affects the industry in Scotland. Consequently, only brief attention will be given to the more general licensing and fiscal policies.

In the context of industrial policy the North Sea oil and gas industry displays certain unique features. For instance, the Government can control, to a large extent, the level of industrial activity and its rate of growth. All companies wishing to explore in the UK sector of the North Sea have to obtain licences from the Government and if commercial discoveries are made then production licences are also required. Because of the economic rent generated and the fact that the UK Exchequer takes about eighty per cent of the value added from production, the tax regime is also a major influence on activity levels. Further, there are important state concerns in the form of Britoil (formerly BNOC, the British National Oil Corporation) and the British Gas Corporation (BGC), which have been very active in the North Sea.

A major concern of this chapter is the involvement of Scottish industry and how policy has affected that. The licensing and taxation regimes, coupled with geological factors and world energy prices, provide the framework which determines the aggregate level of North Sea activity. However, the essentially free market policies of the UK oblige domestic companies to compete with imports of goods and services or with foreign companies with branches in Scotland. Thus a key objective of industrial policy within Scotland has been to maximise the involvement of Scottish industry in the North Sea developments.

The measures which fall within this definition of policy can be classified into three groups: (a) general, (b) industry-specific and (c) infrastructure support; and these are discussed in turn below. The general measures embrace regional and industrial assistance. The industry-specific measures include special legislation, initiatives on matters such as production platform sites, the activities of the Offshore Supplies Office and specific oil-related activities of bodies like the Scottish Office, the Scottish Development Agency, the Highlands and Islands Development Board and various local authorities. Infrastructure support covers investment in roads, harbours and airports, training, research and development. In addition there are other relevant policies covering, for example, health and safety legislation,[10] but they lie outwith the scope of this chapter.

Before considering these various policy measures, a brief discussion of the implications of the macroeconomic policy framework is necessary.

The main legislation is the responsibility of the UK Department of Energy, which (surprisingly, perhaps) does not have a Scottish counterpart although the Scottish Office is regularly consulted on issues affecting Scotland. However, the advent of North Sea oil was in part responsible for the creation of the Scottish Economic Planning Department (SEPD) (now known as the Industry Department for Scotland) and responsibility for relevant North Sea oil matters is vested in its energy division.

Considering the legislative framework, it is sensible to begin with exploration licensing. The number and size (acreage) of licences are a major influence on the level of exploration drilling. Applicant companies are required to submit proposed work programmes, including the number of wells to be drilled, so the Department of Energy's discretion in allocating licences can be important. Virtually all the licences have been made on a discretionary basis, although there have been three small experiments with cash tenders.

To date there have been eight licence rounds for the UK Continental Shelf (including non-North Sea areas). Their timing and the number of blocks awarded in each case (in parentheses) are: 1964 (348 blocks), 1965 (127), 1970 (106), 1972–73 (282), 1976–77 (44), 1978–79 (42), 1980–81 (90) and 1982–83 (seven tender blocks allocated but others to be finalised). These rounds represent a rapid rate of licensing, and a large proportion of the UK sector of the North Sea has already been covered, although there remain virgin territories particularly off the West Coast around Rockall. The high levels of licensing and exploration activity in the UK sector contrast sharply with the slower and more moderate policies of other North Sea countries. Norway, for example, with a continental shelf much greater than that of the UK, has only licensed 55 blocks to date (compared with 1046 by the UK) and has deliberately pursued a policy of slow exploration and development in order, among other things, to allow time for the maximum involvement by Norwegian firms. It should be remembered, though, that with the Ekofisk field alone, Norway became self-sufficient in oil.

However, licensing policy is a fairly crude way of controlling exploration drilling and only one of a number of factors, including taxation, relative attractiveness of other offshore provinces, oil and gas prices, availability of rigs, and so on. The complications can be seen from the low level of exploration drilling over the period 1978–80 (Table 10.1), despite the fifth and sixth Licence Rounds in 1976–77 and 1978–79 and the price rises in 1978–79.

Assuming commercial discoveries, companies will base their production plans on expected returns and costs. The revenues are a function of production rates, world market prices and the tax regime. The costs are capital and operating costs, net of investment grants and other assistance. Obviously the UK has little influence on world market prices, although as the major non-OPEC trader of crude oil on the world market (and one of the leading producers) the UK, primarily through the British National Oil Corporation, appears in 1983 to have had a significant influence on crude prices, by holding them up rather than allowing them to continue to fall. On the other hand, the Government exerts more direct influence through the tax regime. This was very generous in the early years and encouraged the development of many fields in the period to 1976. Since then the regime has become more punitive and in 1981 and 1982 some oil companies appeared to be deliberately postponing or abandoning field development programmes in protest at the high Government tax take. In response, the 1983 Budget included generous concessions for the oil companies and the current indications are that more new fields will be developed in the near future, although uncertainties over oil prices may be a deterrent.

In passing, the UK Government has power over production levels, which are commonly described as depletion controls. Under the terms of petroleum production licences, development work and the production of petroleum may be carried out only with the consent of the Secretary of State for Energy or under a development or production programme approved by him. Most fields operate under temporary consents for three to six months at a time. In practice, however, the Secretary of State has interfered with the companies' own plans on only two significant occasions. The first was in delaying the development and production of BNOC's Clyde field and the second was in holding down production from certain oil fields with associated gas until such time as gas production facilities were installed to eliminate the need to flare gas. Because exploration drilling has been so successful the companies involved have wished to develop the fields quickly and UK Government policy has supported that objective, mainly on the grounds that a high level of production would result in substantial balance of payments advantages and in substantial increases in Government revenues. Successive Governments have given assurances that there would be no interference with production levels from existing fields.

There has been considerable discussion about the appropriateness of this depletion policy, culminating in a report by the House of Commons Select Committee on Energy.[11] However, in the present context only two specific questions are relevant: what are the policy implications for Scotland; and what influence have Scottish bodies had on the policy?

Regarding the former, the preceding section outlined the link between the level of offshore activity and onshore developments, such as supply base, platform and module yards, and a wide range of support services. A rapid rate of offshore development has resulted in significant employment creation at a time when Scotland's more traditional industries have been shedding labour.

In earlier work[12] the present author has discussed the differing viewpoints of different parts of the UK. Briefly, three distinct attitudes can be identified, depending on whether the focus is the UK, Scotland or the local community. From the point of view of the UK economy, past policies appear to have been appropriate because of the substantial Government revenue and balance of payments benefits. From the point of view of Scotland, a medium to high level of activity was desirable, in order to provide a strong market for Scottish goods and services but also to provide time for Scottish companies to establish a competitive position in the industry. Most local communities would have preferred a much slower and possibly lower level of activity, to allow time for the provision of supporting infrastructure such as houses and schools. Communities like Shetland and Easter Ross have suffered because of the scale and rapid build-up of oil-related developments there, particularly during the development phase.

These three viewpoints could never be compatible and most people would probably agree that the UK needs should be paramount. The implication then is that UK policy would have some detrimental consequences for Scotland and the local areas affected but there are mechanisms for compensating those adversely affected (although, unfortunately, they have not really been used in this instance). As far as Scotland is concerned, the main problem has been the short period of time in the early years for Scottish firms to establish themselves in the industry but on the other hand the high level of demand for goods and services has been a positive feature. It would therefore be difficult to conclude firmly that UK policy in this respect has worked against the interests of Scottish industry.

Regarding the second question, there is little specific evidence to suggest that the Scottish Office or other Scottish policy-making bodies have had any major influence over UK depletion or taxation policies, but if it is accepted that there was little divergence of viewpoint then that has not been a problem. In fact there has hardly been a period when one of the Energy Department ministers was not a Scottish MP, so Scottish considerations will undoubtedly have been aired at the political level. The Secretary of State for Scotland is also, of course, a member of the Cabinet and there are interdepartmental working groups of officials on which the Scottish Office is represented.

However, there is evidence to suggest that the North Sea involvement of Scottish (and UK) firms has been disappointing, which may be a criticism of the industrial policy measures outlined earlier, and the remainder of this chapter concentrates on these policies.

The Offshore Supplies Office (OSO), which is part of the Department of Energy, publishes annual figures on the share of UK North Sea orders won by UK firms. The figures are calculated from returns made to

343

the OSO by the oil companies for all orders placed with a value exceeding £100000. The latest figures are shown in Table 10.4 and suggest that the UK share is over seventy per cent, which has been accepted by Government ministers as a reasonable achievement. However, there is evidence to suggest that the OSO figures may be an overestimate and that consequently UK involvement is less encouraging. The main difficulties with the OSO calculations are the definition of 'UK' firms and the coverage of sub-contracts. Many of the oil-related firms operating in Scotland are subsidiaries of foreign companies, particularly from the USA. Although the OSO believes that their system of reporting overcomes these difficulties and that therefore their figures are an accurate reflection of UK content, their refusal (on confidentiality grounds) to allow outsiders access to the data makes it impossible to confirm this.

Table 10.4. UK share of North Sea expenditure (per cent).

	OSO	author
1973	35·0	30·5
1975	51·7	44·4
1977	65·0	52·3
1980	70·8	52·6
1982	72·2	49·4

The author has attempted from various sources to calculate alternative estimates of the UK share of the market, and these are also shown in Table 10.4. The main source is the employment data given earlier to which a gross output per employee multiplier has been applied to produce an estimate of total expenditure. This is then compared with official estimates of North Sea-related expenditure (given in the annual Brown Book). The gross output figures are higher than the UK averages for the engineering and construction industries to allow for the possibility that the employment data are not comprehensive but it may be that there are still some gaps in the coverage. Also, these estimates are of actual expenditure in any year whereas the OSO's are of orders placed and there will be a time-lag before orders become expenditure. Nevertheless, it is useful to compare the figures, and the table shows significant differences, for example, either a 72 per cent share or a 49 per cent share in 1982. It may be that these represent the upper and lower limits of the feasible range, although the author believes that the actual figures must be closer to the bottom end of the range. If the actual figure was 60 per cent in 1982, that implies a disappointing UK performance, particularly when it is remembered that the North Sea market has existed for ten to fifteen years.

General Policy Measures. A threefold classification of industrial policy measures was given earlier: (a) general, (b) industry-specific and (c) infrastructure support. Taking these in turn, the general measures are those industrial and regional aids which apply to manufacturing industry as a whole and not just North Sea oil and gas. These were described in Chapter 2. In terms of regional preferential assistance most aid now comes in the form of regional development grants and expenditure by the Scottish Development Agency (see below) and, to a much lesser extent, the Highlands and Islands Development Board (see below). It is not possible to obtain separate figures on regional development grants for the North Sea oil and gas industry but assistance must have been substantial in the light of the massive investment by the industry.

For example, over the five years 1978–82 UK North Sea expenditure was approximately £18 billion, and if a quarter of that were spent in Scotland it will have accounted for a substantial share of the sums shown in Chapter 2. However, there are two interesting points peculiar to the North Sea industry. The first is that until recently all of Scotland was a designated area, eligible for regional assistance. The Aberdeen travel to work area was downgraded to intermediate area status in the 1970s and a major review in 1979 changed the status of other important oil-affected areas. These changes included the further downgrading of the Aberdeen area to a non-assisted area and the designation of areas such as Orkney, Shetland, Montrose and Peterhead as non-assisted areas.

Not surprisingly there was an outcry at the proposals from the Secretary of State for Industry (note, not the Secretary of State for Scotland) and in response the Scottish Office commissioned a special study of the problems of the oil-affected areas facing downgrading.[13] The study report highlighted both the problems of non-oil industries in these areas and also the poor long-term prospects of areas like Shetland after the main development phase. Following the study, the Government announced in June 1982 a few changes to the original proposals, including the retention of intermediate area status for Orkney, Shetland, Nairn and Forres. The changes took effect in 1980 and 1982, so it is too soon to assess the impact, but they will certainly create problems for non-oil firms in the areas affected and some of the areas downgraded, like Fraserburgh (with an unemployment rate well above the Scottish average), have experienced little benefit from the North Sea developments.

The second point concerns the eligibility of certain oil-related developments for regional aid. There has been a prolonged debate about whether or not the oil and gas landfall terminals could be classified as manufacturing activity. The eventual decision was that they could be, which made them eligible for regional aid and also for industrial derating. Although this had no influence on the choice of locations for the terminals, it has obviously increased the profitability of the operations and may influence future decisions, for example between offshore loading and pipelines.

Specific Measures. These are probably of more interest in the present context. However, it is difficult to present a coherent picture because of the different bodies and objectives involved. If we begin with the institutional side, the main bodies are the Offshore Supplies Office (OSO), the Scottish Office (SO), the Scottish Development Agency (SDA), and the Highlands and Islands Development Board (HIDB).

The OSO is part of the Department of Energy. In the early 1970s the Department of Trade and Industry (as it then was) commissioned a consultancy study into the prospects for the UK offshore industry.[14] This study (known as the IMEG study) was completed in 1972 and its conclusions fell into three main groups:

(a) the setting up of an independent Petroleum Industries Supply Board;

(b) the encouragement of new British manufacturing and contracting industry and of partnerships with foreign companies to secure know-how and experience for British interests;

(c) other recommendations such as the monitoring of the procurement pattern of the oil companies, the provision of credit and the encouragement of research and development, training and education.

The Government accepted most of the recommendations, but no separate Supply Board was created; instead, the tasks fell to a special unit within the Department of Trade and Industry, to be known at the Offshore Supplies Office. The Office was set up in January 1973 and was transferred to the Department of Energy in early 1974, shortly after which its headquarters were transferred to Glasgow. The OSO's early tasks were aimed at identifying the size of the likely market, informing UK companies of the opportunities and the performance standards required, and helping to encourage an acceptable UK capability through identification of sources of expertise with which to associate, and of finance, and monitoring orders placed by the oil companies. To undertake these tasks the OSO created specialist posts of venture managers and audit engineers, the main responsibility of the former being to identify opportunities and encourage domestic participation, and of the latter, to monitor the orders of the operating companies.

Through a voluntary agreement reached in 1975 with the UK Offshore Operators' Association, known as the Memorandum of Understanding, UK industry is given an opportunity to compete on an equal basis with foreign firms for North Sea orders. This is generally known as 'full and fair opportunity'. The OSO discusses the companies' bid lists with the operators prior to the bid documents being sent out and, if they feel that a UK capability has not been given the chance to tender, they suggest the addition of suitable firms. On the receipt of bids they have to be satisfied that the UK tenders have been fairly treated and that if a UK bid is competitive in terms of price and delivery, it receives the contract. The OSO has no legal powers to insist on UK firms winning contracts and does not exclude foreign firms from bidding for such work, in contrast to the more protectionist offshore policies of, for example, the United States and Norway.

In the context of UK industrial policy, the OSO is unique, and it is interesting to note that other industries have both complained about the special treatment awarded to the North Sea oil and gas industry, and requested that similar bodies be set up for their own industries. Certainly, the experience of the OSO merits detailed consideration as a more general measure of industrial policy. The Office itself regards its work as successful and points to the doubling of UK participation shown in Table 10.4 above. To quote Forrest and Taylor:[15] 'The implementation of this policy has contributed greatly to the increase in the UK share of the market ... We have been judged as over-protective of UK industry by some and as not doing enough by others; too tough on the oil companies, yet not nearly as tough as many other countries ... Irrespective of this, I hope it is possible to form a balanced view and to hold that the Offshore Supplies Office has done no more than promote and defend the legitimate aspirations of our offshore industry. Our role is definitely not protectionist and this is why it has received the support of successive UK Governments and has stood the test of time.'

The present author concurs with the view that the OSO has contributed substantially to the increase in UK involvement, particularly through the monitoring functions and the increasing awareness of the offshore market. Without detracting from that view, two qualifications can be made. The first is the belief, expressed earlier in this chapter, that the UK share of the offshore market is not as high as official figures suggest. Further, there remain key, high-technology sectors with a minor UK presence, and these tend to be the sectors with good export opportunities.

Secondly, it is possible to conclude that the OSO could have been more active in promoting a UK capability in these sectors. To quote Forrest and Taylor again: 'In general the more successful companies in the oil equipment and services supply business were those, often created for the purpose, whose only activity was to meet the offshore business needs. While many large conglomerates also entered the field and some have found the business worthwhile, other lost heavily. Such companies often appeared as lacking total conviction in the offshore sector ... (for example) the steel suppliers were slow to adapt their operations to supply the full range of high quality steel goods for offshore use as were shipyards in their approach to the offshore market.'

A recent study by two academics, Cook and Surrey, from the University of Sussex lend support to this author's views. For example, they conclude that 'the main roles of the OSO were those the Civil Service is well able to perform – auditing the quarterly returns, monitoring the performance of British firms, and where possible, mediating to clear blockages involving, for example, planning regulations and industrial arbitration ... The Government's role remained essentially that of monitoring, auditing and persuading, rather than the more entrepreneurial one, as envisaged by IMEG, of establishing domestic capabilities in high-risk, potentially high-return activities requiring specialist facilities and know-how.'[16]

According to the OSO the areas where UK capability is most lacking are generally those involving heavy capital expenditure, e.g. for drilling rigs and pipelaying barges. Also, other areas with a low domestic capability are largely those where the UK market is a small proportion of the total world market and where the UK market alone might not support a British capability.

Given the depressed state of Scottish and UK industry in the 1970s, and the almost intractable problems of industries like steel and shipbuilding, it is not surprising that many firms were reluctant or found it very difficult to break into the offshore market. The implication is that to establish a worthwhile and lasting UK presence in these sectors of the market, special initiatives were necessary. Unfortunately, these initiatives have been too few. The OSO tried during its early years but has two spectacular disasters, since when it has adopted a much lower profile. Similarly, the Scottish Office, also involved in one of the disasters, has taken a less active role in this regard. However, given the responsibilities of both the Scottish Office and the Department of Energy, it was probably more appropriate for other bodies to pursue such special initiatives. The obvious body is or was the Scottish Development Agency but, surprisingly, the Agency has until recently taken only a relatively minor interest in the North Sea developments, in contrast with the activities of its northern counterpart the Highlands and Islands Development Board.

Criticism of the lack of initiatives of the main industrial policy bodies in Scotland is difficult when the bodies have taken initiatives which proved unsuccessful and attracted considerable public disapproval. However, the author's view is that some of the initiatives were ill-chosen and that the bodies involved should have persevered with others, despite the results of their early efforts.

The best example is probably the production platform *débâcle*, which has important lessons for the abilities of public bodies in this sphere. This was a joint Scottish Office/Offshore Supplies Office initiative, following the introduction of special legislation in the form of the Offshore Petroleum Development (Scotland) Act, 1975. Prior to that there had been concern in some Government circles that there were insufficient production platform sites in Scotland and that consequently important orders were being lost abroad, notably to Norway and France. A major factor had been the success of some groups in preventing or delaying planning permission being given for platform sites in rural areas, the outstanding example being Drumbuie on the West Coast.

One purpose of the 1975 Act was to circumvent this procedure. Initially the main proponents were the Department of Energy and the Offshore Supplies Office. Their forecasts of future production platform demand eventually convinced the Scottish Office that there was a need for special legislation. At the time there was some opposition on the grounds that the Department of Energy's forecasts were exceedingly optimistic and that also the benefits of platform construction in Scotland were not clear-cut,[17] but these arguments were largely ignored. Using the Act's powers of compulsory purchase of land, the Scottish Office bought and constructed two platform yards at Portavadie in Argyll and Hunterston in Ayrshire. The estimated costs in 1976 were £16 million and £5 million respectively.

The former was leased to a potential builder, Sea Platform Constructors, along with an adjacent labour camp for 450 people, also built with government money. Sea Platform Constructors never received an order and eventually gave up the lease on the yard but unfortunately the yard had been built with their particular design in mind and the Scottish Office were unable to find another company to take over the lease. Thus the Portavadie yard has never been used and for some years after a working group, plus consultants, attempted to find an alternative use. A complication is that an error or oversight in the agreement with Sea Platform Constructors means that they continue, at least nominally, to be the owners of the labour camp and they have been reluctant to give that up, seeing it as an opportunity to recoup some of their own expenditure. To date the cost to the Government has been about £45 million (in 1983 prices). The yard is now to be reinstated to its original condition.

Hunterston has had a similarly embarrassing history, although in 1980 the lessee of the yard, Ayrshire Marine Constructors, obtained an order – ironically for part of a steel platform (the yard had been built for concrete platforms needing the deeper water of the West Coast). Two other yards, one steel and one concrete, have gone out of business through lack of orders, and activity and employment in the others have fluctuated substantially. Also, the established builders have claimed that Ayrshire Marine had an unfair advantage over them by having access to a subsidised yard. Since completion of the first order the company has so far been unsuccessful in obtaining further work.

Other provisions of the 1975 Act have been used to control platform construction activity offshore, specifically in two designated areas in the Sound of Raasay and Loch Fyne. Concrete platforms are built vertically and the final stage of operations requires deep water offshore. This means inevitable interference with fishing and other marine activities and the Act has reduced these problems to a minimum.

Certainly the unique nature of concrete platform construction necessitates special planning measures. However, with hindsight, the onshore provisions of the Act have proved both unnecessary and costly. They raised questions in Scotland about the advisability and ability of Central Government 'interfering' or intervening in the oil industry, and cast unnecessary doubts on the suitability of the existing planning system. Regarding the latter, it is probably fair to conclude that the established system would have resulted in a better outcome than that generated by the 1975 Act, in terms of the supply and demand of sites, but prior to its introduction there was a great deal of confusing speculation about platform sites and no apparent means of controlling their number. The oil companies' own forecasts of platform demand were also optimistic and the Government was keen to ensure that orders did not go abroad for reasons of lack of domestic capacity.

Regarding the former criticism, the evidence tends to support the view that the Scottish Office did not have the in-house abilities to control the platform sector of the industry. Indeed, given the complex nature of the oil industry and its vast size, it would have been most surprising if they had had such expertise. Therefore the real mistake was probably to rely on the advice of other Government bodies – the Offshore Supplies Office and the Department of Energy – who were in reality in a similar position and also were biased parties in the sense of wanting to see a large number of platform sites in Scotland.

One unfortunate consequence of the criticisms of the 1975 Act and the waste of money at Portavadie has been a marked reluctance on the part of the Scottish Office to take innovatory measures in other aspects of the North Sea oil industry. Since 1978 the Scottish Office has taken a largely passive stance, reacting to proposed developments rather than promoting or encouraging. This is in contrast to the active period of the early 1970s, exemplified by a series of helpful planning guidelines and discussion. Of course, the change in attitude is also partly attributable to the steady move from the development phase to production, which reduces the uncertainties involved.

The Scottish Development Agency is in a much better position to undertake such initiatives. It has been very active in a number of sectors and areas. However, its involvement in the North Sea has been surprisingly small, given the existing importance of the industry to Scotland and the substantial export opportunities to other offshore provinces. The Agency's oil-related activities have mainly been confined to a few investments in oil-related companies, participation in exhibitions and trade shows and, recently, the promotion of some infrastructure projects (see below).

The SDA was set up in 1975 but it was only in 1983 that a small team of two staff was established within the Planning and Projects Directorate to cover the energy sector, including North Sea oil and gas. Similarly, the Agency has, at the time of writing, just commissioned a consultancy study of a strategy for Scotland's offshore technical base – a much needed exercise but a few years late. It may be that their view is that a special SDA effort was not needed because of the activities of the OSO and the Scottish Office, and it is true that there could appear to be too many bodies involved, but the argument presented above is that after 1976 or 1977 these other bodies adopted a passive approach and the SDA would appear to have been the appropriate body to fill the gap.

This is in contrast to the HIDB which has taken a vigorous approach to the promotion of oil-related developments within its area and, as can be seen from Figure 10.2 and Table 10.3, the Highlands and Islands have been heavily involved. Unlike the SDA, regular sections of the Board's annual reports are devoted to the North Sea. To take the 1980 report as a typical example: 'Throughout the year we continued to promote and encourage oil, gas and petrochemical developments at Nigg Bay. Considerable efforts were made to maintain close contact with potential commercial developers and the responsible departments of state and public corporations to ensure that the development potential of Nigg Bay was fully recognised. . . . We have been actively involved with Highland Regional Council to promote the use of service facilities in Caithness to support exploration and production activities in the Moray Firth. The two bodies have formed a Caithness joint working party who have prepared promotional material and made contact with a number of oil companies . . .'.[18]

As with many policies, it is difficult to assess their specific impact because of uncertainty about what would have happened in the absence of policy action. In the case of the Highlands, it may well be that the platform yards and other oil-related developments would have been located in the Moray Firth area without HIDB and local authority action but the evidence suggests that their efforts have had an influence, at the very least in relation to the geographical distribution of activity within Scotland. Similarly, the North East Scotland Development Authority (NESDA), the development arm of Grampian Regional Council, have been very active and successful in promoting their own area for inward oil-related investment, and other local authorities in Scotland have pursued similar strategies.

Infrastructure Support. Three aspects merit mention in the present context: physical infrastructure, training, and research and development. Regarding the first, there are now over 1100 oil-related firms in Scotland, eighty per cent of them being new starts as far as Scotland is concerned.

About 800 of these firms are located in the Aberdeen area, a concentration which is typical of the international oil industry and which occurs also in Houston and Stavanger, for example. The influx to the Aberdeen area and other parts of the North of Scotland has put great pressure on infrastructure and has led to substantial capital investment by the authorities concerned. This investment has undoubtedly helped the development of the industry and encouraged foreign firms to locate in Scotland. The most noticeable facilities are the airports and harbours but there has also been considerable spending on housing, schools, roads and so on. Local authorities have been particularly active in the provision of industrial estates and advance factories.

On the training side there has also been considerable Government spending, mainly through the Offshore Petroleum Industry Training Board and the provision of facilities for training divers and helicopter pilots (two skills in short supply in the 1970s). However, these facilities took a relatively long time to appear, and there still appear to be deficiencies, for example regarding divers and firefighters.

The research and development picture is much more depressing and is undoubtedly one of the weak points of industrial policy as far as the North Sea is concerned. The long-term technological implications are discussed in more detail later in this chapter but, in summary, the UK has a disappointing record in offshore technology and the level of Government support for research and development is well below that of our competitors.[19] Both France and West Germany, with small offshore areas, spend considerably more than the UK on offshore research and as a consequence French and German companies are well established in the international offshore industry. The most striking comparison is with Norway, a country of less than five million people, where government support for offshore research and development is currently three times greater than that in the UK.

The visitor to Norway cannot fail to be impressed by the research centres there. Trondheim, for example, has just completed a new deep water test tank and a two-phase pipeline test station. Bergen has a new underwater training and research centre. No such facilities exist in Scotland and those in England are generally inferior to their European counterparts.

Mention was made earlier of the SDA's lack of interest in the North Sea. However, in this specific instance, the Agency's record has been better because they have strongly promoted the setting up of facilities in Scotland such as a hyperbaric facility and a UK deep water test tank. Unfortunately these proposals have not yet received the necessary industry and government support, although they may do in the near future.

Case Studies

A feature of most of the chapters in this book is case studies of firms involved in the particular industries. This chapter looks briefly at three examples. There are over 800 oil-related firms now located in Scotland (i.e., firms for which the North Sea is their main or sole market), plus many others with smaller interests in the industry. Consequently it is difficult to choose a few which are representative of the industry and illustrate the industrial policy concerns of the chapter. It is hoped that these three are reasonably representative: the Wood Group, RGC Offshore and the Weir Group. The first has been an undoubted success in the North Sea. The second has had mixed fortunes, but is currently doing well; and most observers would probably agree that the third has struggled to establish a sound North Sea presence. Two of the three firms are indigenous Scottish firms which diversified into the offshore industry and the third was set up specially for North Sea work.

The Wood Group, Aberdeen. This company has grown, in little over a decade, from being a medium-sized firm involved in traditional local industries to one of the leading and largest Scottish oil-related firms with growing overseas interests. In 1970 there were about 600 employees, principally in fishing and ship repairing, but also providing support services to other traditional industries in the North of Scotland such as whisky distilling, agriculture and paper-making. Annual turnover was approximately £4 million. By 1975 employment had increased to about 1350 and turnover to £16 million. The range of activities had been extended to cover onshore and offshore logistic services to the North Sea oil industry as well as offshore engineering services. By 1980 employment had risen to over 2400 and turnover to £61 million. The current figures are approximately 2600 and £80 million respectively. Oil-related services have been further extended into petrochemical engineering and various high-technology areas. The traditional industry interests now represent less than 25 per cent of the group's turnover.

The John Wood Group is notable both for its successful entry into the North Sea industry and for its commitment to its traditional activities, particularly the fishing industry. Similar companies in Aberdeen have allowed the latter to be replaced by oil-related activity, often through the sale of industrial premises and space to oil service companies.

This continued spread of interests has been difficult to maintain because of the impacts imposed on the local Aberdeen economy by the oil industry. For example, wage rates in the oil industry – both onshore and offshore – are much higher than in most traditional industries, with the consequences that the latter have suffered substantial losses of labour and have had to face higher wage bills than their competitors elsewhere in the UK. The oil industry impact embraces other inputs such as factory and office space, repair facilities and transport. Despite these problems, the John Wood Group has been reasonably successful in the traditional sector, despite the recession and the EC Common Fisheries Policy, and has spread these interests over a wider part of Scotland, rather than concentrating on Aberdeen.

Regarding North Sea oil involvement, the Group operates in three divisions: engineering, oilfield logistics and supplies, and drilling services. Over thirty specialist companies fall into these divisions. Wood Group Engineering, the largest division, has sixteen trading companies. Through a combination of internal development and acquisition, it has become one of the major petrochemical engineering concerns in the UK. The initial emphasis on the provision of technical skills has developed into the conception, design and manufacture of complex offshore systems and products. The Oilfield Logistics and Supplies Division grew from the group's traditional marine activities and facilities, for example by converting quayside premises in Aberdeen into one of the first oil supply bases. The division has recently opened a similar base in England (Great Yarmouth) and has undertaken consultancy work overseas. Wood Group Drilling Services is the newest and fastest-growing division. This sector of the North Sea market was dominated by foreign companies but in the late 1970s the Group board decided to break into the market and this has been done successfully, mainly through joint ventures.

In 1982 the Group took an unusual step, by demerging the traditional industry activities into a separate parent company, known as JW Holdings. Thus the John Wood Group is now concerned exclusively with the oil and gas industries. According to Ian Wood, the chairman and managing director, 'this move consolidated our identity and corporate profile as supplier of services and products to the world's energy industries and our goals are set accordingly. We are continuing the expansion of our range of products, engineering contracting and specialist services, particularly in the high technology engineering field . . . the Group's overall goal is to consolidate our status as an international energy industries manufacturing and service company and we believe we are now well on the way to achieving this.'[20]

There can be little doubt that the main reason for the Group's success has been the ability of Ian Wood and his senior management to identify new opportunities and be willing to take appropriate risks. At a seminar in Edinburgh in 1981, Mr Wood provided some excellent insights on how they had built up their North Sea involvement:[21]

'We started off as raw beginners and it was extemely difficult to analyse and market the technical requirements of North Sea oil satisfactorily where the technology and products were all so new to us. To try and overcome the major problems encountered in the early part of the learning curve, there are at least three different strategies which local companies can adopt and we, in fact, have had varying experience of all three.

'The first is to buy oil expertise by taking on a number of very expensive, but highly experienced, offshore oil managers to provide the basic credibility and technology and also the basic training for the traditional management and staff. It is our experience that success here depends entirely on the calibre, tact and honesty of the personnel taken in. Basically, established local management is resentful of such new personnel who are inevitably given a privileged position and paid (particularly if they are American) substantially in excess of anyone else in the company. In many cases, such specialists are employed for only a reasonably short period of time and it is therefore important to try and ensure that as much as possible of their experience and know-how is passed on to the indigenous management.

'The second strategy is by a process of joint venture with a company which has the technological experience and know-how. Our experience in Aberdeen is that such joint ventures have less than a 50/50 chance of long-term success mainly because in a situation where the local company has no technology, any joint venture with an experienced partner appears to be a relatively cheap and safe way of getting into the specialist market. In the long term, however, it can be very expensive and an ongoing contribution from both participants is an essential ingredient to success. Problems have also arisen where the level of investment and rate of return aspirations have been incompatible between a large outside company participating with a small local company and it is important that this factor is also taken into account.

'We have two very successful joint ventures which have survived the test of time and at least two of those which failed left us with the door just wide enough open to follow up and proceed on our own. We are now facing the interesting experience of the joint venture situation "in reverse" where we now find ourselves as the participant with the experience and technology having discussions with local companies either elsewhere in the U K or abroad who have the local presence and facilities.

'The third strategy for the larger local company is the acquisition of one or two smaller specialist companies, particularly those with really good experienced management. This is certainly a strategy that we have employed with some success over the past four or five years and one which we intend to continue to exploit.'

Mr Wood has been a frequent critic of Government industrial policy as it has affected the North Sea. His Group has suffered substantially from the withdrawal of development area status from Aberdeen and other parts of the North of Scotland. From the above descriptions of the Group's activities and strategies, it is difficult to identify impacts of the specific policy measures outlined earlier in this chapter. There has been very little public-sector assistance to the John Wood Group but that has not inhibited their success. However, most other companies have not been as successful, which raises the question as to whether a more active industrial policy could have helped them.

RGC Offshore, Methil. This company began operations in 1972 under the name Redpath Dorman Long (North Sea) Ltd. It was formed as a joint venture of Redpath Dorman Long (RDL), a wholly-owned subsidiary of the British Steel Corporation, and an Italian consortium of Saiper Interconsult and Micoperei, with shareholdings of 55 per cent and 45 per cent. The intention was to construct jacket structures, decks, modules and piles for North Sea production platforms. A coastal site at Methil – a former colliery – was chosen and cleared, the area also being a declining coalmining district with a good supply of skilled labour and special development area status.

The Italian consortium withdrew in 1975, at which time the company became wholly BSC-owned. In 1978 BSC sold a substantial part of its shareholding to a Dutch company, Grootint, with the Edinburgh financial firm North Sea Assets and the Scottish Development Agency alos taking smaller stakes. The name was changed to Redpath de Groot Caledonian (RGC), with the issued share capital being held by RDL/ BSC 48 per cent, Grootcon 43 per cent, North Sea Assets 5 per cent and the SDA 4 per cent. Grootint withdrew in 1981, with their shares being taken up by the other partners and the company renamed again as RGC Offshore.

RGC lost considerable sums of money in the early years. By 1980 the accumulated losses were about £16 million, which was the main reason for the withdrawal of the Italian and Dutch partners. Since the latter event, however, the company has done well and has started to make good profits. The early losses were mainly attributable to specific contracts for the first large steel platform jackets to be installed in the North Sea and the company underestimated the time required to fabricate them. They were also fixed-price contracts which did not adequately compensate RGC for design changes. Industrial disputes, low productivity and late deliveries also created problems. A loss was also made in 1980–81, primarily because of the depressed market.

Over the last three years, however, RGC has been able to shed its reputation for late deliveries and poor labour relations. Of the three steel platform yards in Scotland, it has been the most successful in obtaining new orders, has met delivery dates and become profitable. It is difficult to identify the precise reasons for the dramatic changes in fortunes but they include new management, better project control, more active marketing, diversification into module manufacture and piles, and investment in new, covered facilities.

In relation to industrial policy in Scotland, regional grants were certainly an important factor in the choice of the Methil site. The main stimulus came from the state-owned British Steel Corporation, which had indirect interests in providing the steel for North Sea facilities and was eager to have a more direct involvement. The Government's eagerness to have platforms built in the UK rather than abroad, as described earlier, also encouraged RGC/RDL to set up a yard in competition with the two American-controlled yards in the Highlands.

However, that latter policy led to excess capacity in the platform fabrication industry, which was a contributory factor in RGC's problems in the 1970s, although its two main UK competitors did well over that period. More generally, the overall level of offshore activity and the flow of platform and module orders are critical factors affected by policy. In other words, industrial policy determines the size of the market but does little to affect RGC's market share (nor, indeed, those of the competitors). More recently, the SDA's small stake in the company and their support for the module diversification programme have helped the company's performance, although it is probably fair to conclude that the programme would have proceeded without the direct support of the Agency.

The Weir Group, Glasgow. This company is an interesting example of one of Scotland's leading engineering companies which has failed to establish a major presence in the North Sea, despite appearing to be in a strong position to do so in the early 1970s. This is in marked contrast with the Wood Group, for example, which did not really have a suitable engineering base at that time but now has. One of the disappointments of the North Sea oil industry from Scotland's point of view has been the failure of some of the major engineering firms to make a major impact. A consequence has been that much of the equipment needed has been provided by US firms like Baker Oil Tools, Cameron and Vetco, albeit from plants set up in Scotland. North Sea-related employment as a percentage of total Scottish employment in engineering and allied industries is less than 10 per cent and that proportion fell during the 1970s.

Weir Group turnover in 1982 was nearly £137 million and employment 4700. The Group operates in three main divisions: engineering (accounting for about 70 per cent of turnover), foundries and engineering supplies (23 per cent) and desalination and heat exchange (7 per cent). The largest of the engineering division companies, and the largest company in the Group, is Weir Pumps. Its main products are pumps, with associated equipment and systems, for power stations, oil production, ships, water supply and other industrial uses.

The North Sea accounts for less than ten per cent of the Group's turnover. Although important orders continue to be won, it seems reasonable to believe that the involvement could have been higher. Unfortunately the Group has had major problems, unconnected with the North Sea, which have constrained its ability to invest in new markets.

The Group also tried to enter the North Sea market fairly late, by which time some of its competitors were well established. There was a fairly common view in the Scottish engineering industry in the late 1960s and early 1970s that the North Sea would be a temporary market and consequently many firms were reluctant to get heavily involved and adapt their products to the new environment.

Apart from Weir Pumps, the Group has set up a few joint ventures to try to increase its market penetration. These include Wood-Weir Engineering services (with the Wood Group), set up in 1974, and Weir-Houston (with Houston Engineers Inc. of the USA). The most recent joint venture is Ayrshire Marine Constructors, a company set up in conjunction with Chicago Bridge of the USA to build steel platform jackets and related structures. AMC have leased the Hunterston platform yard, which was established with Government money (see the earlier section on specific measures), but have won only one order, a gravity structure for the Maureen field, on which they made a considerable loss. Thus this new venture of Weirs has further exacerbated their problems.

The engineering chapter details various specific measures designed to restructure and help that industry. None of these has been directed at the North Sea industry and consequently from that perspective the Weir Group has benefited little.

Technological Change and Export Opportunities

The offshore oil and gas industry projects a high-technology image. In many respects this is inaccurate because much of the equipment and systems used offshore are standard items which have been used onshore for many years. However, there are some areas of operation, e.g. subsea production, where major technological advances have been and continue to be made.

The early years of North Sea development were dominated by US and other foreign firms. The main centre of the offshore industry was the Gulf of Mexico, and the oil companies were very dependent on US technology and experience. Over time that dependence has diminished in the North Sea, although there is still a substantial American presence on both the producing and supplier sides. In the UK sector French, West German, Norwegian and other foreign firms also have significant involvements. A common approach in the 1960s and early 1970s was simply to transfer proven Gulf of Mexico techniques to the North Sea. However, there are major differences between the Gulf of Mexico and the North Sea, particularly in relation to environmental conditions and water depths, such that substantial changes and innovations in operating methods and equipment have been necessary. Consequently the North Sea has been at the forefront of important technological developments, and other offshore provinces are now looking to the North Sea, rather than the Gulf of

Mexico, for appropriate experience.

As more and more countries search for oil and gas in efforts to increase domestic energy production, export opportunities for offshore equipment and services increase substantially. Can Scottish firms with North Sea experience take advantage of these opportunities? If the Offshore Supplies Office's estimate that UK industry has more than a seventy per cent share of the UK North Sea market is accurate, then the answer should be yes. However, this optimism may not be wholly justified. Two reasons for a more pessimistic view will suffice.

To quote Ian Wood again,[22] 'there is a strong belief in the UK, fostered by both this and the previous Government, that UK industry has done well in the development of North Sea oil. I personally believe this is a dangerous myth and one which both the Government and the Grampian Region should self-critically re-examine urgently. Far too many of the successful North Sea performers are the incoming international companies who are simply operating a local UK base to cater for North Sea oil – they are not building up genuine UK technology and know-how to be applied in further expansion overseas. Such was our Government's haste to get the oil out of the ground as quickly as possible that far too little attention was paid to the build-up of genuine UK oil technology and manufacturing know-how to provide an important new indigenous addition to the UK's failing industrial base. The Government's initial impetus through the Offshore Supplies Office to try and ensure that UK industry did play a meaningful part in this new industrial revolution has now substantially waned. As a result, any present realistic assessment of the number of UK companies who have the know-how, technology and manufacturing skills to expand into the offshore industry worldwide, would provide a pitifully small number, nowhere near the level of presence and influence that should have been achieved from our privileged frontier starting position.'

It is worth remembering that this is the considered view of one of the most successful Scottish businessmen involved in the North Sea, whose group has been very active in seeking out overseas markets. It is a view which is shared by many other Scottish businessmen, including some who have not been successful in the North Sea.

Secondly, the author has recently completed a study for the Ocean Industry Development Office in Canada (the Canadian equivalent of the OSO) to identify offshore-related firms in Western Europe which might be interested in locating in Nova Scotia and/or establishing joint ventures with local firms there. The first gas field offshore Nova Scotia is being developed and oil production offshore Newfoundland is expected by 1990. The Canadian authorities regard the North Sea as the best location for appropriate expertise and are eager to encourage interested firms to set up facilities in Nova Scotia and Newfoundland.

The study involved contacting over 300 firms in Western Europe, with detailed interviews with 120 of them. Of those, just under 30 have so far established a presence in Nova Scotia. Most of the firms approached – 230 – were from the UK but the level of positive interest from them has been very disappointing in comparison with that from France and Norway. Further, the Canadians are particularly keen to attract medium-to high-technology firms, providing skills which are not available locally, but most of the UK firms seriously interested in Nova Scotia do not fall into those categories. They are more of the 'rope, soap and dope' type, providing fairly standard services and goods.

Generally, the latter can usually be provided domestically in Canada and the other export markets, although there may well be a learning period of a few years. These countries are deficient in the medium- to high-technology sectors, which is where the long-term export opportunities for Scottish firms lie. Unfortunately the evidence suggests that Scottish involvement in these sectors of the North Sea market is limited and that foreign firms are still responsible for much of the real technological development in the North Sea.

There are important exceptions to this generalisation, of course, and UK firms like Ferranti, Marconi and Osprey Electronics have been involved in major new advances in technology. On the whole, however, the position is not as encouraging as official statistics might suggest.

Is there a role here for industrial policy? Certainly, as discussed in Chapter 9, the Government has sponsored a range of special schemes for high-technology industries, although none has been specifically directed at the export potential of the North Sea. As noted earlier, the Scottish Development Agency have recently commissioned a consultancy study to produce a strategy for the development of the offshore industry's technical base in Scotland. The main justification for the study was the belief that the contribution currently made by the offshore industry to the Scottish economy will only be maintained and strengthened in the longer term if firms based in Scotland increase their penetration of offshore markets in other parts of the world. To do this, domestic industry will have to be able to offer a comparative advantage over international competition, but there is concern in the Agency that a sufficiently strong technical base has not yet been established in Scotland. The study is intended to prepare a strategy for its development in Scotland.

A key area in which industrial policy in Scotland has been deficient is in support for research and development, particularly in relation to the link between the two. The contrast with Norway, for example, is very marked. In 1980 the Royal Norwegian Ministry of Petroleum and Energy introduced a system of 'technology agreements' which were to be signed by the Ministry with individual foreign oil companies. These are intended to ensure that state-of-the-art technology would reach Norwegian research institutions and industrial companies. The oil companies are encouraged to place research contracts with the Norwegian institutions and companies. It was intended that such technology agreements would be taken into account in the Ministry's allocation of future exploration and production licences, although the importance of that intention is difficult to assess.

To date, spending under these agreements has exceeded £200 million. Further, there has been massive public spending on the research institutions to provide them with the necessary facilities and staff. Petroleum technology research centres have been set up in Stavanger and Trondheim. In Trondheim there are also a new deep water test tank (ocean laboratory) and a two-phase pipeline flow facility. In Bergen there is a Norwegian underwater technology centre. The Royal Norwegian Council for Scientific and Industrial Research (NTNF, the equivalent of the Science and Engineering Research Council) has recently produced a fifteen-year plan for Norwegian offshore research and development, financed in part by another £200 million from foreign oil companies. NTNF has set up eleven planning groups to help define priorities and possibilities, and the four main strategies are concerned with better extraction techniques, reductions in development costs, improvements in safety standards, and a strengthening of the competitive position of Norwegian industry at home and abroad through a commitment to advanced technology.

Norway is probably the outstanding example of this approach, but similar programmes are under way in all the other North Sea countries, including France which has a tiny offshore market of its own. In contrast, public sector research and development in Scotland is on a very small scale and is sporadic and poorly coordinated. Hardly any of the facilities set up in Norway in recent years exist in Scotland (or indeed the UK) and the Scottish Development Agency has so far been unsuccessful in its efforts to promote hyperbaric and deep water test tank facilities. This certainly appears to be an aspect of industrial policy which requires strengthening if Scottish industry is to be encouraged to compete in overseas markets.

Conclusions

In a period of about fifteen years, a major new industry has been established in Scotland. The offshore oil and gas industry makes substantial contributions to the UK economy. Within Scotland it employs directly over 80000 people and involves at least 1000 firms. In most respects, therefore, it has been a success story.

Industrial policy in terms of licensing, taxation and related matters has undoubtedly facilitated the development of the industry and encouraged it to grow at the rate it has. There have been occasional problems, but that is not surprising, and generally the difficulties have not been major. The North Sea is now regarded internationally as one of the world's major oil and gas provinces and its influence on world energy markets continues to increase.

Within Scotland, the benefits are not as great as those related to Government revenue and the balance of payments, because of the nature of the industry, but equally they should not be underestimated. Geographically, Aberdeen and the North of Scotland have attracted most of the onshore activity, whereas the Central Belt – embracing the bulk of Scotland's unemployment and economic problems – has had a relatively small involvement. However, this issue of geographical imbalance has not created serious difficulties and there has been considerable public investment in the necessary supporting infrastructure in the oil-related areas.

The public bodies involved have all been active in promoting Scotland as a centre for North Sea and other offshore-related firms. The number of firms involved and the scale of activity demonstrates the success of these efforts. It is within this overall, encouraging framework that the chapter has highlighted certain deficiencies in industrial policy which have implications for the future of the industry.

The two main areas for policy improvement are to increase Scottish involvement in the North Sea and to help Scottish firms compete better in foreign markets. Regarding the former, the official estimates indicate that UK industry currently has about a seventy per cent share of the UK-sector market. The author believes this to be an optimistic estimate, but, in any case, there remain important parts of the North Sea market in which Scottish and UK involvement is low. To overcome the barriers to greater involvement, special efforts are required. In the early 1970s some of the public bodies involved, notably the Scottish Office and the Offshore Supplies Office, were very active in this regard, e.g. in relation to production platform construction. Unfortunately, some of these efforts were unsuccessful and attracted considerable criticism, in the industry itself, in political circles and in Scotland generally. As a consequence, the public bodies involved with the North Sea have taken a more passive stance.

The author believes that much of this criticism was misguided and that it was, and still is, necessary for the public sector to take special initiatives to increase Scottish involvement. The opportunities include rig ownership and operation, drilling equipment, the construction of rigs and supply boats, the inspection, repair and maintenance of such vessels, and pipelaying. It is probably easier for the Scottish Development Agency and the Highlands and Islands Development Board, rather than Government departments, to promote these initiatives, and one disappointment of the last few years has been the SDA's relative lack of interest in the North Sea, in comparison, for example, with its efforts in the electronics and health-care sectors.

Turning to the future, activity in the U K sector of the North Sea will eventually decline as reserves are depleted. The timing of the downturn and the rate of decline are uncertain but much more planning has to be done for what might be described as the post-oil era. The author believes that Scottish firms have great opportunities in offshore markets throughout the world, given their North Sea experience. However, the evidence suggests a disappointing response to these opportunities to date, and again there is a need for a more active industrial policy to improve the technological capabilities of Scottish firms and to encourage them to seek out the export markets. This would include a greater research and development effort in Scotland and possibly the formation of a group exclusively concerned with oil-related export promotion.

NOTES AND REFERENCES

1. D.I.MacKay & G.A.Mackay, *The Political Economy of North Sea Oil*, Martin Robertson (Oxford), 1975.
2. See, for example, G.Arnold, *Britain's Oil*, Hamish Hamilton (London), 1978 and M.Jenkin, *British Industry and the North Sea*, Macmillan (London), 1981.
3. Department of Energy, *Development of the oil and gas resources of the United Kingdom*, HMSO (London), annual.
4. The two maps have been reproduced with the kind permission of NESDA (the North East Scotland Development Authority).
5. See, for example, G.A.Mackay *et al.*, *The Economic Impact of North Sea Oil on Scotland*, HMSO (Edinburgh), 1978 and T.M.Lewis & I.H.McNicoll, *North Sea Oil and Scotland's Economic Prospects*, Croom Helm (London), 1978.
6. See the series of occasional papers produced by the Social Science Research Council's North Sea Oil Panel.
7. C.Baxter, *North Sea Oil: the Economic Impact on Scotland*, a paper presented at the SSRC North Sea Oil Panel seminar in 1981.
8. Mackay *et al., op. cit.* (n.5), p.99.
9. Baxter, *op. cit* (n.7).
10. W.G.Carson, *The Other Price of Britain's Oil*, Martin Robertson (Oxford), 1982.
11. House of Commons Select Committee on Energy, *North Sea Oil Depletion Policy*, House of Commons Paper 337, HMSO (London), 1983.
12. MacKay & Mackay, *op. cit.* (n.1), chapter 6.
13. S.McDowall & H.M.Begg, *Industrial performance and prospects in areas affected by oil development*, Economics and Statistics Unit, Scottish Office, Research Paper 3, 1982.
14. International Management and Engineering Group, *Study of Potential Benefits to British Industry from Offshore Oil and Gas Developments*, HMSO (London), 1972.
15. K.P.Forrest & P.R.Taylor, *The Industrial Impact on the Scottish Economy*, paper presented at the SSRC North Sea Oil Panel seminar in 1981.
16. L.Cook & J.Surrey, *Government Policy for the Offshore Supplies Industry*, University of Sussex, Science Policy Research Unit, Occasional Paper no.21, 1983, pp.22–23.

17. See G.A.Mackay & N.F.Trimble, *The Demand for Production Platforms and Platform Sites, 1974–80*, University of Aberdeen, Department of Political Economy, North Sea Paper no.3, 1975.
18. Highlands and Islands Development Board, *Annual Report*, 1980, p.39.
19. Cook & Surrey, *op. cit.* (n.16).
20. I. Wood, *Offshore Oil – Problems and Opportunities for Local Industry*, paper presented at the SSRC North Sea Oil Panel seminar in 1981.
21. *Ibid.*
22. *Ibid.*

11

THE FINANCE SECTOR

ANDREW D. BAIN AND RICHARD G. REID

No modern economy can operate efficiently without a healthy financial sector. The financial sector oils the wheels of economic activity and is responsible for supplying all the other sectors of the economy with the financial facilities they need. In addition, financial institutions make a contribution to value added in their own right, something which is particularly valuable if the services they provide are marketed beyond the boundaries of the country concerned, and they are an important source of employment. The sector's success in carrying out its functions has a profound effect upon the performance of the economy at large.

This chapter begins with a brief description of the financial sector in Scotland as it is today. An examination of its performance in recent years follows. Aspects of performance include its growth, the rates of return which financial institutions have been able to earn, and their capacity to innovate and adapt in response to change. Next, the Scottish financial sector as a provider of services to the rest of the economy, particularly industry, is considered, and the chapter concludes with a brief discussion of some of the activities of the Scottish clearing banks.

The Finance Sector Today

Sector Overview. In 1980, the most recent year for which figures are available, the Banking, Insurance and Finance sector[1] accounted for a little under seven per cent of Scotland's GDP. This was in fact greater than normal – boosted by the high level of interest rates prevailing in that year – and Table 11.1 shows that a more normal figure would be in the range 5·5–6·0 per cent. Statistics for employment (Table 11.2) show that the sector now employs some 80000 people, a figure which has risen by about twenty per cent over the last five years.[2] Nevertheless, at 4·2 per cent of total employment in Scotland, the share of employment is considerably less than the share of value added.

Tables 11.1 and 11.2 also show comparable figures for the UK, and from this it is clear that the sector is less important within Scotland than in some other areas. However, for the UK as a whole the finance sector is heavily concentrated in London and the South-East of England, and in terms of regional concentration Scotland ranks behind the South of

Table 11.1. Banking, insurance and finance sector's share of GDP (per cent).

	1971	1976	1977	1978	1979	1980
Scotland	5·6	5·5	5·7	5·4	6·1	6·8
UK	7·3	7·9	8·2	8·0	8·4	8·8

Sources: *Scottish Economic Bulletin*, Summer 1982;
National Income and Expenditure, 1982.

England, East Anglia (which has a strong insurance representation) and the North-West, but ahead of other regions.[3] The rate of growth of employment in the finance sector in Scotland compares favourably with that of other sectors, both in Scotland and in the rest of the UK.

Because not all parts of the system offer competing and comparable services it is convenient to consider them under three headings: deposit-taking institutions, investing institutions, and specialist financing bodies and agencies and other sources of finance.

Table 11.2. Employment in banking, insurance and finance sectors (thousands).

	1971	1976	1977	1978	1979	1980	1981
Scotland	65	75·8	76·2	77·9	81	81	80
(% total Scottish)	(3·3)	(3·7)	(3·8)	(3·8)	(3·9)	(4·0)	(4·2)
UK	976	1103	1145	1200	1233	1255	1240
(% total UK)	(4·4)	(4·9)	(5·1)	(5·3)	(5·4)	(5·6)	(5·9)

Sources: *Scottish Economic Bulletin*, Summer 1982; *National Income and Expenditure*, 1982; Department of Employment.

Deposit-Taking Institutions. The first group covers the clearing banks, Trustee Savings banks, merchant banks, the branches of non-Scottish banks, building societies, and the National Savings Bank (NSB). Table 11.3 provides information on the customer balances, branches and number of employees of the three most important categories. It shows that the clearing banks dominate the group with just over fifty per cent of total customer balances and by far the largest shares of employment and branch coverage, 82 and 68 per cent respectively.

The three clearing banks – the Bank of Scotland (BS), the Clydesdale Bank (CB) and the Royal Bank of Scotland (RBS) – are the most important financial institutions in Scotland catering through their branch networks for the general deposit-taking, lending and money transmission needs of the economy. In terms of balance-sheet size (Table 11.4) BS and RBS are similar, both being roughly twice the size of CB; they each have over 550 branches in Scotland compared to CB's 380, and both employ

Table 11.3. Deposit-taking institutions, end 1981.

	Customer balances (£m)	Branches	Employees
Clearing Banks[1]	4820	1536	24896
Building Societies	3420	423	2538
TSBs	1087	287	2752
	9327	2246	30186

[1] U K Private and Public Sector Sterling Deposits
(excluding Certificates of Deposit).
Sources: Committee of Scottish Clearing Banks; Building
Societies Association Bulletin; TSB Annual Reports.

over 9000 staff, compared to CB's 5500. The clearing banks' activities
are not, of course, confined to Scotland, or indeed the UK; nevertheless,
in August 1982 their lending to UK residents amounted to £5.2 billion,
with just under thirty per cent of this going to the services sector, with
manufacturing and other production each receiving about twenty per
cent of the total, and with personal lending accounting for twenty-five per
cent. Each of the clearing banks provides a range of financial services,
either directly or through subsidiary or associated companies.

Table 11.4. Scottish clearing banks: balance sheet totals (£m).

Royal Bank of Scotland (December 1981)	4071
Bank of Scotland (February 1982)	3683
Clydesdale Bank (December 1981)	1907
	9661

Sources: Annual Reports.

   The clearing banks' strongest competitors for personal savings in the
retail deposit market are the building societies. They have shown a very
rapid growth over the past decade and the number of building society
branches has increased from 107 in 1970 to 423 in 1981. Shares and
deposits at the end of 1981 stood at £3420 million, representing six per
cent of total UK building society deposits. The bulk of building society
activity in Scotland is carried out through the branches of societies with
headquarters in England, and in 1980 less than fifty branches were of
Scottish societies. Thanks to amalgamations within the building society
movement, as a result partly of the relatively high costs of operation of
small societies, their number has been dwindling, and now only the
Dunfermline Building Society, with assets in excess of £160 million and

some branches in England, is a substantial force, though even it accounts for under five per cent of shares and deposits held in Scotland. The growth in building societies has, of course, been associated with saving for house purchase and the spread of owner-occupation in Scotland. Although specialised in their lending, building societies now provide a range of facilities for depositors, including limited money-transmission services.

In common with TSBs throughout the United Kingdom the banks in Scotland have undergone a process of rationalisation in recent years, and the 22 member banks which existed in 1969 have now been brought together into four groups: the West of Scotland, Tayside and Central, Aberdeen, and South of Scotland banks. Further amalgamation to form a single Scottish TSB took place in 1983. The TSBs operate through nearly 300 branches and have over 2700 employees. In recent years they have moved away from their traditional role as savings banks pure and simple, into the provision of chequing and money-transmission services for their customers and of loans to both individuals and small businesses. In these sectors of the market they are in direct competition with the clearing banks, and during the last decade their customer balances have approximately doubled.

There are four Scottish merchant banks of which much the largest is the British Linen Bank (BLB), a subsidiary of the Bank of Scotland, with assets of some £400 million (January 1982). The bank took its present form in 1977. Next in size is Noble Grossart with assets of just over £30 million, followed by the James Finlay Corporation and McNeill Pearson. These banks specialise in corporate advice and specialised lending, including also the provision of limited amounts of equity finance. In addition to the Scottish merchant banks there are numerous branches of English-based banks, including some of the clearers and merchant banks, and a considerable number of foreign banks – amounting to about thirty in all. Many of these came to Scotland between 1973 and 1979 in the wake of companies from their own countries which have had branches or subsidiaries in Scotland or, more recently, have been participating in North Sea oil operations. Once established in Scotland they do not, of course, confine their activities to servicing existing customers, and compete with the clearing banks for corporate and larger-size private business. The incomers also include several banks which deal primarily with the Asian and Irish communities. No data on the scale of deposit-taking or lending by these banks in Scotland are available.

The headquarters of the National Savings Bank is located in Glasgow, having moved there in 1966. It has about 3500 employees at its headquarters, and provides deposit and withdrawal facilities through the Post Office system. Since all the funds collected are channelled directly into Government securities it has little impact on the Scottish financial system.

Investing Institutions. A notable feature of Scotland's financial sector is the number and strength of its investing institutions – Scottish-based life assurance companies, investment and unit trusts, and, to a lesser extent, general insurance. At the end of 1981 the worldwide assets managed by these institutions amounted to over £15 billion and about 7500 people were employed by them in Scotland. This employment is important not only on account of the substantial numbers, but also because a relatively high proportion require professional qualifications.

At the end of 1981 the nine Scottish life offices handled funds of some £10 billion. The largest is the Standard Life (£4.0 billion), followed by Scottish Widows (£2.1 billion) and the Scottish Amicable (£1.3 billion). Standard Life does a substantial part of its business in Canada, Scottish Amicable has activities in Australia, and several offices engage in business in the Republic of Ireland. The funds held in respect of this non-UK business are not segregated, but probably accounted for about £1.3 billion of the total. About 80–85 per cent of the Scottish life offices' UK business is done in England and Wales, with the balance in Scotland. Employment in 1981 averaged nearly 7500, of whom about 4700 were resident in Scotland.

None of the Scottish life offices engages in 'industrial' insurance, i.e. door-to-door collection of small premiums. Their share in 1981 of the ordinary long-term premium income (at home and overseas) of UK life offices was a little over 15 per cent, and of UK business just under 15 per cent. Their share of assets was slightly higher – 16·1 per cent of the net assets of all long-term insurance (including industrial), and 17·4 per cent of the book value of ordinary insurance funds. As is to be expected, the offices invest widely in government securities, other fixed-interest securities, ordinary shares and property, the proportions varying substantially between offices. On average ordinary shares and property account for about half of the offices' total assets.

Scotland has only one significant general insurance company, General Accident, whose Head Office is in Perth. It is the fourth largest composite insurance company in the UK, and, in terms of UK general premium income, it is the leading company. In 1981, General Accident's UK gross general premium income was £497 million, almost 7 per cent of the total UK premium income; at £241 million its share of motor insurance was over 11 per cent. World-wide net premium income exceeded £1 billion, but only about forty per cent emanates from the UK, and around ten per cent of this from Scotland. In addition, long-term business premium income exceeded £100 million.

World-wide assets at the end of 1981 amounted to nearly £2.5 billion, including general fund investments of nearly £1.5 billion and long-term fund investment of nearly £700 million (all at book value). Assets held in respect of overseas business must often be invested in the country or

369

currency concerned, and the management of these assets is usually in the hands of the relevant subsidiary. UK funds managed from the Head Office probably amounted to about £1.5 billion at the end of 1981.

Of General Accident's 11000 UK employees, some 2250 live in Scotland, and it is a major source of employment in Perth.

Forty-one of the fifty-one Scottish investment trusts were run by twelve management groups (the remainder being independent companies), most of which also manage unit trusts, pension or other funds. Total assets of the investment trusts amounted to £3.1 billion, just over 35 per cent of the UK total. The largest groups were Ivory and Sime (£401 million of investment trust funds), Baillie Gifford (£285 million) and Martin Currie (£271 million) in Edinburgh, Murray Johnstone (£324 million) in Glasgow, with the Alliance Trust (£245 million) in Dundee also having over £200 million under management.

Many of the Scottish trusts have traditionally had a very strong overseas component in their portfolios, holding a larger proportion of their funds abroad, particularly in the United States, than their English counterparts. Table 11.5 shows that this is still the case: at the end of 1981 the Scottish held under half of their equity assets in the UK, compared with 55 per cent for all trusts (or 60 per cent for English trusts), while North America accounted for 37 per cent of Scottish trusts' funds, compared with 27 per cent overall (just over 20 per cent for English trusts).

Table 11.5. Investment trusts: geographic distribution of equity assets, end 1981 (%).

	UK	N. America	Japan	Others
Scottish Trusts	47	37	9	7
All UK	55	27	8	9

Source: Wood, Mackenzie and Co.

In contrast with investment trusts, authorised unit trusts are not at present well represented in Scotland, with only £150 million out of a UK total of £5.6 billion at the end of 1981. The largest was the Trustee Savings Bank Scottish Unit Trust (£82 million), managed by Murray Johnstone. At one time about half of the funds of the Save and Prosper Group trusts (the largest group) were managed by Ivory and Sime; they are now managed by the group itself, though Ivory and Sime investment trusts continue to hold a substantial interest in the management company.

The institutional fund managers, the investment departments of the clearing banks, and two major self-administered pension funds also manage a very substantial volume of investment capital. In 1981 total pension fund monies (excluding insured pension funds which form part of the balance sheet of the insurance companies) amounted to £2 billion, of which some £850 million represented self-administered funds (including those of the clearing banks and General Accident). This total had certainly risen to a figure in excess of £2.5 billion by the end of 1982.

In addition these fund managers were responsible for about £650 million of other funds (e.g. private clients, charities, and exempt unit trusts) at the end of 1981, which had risen to over £800 million by the end of 1982. Broad estimates suggest that both pension and other funds under management at the end of 1981 were about three times their level five years earlier.

Simply adding together the funds under management of the insurance companies, investment and unit trusts, and fund managers would lead to an over-estimate of the total funds under management in Scotland. There is a danger of overlap: for example, insurance companies hold shares in investment trusts, investment trusts in specialised overseas funds, and pension funds in exempt unit trusts. However, the overlap is probably not large, and a total of £16.5 billion for funds under management at the end of 1981 is unlikely to be wide of the mark. By the end of 1982 the corresponding figure will certainly have been over £20 billion.

Other Sources of Finance. Although the separate British stock exchanges were amalgamated into a single national exchange in London in 1973 there remains a trading floor in Glasgow. There are now 17 stock-broking firms operating in Scotland, of which 15 are Scottish; this compares with 35 firms in 1969–70. There are also two jobbing firms on the Glasgow exchange. The total number of staff directly employed in Stock Exchange business fell from 1272 in 1970 to 1007 in 1980. Apart from the increasing focus on London there have been three reasons for the declining number of brokers; first the growth of institutional investors who make use of London brokers for the greater part of their business, secondly the blurring of distinctions within the financial system, with brokers increasingly offering a range of financial services, and thirdly the advances in communications and data processing. These have tended to lead to resources being concentrated in fewer firms.

The demands placed on the Stock Exchange by Scottish-based companies has fallen, as the number of listed companies in Scotland has declined – from about 170 in 1970 to 100 in 1982. This reduction has been due largely to merger activity, with control in 51 of the 66 takeovers passing outside Scotland. Moreover, although they are registered in Scotland, many of these companies are nationally and internationally oriented, and their shares are largely traded and owned outside Scotland. There are hopes that the primary business of the Glasgow exchange can be enlarged through USM listings, which might be more appropriate for many local companies, but as yet this kind of business has not developed. Stock exchange activity in Scotland at present tends to be heavily reliant on secondary market dealing for private customers.

There are a number of institutions providing long-term finance to companies in Scotland, mainly to smaller companies or to those with special needs. The largest of these is the Industrial and Commercial Finance Corporation (ICFC), owned by the Bank of England and the clearing banks, which makes medium- and long-term loans to small and medium-sized enterprises, sometimes with a minority equity stake. In Scotland it has three branches, and investments outstanding total about £50 million.

Another group comprises organisations set up by private bodies to participate mainly in the financing of new or high-technology business. The British Linen Bank has an associate company, Melville Street Investments, which makes long-term capital available to proven companies. The Finlay Corporation's two funds, Scottish Offshore Investors (SOI) and Scottish Allied Investors (SAI), make long-term loans, usually combined with equity stakes, in expanding industries, particularly in the energy field in the case of the former. All banks participate in the loan guarantee scheme for small firms, which by March 1982 had issued guarantees of £6 million in Scotland.

Most venture capital finance is provided on a joint basis by a number of institutions involving often the ECSC, the SDA and a variety of private organisations such as the Norwich Union Life Assurance Co.; the Scottish Northern Investment Trust; Ivory and Sime; Hodgson and Martin; Moracrest Investments; and the Scottish clearers. The BLB now has its Creative Capital Fund and the RBS joins the Finlay Corporation and the Scottish Western Trust in SAI. Other groups generally look for investment possibilities in high-technology areas, but not specifically in Scotland – involved here are Advent Technology; Ivory and Sime; and Murray Johnstone.

Performance

Clearing Banks. Turning now to the performance of some of the more important parts of the financial sector, the Scottish clearing banks will be considered first. One approach is to look at their profitability, and to compare it with the London clearing banks which are engaged in similar business south of the border. Measures of profitability are shown in Tables 11.6 to 11.8 for the period 1977–81.

One measure of overall profitability is the pre-tax return on assets, which shows the ability of the bank to earn profits on its assets as a whole. Table 11.6 shows that in 1977 and 1978 the profitability of the Scottish banks[4] was significantly higher than their English counterparts, but that, with the exception of CB, profitability rose less than for the London clearing banks in 1979, and since then average pre-tax returns on both sides of the Border have been very similar.

The pre-tax return on banks' assets is, however, influenced by the

Table 11.6. Scottish clearing banks: pre-tax returns (%) on average assets, in comparison with London clearing banks, 1977–81.

	1977	1978	1979	1980	1981
Bank of Scotland	1·59	1·57	1·57	1·37	1·19
Clydesdale	1·47	1·94	2·44	1·62	1·31
Royal Bank of Scotland	2·10	1·70	1·84	1·52	1·31
SCB average[1]	1·72	1·74	1·95	1·50	1·27
Barclays	1·29	1·62	1·95	1·56	1·32
Lloyds	1·31	1·29	1·72	1·55	1·62
Midland	1·53	1·60	1·76	1·02	0·70
National Westminster	1·33	1·48	1·72	1·29	1·27
Williams and Glyn's	1·25	1·47	2·16	2·04	1·80
LCB average[1]	1·34	1·49	1·86	1·49	1·34

[1] Unweighted.
Sources: Scottish clearing banks; W Greenwell & Co.

composition of their liabilities. Banks with a high ratio of shareholders' funds, on which no interest is payable, might be expected to earn relatively high margins overall. The comparison between the Scottish and English clearing banks in this respect is complicated by the fact that the latter have traditionally obtained a higher proportion of their retail deposits in the form of non-interest-bearing current accounts; nevertheless, the Scottish banks do have the stronger equity base – their equity/deposits ratio averaged 7·85 per cent in 1981, compared with 5·59 per cent for their English counterparts, and the free equity/deposits ratio were 3·31 per cent and 2·65 per cent respectively.[5]

Table 11.7 measures profitability as the pre-tax return on shareholders' funds. The trends are very similar to those for the pre-tax return on assets, but the Scottish clearing banks' stronger equity bases have resulted in average returns on shareholders' funds in recent years which have been lower than those of the English clearers. In terms of the growth of profitability over the five-year period from 1976 to 1981, the Scottish clearing banks have done less well. Table 11.8 shows that the profits of the English clearing banks increased at a compound rate of 19 per cent per year. None of the Scottish clearing banks achieved this level: their average was only 11 per cent.

A second indicator of performance is the growth of the Scottish clearing banks' business. Table 11.9 shows that in the five-year period from 1976 to 1981 the total liabilities of the Scottish clearing banks grew at almost exactly the same rate as those of the London clearing banks, i.e. by a factor of 2.2. However, the Scottish clearing banks' growth was

Table 11.7. Scottish clearing banks: pre-tax returns (%) on average shareholders' funds, in comparison with London clearing banks, 1977–81.

	1977	1978	1979	1980	1981
Bank of Scotland	22·2	21·0	21·2	19·7	17·5
Clydesdale	26·5	33·7	38·3	23·9	20·7
Royal Bank of Scotland	27·9	24·1	23·5	20·1	18·5
SCB average[1]	25·5	27·6	27·7	21·2	18·9
Barclays	27·7	30·9	34·0	27·9	26·6
Lloyds	22·0	18·7	24·5	22·2	24·8
Midland	29·4	26·9	28·9	18·1	16·6
National Westminster	23·2	24·7	30·8	24·5	24·5
Williams and Glyn's	19·0	21·0	27·7	24·5	22·9
LCB average[1]	24·3	24·4	29·2	23·4	23·1

[1] Unweighted.
Sources: As for Table 11.6.

Table 11.8. Scottish and London clearing banks: growth of pre-tax profits, 1976–81 (% per annum).

Bank of Scotland	12·0
Clydesdale	16·4
Royal Bank of Scotland	7·1
SCB average[1]	11·0
LCB average[1]	19·0

[1] weighted.
Source: Scottish Clearing Banks;
Wood Mackenzie and Co.

Table 11.9. Scottish and London clearing banks: balance sheet growth, 1976–81 (mid-December).

	Total liabilities			Sterling deposits of U K public and private sectors (excluding CDs)				
	1976 (£m)	1981 (£m)	Growth factor	1971 (£m)	1976 (£m)	1981 (£m)	Growth factor 1971–81	1976–81
SCB	4197	9309	2·2	1073	2397	4820	4·5	2·0
LCB	35032	76909	2·2	10779	21760	41056	3·8	1·9

Sources: *Financial Statistics*, December 1977; *Bank of England Quarterly Bulletin*, 1982.

founded to a greater extent than that of their English counterparts on sterling deposit and lending business.[6] Over the ten-year period from 1971 to 1981 the Scottish clearing banks had a growth factor for sterling customer deposits of 4.5, compared with 3.8 for the London clearing banks, and in the last five years the Scottish growth factor of 2.0 still exceeded the corresponding English level (1.9).

In comparison with the building societies, the Scottish clearing banks have fared less well (see Table 11.10). While the figures for building society deposits in Scotland in 1971 are somewhat uncertain (and may well be greater than that shown in the table) it is clear that building society deposits over the ten-year period have grown faster than those of their clearing bank competitors, and the same remains true for the last five years. The Trustee Savings banks, however, have grown considerably more slowly.[7]

Table 11.10. Deposit growth: Scottish clearing banks, building societies and trustee savings banks.

	Deposit balances outstanding (end of year, £m)			Growth factor	
	1971	1976	1981	1971–81	1976–81
Clearing banks	1072	2397	4820	4·5	2·0
Building societies	511[1]	1446	3420	6·7	2·4
Trustee savings banks	565	763	1087	1·9	1·4

[1] This figure may well be an underestimate of building society deposits at that time (see footnote 8).
Sources: Clearing banks – as for Table 11.9; *Building Societies Association Bulletin*, April 1982; *Trustee Savings Banks Yearbooks*.

Other aspects of performance which require some comment are the flexibility of the banks' responses to a changing environment, their innovativeness and their ability to exploit opportunities. Three aspects will be touched on – the response to technological developments, the degree of involvement in international and foreign currency business, and the provision of corporate financial services. Some further information concerning the international and merchant banking aspects of the banks' business will be found at the end of this chapter.

Developments in information technology have wrought a revolution in the mechanics of retail banks. All of the Scottish clearers have been well to the fore in adopting new equipment and in experimenting with new facilities. For example, RBS took the lead in installing automatic cash dispensing facilities for its customers, BS is experimenting with home banking facilities, and CB with point-of-sale facilities.

However, the banks' policies regarding involvement in international banking have differed significantly, as shown in the Appendix to this chapter. CB, which is a wholly-owned subsidiary of the Midland Bank, has the least direct involvement of the three, although customers who require services which CB does not provide itself can be directed elsewhere in the group. BS has gone farthest on the international side. It is involved in international lending, and particularly energy lending, through shareholdings in two associate banks, Banque Worms et Associés and the International Energy Bank. In addition, its own international division includes a cadre of senior staff and specialist expertise in the oil industry. As a result it has the capacity to initiate and lead international loan operations.

RBS at present occupies an intermediate position. In 1981 the Royal Bank Group sought to implement an agreed merger with Standard Chartered Bank, which would have provided the Group with wide-ranging international connections and involvement. After a competing proposal from the Hong Kong and Shanghai Banking Corporation the proposed mergers were referred to the Monopolies and Mergers Commission, which recommended that neither should be allowed to proceed. Since then the Royal Bank Group has been reassessing its strategy, but no alternative proposals have been revealed.

None of the Scottish clearing banks has followed the route taken by the English clearers of making substantial acquisitions abroad. It is doubtful if they would have much to gain from doing so. Access to the branch network and resources of a major international bank would be advantageous, but none of the Scottish banks could contemplate an acquisition on the necessary scale. Moreover, the margins to be earned on international business, particularly participations in syndicated loans, have been very variable in recent years, while the risks are not to be ignored. The BS strategy, of a more limited incursion based on specialised expertise, which may be expected to generate direct lending business at a satisfactory return, seems more likely to be rewarding. The possibility that some corporate business in Scotland may be lost, through failure to match the range of connections and services provided by some non-clearing bank competitors, may be unavoidable.

All the banks provide some corporate finance facilities within their main organisations, but more complex matters require the services of specialists. Again, CB would not generally provide these services in-house, though they are available within the Midland Group. RBS has strengthened its corporate finance division and recently transferred some of its staff to a separate subsidiary with the object of developing into a fully-fledged merchant bank. BS already has the British Linen Bank as a merchant bank subsidiary, operating independently of the main bank and actively seeking business in England as well as Scotland.

BL's success, and that of Noble Grossart before it, have demonstrated that opportunities in merchant banking exist in Scotland for a dynamic management to exploit. Merchant banks based in Scotland, with their short lines of communication and range of expertise on hand locally, should be in a strong position to compete with the Scottish branches of City or other merchant banks.

Judgement on these aspects of the Scottish clearing banks' performance must inevitably be qualitative. On technological development all seem to be performing well. CB has been constrained in its direct involvement in international and merchant banking activities by its membership of a group which provides these facilities in other ways. The strategic development of RBS was interrupted by the abortive merger proposals, though on the merchant banking side developments are now in train. BS has committed substantially more resources than the other banks to building up its international and merchant banking expertise. In recent years, however, BS has been the least profitable of the Scottish banks (see Table 11.7, above); it may be no coincidence that the gap appears to be narrowing.

Table 11.11. Building societies and TSBs:
deposits in Scotland and the UK, 1971–81.

	1971	1976	1981
Building Societies:			
shares and deposits (£m)			
Scotland	511	1446	3420
UK	12176	26101	57146
Scottish %	4·2	5·5	6·0
TSBs: deposit balances (£m)			
Scotland	565	763	1087
UK	2779	4272	6095
Scottish %	20·3	17·9	17·8

Sources: *Building Societies Association Bulletin*, April 1982;
Trustee Savings Banks Yearbooks; Financial Statistics.

Building Societies and Trustee Savings Banks. It is clear that the building societies as a whole have been consistently successful in increasing their share of the deposit market in Scotland[8] during the last ten years. As already seen, Scottish-based building societies account for only a small proportion of the total. Table 11.11 shows comparative figures for the UK, from which it is apparent that building society growth in Scotland has exceeded the national average, though the proportion of UK deposits held through Scottish branches is still well below Scotland's share of UK population.

The performance of TSBs presents a striking contrast. Deposit growth has been comparatively slow and they have lost market share, as shown in Table 11.10. Moreover, between 1971 and 1976 the TSBs in Scotland fared much less well than their counterparts in England, though since that time their performance has run in parallel (Table 11.11). Nevertheless, the TSBs in Scotland still account for nearly 18 per cent of total TSB deposits in the UK, and the new Scottish TSB has over 10 per cent of the sterling customer balances of Scottish deposit-takers under its control. During the first part of the period under review the TSBs continued to operate in their traditional role, providing savings but not lending facilities to their customers. Since then the progressive amalgamation into stronger units and their gradual development of lending functions and other banking facilities has put them in a position to compete on more equal terms with the other major deposit-takers.

Scottish Life Offices. During the last ten years premium income of ordinary life assurance business in the UK multiplied by a factor of nearly 5, while the value of long-term funds rose to nearly 4 times its previous level. In aggregate, the Scottish life offices conformed to this general pattern, though, as Table 11.12 shows, their market share of the world-wide premium income of UK offices rose from 14 per cent to over 15 per cent, and of the UK premium income from 13 per cent to nearly 15 per cent, in the period. Between 1971 and 1981 the Scottish offices' share of total funds (at book value) rose by about one per cent from 16·3 to 17·4 per cent; market value figures for UK offices in 1971 are not available, but the figures for 1976 and 1981 show that the Scottish offices have increased their share of the net assets of UK long-term funds slightly. There was considerable variation between offices, with the Scottish Equitable showing a particularly rapid growth of funds, and the Life Association of Scotland, Scottish Amicable and Scottish Equitable all raising premium income by a factor of over 8.

In terms of their expenses the Scottish offices also appear to be extremely competitive. Compared with a national expenses ratio (management expenses plus commission as a percentage of premium income) in 1981 of 21·5 per cent, the ratio for the Scottish life offices as a whole was just under 15 per cent. The expenses ratios for large offices are generally considerably below those for the smaller offices, but in 1981 only two of the Scottish offices were above the national average.

Finally, the Scottish offices have generally served their policyholders well. Figures published in the *Economist*[9] show how policyholders paying an annual premium of £100 for a with-profits policy would have fared with a large number of UK offices. Five of the eight Scottish offices which quoted the proceeds of a whole-life policy taken out forty years before were above the median, as were six of the seven quoting the proceeds at maturity of a 25-year endowment policy, though only half of the Scottish offices were above the median proceeds of a 15-year policy taken out in 1972, payable on the policy-holder's death in 1982. Out of the top ten UK offices for each of these periods, the numbers of Scottish offices were 4, 4 and 2 respectively.

Overall the performance of the Scottish life offices, whether judged by their growth, their expenses or their returns to policy-holders, must be regarded as very satisfactory.

Table 11.12.Scottish life offices compared with UK offices (ordinary business).

	1971	1976	1981
Premium Income:			
UK and overseas			
Scottish Offices (£m)	237	506	1272
UK Offices (£m)	1694	3642	8320
Scottish %	14·0	13·9	15·3
UK only			
Scottish Offices (£m)	192	416	1057
UK Offices (£m)	1478	2982	7143
Scottish %	13·0	14·0	14·8
Long-term Funds (Book values)			
Scottish Offices (£m)	2089	3721	8688
UK Offices (£m)	12800	23200	49800
Scottish %	16·3	16·0	17·4
Net Assets[1] (Market values)			
Scottish Offices (£m)	2549	3892	9851
UK Offices (£m)	n.a.	24487	61102
Scottish %	n.a.	15·9	16·1

[1] Includes industrial insurance funds
Sources: All Scottish figures are taken from *Scottish Life Offices' Annual Reports* and additional information supplied by the companies. Premium income: UK and overseas, from *Life Assurance in the United Kingdom.* UK only, from *Insurance Premiums in the UK, 1960–1981*, BIA, October 1982. Long-term funds: *Life Assurance in the United Kingdom.* Net Assets: *Financial Statistics.*

General Accident. Over the last decade General Accident has broadly held its position in the general insurance market. Its share of the world-wide general premium income of British insurance companies rose from 9·2 per cent in 1971 to 10·6 per cent in 1980. In contrast, in the five years to 1981, its share of the UK market seems to have fallen slightly – from 11·5 to 11·3 per cent – for motor insurance, although it rose from 5·7 to

6·2 per cent for fire and accident insurance. At the end of 1981 General Accident was still the largest general insurance company in terms of its UK premium income, though again its market share of the top six companies had fallen slightly over the previous five years – from 32·2 to 30·3 per cent for motor insurance and with little change in fire and accident insurance.

Investment Trusts. One measure of an investment trust's performance is the total return on net assets. This shows the growth in value of a shareholder's investment over the period in question, but makes no allowance for risk – which may differ from one trust to another – or for the shareholder's own preferences regarding the balance of the trust's investments (e.g. country or currency composition). To the extent that shareholders choose to hold shares in trusts because of their characteristics in these other respects, the total return may be misleading as a guide to how well the trusts have served their shareholders' interests.

Table 11.13. Performance of Scottish investment trusts relative to the size-weighted growth of net assets of all UK investment trusts.

	Number of trusts		
	10 years	5 years	1 year
Above UK average	7	9	24
Below UK average	31	31	18
Total trusts	38	40	42

Source: *Investment Trust Yearbook*, 1982.

Table 11.13 shows the performance of Scottish-managed trusts over ten-year, five-year and one-year periods up to the end of 1981. For both the ten-year and five-year periods only a minority of the Scottish trusts performed as well as the average of UK investment trusts. This is as least partly due to the high overseas weighting in their portfolios – the Scottish trusts were adversely affected by the relative poor performance of US shares, and by the abolition of exchange control and the disappearance of the premium for investment currency in 1979. More recently the high overseas weighting has been a source of relative strength, and over half of the Scottish trusts out-performed the average in the year to the end of 1981.

The last two years have seen a number of new developments amongst the investment trusts. New trusts with specialist objectives, such as East of Scotland Onshore, Japan Assets and Murray Technology, have been floated, and several trusts have increased the weight of unquoted and smaller companies in their portfolios. Some of the larger trusts have been restructured to give them more clearly distinguished investment objectives. Thus, while it is generally held that the increase in share ownership by life assurance and pension funds, which are of a size to achieve all the advantages of diversification at low cost themselves, has led to a reduced role for investment trusts in the capital market, the Scottish fund groups have in recent years demonstrated a continuing capacity to innovate and to provide specialist investment services to institutional as well as private shareholders.

The market value of investment trust shares in recent years has typically stood at a considerable discount on the underlying asset values. This has left them vulnerable to takeover bids, with a view to liquidating their portfolios or amalgamating them with other funds, and to pressures to convert into unit trusts in order to eliminate the discount. Scottish trusts have been by no means immune from these pressures, and while new trusts have been created others have disappeared.

Independence and Performance. There is a close connection between the independence of the Scottish financial institutions and the finance sector's performance. But it is a two-way relationship: for while independence may sometimes aid performance, a satisfactory performance is often the best guarantee of continued independence.

Both IDS and the SDA acknowledge the importance of the health of the finance sector for the well-being of the Scottish economy. The finance sector is seen as an important, and growing, source of employment – of special significance because it offers opportunities to people with high professional or other qualifications. The advantages which other sectors derive from the presence of a strong finance sector are also recognised.

The creation of further job opportunities and the maintenance of a diversified finance sector depend on its performance. Head-office employment in insurance depends on the success in winning business of the Scottish-based companies, the ability of fund management groups to increase the range of their business depends on their investment expertise, and the scale of the clearing banks depends on how far they are able to penetrate new markets. High performance and growth of market share go together.

Any loss of independence could threaten both performance and employment – performance, because the opportunity to respond to business opportunities may be constrained as a result of membership of a large group, and employment because loss of control may lead to the transfer of head-office functions (as occurred with composite insurance companies in the 1960s). For these reasons IDS and the SDA expressed anxieties about the possible consequences of the merger proposals involving the Royal Bank Group. A similar threat, though on a smaller scale, exists in connection with fund management activities, where the takeover of a fund would probably be associated with an immediate loss of employment.

Some parts of the finance sector depend on ready access to a wide range of expertise – there are significant external economies of scale. The sector as a whole could therefore be vulnerable to any appreciable contraction in a major component part. Though there is no indication that the viability of any part is threatened at present, it is a danger against which the authorities should be on their guard.

Financial Provision for Industry and Commerce

The description of the finance sector earlier in this chapter has already touched upon many of the facilities which are at the disposal of industry and commerce. In considering their adequacy the characteristics of the enterprises which need to be financed must also be borne in mind – in particular, the substantial proportion of Scottish enterprises which are branches or subsidiaries of other companies. Moreover, the integrated nature of the British financial system, and the ease of access to facilities in the City which many companies enjoy, are also relevant factors.

Independent firms generally make greater demands on local financial facilities than the branches or subsidiaries of firms based elsewhere in the United Kingdom or overseas. Branches and subsidiaries require the services of a clearing bank, mainly in connection with payments and receipts (in foreign currencies as well as sterling) and with payroll services. But their demands for financing are often limited, because this aspect of their business is typically controlled centrally by the parent company, the bulk of liquid balances are held centrally, and capital is provided by the parent either as additional equity or on inter-company loan account. When local financing of a subsidiary is required it is usually arranged by or at the instigation of the parent, and is dictated more by the financial policy of the group as a whole than by the needs of the particular subsidiary. Scottish financial institutions have a chance of winning a share of this business, but they are hardly in a position to expand it. Business opportunities within Scotland for the finance sector are to be found mainly with the independent companies.

The large Scottish-based companies generally make considerable use of the facilities available in Scotland, but in addition they tend to look to the City for some of their specialised requirements. For example, most large companies would expect to consult merchant bankers in the City, rights issues would be handled by London as well as Scottish brokers, and major leasing deals would involve companies based in the south. It is thus the small and medium-sized independent enterprises that have most to gain from the existence locally of a wide range of financial facilities and advice.

The high degree of integration within the British financial system helps to ensure that the terms and conditions on which finance is available do not differ greatly from one part of the country to another. Nevertheless there are advantages of convenience, local knowledge and expertise, and commitment which might be expected to arise from the presence of a strong finance sector.

The Scottish clearing banks are much the most important source of external finance for industry and commerce in Scotland. Table 11.14 shows the breakdown of their advances in August 1982. The shares of the manufacturing and other production sectors have been falling in recent years, whilst that of the personal sector has been rising – a trend which applies equally to the English clearing banks. A declining share for a sector does not, of course, denote any shortage of finance: the actual level of advances to industry and commerce has risen rapidly and there is no evidence that the total lending of the Scottish clearing banks has been constrained by a shortage of funds.[10]

Table 11.14. Scottish clearing banks' advances, August 1982.

	£ billion	% of total	% increase since August 1979
Manufacturing	1·02	19·5	55
Other production	1·07	20·4	67
Services	1·51	28·9	84
Financial	0·35	6·7	25
Personal	1·28	24·5	161
Total	5·23	100·0	81

Source: *Scottish Economic Bulletin*, No. 26, 1983.

It is sometimes alleged that the Scottish clearing banks have provided inadequate support for Scottish industry. *A priori* argument, and what little evidence there is, do not support this charge. Indeed, the evidence would seem to suggest that by and large the Scottish clearing banks provide a satisfactory service to their industrial and commercial customers. Of course, not every request for finance is granted, and there will always be some dissatisfied customers. But with three clearing banks competing for business, and with the TSBs beginning to lend to the smaller businesses, customers are not tied to a single source of funds, and if one branch manager is overcautious they would have to be unlucky not to find another prepared to take a different view of a fundamentally sound lending proposition. For the business of medium-sized firms there is also strong competition from the branches of English and overseas banks, but no evidence that the clearers' dominance in this business has been seriously eroded.

Like other banks in Britain, the Scottish banks have adapted to meet their customers' needs. As well as the traditional overdraft, firms can make use of term loans, project loans with repayments tailored to the cash which the project is expected to generate and security tied to the characteristics of the project concerned, bill finance, finance for leasing rather than direct ownership of capital assets, performance bonds, and so on. The Scottish banks have acquired the necessary expertise and in some instances, particularly in connection with both offshore and onshore North Sea oil activities, played a leading and innovative role.

The Scottish banks have two important advantages over their competitors: their lines of communication are short, and they have a long-term commitment to the economy. The first means that they are usually in a position to give customers an answer quickly, something which is often important in a competitive situation. The second gives their customers confidence, for they know that the banks must consider the consequences of their decisions for the community to which they belong, rather than simply having regard to their own commercial interests. If a company has the misfortune to get into difficulties, it may expect its Scottish clearing banker to show more tolerance than an outside competitor. Indeed, there have perhaps been occasions when Scottish banks can be seen with the benefit of hindsight to have been more tolerant than companies deserved.

Scottish firms also have easy access to foreign currency financing if it it required for international investment or other purposes. All the clearing banks can provide Eurodollar loan facilities, though probably on a syndicated or shared basis if the sum involved is large.[11] Beyond that, their experience of acting as lead managers for syndicated loans varies. Scottish firms, who prefer to obtain a large loan from one single lender, can also approach some of the major international banks (such as The Hong Kong and Shanghai Banking Corporation or the Standard Chartered Bank) through their Scottish branches.

Beyond the supply of finance itself all the major banks are in a position to provide corporate financial advice, though, as the final section of this chapter shows, the resources committed to this kind of activity vary from bank to bank. In addition there are the specialist merchant banks and financial advisers capable of devising and arranging the financing of new or reconstructed enterprises. A good example is one company which, with the help of an independent financial adviser, rose like a phoenix from the ashes of the Carron Company. The specialist advisers, and the Scottish-based merchant banks, display a combination of financial skills and entrepreneurial flair which has enabled them to handle small and medium-sized operations, though the very large deals may still be beyond their reach.

As with companies elsewhere in Britain, business in Scotland suffers from a dearth of new long-term loan capital at a fixed rate of interest, for which the banks' variable-rate term loans are not an entirely satisfactory substitute. But this reflects not a lack of supply but a justifiable reluctance on the part of the firms themselves to enter into commitments to pay what seem high rates of interest for twenty or more years. The terms demanded by the institutions for long-term capital in Scotland are, of course, no different from those in the rest of the country, and the rate of interest is set largely by the prevailing yield on gilt-edged securities. High long-term real rates of interest (when judged by the current level of price inflation) are a world-wide phenomenon at present, a legacy of inflation which has led investors to seek protection from the possibility of a resurgence in future. Suppliers of capital, who can invest their funds elsewhere at these high rates of interest, cannot be expected to lend at a lower rate in Scotland.

For equity capital the diminishing number of listed companies in Scotland have access to funds through the UK capital market on the same basis as any other UK companies. Smaller and unlisted companies are not immune from the problems that beset their counterparts elsewhere – low profitability has diminished firms' ability to augment their own equity for expansion, and shares in the generality of unlisted companies are unattractive to most institutional investors. However, the diversity of the financial sector in Scotland means that Scottish firms have within easy reach a wider range of sources of equity capital to tap than in any other non-metropolitan region of the United Kingdom. ICFC is well represented, the SDA provides more extensive facilities than are available elsewhere, the clearing banks have subsidiaries which can make limited amounts of equity available to clients, some of the fund management groups take a special interest in investment in unlisted companies, and competition between venture capitalists for projects to support has increased in recent years. Moreover, the loan guarantee scheme for bank loans is available to help businessmen to increase their borrowing when, in other circumstances, an expansion of their equity base might have been preferable. The provision of finance for small firms and new ventures is discussed more fully in Chapter 3.

All this does not mean that firms can be sure of obtaining finance cheaply or easily at any time. Finance is certainly not cheap; but that, as already noted, is an international problem. Nor is it necessarily available, if the financial institutions judge that the proposal does not match up to their normal lending or investing criteria. Financiers may judge that a company which is in trouble does not warrant further support, or that the management of a new or young company has weaknesses or is too vulnerable to misfortune, or that prospective profits are too speculative to compensate for the risk of loss. They will not take account of social benefits which may be held to justify investment even if the risks are high and rewards only modest.

Nor should they be expected to do so. If the Scottish financial institutions were to behave as local philanthropists, at the expense of their depositors, shareholders, policy-holders or pension-scheme members, they would soon lose their credibility and their business. The contribution they make to the Scottish economy would suffer, as would their ability to provide support on those occasions that it is warranted. When deficiencies in management are the source of a firm's problems, the Scottish financial sector is well-placed to give advice and help to remedy perceived weaknesses – a precondition for the supply of finance. In other cases, where the prospective profitability of a proposed development is insufficient to attract support, but social benefits might be expected to accrue if the project went ahead, the responsibility for financing, or for raising the prospective return to private capital by means of grants, lies with the Government on behalf of society as a whole rather than with the private financial institutions.

Overall it is difficult to point to any major deficiencies in the supply of finance for firms in Scotland today. A reduction in the cost of funds would be welcome – but that is not in the hands of the Scottish institutions. A wide range of institutions are looking out for lending and investing opportunities, and are in active competition – sufficient to ensure that margins are not excessive. For those businesses seeking help in raising funds Scotland is well endowed with financiers who have the expertise and contacts needed to arrange a suitable financial package.

Appendix:
The Scottish Clearing Banks:
Corporate Finance and International Activities

The Scottish clearing banks today are all the product of amalgamations from among the survivors of the many banks formed in Scotland, mainly in the eighteenth century. All now have links with English clearing banks: CB is a wholly-owned subsidiary of the Midland Bank, Barclays Bank has a 35 per cent holding in BS, and Lloyds Bank holds 16 per cent of the shares in the RBS Group – whose principal components are RBS itself and Williams and Glyn's, the smallest of the English clearing banks.

In their main clearing bank functions the banks tend to operate in a similar manner. They all provide a full range of clearing bank facilities and services to their customers through extensive branch networks, all have divisional or regional structures for domestic banking, and in each case there is a distinct international division. To assist their smaller corporate customers they all have subsidiaries able to make equity investments in small companies. There are, of course, differences of emphasis and detail, for example in the priority attached to certain ancillary activities. But the most important differences amongst the three clearing banks exist in connection with their approach to and resources employed in corporate finance and international activities.

On the corporate finance side BS has made the most substantial development, with its subsidiary, the British Linen Bank, as a fully-fledged merchant bank. It has four offices (Edinburgh, Glasgow, London and Birmingham) employing over 120 people. In addition to the Chief Executive there are eight other executive directors. While relations with the parent bank are close it seeks business independently and has recruited a significant proportion of its senior staff from outside the Group. Total assets at the end of January 1982 amounted to nearly £400 million. The British Linen Bank has experienced very rapid growth in its deposits (up 29 per cent in 1981) and loans (up 40 per cent in 1981). Its bills are eligible for rediscount at the Bank of England, it has substantial interests in leasing, both on behalf of the Group and for customers, and company promotion activities have included a leading part in the privatisation of the British Transport Hotels. Through associate companies it assists with equity financing for small companies and also provides venture capital.

RBS is now following a similar route, having recently formed its corporate finance division into a separate subsidiary, National Commercial and Glyn's Ltd, which does not yet have full banking status. Previously the division was part of the responsibility of an executive director, with fifty staff including two of AGM or higher rank. As with the British Linen Bank, a high proportion of the specialist managerial staff has been recruited from outside the bank.

The Midland Group has its own merchant bank (Samuel Montagu) and CB have not found it necessary to make provision for specialist corporate finance functions. Such advice as is required from a clearing bank is available through its branches and chief offices.

Similar differences between the banks exist in regard to their international activities. The Bank of Scotland has two important holdings (15 per cent) in associate banks, Banque Worms et Associés (Genève) and the International Energy Bank. Its own international division employs 430 people, of whom over fifty are overseas, and it has branches in New York and Hong Kong and representative offices in Houston, Los Angeles and Moscow. The division includes nine members of staff of AGM or higher rank. Apart from servicing domestic customers the division has built up a significant expertise in lending to the oil industry and in international lending. The Bank took the lead in studying the feasibility and possible financing of the proposed North Sea gas-gathering pipeline. Amongst recent activities are the issue of $100 million floating rate notes in the US and $50 million of capital notes in the Eurobond market. Both these issues count as subordinated loan capital for the Bank and strengthen its capital base. While the relative profitability of domestic and international business fluctuates from year to year, international activities normally account for between 10 and 15 per cent of the Bank's profits.

RBS's international banking activities are less highly developed, though substantial resources are involved. Its international division employs 375 staff, of whom about 225 are in the UK, with branches in New York and Hong Kong, an agency in San Francisco, and four representative offices in the USA. The division forms part of the responsibility of one of the executive directors, and has two other staff of AGM or higher rank. It provides a full range of international banking services to its customers, and participates in international lending, though it has only rarely acted as 'lead manager' (i.e. organising and syndicating a loan). International activities accounted for approximately 20 per cent of *Group* pre-tax profits in 1981–82.

In 1981 the RBS Group sought to implement an agreed merger with the Standard Chartered Bank, and contested a takeover bid from the Hong Kong and Shanghai Banking Corporation. In the event, following a report of the Monopolies and Mergers Commission which recommended that neither merger should be permitted, these proposals were abandoned. Both would have given the Royal Bank access to an extensive international branch network, and, as part of an enlarged group, greater participation in international lending business.

The international business of CB is handled by a division known as Clydesdale Bank International employing 205 staff, all of whom are in the UK under the leadership of a Chief Manager who is of AGM rank based in Glasgow. CB International forms part of the responsibility of a General Manager. It has not been involved as the lead manager although on occasions it has acted as co-manager in international lending operations. In addition to the facilities which CB International provides itself for domestic customers the world-wide range of services available through the Midland Group can also be put at their disposal.

NOTES AND REFERENCES

1. The statistics are for Order XXIV of the 1968 SIC. As well as insurance, banking and other financial institutions, they include other business services.
2. About 75 per cent of the employees are in Insurance, Banking and Other Finance (MLH 860–862) – see M. Gaskin, *Employment in Insurance, Banking and Finance in Scotland*, Scottish Economic Planning Department, ESU Research Papers, no.2, 1980, Table 3.5.
3. *Ibid.*, Table 3.1.
4. Note that the year end for BS is February of the year subsequent to that shown in Tables 11.6 to 11.8.
5. Equity is defined as shareholders' funds less goodwill and minority interests; free equity is after deduction of trade investments and fixed assets. Figures are weighted averages (supplied by the Bank of Scotland).
6. A relatively high proportion of foreign currency business is low-margin wholesale deposit-taking and lending. Growth figures are also liable to

distortion as a result of changing allocations of business between the clearing banks and their subsidiaries.

7. Note that the figures for clearing bank deposits include deposits taken through English branches, whereas those for the building societies and Trustee Savings banks refer only to Scotland. The London branches of the clearing banks are important, holding the accounts of some very large companies, and evidence to the Monopolies and Mergers Commission by the Royal Bank of Scotland indicated that up to 20 per cent of their total domestic deposits might be held through London branches at any time. However, there are no comparative figures for other banks, and there is no way of establishing the trend in English business over the last ten years.

8. This statement holds even if the figure of £511 million for 1971 is an underestimate. It is derived from a current estimate of building society deposits in Scotland, adjusted for the estimated increase in each of the preceding ten years. The reason for caution is that, if carried back further, this procedure gives a suspiciously low estimate for the opening year.

9. 10–16 July 1982, p.87.

10. With their strong capital ratios and access to wholesale funds in London there is no reason why lending should be constrained in this way.

11. The possibility of sharing a large loan with an associated English clearer is always present.

12

CONCLUSIONS: THE WAY AHEAD

NEIL HOOD AND STEPHEN YOUNG

The foregoing chapters have combined an examination of the recent performance of respective sectors with some analysis of the principal policy issues which have contributed to their prosperity or lack of it. Against this background, the present and final chapter begins with some summary comments on performance in the sectors studied, followed by a review of the dominant factors which have affected sectoral performance. The contribution which industrial policies have made in each case are summarised and assessed and thereafter the pointers to future policy are considered. Finally, and controversially, a series of alternative scenarios for industrial policy in Scotland are outlined.

Industrial Performance and Dominant Sectoral Influences

Introduction. Employment performance within the *manufacturing* industries studied has been almost universally dismal, characterised most notably by Scotland's traditional lifeblood – the engineering industry. This latter sector, which accounts for nearly half of Scottish manufacturing employment, lost over 90000 jobs (a loss of 29 per cent) between 1971 and 1981. Moreover, among the small number of expanding subsectors – aluminium and aluminium alloys; other mechanical engineering n.e.s.; radio and electronic components; computers; radio, radar and electronic capital goods and aerospace equipment – only 4200 jobs were gained (and this was before the closure of the Invergordon aluminium smelter!). Even in electronics there was no overall growth in jobs in the 1971–81 period, although the position was clouded by definitional problems in the switch-over from electro-mechanical to electronic products. It seems that employment in electronics increased significantly in the early 1980s, and the number of announcements of new and expansionary projects in this period does promise further employment growth.

By contrast with the catalogue of employment losses in most of manufacturing industry, in the *service* sectors of banking, insurance and finance, employment went up by 15000 (an increase of 23 per cent) over the 1971 to 1981 period.

Understandably, jobs and job prospects dominate discussions on industrial performance. Yet the economic health and prosperity of the country is most strongly associated with the international competitiveness of Scottish industry. Little information is available on the trade or innovative performance of Scottish firms and most of the discussion in the sectoral chapters concerns levels and growth of output, productivity, and capital investment; openings and closures of enterprises; the relative contribution of indigenous and foreign enterprises etc. On this basis, performance is seen to be very patchy, with few 'laser beams' penetrating the murkiness. The electronics industry undoubtedly stands out in terms of a number of criteria and contributes to the healthy performance of the foreign *vis-à-vis* indigenous manufacturing sectors. Partly because of the latter point, of course, the depth of this industry within the economy is still open to some doubt. Within other sub-sectors, some bright signs can be observed both in terms of past performance and future potential: bottled malt whisky represents one of these; wool textiles, quality garments and knitwear are perhaps others. There are, too, some encouraging signs within the small-firm sector, although a much longer period of time will be needed before a realistic evaluation can be made. In other sub-sectors where overall performance may have been relatively poor, isolated examples emerge of companies bucking the trend. Too often, as in engineering, however, the picture emerges of lack-lustre performance by leading companies within highly concentrated industries. And the sectoral chapters highlight some major problem areas relating both to past performance and future prospects. These include:

The failure of many engineering companies to capitalise on oil-related work, both in the U K and abroad.

More general product and market adjustment difficulties faced in the traditional engineering sectors.

The emergence of important threats to the future of the whisky industry – exports of bulk; the expansion of competitor countries and competitor products; the conservatism of the industry.

The need to extend processing activities and increase value added within natural resource-based industries; but equally the poor past experience of large capital- and energy-intensive projects in these industries.

The traditional nature of the food and fish processing sector – lack of expansionist ambitions among companies; limited markets; traditional, undifferentiated products.

To these sectoral problems should be added the management weaknesses of Scottish industry, which are largely cross-sectoral. One recent study of medium-sized companies in Scotland indicated that only a third of firms undertook formal planning, and where planning did take place it tended to be merely document-oriented: many companies appeared to be ignorant of the market and the technological environment surrounding their businesses.[1] Even this study found, however, that planning was most

| | Macro level | | | | | Micro level | | | | | |
| | | | | | | Sector-specific | | | Firm-specific | | |
	Economic climate	Trade-related	Factor costs	Govt. policy	EC dimension	Technology	Capacity	New entrants	Investment	Performance	Management
Small firms	●●●		●	●●				●	●●	●	●●
Foreign-owned	●●	●●	●	●●	●	●●●	●●	●	●	●	
Engineering & metals	●●	●●	●	●	●	●●	●●●	●●●	●●	●●	●●
Food, drink & tobacco	●●	●●	●	●	●●●	●	●●	●●	●●	●	●●
Textile & clothing	●●	●●●	●		●●	●●	●●●	●●●	●●	●●	●●●
Natural resource-based	●●●	●●●	●●●	●●●	●●●	●	●●	●	●	●●	●●●
New high technology	●●	●●	●	●●	●	●●●	●●	●●	●	●	●
Oil & oil-related	●●	●	●●	●●●		●●●	●	●	●●●	●●●	●●
Finance	●●●	●●	●	●		●●		●	●●		●●●

Figure 12.1. Principal factors influencing the study sectors over the past decade (●●● = major influence).

unsatisfactory among companies in some of this country's traditional industries.

Dominant Sectoral Influences. Each of the chapters have commented on the principal forces which have shaped the sectors over the study period. These reviews in turn serve to provide an indication of the scope for policy, and the policy options at various levels. Figure 12.1 summarises the chapter contents, albeit in a qualitative manner, distinguishing between forces operating at the macro and micro levels. Within the former, three issues dominate – namely, the effects of the economic climate, trade-related factors, and the role of Government policy in general. The chapters have shown how these latter two influences occur in both positive and negative forms. For instance, Government policy has had a positive effect on the small-firm sector in recent years, although the extent of that effect is probably exaggerated to date. In contrast, Government policy has played a more negative role in aluminium. The food, drink and tobacco sector and the natural resources sector display some of the strongest negative effects arising from EC policies, especially in whisky and fisheries.

Micro influences distinguish between those occurring at sector and firm levels. Of the former, three have been selected for emphasis. The pace of technological change has influenced UK sectoral competitiveness in certain cases, as has the emergence of excess capacity on a UK and European scale in particular industries. Equally, the emergence of new entrants, invariably from overseas, has dominated sectoral strategy in others. The two sectors where these issues emerge with greatest strength are engineering and metals, and textiles and clothing. Both have been particularly affected by the shift of competitive advantage away from the UK, largely to developing countries, and by the consequent emergence of overcapacity. Chapters 5 and 7 emphasise the importance of higher-technology and higher-value-added products in the success of the residual parts of both sectors. Technological changes have been notable in both cases, but this influence has been predominant in two other sectors, namely the foreign-owned, and oil and oil-related sectors. In the former, Chapter 4 drew attention to the relationship between loss of technological advantage in some major US corporations and employment decline in Scotland from the mid 1970s.

At this level of aggregation, the most difficult factors to identify are those at the firm-specific level. Three variables are included, although two of them – investment and performance – are partially externally determined. The firm-specific variables are incorporated, however, to give some indication of the extent to which managerial decisions, and especially those relating to corporate strategy, might be deemed to have exerted a significant influence on the prosperity of the sector. So, strategic problems in the areas of marketing, diversification and internationalisation were shown to be important in determining the health of the engineering and metals sector in Chapter 5. Several of these managerial dimensions were featured in the company cases within that chapter. Again, within textiles and clothing, marketing and product development were found to be recurring themes in each of the three sub-sectors considered. Equally, strong weight is placed on management-related variables in the finance and natural resource chapters, though heavily tempered by macro considerations in both cases.

Taking an overview of the summary material in Figure 12.1, it is possible to compare and contrast the study sectors on a variety of bases. A starting point is the relative weighting to be given to macro and micro factors in influencing sectoral performance. At one end of the spectrum is the natural resource-based sector where global sets of factors dominate even within the general macro group: world demand, exchange rates, trade policy, factor costs and EC policies are all part of the complex mix of determinants in this instance, with the Wiggins Teape case in Chapter 8 amply illustrating the way in which these impact at corporate level. Textiles and clothing as a whole display some similar properties, but on a less dramatic scale in the Scottish case, in view of the specialities within the residual sector. In terms of balance, thus, textiles possibly falls more clearly into the other extreme in Figure 12.1, namely, where micro issues dominate. It shares this group with engineering and metals and, although often in a very different way, with the oil and oil-related sector. In the latter case, of course, the market growth element has been very much stronger than in either of the other two sectors, but corporate success has often been largely determined by the presence or absence of strategic commitment to this demanding market.

The other industries do not fall neatly into either of these broad groupings, in that the relative balance is not readily determined. In aggregate terms, the health of the small-firm sector is probably largely determined by the general economic climate and supportive Goverment policy on the macro side, with a major input of managerial interest on the micro side. The sector has received conflicting signals and, as Chapter 3 points out, will require both expansionist macro policies and positive discrimination before its overall role changes in any significant way. Perhaps the macro/micro balance is at its finest in the foreign-owned sector. The flows of new projects and reinvestment schemes have been affected by the recession, although probably less so than in all the other sectors except oil. Exchange rates and the continuation of positive Government inducement policies have continued to be critical. However, the evidence in Chapter 4 and elsewhere suggests that sector and firm-specific variables are absolutely vital in determining the pattern and rate of flow of mobile projects. At the corporate level, the longer-term health of the sector is much conditioned by international strategic decisions and by the real or perceived performance records of affiliates within Scotland.

In many senses, the finance sector is a special case by dint of the distinctive influences on performance which are exerted by Government macro policies and the economic climate, at home and abroad. Certain sections of the finance sector, as Chapter 10 showed, have been strongly influenced by market niche strategies and positive and negative attitudes towards internationalisation. Within this sector then, many of the inter-firm variations in performance must be largely attributed to a positive balance in firm-specific attributes, which have combined with the sector-specific skills of speed of adoption of technology and ability to handle new competitive threats.

Overall, this balance of macro/micro influence within the sectors is of considerable importance in determining the extent to which industrial policy could make a contribution towards improved performance. A distinction has to be made between sectors where there is scope for such policy initiatives in the abstract, and where UK and Scottish policy has actually been applied.

A further basis for considering the study sectors lies in the extent to which they have been effectively linked into the international economy. Several of the chapters have specifically drawn attention to this question, emphasising the need to judge Scottish-based industries by standards of international competitiveness. Excluding the small-firm sector, the others fall into quite distinct categories. At the end of the spectrum which is most integrated into international trade are the foreign-owned, textile and clothing, whisky, finance and high-technology sectors. The first and last of these have a considerable degree of overlap, while the form of international link varies substantially. So, textiles and clothing and whisky are export-oriented and not linked into international production networks to any significant degree.

In contrast to this group are the other sectors with either minimum export records or with firms in the fairly early stages of establishing overseas operations. The food sector (excluding whisky) has high UK market dependence, but perhaps the problem of greatest concern is in the oil and oil-related sector, where the export prospects are as yet largely unrealised. For some parts of the oil-related sector, there are, however, considerable opportunities in emerging oil markets, provided companies commit themselves to following the market into locations such as Canada, China and so on. There is little doubt that the problem of operating from a home market which has a persistently low rate of growth and the need to internationalise business operations are two of the key strategic challenges also facing engineering enterprises. For much of the engineering and metals sector, it may in fact be already too late to respond, since the cycle of competitive advantage has already moved away from the UK at the lower-technology end of their business. Belated efforts to diversify and/or upgrade to higher-value activity are being made.

The Contribution of Industrial Policy

One of the principal themes in this book has been a consideration of the contribution made by industrial policy to the development and performance of the sectors. The individual chapters show how difficult an exercise this is. Some of the policies are of marginal relevance to the sectors, while others are so fundamental as to make it difficult to understand the sector in their absence. Alongside this, of course, the contributors themselves have different perspectives as exemplified, for example, by comparing Chapters 4 and 11. In the former, a strong case is made for both Scottish and UK policy initiatives, while in the latter a much more market-

	UK Dimension					
	Efficiency-centred				Innovation-centred sectoral schemes	
Sector	Assistance under Industry Act 1972	Other investment assistance	Institutional support	Other		Other
Small-firms	Limited contribution	Many sector-specific schemes	DTI information service	Advisory services	Marginal, but growing	Several schemes to facilitate expansion
Foreign-owned	Substantial contribution in most cases	Significant at the margin	DTI; IBB; FCO on attraction & support	—	Relevant in high-tech firms	Marginal through MMC, Inland Revenue etc.
Engineering & metals	Differential impact	Several sector-specific schemes	NEDO	—	Wide variety (MAP; CADCAM; FMS etc.)	Export assistance
Food, drink & tobacco	Impact varies widely by MLH	Several sector-specific schemes	FFB	—	Especially led by EC trading links	Consider influence through UK macro policies
Textile & clothing	Impact varies widely by MLH	Several, sector-specific schemes	Several including NWTEC	—	On limited scale	—
Natural resource-based	Impact varies by sector	Several sector-specific schemes	Several including FC, SFIA, ETSU	—	Many in individual sectors (especially fish-related)	Dominant influence from UK policies on energy prices; exchange rates etc.
New, high-technology	Substantial contribution	Significant at the margin	DTI; IBB	—	Wide variety	Future support following Alvey Committee recommendations
Oil & oil-related	Very substantial	Dominantly private sector	Several, including OSO	—	Dominantly private sector	Training; export promotion etc.

Figure 12.2. Principal industry policy initiatives applied to the study sectors.

oriented approach is taken. In most cases, the industrial policy dimension is quite limited and has not been subject to formal assessment. In some others, including a number where the SDA has been quite active, some of the initiatives are either so recent or so diffuse as to belie any effort to objectively assess their outcome.

Even given these limitations, it is necessary to take an overview in this final chapter. There are two stages to be considered, the first to summarise what has happened, and the second to comment on its effec-

	Scottish Dimension			EC Dimension
	Efficiency-centred			
Institutional support	Co-ordinating activity	Financial support	Innovation-centred sectoral initiatives	
SDA (SBD) advisory services	Underdeveloped to date	SDA & local loan schemes	Underdeveloped to date	Implementation of EC loan schemes
LIS/IDS	LIS/IDS	Limited, but growing	SDA sectoral promotion and development schemes	Principally through limitations on competitive bidding for projects
—	—	SDA investments & loans	Marginal SDA sectoral involvement	Limited
—	—	SDA investments & loans	In early stages	Strong EC influence through CAP; FEOGA; competition policy etc.
—	Joint marketing scheme for wool textiles	SDA investments & loans, initially on large scale	SDA sector studies & quality garments project	Strong EC influence through MFA
SFPDG	SFPDG	SDA & HIDB	—	Strong EC influence through CFP
SDA/IDS	SDA/IDS	SDA investments & loans	Major SDA initiatives	Limitations on competitive bidding; new microelectronics programme Esprit
SO/HIDB principally	SO/HIDB principally	Considerable in terms of local & national infra-structure	Marginal SDA sectoral involvement	Limited

tiveness within the relevant Scottish sector. Figure 12.2 is designed to aid the first of these stages. The categorisation employed is broadly in line with the strategic aims of the then DoI as outlined in Chapter 2 (Figure 2.1) in order to provide continuity in the analysis.

Viewing the data in Figure 12.2 as a whole, some important issues emerge. Within the confined limits of UK-level industrial policy, the relative attention and the mode of operation has varied quite widely in the area of efficiency-centred measures. At the two extremes lie small firms and oil as regards direct financial support in the past, although both are changing now in quite opposite directions, as more small-firm schemes continue to emerge and oil projects receive progressively less automatic grant aid. Of course, the financial orders of magnitude remain of a different order. Most interesting, perhaps, are comparisons of the forms of institutional support which have operated at UK level. Most directly interventionist has been the OSO approach for oil, setting an example which could well be transferred, for instance, to the small-firm sector if there was a genuine desire to change radically its contribution in areas such as public purchasing. The OSO approach differs in other regards, including the specific objectives which it has been designed to achieve and the use of widely publicised measures showing progress to these ends. For these reasons, the approach to oil really stands out within the study sectors. Quite different are the marketing initiatives of food and drink and of textiles and clothing, which have had less specific remits, and where some of the benefit will remain intangible in any event. The most formal and all-embracing institutions are in the natural resources sector while, conversely, the foreign-owned sector has been approached by relatively informal inter-departmental liaison mechanisms. It would not be particularly valid to argue that any one of these different types of structure would be effective for all sectors. What they do highlight is that even within the ill-defined industrial policy mechanisms of the UK, quite different approaches have evolved to meet different sets of objectives.

The individual chapters drew attention to the various types of innovation-centred schemes. These were shown to be most prevalent in the engineering and metals sector (and by extension, in the foreign-owned and high-technology sectors) and to have played some role in the textiles and natural resources sectors. Small firms and oil again stand out in this regard, the former because of the relatively small numbers of projects directed to innovation in this sector as such, the latter because of the balance of the technological thrust coming from massive demand-led pressures through the private sector.

The special focus of this book has been on the secondary tier of industrial policy based on Scottish initiatives. In the interpretation of this dimension of Figure 12.2, some care should be taken. It was shown in Chapter 2 that the IDS played an important initiating, sponsorship and coordinating role in these matters. However, in the first of these categories, the IDS implements many UK initiatives, while the SDA is both the prime mover and the delivery mechanism for much of the 'Scottish dimension'. As such, it is the SDA which features frequently in Figure 12.2, not the IDS.

The three sectors which emerge as having attracted special attention, and where the Scottish dimension is most developed, are small firms, the foreign sector and high technology. All three have had quite substantial institutional support in an attempt to add value to UK schemes. LIS is the sole body with an effective coordinating remit to date, although there is a growing need for this in the small-firm sector. The high-technology and related foreign sectors are the only two where strong links can be argued to exist across both the efficiency and innovation-centred projects within Scotland. The other two industry groupings where institutional and coordinating links are strongest are oil and, very recently, forestry, but not in the other parts of natural resources. For the former, the activities have, however, been more in the coordination and facilitating of major projects, rather than in determining a strategic direction for the sector. The UK and world theatre frequently dominate in oil matters, leaving Scotland as a policy-taker rather than a policy-maker. In forestry, the embryonic activity of SFPDG begins to mirror some of the activities of Scottish sector working parties such as were proposed for engineering in Chapter 5. As such, it constitutes an important experiment in bringing the major interest groups together to resolve sectoral problems. It is regrettable that it has taken so long for this type of mechanism to emerge, since among the many sectors which could have benefited from its earlier adoption are food in general and the fishing industry in particular. In both sectors, there has been little structured effort to build vertical linkages and add value within Scotland.

Almost all of the other Scottish-centred activity revolves round SDA equity and loan activity on the financial side and projects emerging from sectoral studies on the side of the innovation-centred initiatives. Three of the sectors have had marginal attention under the latter heading, namely small firms; engineering and metals; and oil. In small firms, the SDA have commissioned extensive reviews of the development prospects of small firms, as part of major area studies, thereafter applying that frame of reference for follow-up advisory work. In any event, it could well be counter-productive to introduce any more general schemes for small firms within Scotland at this stage. As Chapter 3 suggested, one of the first priorities should rather be to assess the effectiveness of what is already being done. Engineering and oil are in a different position, and both could perhaps gain from more sectoral work at SDA level, although this is now beginning to emerge, as indicated in Chapter 9. In part, this poses the perennial problem of priorities, resources and, especially in oil matters, lines of demarcation between Government bodies.

The EC dimension is shown in Figure 12.2 to have impacted most directly on food, drink and tobacco; textiles and clothing; and parts of natural resources. In the whisky and fishing industries, the EC effect is much stronger than either UK or Scottish effects. The limitations on national action emerged in the consideration of both these industries, and with particular force in the textile chapter. Much more creative thinking and energy would seem to be required on the part of the UK to enable appropriate sectoral initiatives to be sustained within the boundary conditions specified by the EC. The foreign sector is perhaps the one where the prospect of further EC limits on competitive bidding for mobile projects is greatest. If, as is sometimes argued, technological change in the next decade makes projects more mobile against a background of continued high unemployment, this could be quite important for LIS activity. Recent EC interest in the Hyster case reinforces this view.

The Effectiveness of Expenditures on Industrial Policy. By far the largest proportion of expenditure on what is defined as industrial policy in this book comes under the heading of regional financial assistance, and, as Chapter 2 indicated, Scotland has fared relatively well in the past in terms of its share of total UK spending. This has had a positive effect on jobs generally, and the emergence of the electronics industry was linked strongly to regional policy. The criticisms of regional policy instruments in terms of lack of selectivity, etc., are as valid in Scotland as elsewhere. Most of the industry chapters in this volume did not, in fact, attempt to assess the impact of regional aid on the sectors in Scotland, but some of the problems and controversies did emerge: the very high levels of assistance to certain foreign-owned firms, the concentration of payments to large enterprises and to locationally-tied oil projects, the arbitrariness of eligible areas, the limited assistance available for certain projects in the forest products industry, and so forth. And as a recent DTI study suggested for the UK as a whole, some of the problems of the Assisted Areas have been relatively unaffected by regional policy.[2] Such problems include: an unfavourable rate of product innovation; a relatively low rate of employment in the business services sector; occupational structures with a low proportion of managerial and professional jobs; and a high level of dependence for manufacturing employment on branch plants of national and international companies, whose UK headquarters and R&D facilities are concentrated in the South-East.

Despite the problems, the benefits of regional policy to Scotland cannot be doubted. Moves to more selectivity and cost-effectiveness would not, nevertheless, be opposed, were it not for the much poorer Scottish experience with other schemes of assistance which were of growing importance into the early 1980s. Thus, the engineering chapter of this book showed disturbingly low take-up in Scotland for many of the sectoral schemes of assistance and also for certain of the measures designed to promote innovation in industry. Finally, for the invariably recent small-firm schemes, Scottish up-take levels are not readily determined. In Scotland, as elsewhere, of course, there has been very little evaluation of the effectiveness of such schemes.

Turning to the specifically 'Scottish dimension', the impact of industrial policy is very constrained by the fact that the proportion of total identifiable public expenditure in Scotland in this area is so small.

Only 20 per cent of SDA spending is outwith industrial property, land reclamation and environmental improvement. In short, the cost side of the 'Scottish dimension' equation was probably around £35–40 million in 1981–82 and is in the area of 5 to 7 per cent of total identifiable public expenditure in Scotland on industry, energy, trade and employment (see Chapter 2, Table 2.2). It should be remembered, moreover, that some of this expenditure constitutes investments and is thus recoverable.

By what criteria, then, should this modest expenditure be evaluated? It has to be recognised immediately that since a proportion of it goes in planning (sectoral studies), advisory services (small firms) and pro-motional activity (LIS), there is a high element of the intangible built into the contribution. Equally, there is the unanswerable problem of what would have happened in the absence of this Scottish industrial policy. No one can truly address that question, and value-judgements must prevail. For example, while loan and equity sources of finance may in theory have been available from private sector sources, the individual circumstances or stage of development of some firms receiving SDA support might have precluded any other source of aid.

Bearing all these considerations in mind, it could be argued that benefit might be sought in the following areas:

First, there is the question as to whether the Scottish dimension acts as a purposeful means of coordinating regional effort, thereby enabling existing resources to be deployed to better effect while bringing them to bear on a common set of problems. At a sectoral level, this has been con-fined largely to small firms and the foreign-owned and high-technology sectors, although it has recently emerged elsewhere. It would be difficult to conceive of such a role emerging in Scotland in the absence of the SDA, although it was also part of the earlier mission of the Scottish Council (Development & Industry). Moreover, some of the most overtly successful Agency coordination has been at area level, outwith the scope of Figure 12.2. But the results under this second heading should not give grounds for complacency. It is all too easy to create the mechanics of cosmetic coordination without actually creating a better delivery mech-anism for the final consumer. Many of the Scottish sectoral initiatives are at relatively early stages, few having run as long as five years, and while the jury remains out on them, the interim verdict might be regarded as positive in the foreign and high-technology sectors; neutral, but poten-tially good in small firms, textiles and foresty; with marginal impact having been recorded elsewhere.

A second area for the assessment of benefit might lie in the extent to which the Scottish dimension fills demonstrable gaps in UK provision. It might be fairly argued that, since 'gaps' are dynamic, as industrial and environmental circumstances change, the greatest single provision lies in the flexibility of the legal framework within which bodies like the SDA and the HIDB operate in Scotland. Taken as a whole, the longest-standing gaps have been perceived of as existing in areas such as finance, sectoral planning (and associated promotion) and coordination. Long-standing though these are in general, some of the gaps have only recently been filled. The greater SDA emphasis on equity involvement in small firms has begun to fill an equity gap; the recent public and private sector co-operation in management buy-outs has also aided in bridging the gap between close-down and the emergence of residual business. It is at least arguable that the existence of a regional dimension to industrial policy, vested in bodies which have some discretionary powers, enables a more sensitive and less bureaucratised response to changing needs. However, if an objective view were to be taken, it might be argued that in its early days the SDA was pushed into gaps which it was not equipped to fill and that, even in more recent years, there has been a temptation to try to fill too many gaps relative to available resources. On the other hand, more robust Agency corporate planning has generally brought a better focus to its activities in the past five years.

Perhaps all the desirable measures of net benefit lie in this third set of criteria. Ultimately, performance must be judged on the basis of having created a more secure sectoral base; improved records in terms of employment, output, productivity, exports and so on, relative to comparable regions or the UK as a whole. While Chapter 1 did outline the relatively better performance in Scotland in a number of variables over the past decade, it is impossible to separate out the industrial policy contribution to this, even if suitable discount rates are applied to 'jobs created' and 'jobs preserved' estimates. Arguing from the negative, since there is no evidence that it has been counter-productive in any sphere, some positive benefit can be reasonably assumed. Another way of proxying this lies in the perception by other UK regions of benefit which is assumed to accrue to Scotland from the activities discussed in this chapter. Of course, this might be more imaginary than real! Much more substantive, perhaps, are some of the fragmentary pieces of evidence emerging from the chapters. For instance, the fairly healthy performance of the foreign sector, the high-technology focus and growing number of spin-off companies might all be partially attributed to regional initiatives. A further investigation of these aspects would require a much more micro approach than is adopted in this volume.

In total, nevertheless, the impact of 'Scottish industrial policy' in terms of the profitability, competitiveness and adaptability of the productive sector in Scotland can only be judged as small. Even if, as is argued here, Scotland has obtained value for money from industrial policy expenditure, the fact that the resources allocated have been so limited is a major constraint. This then raises the question of the desirability and possibility of reallocating Agency resources so as to enhance the industrial policy role. The desirability is, in these authors' views, unquestionable; the possibility is more difficult, given that some of the Agency's activities mirror the increased focus on urban aid at UK level.

The Effectiveness of Scottish Institutions in Industrial Policy. Some of the observations in the preceding section are relevant to the effectiveness of the SDA in the industrial policy area, but it is also necessary to make some assessment of the Industry Department for Scotland and of the links between the SDA and the IDS in this final chapter, even if this is rather tentative and partial. Before proceeding, it should be noted that the basis on which the IDS and the SDA are to be examined must eventually differ. The former, as the Sponsoring Department, must be regarded as promoting the interests of Scotland, maintaining the discretion for action within the relevant Act for bodies like the SDA, determining boundary conditions, and so on. On the other hand, the SDA has ultimately to be judged as an implementing and enabling body, playing a creative role in response to changing economic conditions.

Over the time period of this study, the IDS has operated in two different frames of reference as regards industrial policy, namely pre- and post-1975, the date of establishment of the SDA. Comment is restricted to the latter period. At the broadest level, the IDS has to some degree to be assessed in terms of its ability to represent the economic interests of Scotland in inter-departmental debates about policy measures and resource allocation. While many of these are routine and rarely emerge into the public eye, some indicators are present. For example, on regional policy, Scotland generally did fairly well during the 1970s, as has been shown, at least in part because there was a centralised Scottish interest. Another important criterion by which the IDS should be evaluated is the extent to which it has been able to ensure the uptake of UK industrial support schemes to at least the level predicted from the regional industrial structure. The performance on this count has been mixed, as indicated, although the variations can sometimes be explained by structural or other differences or by the continuation of central management by UK Ministries.

Since 1975, some of the most critical industrial policy missions of the IDS have been related to the functioning of the SDA. There are many aspects to this, not least of which are the effective monitoring of Agency activity, the provision of appropriate guidance on probable UK and EC response to proposals and the defence of the scope for selected discretionary powers. It is arguable, and perhaps inevitable, that the period since 1975 has witnessed the IDS in a more reactive role than in former years, as the SDA grew in experience and credibility with the private sector. While it would therefore be unrealistic to expect a strongly pro-active role from a department which was sponsoring a major development agency, the IDS probably is at its weakest when its involvement in the planning of a Scottish industrial strategy is under review. A stronger hand in this area would probably have helped the strategic development of the SDA in the first five years of its existence and might have acted as at least some counter-weight to the vagaries of political whim during the earlier part of that period. In part, of course, this was a learning experience both for the IDS and the SDA, but the former was markedly lacking in its development of industry-specific knowledge and associated policies before the formation of the SDA. It is ironic that, historically, the Scottish Office was a pioneer in regional planning and was involved in the commissioning of the Toothill Report on the Scottish economy in 1961, in the preparation of the Scottish Plan to fit into the 1965 National Plan, and so on.[3] In addition, until the end of 1983, the department was titled the Scottish *Economic Planning* Department.

A similar overview of the SDA would suggest some rather different criteria of performance. On the accounting front it is possible to take a view on the annual accounts, returns on investment, etc. Such a frame of reference is, however, far too narrow for this purpose, and while indifferent performance has been recorded by a number of these measures, especially in its early years, other measures must be preferred. One of the most basic, yet least tangible, must be the SDA's ability to design and effectively implement projects which resolve or ameliorate specific industrial and economic problems. The capability to do this within the scope of the Act is a measure of considerable importance, but it requires each project to be assessed, at least internally. This immediately complicates matters, since much of the work which the SDA does in the industrial policy field has several objectives and involves a number of co-operating bodies. Moreover, the SDA may legitimately initiate a project, but not necessarily remain the central driving force over its whole life span. Part of its success will, therefore, be measured through project management skills, both at entry and departure.

A number of the chapters in this book have shown the type of projects undertaken by the SDA. The emergence of positive signs from some sectoral efforts, but the danger of trying to undertake too many projects with limited managerial resources, are two points which have been made earlier. Of course, not all projects obtain the backing of the IDS or of the UK Government. While this 'checks and balances' role is necessary for the IDS, an equally essential SDA responsibility is to operate as close to the boundary conditions as possible if it deems that such a position is in the Scottish interest.

An important test of effectiveness for the SDA since 1979 has been the willingness of private sector funding bodies to invest in joint projects. By no means all of these fall into the industrial policy area; indeed it was specifically in the context of support for individual firms that the SDA had to live down its reputation of its early years. The Agency has now begun to attract more private sector support, although often on a token scale and largely because it has been moving closer to prospects with high private sector interest, rather than the reverse.

There is no doubt that in its initial years the activities of the Scottish Development Agency were viewed sceptically in many quarters in Scotland. Some of this criticism came from vested interests, such as local authorities and New Towns who felt their powers being usurped; some came from the private sector, whether small businesses who doubted the relevance of the advisory services of the Agency, or larger enterprises, who, in their view, could see competitors being supported (and in this regard 'industrial policy' had a bad name in Scotland, since its manifestation was largely in the bailing out of dud businesses); some, too, came from the more prosperous or northern areas of Scotland who alleged a Strathclyde bias in the Agency's activities. There is still anecdotal evidence of such views, but overall there is a much greater acceptance of the contribution that the Agency may be able to make in Scotland, and this matches the judgements made by the authors in this chapter.

As is implied above, institutional effectiveness also requires efficient and harmonious relationships between the two major institutions in Scotland. It is in this area that there is perhaps room for greatest improvement. From the perspective of the Agency, the IDS may be seen as being largely negative in its contribution. From the IDS side, the criticism of the Agency could be that it tries to behave as if it was independent of statutory and Ministerial control, EC regulations and so forth. At the detailed planning and project level, scope for improving the joint contribution of the two institutions to industry in Scotland lies in better links between the Planning and Projects Division of the Agency and the Economics and Statistics Unit of the IDS. Arguably, the former need not have existed if the IDS had developed differently. For the future, regular interchanges of staff and the greater involvement of IDS personnel in planning and implementing projects should be possible and could produce significant benefits. Similar types of linkages should probably be fostered between other Agency and IDS departments.

The Future of Industrial Policy in Scotland

Suggested Policy Guidelines. Although differences of view are expressed in the chapters and the evidence presented therein is open to some variations in interpretation, the consensus is that the Scottish dimension of industrial policy has been of some benefit and, subject to refinement, could be of even more benefit to that economy in the coming decade. But such a view is based on a presumption that the boundary conditions will remain similar over that period. As noted earlier, this volume was written during a period when these conditions were under review.[4] As a result, regional policy is to become more selective and designed to achieve more

Sector	Policy direction	Instruments
Small firms	Better monitoring of experimental schemes. Need for IDS/SDA initiative to establish a policy format	Expansion of software services & environmental troubleshooting
Foreign-owned	Greater emphasis on monitoring and affiliate development in existing stock; more specific targeting on projects related to MNE plans; reconsideration of the balance of resources directed to fdi from US	Further SDA direct investment in mobile projects
Engineering & metals	Steps to maximise Scottish benefit from UK schemes; promotion of new UK schemes in Scottish interest	—
Food, drink & tobacco	Major task in developing appropriate schemes to aid smaller food companies expand	—
Textile & clothing	Continued monitoring of sectoral needs and opportunities; increasing linkages within Scottish sectors	Selective assistance for re-equipping in quality garments sector; generic promotional schemes
Natural resource-based	Maintenance of modern fishing fleet at appropriate size; assessment of effects of existing regional policy measures on sector	Expansion of UK fish demand through existing SFIA schemes
New, high-technology	Focus on needs of HTIs and HTCs irrespective of sector; increased university/industry/ Government links; promote awareness of importance of technology and assistance schemes	—
Oil & oil-related	Stronger SDA involvement in aiding overseas expansion of indigenous companies involved in oil	Public sector R&D support for oil-related technology

Figure 12.3. Summary of principal policy guidelines.

Institutional arrangements	Operational guidance	Other
Reappraisal of SDA/ local authority responsibilities	Set of benchmark objectives proposed; reappraisal of advisory services & provision of public sector factory space	—
Development of SDA functions in areas cognate to LIS work (e.g. technology transfer; enterprise development)	Linking of SFA to plant up-grading, local linkages etc.	—
Extension of the administration of UK support schemes within Scotland; NEDO-type approach to engineering in Scotland through EWGs	Development of more firm-specific advisory services	Assessment of impact of public sector purchasing on sector
Need to take steps to maximise Scottish benefit from FFB; scope for further SDA initiatives for SWA	High priority on technical and marketing advice	EC & trade barrier dimensions dominate & limit scope for UK/Scottish initiatives
—	Further emphasis on marketing, promotional & new product projects; facilitating inter-company co-operation	Evaluation of EC limitations placed on UK schemes
Continuation of cooperation through SFPDG for forestry	Continued policy of temporary support in fishing pending further restructuring	—
Continuation & expansion of SDA role, otherwise not discussed in detail	Selective public sector purchasing; development of venture-backed HTCs; interchange of personnel between universities, industry & Government; expansion of firm-specific advice	—
—	Further resources needed to raise Scottish involvement in N. Sea	—

determinable criteria of cost-effectiveness. The related redrawing of the map of regional assistance cannot be expected to benefit Scotland. While the appropriate balance between automatic and selective assistance is yet to be determined, it is probable that there will be an even greater need to preserve the measure of regional discretion in wider aspects of industrial policy which currently exists in Scotland. The existence of the IDS and the SDA could well sustain a measure of institutional advantage in Scotland in the short term, since selective UK schemes will be more readily implemented against a background of sectoral and corporate knowledge of other options. Moreover, in, say, the foreign sector, an effective promotional vehicle could partially offset greater regional expenditure being directed to new entrants such as the West Midlands (although the possibility of development agencies in such areas cannot be ruled out). While some of these issues remain open to debate, it is possible to hypothesise various alternative futures for Scotland in matters of industrial policy.

Most of the individual chapters make the implicit assumption that a fairly similar policy environment will prevail for the immediate future. Figure 12.3 sets out some of the principal policy guidelines which their respective authors would like to see pursued. Some of the authors' suggestions are in direct line with current thinking within the key bodies in Scotland, since they themselves are closely involved with that process. In general, they favour a deeper penetration of existing approaches within their respective sectors as regards policy directions, while stressing more firm-specific aid on the side of operational guidance. More radical approaches are suggested in the oil, small-firm, engineering and foreign-owned sectors. The most fundamental institutional reforms are advocated for engineering and metals, which has not received much attention, outwith rescue missions, in the recent past – and small firms, where the scope for rationalisation between Scottish and sub-regional levels is substantial. Realism has generally prevailed in the matter of recommending further instruments through which to achieve policy goals: a direct reflection, perhaps, of the sensitivity of all the authors to resource-constrained environments.

One of the stated objectives of this book was that of formulating possible new policy initiatives which might enhance the future performance of industry. On first sight, it might appear that only limited progress has been made in this direction and the policy conclusions and suggestions may be a disappointment to some. In fact, however, some quite radical changes are implied in the policy guidelines which are presented in Figure 12.3, and the organisational implications of some of the suggestions are quite profound. For example, constraints on or withdrawal from some of the activities in which the SDA is currently involved on the small-firm side; development of more firm-specific advisory services in engineering; stronger SDA involvement in aiding the overseas expansion of indigenous companies involved in oil, and so forth. There are also implications for the Industry Department for Scotland, which are drawn out most clearly in Chapter 5; here it is suggested that there should be a build up in expertise relating to general support schemes operated in the UK so as to influence the nature of the schemes promoted to the Scottish advantage.

The objective of this book has not been to draw up a plan for the development of manufacturing industry in Scotland. Clearly, a comprehensive plan of this nature would need to consider the interrelationships between sectors, the compatibility of policy proposals for different industries, and so on. This is beyond the scope of the present volume. It is worth noting, nevertheless, that there has been a justification for considering policy and performance on a sectoral basis, despite the fact that the thrust of Government policy has been moving towards more general industrial policies and general support schemes. The chapters in this book have shown that there are genuinely sector-specific problems which need to be considered at that level. One issue which is cross-sectoral concerns the management of Scottish industry – innovation and new product development, marketing and technical advice, etc. Much more consideration needs to be given to ways of tackling the deep-rooted and fundamental problems which exist in these areas. More extensive and intensive management training; inter-company co-operation; public/private sector co-operation into management problems at firm or industry or regional (within Scotland) levels could all have a part to play. And, equally importantly, could be implemented within the framework of 'Scottish industrial policy', whether involving IDS or the SDA, or indeed bringing the Scottish Council (Development & Industry) into a more central role.

Some Alternative Scenarios. The policy suggestions made above have assumed that a broadly similar policy environment will exist in the future. But the question has been begged as to whether this is the most realistic scenario over the next five- to ten-year planning horizon. Figure 12.4 thus sets out a series of alternatives for the future of industrial policy in Scotland. All those outlined in the figure are possible, although scenarios I and V are improbable. The pace of change in national and EC politics places both in that category. Scenario II is also unlikely, although not completely out of the question. This is a highly centralised model where a strong market-centred philosophy prevails; it is much less sensitive to the requirements of regional economies than the present order, and has little to be said in its favour, save the implied commitment to reducing barriers to expansion at UK level. Scenario III is the extreme version of a reaction to other regions expressing their dislike of a 'Scottish dimension'. Instead of creating other regional agencies in the same mould

Figure 12.4. The future of industrial policy in Scotland: some alternative scenarios.

I. *No UK industrial policy; EC level only*

Assumptions: 'Efficiency' support measures totally EC-determined

National industrial policy discretion at minimum level

No scope for region-specific initiatives

II. *UK industrial policy; no 'Scottish dimension'*

Assumptions: No SDA/Industry Department for Scotland

Direct dealings from London with all business in Scotland

UK focus on removing barriers to industrial expansion

III. *UK industrial policy; diminished 'Scottish dimension'*

Assumptions: No SDA

Industry Department for Scotland with progressively reduced powers, acting exclusively as local presence for UK Ministries

IV. *Status quo; enhanced 'Scottish dimension'*[1]

Assumptions: Existing institutional framework adequate

Progressively finer tuning of UK policies to local needs

Maintenance of limited element of discretionary power at regional level

V. *A Scottish industrial policy; independently determined*[1]

Assumptions: SDA/Industry Department for Scotland developing distinctive schemes across whole spectrum of activity

Responsibility to devolved Government in Scotland

---

[1] Either of these could be associated with the formation of other regional agencies in the UK in the same mould as the SDA.

as the SDA, these are removed, employing IDS as a concession to regional focus in Scotland. The predominant view taken in this book is that both cases II and III would be to the clear detriment of the Scottish economy in the long and short term. As presently constituted, for example, IDS could not act as a proxy to the SDA in terms of the benefits discussed earlier. The generation of such benefits presumes a type of pro-active role associated with a quango, rather than the reactive role identified with a Government department.

Realistically, the most that can be hoped for is some version of scenario IV. Even here, however, certain provisos need to be made. If, for instance, other regional agencies were set up within the UK, this could have a detrimental effect on Scotland, particularly in the area of inward investment attraction. Equally, the presumed benefits from an enhanced Scottish dimension would depend on the allocation of resources to industrial policy in Scotland. The maintenance of the existing institutional framework would not be especially useful if resources allocated for industrial policy purposes were substantially cut.

Industrial Policy and the Employment Problem. The scenarios for industrial policy in Scotland outlined above are important in another sense, namely in establishing the possibilities for independent job creation. Within the dimensions of Figure 12.4, only scenario V, which permits independent policy formulation, could conceivably lead to significantly different job prospects in Scotland as compared with elsewhere in the UK. And such job prospects would not be primarily a function of industrial policy but rather of macroeconomic policy. Eliminating the possibility of a devolved Government in Scotland with independent tax-raising powers, employment and unemployment in Scotland will remain at the whim of UK and international macroeconomic policies.

In discussions on the future level of employment, views vary considerably: many believe that the job losses over the last decade will never be replaced; concurring with this view to some extent are those who argue for reductions in the length of the working week, a lowering of the retirement age, and so forth. And, as has been shown in this volume, the so-called sunrise industries have yet to make much in the way of a contribution to job creation. Others see the solution in the creation of a bedrock of self-employment – but even to increase the size of the small-firms sector in Scotland to something near to that in other industrialised countries will take many years and require fundamental attitudinal changes. There are, fortunately, signs that (a new) Keynesianism may be making a comeback.[5] As has been remarked: 'In the end we cannot escape from the present depression without a large increase in demand and there is no likelihood of such an increase without an initiative on part of governments. It is pure fantasy to suppose that output will recover of itself'.[6] The one hope for the Scottish unemployed is that such expressions make their way into policy in the not too far distant future. It is interesting, nevertheless, that as at 1983 there were indications of significant divergences in the responsiveness of different national economies to a very modest stimulus to economic activity, with the United States in the vanguard of recovery. The challenge in Scotland is to recapture the innovative and entrepreneurial spirit which makes this possible in the USA.

NOTES AND REFERENCES

1. The *Scotsman*, 21 December 1983, quoting a study by Arthur Young, McLelland & Moore in association with the Department of Business Studies, University of Edinburgh.
2. Department of Trade and Industry, *Regional Industrial Policy: Some Economic Issues*, HMSO (London), 1983.
3. M. Keating & A. Midwinter, *The Government of Scotland*, Mainstream Publishing (Edinburgh), 1983, chapter 9.

4. *Regional Industrial Development*, Cmnd 9111, HMSO (London), December 1983.
5. J.Meade, 'A New Keynesian Approach to Full Employment', *Lloyds Bank Review*, no. 150, October 1983, pp.1–18.
6. Sir Alec Cairncross, 'Is Employment Policy a Thing of the Past?', *The Three Banks Review*, no. 139, September 1983, p.17–18.

ABOUT THE AUTHORS

Neil Hood, M A, MLitt, is Professor of Business Policy at the University
of Strathclyde, Associate Dean of the Business School and co-
Director of the International Business Unit. He has held a variety of
posts in business and academic life in the UK and abroad. He has
researched and published widely, largely in international business,
marketing and industrial development.

Stephen Young, Bcom, MSc, has worked as an international economist
with the Government of Tanzania and with a British food organisation. His academic career has included posts at Paisley College of
Technology, Louisiana State University and the University of Texas,
and he is presently Senior Lecturer and co-Director of the International Business Unit at Strathclyde University.

The editors have worked on a large number of projects for regional,
national and international agencies. As a result, they have co-
authored a range of books including *Chrysler UK: A Corporation in
Transition* (Praeger, 1977); *The Economics of Multinational Enterprise* (Longman, 1979); *European Development Strategies of US
Owned Manufacturing Companies Located in Scotland* (HMSO,
1980); *Multinationals in Retreat: The Scottish Experience* (EUP,
1982); *Multinational Investment Strategies in the British Isles*
(HMSO, 1983).

Andrew D. Bain, M A, PhD, was Walton Professor of Monetary and
Financial Economics at the University of Strathclyde. He is the
author of several books and articles in economics, notably *The
Control of Money Supply* (Penguin, 3rd edition, 1980), *Company
Financing in the UK* (Martin Robertson, 1973) and *The Economics
of the Financial System* (Martin Robertson, 1981). He was a member
of the Committee to Review the Functioning of Financial Institutions (Chairman: Sir Harold Wilson) which reported in 1980. Since
mid-1984 Professor Bain has been the Group Economic Adviser at
the Midland Bank.

David Bell, M A, MSc, was educated at Dornoch Academy, Aberdeen
University, and the London School of Economics. He is currently
senior research fellow at the Macroeconomic Modelling Bureau,
University of Warwick, working on forecasting models of the UK
Economy. He was previously employed at the Fraser of Allander
Institute, University of Strathclyde, to forecast and analyse trends in
the Scottish economy. His publications include articles in *Economica*

and *Oxford Economic Papers* as well as many contributions to periodicals and newspapers of a less academic nature.

David Crichton, MA, graduated from Edinburgh University in 1977 with an honours degree in Economics and Sociology. He worked in the Department of Political Economy at Aberdeen University, publishing a number of papers on the comparative effect of oil taxation systems worldwide. He worked for the Scottish Development Agency from 1979 to mid-1984 and was involved in strategy development and project formulation in both the textile and offshore oil and gas industries.

John R. Firn, BA, NDA, SDA, began his career in agriculture, studying at the Edinburgh College of Agriculture, and then graduated in Economics at the University of Sussex in 1967. He joined the Department of Social and Economic Research at the University of Glasgow, where he lectured in Applied Economics. In 1977 he joined the Scottish Development Agency as industrial sector economist, and from 1982 to mid-1984 was Head of Industrial Programmes Development with responsibility for the Agency's industrial policy and sectoral reviews. He has also undertaken research on the Indian economy, and was an Associate Fellow of the Institute of Development Studies from 1969– 1971. His main interests are in industrial and regional economics, on which subjects he has published widely.

David M. Henderson, MA, is currently Head of Project Development at the Highlands and Islands Development Board, where he has previously held the positions of Head of Industrial Strategy and Senior Economist. Prior to joining the HIDB in 1975, he lectured for six years in business economics at Heriot-Watt University. A native of Inverness and an economics graduate of Aberdeen University, he studied in the USA and worked for an electricity corporation in Canada before returning to Scotland. Previous publications include a major study of the economic impact of tourism, with particular reference to Tayside.

Tony (G.A.) Mackay, BA, MA, is an economic consultant. He was previously a partner in PEIDA, the Edinburgh-based firm of economic consultants. He is a graduate of Kent and Reading Universities. From 1969–81 he was on the staff of the University of Aberdeen. One of his main research interests is North Sea oil and gas, on which he has written many books and articles, including *The Political Economy of North Sea Oil* (with D.I. MacKay, Martin Robertson, 1975), and *The Economic Impact of North Sea Oil on Scotland* (HMSO, 1978).

Richard G. Reid, MA, MSc, is the economist for the Scottish Provident Institution. His first degree was from Aberdeen University and he was formerly a research assistant in the Economics Department of

Strathclyde University.

Alan Reeves, BA, BPhil, PhD, graduated in economics at the Universities of Reading and York. He is senior lecturer in economics at Paisley College and has spent two years recently as research fellow on an international business research project at Strathclyde University. His main interests are in industrial economics and international business.

David Roberts, BSC, MF, is a graduate of the University of Wales and the University of British Columbia. He worked for the Swaziland Development Bank before joining the Scottish Development Agency in 1980, where he has been involved in sectoral strategy development and project formulation in the electronics, printing and forest products industries.

Drummond B. Small, BA, MInstM, is an honours graduate in Business Organisation of Heriot-Watt University. He undertook research into the advisory needs of small firms before joining the Small Business Division of the Scottish Development Agency. He is currently an Industrial Project Officer with the Agency's Planning and Projects Directorate. His responsibilities include the identification, development and monitoring of projects in the food and drink industries.

Lawrence D. Smith, BSC, is Reader in Agricultural Economics in the Department of Political Economy, University of Glasgow. He has done several studies of aspects of the Scottish food industry for the Scottish Development Agency.

INDEX